# *Writing for College*

# Writing for College
## A PRACTICAL APPROACH
### THIRD EDITION

**Robert E. Yarber**
*Emeritus, San Diego Mesa College*

**Andrew J. Hoffman**
*San Diego Mesa College*

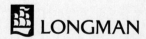 LONGMAN

An imprint of Addison Wesley Longman, Inc.

New York • Reading, Massachusetts • Menlo Park, California • Harlow, England
Don Mills, Ontario • Sydney • Mexico City • Madrid • Amsterdam

Executive Editor: Anne Elizabeth Smith
Project Coordination, Text and Cover Design: Ruttle, Shaw & Wetherill, Inc.
Electronic Production Manager: Angel Gonzalez Jr.
Manufacturing Manager: Helene Landers
Electronic Page Makeup: Ruttle, Shaw & Wetherill, Inc.
Printer and Binder: RR Donnelley & Sons Company
Cover Printer: Phoenix Color

**Credits**

Page 10, V. S. Naipaul. *India: A Million Mutinies Now.* Viking, 1990.

Page 19, "602 pounds of pot seized by agents." *The San Diego Union-Tribune* 9 June 1994: B–3.

Page 20, Malcolm X. *The Autobiography of Malcolm X as told to Alex Haley.* Ballentine Books, 1965.

Page 22–23, Deems Taylor. *Of Men and Music.* Simon & Schuster, 1937.

Page 23–24, Stanley Elkin. *The Franchiser.* Farrar, Straus, Giroux, 1976.

Page 201, Talcott Parsons. *The Social System.* Free Press, 1952.

Page 254, From *Reader's Guide to Periodical Literature.* May 1983. Copyright © 1983 by H. W. Wilson Company. Material reproduced by permission of the publishers.

Page 262, Richard Grenier. "Language Barriers to Leaving the Barrio." *Insight* June 15, 1992: 22.

**Library of Congress Cataloging-in-Publication Data**

Yarber, Robert E.
    Writing for college : a practical approach / Robert Yarber, Andrew Hoffman. —3rd ed.
        p.        cm.
    Includes bibliographical references and index.
    ISBN 0–673–46795–3 (student edition)
    ISBN 0–673–55183–0 (instructor's edition)
    1. English language—Rhetoric.  2. Report writing.  I. Hoffman, Andrew [date].  II. Title.
PE1408.Y37        1996                                95–12193
808'.042—dc20                                         CIP

99 00 01 -DOC- 9 8 7

To Cathy, Sean, Alex, and Mary Roberta.


All happy families resemble one another. . . .

—Leo Tolstoy

# Brief Contents

# Detailed Contents

CHAPTER 8    *Writing Effective Sentences*    *160*

CHAPTER 9   *Using the Right Word*      192

# *Preface*

The principle governing this revision of *Writing for College* remains the same as that of the previous editions: to present a process-oriented writing textbook for college freshmen. Like its predecessors, it offers a sound, workable, and contemporary approach to writing that blends traditional organization and terminology with current findings in composition.

In preparing this revision, we have benefitted from the experiences and suggestions of instructors throughout the country who have used *Writing for College* in community colleges and universities. Whenever possible, we have incorporated their ideas and observations. The result, we believe, is a useful and practical textbook that will meet the needs of today's students and their instructors.

## *Features*

Previous users of *Writing for College* will recognize features in this revision that carry over from the first two editions:

- Writing is presented as series of manageable steps that can be mastered by even the least confident student.
- A jargon-free style invites and reassures students rather than intimidating or threatening them.
- Abundant exercises and writing assignments, arranged in escalating levels of difficulty to reinforce and strengthen writing skills, accompany each chapter.
- Throughout the text, revision is stressed as an integral part of the writing process. Chapter 7, for example, offers detailed comments and analyses of the revision process.

## New Features

In response to suggestions by several users of the previous editions, the following new features have been introduced:

- The discussion of the term paper and documentation techniques has been updated to conform to the 1995 edition of *MLA Handbook for Writers of Research Papers.* In addition, a new term paper has been included.
- Exercises designed for use in a CAI classroom have been added, most of which can be adapted for use in non-CAI classrooms.
- New exercises and examples of student and professional writing have been added.
- The emphasis on the importance and awareness of audience in the writing process has been expanded.
- Most model essays have been replaced by essays written on topics more relevant to the contemporary student.
- Chapter 1 (On Writing: A Preview) now includes a discussion of the role of computers in the classroom.
- Chapter 2 (Generating Ideas and Getting Started) includes an expanded discussion of prewriting techniques.
- The explanation of the classification paragraph has been simplified in Chapter 3 (Writing Paragraphs).
- The order of chapters has been changed so that Chapter 7 (Revising and Editing the Essay), Chapter 8 (Writing Effective Sentences), and Chapter 9 (Using the Right Word) now form a block of chapters dedicated to the revision process.
- Chapter 9 (Using the Right Word) now has a section on how to avoid sexist language.
- The discussion of plagiarism has been expanded to include sloppy documentation practices and inadequate paraphrasing.
- The allusions and references have been updated throughout the text.
- The list of writing topics has been expanded to 300.

## Organization of the Text

Chapter 1 employs a sympathetic tone and encourages the student to begin writing immediately. Chapter 2 offers practical solutions to the two problems every writer faces: coming up with ideas and getting started. Because the student must master the paragraph early in his or her college career, and because it is the building block for longer assignments, Chapter 3 introduces the student to the strategies for developing successful paragraphs. Chapter 4 gives detailed suggestions for choosing and limiting a topic, determining purpose and audience, gathering material, and writing a thesis statement. Chapter 5 presents the most important organizational patterns available to the writer, as well as suggestions and models for writing outlines. Chapter 6 explains and illustrates the most helpful patterns for developing the expository essay.

Because the process of revision actually involves making choices at the levels of the word and the sentence, as well as the paragraph and essay, we have created a block of chapters devoted to the revision process. Chapter 7 demonstrates the importance of revising, editing, and proofreading, using detailed comments and an extensive analysis of a student-written essay. Chapters 8 and 9 move from the larger to the smaller units of discourse: the sentence and the word.

Since much college writing requires that the writer persuade the reader to take a specific course of action or accept a particular point of view, Chapter 8 considers the problems unique to persuasive writing. Instructors who require students to include research in their writing can look to Chapter 11. This chapter includes an extensive list of reference materials and shows students proper documentation technique based on the *MLA Handbook for Writers of Research Papers*, Third Edition. This chapter also offers an innovative approach to the term paper by teaching the student a "search strategy," a step-by-step process of collecting and evaluating information on various topics. Two sample term papers are included, one written to MLA requirements, the other to a form more suited for the sciences. Since essay examinations, business letters, and résumés are also important writing tasks, Chapter 12 provides practical and detailed suggestions for mastering these skills.

## Exercises and Writing Assignments

The act of writing daunts many students who believe that they have nothing to say. They do not know how or where to begin when faced with writing tasks; consequently, they ignore the process of writing, emphasizing instead only the finished products. The exercises and writing assignments in *Writing for College* enables students to start writing with success immediately by beginning with manageable tasks and by developing meaningful ideas.

## Computer Exercises

Computers continue to have a profound impact on the modern world, and today's classroom is no exception. Many universities and colleges have or are planning to have classrooms in which students use computers not only as expensive typewriters but as integral learning tools.

While there is no standard CAI classroom, the exercises in *Writing for College* assume that information can be exchanged electronically, at least from the teacher to the student, and hopefully back again. Overhead projectors are also mentioned: this device is able to project the contents of the teacher's screen via an overhead projector so that all students can view the same screen. A "broadcast" function that puts the same screen on all computer screens could accomplish the same task.

## Acknowledgments

This third edition of *Writing for College* is a result of advice and criticism from reviewers and readers of the second edition manuscript, and of a new partnership between coauthors who share a vision of what this text should be. We would like to express appreciation to Professor Al Krahn of Milwaukee Area Technical College for his contributions to the term paper chapter. Virginia Tiefel, head of undergraduate libraries at Ohio State University, generously supplied information about the search strategy explained in Chapter 11. Devin Milner and his staff at the San Diego Mesa College library were patient, enthusiastic, and willing to let us into the library when it was supposed to be closed.

We would also like to express our gratitude to our students at San Diego Mesa College, without whom there would be no book. We would like to single out J. R. Salazar and Anna Kalina for allowing their names to be used in connection with their writing, an act of bravery indeed.

Finally, it is our pleasure to again thank our wives—Mary and Cathy—both of whom are English teachers themselves. They are the ones who encourage, cajole, and inspire us daily.

*Robert E. Yarber*
*Andrew J. Hoffman*

I am happy to welcome Andrew J. Hoffman as coauthor of *Writing for College*, Third Edition. Andrew brings to this revision a thorough grounding in rhetorical theory as well as extensive practical classroom experience. More important, he understands the writing process and the needs of college writers. This revision has been immeasurably strengthened by his many insights and contributions.

*R.E.Y.*

# 1

## On Writing:
## A Preview

# Why Write?

You have probably been told by your high school and college instructors that writing is an important and practical skill. Nevertheless, you may not be convinced that the ability to write will be important in your own future. If so, you will be surprised at the results of a survey by the National Institute of Education. More than four thousand working men and women who had graduated fifteen years earlier were asked to name the courses they would have taken in college if they had known then what they know now. The designers of the survey expected people to name courses in computer science, mathematics, or business. But the courses most often mentioned by the respondents were courses in writing.

If you already have a job, you are probably not surprised at their answer. Many jobs require the ability to write. Corporate leaders agree that despite the increasing use of the telephone and the computer, much information must still be communicated in writing. Some ten million Americans—managers, engineers, sales representatives, and countless others—write regularly as part of their jobs. Summaries, reports, proposals, letters, and speeches are required in today's work world. The ability to write, therefore, is a marketable skill, and the individual who is successful in his or her profession is almost always the one who can communicate successfully in writing.

Your success in college is determined, to a great extent, by your ability to write. Almost every class requires writing of some kind; summaries, exams, reports, critiques, essays, and term papers are typical assignments. Regardless of the specific assignment, your instructors expect you to write clear, well-organized prose without too many surface errors. They want you to be able to develop an idea in a logical and convincing way without losing the reader in the process. They expect your writing to be interesting as well as coherent, and sincere as well as correct. That is the kind of writing emphasized in this book, and those are the qualities your writing will acquire if you follow the suggestions of your instructor and this text this semester.

Writing communicates your thoughts and feelings to others; it also tells you something about yourself. It helps you know who you are, what you believe, and what your purposes are. Maybe this is what Eldridge Cleaver had in mind in his autobiography, *Soul on Ice:* "I started to write . . . to save myself . . . I had to seek out the truth and unravel the snarled web of my motivations. I had to find out who I am and what I wanted to be, what type of man I should be, and what I could do to become the best of which I was capable."

## How Is Writing Different from Speaking?

As a speaker of English, you already have a grasp of the structure of the language. This knowledge of the way the language works will help you as you become a better writer. Of course, there are several differences between speaking and writing, some of which are obvious.

When you speak, your audience is in front of you. As a result, you can rely heavily on gestures, facial expressions, and even body language to convey your meaning and to detect the reaction of your listener. You can take shortcuts by using incomplete sentences or single words without confusing your listeners. Depending on the audience, you can use specialized language, dialect, slang, or even profanity. You can repeat a word or an entire sentence if it is not understood, or you can pause dramatically, whisper, or shout to convey a particular impression or point. Finally, you don't have to rewrite or edit your words as you speak, and as a result your speech is usually more direct and simple than your writing.

You have few of these advantages when you write. Although you can revise or censor yourself before you write the words on paper (have you ever said something for which you were immediately sorry?), the lack of an immediate audience presents some challenges.

To begin with, your writing must be more organized than your speech, because when you talk, you can change the subject, repeat yourself, wander off to a different topic, and then finally return to the original idea. When you write, you have to use punctuation, word choice, and sentence structure to convey shades of meaning instead of gesture or voice emphasis. To avoid confusing your reader, you have to select your words carefully and arrange them in sentences that follow each other in a particular order. Instead of using slang or terms known only to a certain group, you have to use words that are understood by most readers. Instead of using bits and pieces of sentences, you have to use complete sentences to avoid distracting readers.

## What Is Good Writing?

It would be impossible for everyone to agree on a definition of good writing, just as it would be impossible to agree on the precise definition of a good film or a good song. The problem is complicated because we have to write for different situations, purposes, and audiences. Nevertheless, most effective writers would probably agree that good writing has several important characteristics.

Good writing, like a good film or song or friend, is not boring; it keeps your interest by what it says and how it says it.

Good writing is easy to follow because it follows a plan. In the case of an essay, this means that it sticks to one dominant idea, which is supported or developed by enough facts and details.

Good writing presents ideas that are fresh and original, not hand-me-down, tired ideas borrowed from someone else. As a result, it sounds like its author rather than sounding generic.

Good writing uses language that is right for the job—formal when required and informal when appropriate. The writer uses words that are precise and vivid and exact, avoiding worn-out expressions and clichés.

Good writing is free of serious mistakes in grammar, spelling, and punctuation because those errors get in the way of the writer's ideas and distract the reader.

## What Do Good Writers Do?

If all of this sounds overwhelming and impossible to achieve, you should realize that all writers, even professionals, face the same problems: How do I get started? What can I write about? What is it I really want to say? How should I say it?

Good writers solve these problems in ways that are as different as their personalities. Some prefer a typewriter to a yellow pad; others choose a word processor. Despite their individual quirks and writing habits, they share several traits. Before they begin to write, they make certain that they understand the kind of writing called for. In college, this means understanding exactly what the assignment requires. Good writers probably spend more time on prewriting—thinking, dreaming, making lists, and so on—than they do on the actual writing. They decide who their audience is, the tone they will take, and the level of language they will use. Before beginning a first draft, they often work on focusing what they want to say. They put their main or controlling ideas into one sentence before they begin to write. This sentence is known as the thesis sentence.

Many good writers have a plan or organization in mind before they write; others let the ideas take shape as they write, and rearrange after the first draft. In both cases they present their ideas in a pattern that will make sense to their readers. They often make changes in wording, in sentences and paragraphs, and in entire sections of their pages as they subtract, change, or add material. Finally, good writers respect their readers; they go over their work carefully and correct mistakes in grammar, punctuation, and spelling.

# Writing: The Three Stages

In the chapters that follow, you will be introduced to the three stages of writing: *prewriting, writing,* and *revising.* Although each stage involves certain distinct activities, you will find that the three stages often overlap. The first step often takes more time than the act of writing itself. **Prewriting** is a time in which you mull over past experiences, observe the world around you, interview others who can give you information and ideas, and read articles and books for additional background when necessary. Prewriting can also involve the use of informal and formal techniques for generating ideas on a subject. During this stage you will make notes and tear them up, brainstorm and reject ideas, freewrite time and again, make more notes and rearrange them, and write an outline before finally trying a first draft of your composition. In the course of all this chaos, you will discover that you have more to write about than you originally thought you did.

The second stage of the composing process—**writing**—is sometimes indistinct from the prewriting stage or from the stage that follows. Most writers report than the writing stage goes rapidly if they have spent enough time on the prewriting or "hatching" stage. In other words, after you have decided the purpose of your paper, the audience you are writing for, the main point you want to make, and an organizational pattern that makes sense, the composition almost writes itself.

The final stage—**revising**—is one that many student writers neglect. They are satisfied with their first draft and turn it in to the instructor, only to be disappointed by the grade it receives. Very few (if any) professional writers are content with the first draft they write. The purpose of revising is to remove the warts and blemishes from the paper—to add more ideas, remove weak sentences or irrelevant details, correct misspellings and grammatical errors, and rewrite confusing sentences. In other words, this stage is a time to examine the essay from the reader's point of view—to make sure that it is clear, interesting, well-organized, and free from irritating and confusing errors.

By thinking of the process of writing as three manageable steps, you will become a more confident writer, and you (and your instructor) will notice an improvement in your writing.

# Some Suggestions for This Semester

If you follow the suggestions in this book and those of your instructor, you will become a better writer this semester. These are some tips for improving all your writing, not just the assignments you complete for your writing courses.

### Read

You must have something to write about. If you are a recent high-school graduate, your experiences have probably been limited to your family and friends. Your biases, opinions, and prejudices, and therefore your writing, reflect that limited background. What can you do about it? *Read*. Reading is a way to acquire information, experience, knowledge, and an appreciation for other points of view and other cultures. It is also a way to liberate yourself from fallacies that get in the way of logical thinking and clear writing. Reading is the handiest, most convenient way to expand your mental and intellectual horizons and to stimulate your imagination. If you become an active reader, your writing will be more interesting and stimulating because *you* will be more interesting and stimulating. Equally important, you will see how professional writers put words together into sentences and paragraphs, and you will develop your style.

What should you read? *Everything*. The sports page, the magazines in the dentist's reception room, biographies, history, science fiction, the editorial page, travel books, your textbooks, the cereal box on the breakfast table, anthropology, short stories, novels, scientific writing, poetry, detective thrillers. *Everything*.

If you believe that you need to improve your reading skills, ask your counselor to set up an appointment for you with a reading-skills instructor on campus who can test your reading rate, vocabulary, and comprehension levels and make recommendations for improving your ability in those areas. Visit your library on a regular basis to look over the magazines and newspapers. While some libraries still have card catalogues, many now use computers. These computers contain the same information as card catalogues, and sometimes additional information such as whether a book is currently checked out. Learn the system your library has so you can find the materials you need. Locate the fiction section, the reference books, and the *Reader's Guide*. Tell your librarian what your interests are and ask him or her to recommend some books for you. If you find an author you like, read other things he or she has written.

### Be Nosy About Words

Use your dictionary when you see or hear a word you do not know. Notice the situation in which it was used. In addition to learning its meaning, know how to pronounce and spell it. Make it stick in your mind by reading about its history, variations in its spelling, or other quirks that will give it a personality. Keep a list of the words you have learned and make a point to use them in your conversation and writing.

You should own a college-level dictionary. A dictionary contains much more than definitions. It is a learning tool that you will use in your college classes and for the rest of your life. Among the recommended dictionaries are *The American Heritage Dictionary,* 2nd college edition; *The Random House College Dictionary,* revised edition; *Webster's New World Collegiate Dictionary,* 3rd edition; and *Webster's New World Dictionary of the American Language,* 2nd college edition.

### Take Responsibility for Your Assignments

Make certain that you understand exactly what is called for when you are given an assignment in any class. Instructors are more impressed by a student who asks for an explanation of the assignment than by a student who turns in the wrong assignment.

First impressions are often lasting impressions. This is true in the academic world as well as in the social world. Do not start the semester slowly, thinking that you will deceive your instructor by eventually showing "improvement" over the course of the semester as you gradually show greater interest. Impress the instructor by working hard right from the start. Turn your work in on time and make each assignment represent the very best work you can produce. Even if it does not receive the highest grade, you will have the satisfaction of knowing that you set a standard for yourself and fulfilled it. Your essays should be neatly written and legible. If you type essays written out of class, double space your manuscript. Follow your instructor's guidelines with respect to the heading, margins, title, and manuscript appearance. Before submitting your papers, look them over carefully for mistakes in spelling, punctuation, capitalization, and usage. You will find suggestions for revising your papers in Chapter 7 and a handbook of common usage errors and a guide to punctuation and capitalization at the back of the text.

## An Explanation of the Exercises in This Book

Throughout this book you will find a number of assignments called "Exercises." Some are placed within the various chapters, and some are at the end of the chapter. Most call for a written response, some for a discussion. Your instructor may assign some, many, or all of the exercises.

## An Explanation of the Computer Exercises in This Book

Each chapter contains computer exercises for students working in Computer-Assisted Instruction (CAI) classrooms or laboratories. Some of the exercises require that the computers belong to a network so that information can be shared on a teacher-to-student, student-to-teacher, or student-to-student basis. Many exercises can be adapted to the particular circumstances of your own setup. Some can even be adapted to non-CAI classrooms. Save each of the exercises either on a personal diskette or on a hard disk so that you can have access to them later. Over the course of the semester, you should develop an entire stockpile of ideas that can be developed into essays or term papers. Along the way, you should also become aware that writing requires continual rethinking and revising, and that computers greatly assist this process.

In the exercises, the terms *broadcast* and *overhead projector* are used. *Broadcast* refers to the ability to have a single computer screen shown on all computers at once. Using the broadcast function, an instructor could show the entire class a particular piece of work simultaneously on each student's screen. For rooms without broadcast abilities, an overhead projector combined with a screen projector allows the instructor to project a computer screen onto a large movie screen like a transparency.

## Revising and Editing with a Word Processor

If you write with a word processor, you have joined the growing army of writers who believe that composing on a computer makes the revising and editing process much easier and more efficient. However, some students are holding back out of fear or unfamiliarity. See if your college offers introductory workshops on how to use a computer as a word processor. Some colleges have computer labs that are open to all students so that students without access to computers in their homes may use them at school to do course work, including writing essays.

Computers and word processors have altered and even simplified the act of writing. Using the traditional tools of pen, pencil, or typewriter, most writers in the past took notes, wrote one or more drafts while revising and correcting at each stage, and typed a final copy. Improvements in content, mistakes in grammar, and even typographical errors were sometimes ignored because the author did not want to type another copy, but word processors have changed all of this. Thus, the chief advantage of a word processor is that is allows you to rewrite, correct, change, and revise selected portions of your paper without retyping the whole manuscript.

Just as there are different writing styles for writers who use a pen or typewriter, so there are differing practices for writers who use word processors. Some writers work directly at the keyboard and compose their first draft without stopping to revise or edit, making changes after they have completed their first draft. They then revise and edit entirely on the computer screen, not printing their finished product until they have made all of their modifications and changes. Others write their first draft by hand and then use the word processor for preparing their final copy. Still others write on the screen, print a copy, and then revise with pen or pencil, going back to the word processor for further alterations.

Regardless of the composing style that you adopt, you should not become discouraged by your first attempts to use a computer. For your initial effort, try typing your first draft on the word processor. As you master its keyboard, you will learn that you can move or delete words, sentences, paragraphs, or entire pages; change words, phrases, or sentences; correct punctuation, mechanics, and misspelled words; and copy part or all of the manuscript to use for other purposes.

In addition to revising and editing, the word processor has other uses. In the preparation and formatting of a manuscript it can change spacing and margins, incorporate boldface, automatically italicize words and titles, automatically center material on a page, and close any spaces left by deletions and substitutions.

The advantage of using a word processor will be obvious as you become familiar with its features. The most obvious is that revision is easier: by merely pressing a few keys, you can shift words, sentences, and entire paragraphs around. By putting down ideas as they come, you will be less worried about making mistakes and more likely to draft quickly. You can incorporate additional material and insert it in earlier copy, and because you can get a clean copy whenever you make extensive changes, you will probably revise and edit more than you would if you had to retype continually.

A word of caution: A blown fuse can erase everything, as can power failures and surges of electricity. To avoid such a catastrophe, experienced users of word processors make back-up copies on disks of each session's work and print a copy of their manuscript before beginning to edit so that they have a spare copy. Saving your work every fifteen minutes or so during a writing session is another safeguard.

A final warning: Using a word processor won't make you a good writer. You still need to develop and plan your papers carefully, arranging your ideas in the most effective and logical order, using the most appropriate word choice and sentence structure. But for the last, important stage of the writing process—revising and editing—the word processor can be an invaluable tool.

## E X E R C I S E 1

Discuss these questions with other students in your class.

1. Ritual is often important in helping writers get started. What do you do before you write? Do you like to have music on?

Drink coffee? Do you sharpen all your pencils, clean your room, or play a computer game? Describe your writing rituals.

2. Good writers read. What do you read regularly? What magazines, books, or newspapers? Who are your favorite authors, or what are your favorite types of books?

3. Bring to class an example of writing by a professional reporter or author that you like. What do you like about it? Read the example to the class and see if others like it. If they do not, examine their reasons.

4. What are your strengths as a writer? Try to be specific: mention ideas, vocabulary, organization, or any other aspect of your writing that does not present too many problems for you.

5. What are your weaknesses as a writer? Again, try to be specific: getting started, weak vocabulary, poor spelling, shortage of ideas, and so on.

6. If you have a job, explain the situations in which writing is important.

7. Bring to class some of your own writing that you like. Read it to the class (or have someone else read it) to get their reaction.

---

# E X E R C I S E  2

Two paragraphs by different authors follow. Which is better written? Why? Notice the picture each writer creates, the kinds of words he or she uses, and the way details are arranged.

1. The smell was really bad. You could smell animal skins and their waste products too. There was a swamp nearby where people dumped gasoline and toxic wastes, and the air was so polluted you could actually see the smog in front of you. I just wanted to get away from this poverty and misery and get back to the good side of Bombay. That part, the part I was used to, is an entirely different city. The roads are paved, there is public transportation, and people dress in fashionable, comfortable clothes.

2. The stench of animal skins and excrement and swamp and chemicals and petrol fumes, the dust of cloth waste, the amber mist of truck exhausts, with the afternoon sun slanting through—what a relief it was to leave that behind, and to get out into the other Bombay, the Bombay one knew and had spent so much time getting used to, the Bombay of paved roads and buses and people in lightweight clothes.*

*One of the two paragraphs was written by V. S. Naipaul. Which one?

## E X E R C I S E 3

This assignment calls for you to write one or two paragraphs on each of the following topics. In each case, your job is to make your paragraphs interesting by using vivid and fresh language, clear images, and exact details so that your reader can see your subject. *Remember:* You have no right to bore your reader.

1. Describe one of the following:
   The place you go to study where you get the most work done.
   Your impressions of a recent movie, concert, or television program.

2. Tell what happened the last time you tried to suggest a change in how someone or something operates at school, at home, or at work. It may have been a suggestion about how the teacher could present course material better, what the family could do instead of watching television, or how to get a task at work done more efficiently. What kind of opposition did you face, and how did you deal with it?

3. Write one or two paragraphs explaining one of the following:
   How to grow roses
   How to make a collect call
   How to train parakeets to sing
   How to tune an engine
   How to play a harmonica
   How to avoid being jealous
   How to decorate your home on a tight budget
   How to prepare for a class
   How to wash a dog
   How to complete your income-tax form
   How to plan a baby shower

## C O M P U T E R   E X E R C I S E

Make a curiosity list. Allot two minutes to make a list of all the topics you would like to know more about, school-related or otherwise. After two minutes, look over your list and put an asterisk (*) next to the two items that interest you the most. Then write a paragraph describing how you expect to learn more about each topic. Save your list and paragraphs for future reference.

# 2

## Generating Ideas

## and Getting

## Started

Whether they use a word processor or a lead pencil, coming up with ideas and finding the courage to write those first few words is probably the most common problem writers face. No writer has ever lived who did not at some time find it either difficult to begin or impossible to continue. In one of his journals American novelist John Steinbeck admits, "I suffer as always from the fear of putting down the first line."

Of course, there are many good reasons for writer's block or for a shaky start. Sometimes writers ignore the prewriting stage described in Chapter 1 and jump into the writing stage before they have thought through their ideas. It could be that they have been assigned a topic they do not know anything about or have any ideas on. Or perhaps they worry—particularly if they are students—about the mistakes they will make, and about the red pen they imagine hovering over each line, waiting to pounce on every mistake in grammar or punctuation.

In this chapter you will be introduced to four forms of prewriting that will help you overcome writer's block and develop ideas: keeping a journal, freewriting, brainstorming, and asking questions. In each of these activities you set down ideas and words without worrying about correctness or style. Instead, you put together ideas and relationships that may be valuable to you later. This way it will be easier for you to get started when faced with a writing assignment. Even more important, these techniques will help you to discover and to generate ideas that you can use in your essays, thereby making you a more confident writer.

## Keeping a Journal

To be a good writer, you have to write often. Most good writers write every day. They find that doing so improves their writing just as daily practice improves an athlete's performance.

One of the most popular and effective ways to make yourself write every day is to keep a journal. Keeping a journal has many benefits. It gives you practice in observing and describing details in the world around you. Because you usually do not show it to other people, it creates confidence in your ability to record your impressions and ideas. Your journal can also be a sourcebook for ideas that can be used later in essays and stories. In fact, many famous poets, novelists, and biographers have kept journals to improve their writing and later used ideas and impressions first recorded in their journals in published works.

Here is a journal entry written by a community-college student in Southern California. Notice how she records specific details, as well as her impressions and feelings.

I can't believe college is finally here. Things seem so different from high school. Of course, some things are familiar: the smell of the cafeteria food, the parking lots filled with fancy new cars and old junkers, even some of the faces. But the differences! First of all, buying books just about wiped me out! I couldn't believe it! One of my books cost over $50, and most were over $20. I didn't think I'd be the kind of student to sell my books back at the end of the semester, but now, I don't know. There's a lot of money in those books.

The campus is HUGE. I love walking around it. There are several sculptures around campus, mostly abstracts, but they lend a sort of quiet dignity to the area. Some of the buildings have people's names on them, which seems odd, especially since I have no ideas who these people were. The library is much larger than the one at my old high school, and it's got computers everywhere!

I do miss the intimacy of high school, of knowing everyone, at least by their looks if not their name, of being a real part of a small community. This is different, and a little isolating. But I'm sure I'll make friends and soon enough be a part of this larger, more interesting place.

In keeping a journal, there are a few things to remember. It should be more than a daily accounting of your activities. Nothing is duller than a record of day-to-day routine. ("I got up at eight o'clock this morning. I called Linda to see if she wanted to go skating. I had a hamburger and a Coke for lunch.") Instead, use your journal to record your opinions, your reflections, and your experiences and their meanings. In this sense, a journal is more than a diary.

After you have become accustomed to writing regularly in your journal, you will notice that your writing is beginning to sound like *you*. Every writer has several "voices"; the voice you use depends on your audience. In writing or talking to your clergyman, you use certain words and avoid others; with your family, you use another "voice"; with your friends, still another. In some situations slang is appropriate; in others, a more formal and precise language is more effective. By writing freely and often, you will develop a variety of appropriate "voices," each fitting the situation, yet each sounding like you.

### Some Topics for Journal Entries

Summarize the positions in both sides of some recent conflict.
Take one line from a favorite song or poem. Describe why you
    chose that line, why it has meaning for you.

Defend your decision to go to college rather than join the work force full-time.

Describe your first kiss.

Write a letter to the manager of a restaurant complaining about the poor service you received.

Explain how an important event shaped your life.

Describe some childhood memories. What is the earliest thing you can remember? Tell about the time you were spanked unfairly.

Write an imaginary conversation with a famous person you wish you knew.

## *Freewriting*

Freewriting can best be compared to the warm-up exercises that a team does when it comes onto the playing field. It is an activity that loosens your mind as well as your pen and gets you ready for writing, just as stretching and loosening up gets you ready for playing a game or running a race.

When you freewrite, you force yourself to begin writing immediately. Set a time limit; five minutes will be long enough the first few times, then expand to ten or fifteen minutes as you become accustomed to the technique. Begin writing about anything and everything that occurs to you. If you can't think of anything to write about, write "I can't think of anything to write about" until you get bored and finally think of something to write about. There is only one rule: *don't stop writing.* This means that you can't censor yourself, erase, edit, correct, revise, or worry about the impression you're making. If you can't continue a thought, abandon it and go on immediately to another. Once your time has run out, look over what you have written. Sum up in a sentence the main point of what you have written, and then start freewriting again, using that sentence as your takeoff point. The process is somewhat like the advice given to someone learning how to ride a bicycle: Keep going! You'll have a chance later to repair, correct, and expand any passages you like.

One variation on freewriting is focus freewriting. While this sounds a bit like an oxymoron, focus freewriting can assist you once you know your topic. Most of the rules of freewriting still apply in that you write continuously and avoid censoring yourself on matters of style, punctuation, grammar, spelling, or sentence construction. The focus aspect requires you to keep your mind on your main topic. So, if you know that you are going to write a paper on television, try to focus your thoughts on the broad subject of television. Avoid writing about the floor, what you plan on doing after class (unless TV watching is what you plan to do), or the math exam you're worried about. This time, if you can't think of anything to say, repeat the subject until something new comes to mind. Focus freewriting is a good way to explore the possibilities of a subject you've chosen.

You can also employ looping with focus freewriting. After the freewriting period is over, review what you have written. Underline a phrase you particularly like or find interesting, and repeat it verbatim at the start of a new sheet of paper or computer screen. Use that phrase as the subject for a new session of focus freewriting. You can continue looping with new ideas from each new focus freewriting, or you can return to your first piece of freewriting and choose another phrase to be the focus of a new freewriting session.

The benefits of freewriting are many. Freewriting will not only help you overcome your fear of writing, but it will also help you discover what is on your mind. It will help you clear the hurdle of finding words and putting them down on paper. Don't worry whether these are right or wrong words, but think, instead, of your meaning. It helps to think about topics to write about; give your mind free rein and let it lead your pen. Finally, freewriting is particularly helpful for developing ideas on topics you have been assigned. As you write ideas as they come to you, other ideas will come cascading forth. You will be able to select those that are pertinent to your topic and develop them further.

## E  X  E  R  C  I  S  E      1

Write nonstop for at least five minutes without interruption on one of the following topics. After you have written as much as you can, look over your writing and underline the ideas that could be explored and developed into essays.

| | |
|---|---|
| television | Boris Yeltsin |
| Florida | immigration |
| music | hobbies |
| work | recycling |
| religion | health |

## Brainstorming

Brainstorming is a prewriting technique that is very helpful in generating ideas on a specific topic. When you are assigned a topic for an essay, write down anything and everything that the topic brings to mind.

Write for at least fifteen minutes, putting down all of the words and phrases that occur to you. As in the case of freewriting, don't stop to correct your grammar and spelling—you are trying to get as many ideas down as quickly as possible. Unlike freewriting, brainstorming involves only the list of words and phrases.

Brainstorming is based on the psychological principle of free association; words and images trigger other words and images, and your mind is often led to surprising destinations. As you brainstorm, you will see divisions and aspects of the subject that you had not anticipated, and soon your paper will be filled with a list of ideas connected with your topic. Many ideas won't be usable, of course, but many will fit your needs. Let your imagination race ahead unhampered and don't worry about your thoughts being silly or irrelevant.

If you were assigned to write an essay on "An Important Event in My Life," for example, you might, after a bit of brainstorming, come up with a list like the following:

> my trip to Europe
> getting kicked off the baseball team-pretty depressed
> Meeting Ellen-my first girlfriend
> grandfather dying
> my first job

As you can see, this list is disorganized and haphazard. That's not important at this stage; you can select and rearrange the ideas after listing the words and phrases that come to you as you brainstorm.

## E X E R C I S E · 2

Select one of the following words and, using the brainstorming techniques described above, list as rapidly as possible all of the words and phrases that the word triggers in your mind. After writing for fifteen minutes, look over your list and notice which words and phrases attract your attention. Try to make connections among them, noticing any patterns that emerge as you think about them.

| | |
|---|---|
| cafeteria food | AIDS |
| politicians | rain forest |
| single mothers | guns |
| hospitals | movies |
| minivans | zoos |

## Asking Questions

Another technique writers use to explore a topic is asking questions. The most frequently asked questions are: *who, what, why, where, when,* and *how.* By applying these questions to a topic you can generate material and develop ideas. Of course, not all six questions will apply to every topic, and some topics will suggest additional questions.

By asking questions, you can approach a subject systematically and "shake loose" any ideas that may have been entangled in the background. Asking questions also leads you to answers you had not considered, which helps you to see your topic in a new light.

Kay, a freshman students, developed the following list of questions on the topic of "the destruction of the rain forest":

*Who?* Who is burning down the rain forests? Who is paying them or influencing them? Who stands to gain by doing this? Who is being hurt?

*What?* What is being destroyed in the rain forests? What types of plants and animals are becoming extinct or endangered? What potential medical cures are being lost? What is replacing the rain forests, and what will that do to the environment? What long-term effect will result from the rain forest's destruction?

*Why?* Why is the rain forest being destroyed? Why are the governments of the world not doing more to stop it? Why are people willing to risk environmental disaster? Why is the poverty in some countries so bad that this is the only means that they see to feed themselves? Why have no alternatives been found?

*Where?* Where are the rain forests of the world? Where are they being cut down? Where have rain forests already disappeared?

*How?* How has the rain forest been a part of the world's ecosystem, and how will the world be affected by its destruction? How are people trying to stop the rain forest's destruction? How are people trying to aid the impoverished countries that are destroying their own rain forest? How have the governments of the world cooperated or failed to cooperate on this issue?

As you can see, by asking questions and then trying to answer them, you can often develop a topic when you are uncertain where to start. In the series of questions that Kay asked are the seeds of several essays.

## Narrative and Descriptive Writing

Now that you have learned some techniques for getting your ideas down on paper, you are ready to try your hand at narrative and descriptive writing.

## Writing a Personal Narrative

Narrative writing is the presentation of a series of events in the order in which they occurred, The purest kind of narration—merely a statement of facts without much explanation or description—can be found in newspaper stories. The following example is from a report of a drug seizure along the U.S.–Mexico border in San Diego County.

---

Border patrol agents seized 602 pounds of marijuana and arrested one man yesterday when they discovered drugs during a patrol, officials said.

Agents spotted three men crossing the border illegally about 1 a.m. in a remote area of Campo, officials said. They followed the men, but lost them in thick brush, a Border Patrol spokesman said.

When they resumed the search several hours later, they followed tracks that led them to a man beside three green duffel bags stuffed with 109 pounds of marijuana, officials said. They continued following tracks and discovered another six bags of marijuana hidden nearby in a small storage shed.

—*San Diego Union-Tribune,* June 9, 1994

---

Narration is used in many kinds of writing. Stories, histories, and autobiographies all contain some narrative, usually combined with description and exposition. One of the best-known examples of narration ever written follows:

---

In the beginning God created the heaven and the earth. And the earth was without form, and void; and darkness was upon the face of the deep. And the Spirit of God moved upon the face of the waters.

And God said, Let there be light; and there was light. And God saw the light, that it was good: and God divided the light from the darkness. And God called the light Day, and the darkness he called Night. And the evening and the morning were the first day.

(*Genesis* 1: 1,2)

---

A *personal narrative* is a story taken from your life. It is organized chronologically—that is, it moves along in time from one event to another as they happened. A personal narrative is easy to write because it is about someone you are an authority on: yourself. A personal narrative has a beginning, a middle, and an end. If it is brief (and your first one will be only a couple of paragraphs long), it should be about *one main point* or incident. A personal narrative should give enough specific details and facts for the reader to see and feel the experience, as well as read about it.

In the following personal narrative, Malcolm X, the famed black activist, relates an incident that took place when he was a child. Malcolm moved in with the Gohannas family after his father was murdered and his mother became mentally unstable. In this account, Mr. Gohannas and his friends try to teach Malcolm and Big Boy, Mr. Gohannas's son, how to hunt rabbit.

> The old men had a set rabbit-hunting strategy that they had always used. Usually when a dog jumps a rabbit, and the rabbit gets away, that rabbit will always somehow instinctively run in a circle and return sooner or later past the very spot where he originally was jumped. Well, the old men would just sit and wait in hiding somewhere for the rabbit to come back, then get their shots at him. I got to thinking about it, and finally I thought of a plan. I would separate from them and Big Boy and I would go to a point where I figured that the rabbit, returning, would have to pass me first.
>
> It worked like magic. I began to get three and four rabbits before they got one. The astonishing thing was that none of the old men ever figured out why. They outdid themselves exclaiming what a sure shot I was. I was about twelve, then. All I had done was to improve on their strategy, and it was the beginning of a very important lesson in life—that anytime you find someone more successful than you are, especially when you're both engaged in the same business—you know they're doing something that you aren't.

> —*The Autobiography of Malcolm X,* as told to Alex Haley, New York:
> Ballantine Books, 1964.

Malcolm X narrates this incident chronologically—in the order in which it happened in time. It is a brief story (fewer than two hundred words long), yet it conveys the lesson he learned.

Another personal narrative follows, written by an older student recounting an important event in his life. It, too, succeeds in conveying a strong emotion in relatively few words.

> Grasping my camera, I stood in front of a little Irish pub. The fog was too thick, I thought. There was not enough light for photos. I closed the camera back in its case and slung it over my shoulder. I hoped the fog would burn off later. I wanted to have pictures to show my wife, who had stayed at the inn, and to my grown children, who might not believe that their old man could climb mountains any more.
>
> I remembered how the men in the pub had watched me from behind their pints of Guinness, saying little when I said what I wanted to climb Croagh Patrick. I had heard that the locals climbed Croagh Patrick as a way of doing penance. But the bar-

tender told me that people only did that one day a year, and I was exactly one week late for that one day. But I had laughed that off, and said I wasn't climbing the mountain for penance anyway. I just wanted to do it to say I had conquered the mountain. The bartender didn't speak to me after that. I guess he saw me as another ugly American.

I had no idea how high the climb would be, or how difficult. The climb had started easily—slow, steady, and well marked. Occasionally the ascent steepened, and I had to clutch my knees, pulling my legs up. I stumbled once, and saw I had torn my slacks and even cut my leg. I tried to wipe the blood off, but there was no denying the accident. At one point, I was even crawling on all fours. Why was I doing this?

My wife had said I was trying to deny my age with this assault on Croagh Patrick. I told her I may be fifty, but I'm not old. However, I was starting to feel old. Very old.

After an hour, the land finally leveled off and through the fog I could make out the shape of the chapel to Saint Patrick. I stood there at the top. I had won.

Then, I heard the sound of footsteps. I turned around. It was an old woman and a young boy, both smiling. I waved to her. The boy, perhaps her grandchild or even great-grandchild, seemed shy, tucked away under her coat. I felt humiliated, standing in front of them, torn and bleeding, while neither of them looked the least bit tired.

I asked her if she was coming to see the chapel. She said no, because the chapel was only open one day a year, and that had been last week.

"Why did you climb up here?" I asked.

"Oh," she said, "we just needed to catch a breath of fresh air. It's a wonderful little stroll—if you come up the other side."

I laughed. Later, when I was bandaging my leg, my wife asked me if I was satisfied now that I had conquered Croagh Patrick. I shook my head and laughed. I think I really conquered something in myself.

---

# E X E R C I S E 3

Write a personal narrative about an experience from your life that had particular importance or meaning. Don't just *tell* the reader—make the reader see, feel, hear, and share the incident as it happened to you. Limit your paper to a single main event, and provide details of the experience arranged in an order that makes sense to the reader. Don't wander off into unimportant digressions; stick to the main point. To generate ideas for your narrative, use some or all of the prewriting techniques you have practiced in this chapter.

## REVISION CHECKLIST

### Narrative Writing

*After you write your personal narrative, answer the following questions:*

**1.** *Did I select one main incident and stick to it, or did I wander off into unimportant subtopics and bore my reader?*
**2.** *Did I arrange the events chronologically, in the order in which they happened, or did I jump from the past to the present and back again, confusing my reader?*
**3.** *Did I build up to a certain point or idea, or is my reader likely to put the paper down and ask, "What's the point?"*
**4.** *Did I give examples and details so that the reader could know what I had experienced, or did I just make a series of vague statements, hoping that the reader could read my mind?*
**5.** *Did I check the dictionary when I wasn't sure how to spell a word, or did I just guess, hoping the reader would know the word I had in mind?*

### Writing a Description

Descriptive writing can be compared to a good photograph: it presents a clear picture of an object, a person, or a scene. Good description, however, goes a step further. It appeals to the reader's sense of sound, smell, touch, taste, and sight. It is filled with details that help to create a dominant impression; it has focus. In the following paragraph, notice that the author presents examples and specific details to show the German composer Richard Wagner as a "monster of conceit."

He was an undersized little man, with a head too big for his body—a sickly little man. His nerves were bad. He had skin trouble. It was agony for him to wear anything next to his skin coarser than silk. And he had delusions of grandeur.

He was a monster of conceit. Never for one minute did he look at the world or at people, except in relation to himself. He was not only the most important person in the world, to himself; in his own eyes he was the only person who existed. He believed himself to be one of the greatest dramatists in the world, one of the greatest thinkers, and one of the greatest composers. To hear him talk, he was Shakespeare, and Beethoven, and Plato, rolled into one. And you would have had no difficulty in hearing him talk. He was one of the most exhausting conversationalists that ever lived. An evening with him was an evening spent in listening to a monologue. Sometimes he was brilliant; sometimes he was maddeningly tiresome. But whether he was being brilliant or dull, he had one sole topic of conversation: himself. What *he* thought and what *he* did.

—Deems Taylor, from *Of Men and Music*

Good descriptive writing follows a plan. When you describe something, you supply details about it and arrange those details in a way that makes sense. Several kinds of plans are possible. For example, you can describe an object by starting with its most important feature and then describing other features of lesser importance. You can also follow a spatial order, arranging the objects to be described in some systematic sequence in space. In describing your room, for instance, you can start at the left side and work toward the right, or work from the ceiling to the floor, or from a far wall to a near wall. Remember to follow a plan or design. If your paper is nothing more than a hodge-podge of unrelated details, you will confuse or even lose your reader.

Equally important in description are specific details. Your reader must be able to *see* the object being described. This means that your description must be concrete—you have to supply your reader with specific images instead of vague or general statements.

One way to make your writing specific is to use precise diction. Use words that are sharp and clear. Instead of writing that a character "walked," for example, use a more exact word such as "shuffled," "trudged," "strutted," or "strode."

In the paragraph below, written by American novelist Stanley Elkin, notice how the author creates a dominant impression—darkness and mystery—by his word choice and the kinds of details he selects.

It was a hotel, dark except for the light from an open elevator and a floor lamp by one couch. The Oriental carpets, the furniture, the registration desk and shut shops—all seemed a mysterious, almost extinguished red in the enormous empty lobby. Even the elevator— one of four, he supposed the others weren't functioning—seemed set on low. He looked around for Mopiani but the man had remained at his post. He pressed the button and sensed himself sucked up through darkness, imaging, though it was day, the darkened mezzanine and black ballrooms, the dark lamps and dark flowers in their dark vases on the dark halved tables pressed against the

dark walls of each dark floor, the dark silky stripes on the benches outside the elevators, the dark cigarette butts in the dark sand.
—*The Franchiser*, Stanley Elkin, New York: Farrar, Straus & Giroux, 1976.

The following description, written by a freshman student, describes her impressions of a cemetery. Notice how she uses descriptive details to make a place most people steer clear of seem appealing.

The cemetery in my town is one of the most beautiful places I know. Some people think it strange that I like to take walks there, but if you can stop thinking of Halloween ghosts and goblins, the cemetery seems like a park.

I like the old section of the cemetery the best because of its tall, shady trees, ornate tombstones, and windy, unkempt paths. Few people come here because the graves are over a hundred years old, but when I go there I find I am not alone—there are always birds chattering, squirrels running from this place to that, and once I even saw a small deer that must have wandered in from the nearby forest. There are stone benches in this part, and sitting on them, looking around, I can see the beauty of tombstones built as art pieces, not just slabs that lie flat on the ground.

Some of the wealthier families of the time have small areas devoted strictly to themselves, their plots cordoned off from the others with cast iron fences. Often they have large stone monuments with statues of religious figures on top, and the family name etched in large letters, like "BLANKENSHIP." The family members' names are usually worn down smooth by the weather so that I can hardly read them. Their personal anonymity makes them nonthreatening. I sit on their monument and read a book.

Occasionally a groundskeeper comes by raking leaves or cleaning out the rare trash bin, but mostly I am alone. If I can find a nice sunny spot, I may even take a nap on the grass. The cemetery is really a restful place.

# E X E R C I S E 4

Write a description based on one of the following topics. Before you write, make a list of all the details you can think of. Then, decide on the plan or arrangement that is best for your description.

Make certain that you have not included any details that are off the topic and likely to confuse or distract your reader.

To generate ideas for your description, review the prewriting techniques introduced in this chapter. You can also use a series of questions involving the senses: What do you see? What does the object or person look like? What does the smell or taste like? What is on the left? The right? By asking questions on behalf of your reader, you will make your description more vivid and clear.

| | |
|---|---|
| a room in your home | a public park |
| a TV talk show host | a beat-up old car |
| your best friend | a favorite restaurant |
| a photograph | a pet |
| a scene from your window | the inside of your refrigerator |
| a stranger you noticed something unusual about | a building under construction |

# REVISION CHECKLIST

## Descriptive Writing

*After you write your description, answer the following questions:*

*1. Does my paper concentrate on describing one thing, scene, person, or object, or does it try to describe too much?*
*2. Does my paper have a plan, or does it jump around, confusing my reader?*
*3. Have I given my reader specific details so he or she can see what I am describing, or is my paper just a series of general and vague statements?*
*4. Are my words sharp and clear, or are they too general and vague?*
*5. Does my paper reflect the care I put into it, or is it filled with spelling mistakes or other errors?*

# COMPUTER EXERCISE

Choose a topic for your focus freewriting. Your teacher will allot five minutes; focus freewrite on that topic. Review what you have written, without editing, and start a new paragraph with the word or phrase that you like best.

Now, one twist: Leave your freewriting on your computer screen and switch seats with someone else in the class (if files can be passed from one computer to another, do that). Then freewrite for five minutes based on the new topic given on the screen. Then switch back to your original computer and read your partner's freewriting. Your partner's freewriting may have gone in directions you did not consider.

# C H A P T E R

# 3

# *Writing*

# *Paragraphs*

Most of the writing that you are required to do in college will be in the form of paragraphs. Occasionally—especially when answering questions on exams—your paragraphs will stand alone and be self-contained units. (See Chapter 12 for suggestions on writing single-paragraph responses to test questions.) Usually, however, your paragraphs will be parts of longer pieces of writing. In such cases paragraphs help your reader by breaking down complicated ideas into manageable parts and relating each part to the main idea or thesis of your essay.

Paragraphs have several important jobs in an essay, depending on where they are located. The opening paragraph should catch your reader's attention and present your main idea; the middle paragraphs support and develop your main idea, and the concluding paragraph brings your essay to a close with a sense of completeness.

In this chapter we are going to show how paragraphs can perform each of those functions, beginning with *middle paragraphs*, the paragraphs in the body of the essay that support and develop the thesis statement. (The thesis statement is the sentence containing the main idea and purpose of the essay.) The most important sentence in the middle paragraphs is the *topic sentence*, so we will start with it. Then we will study the important qualities that every effective middle paragraph must have: *unity, coherence,* and *development*.

Finally, we will look at the paragraphs that play other important roles in the essay: *introductory* and *concluding* paragraphs.

## Middle Paragraphs

The job of the paragraphs in the body of the essay—the *middle* paragraphs—is to support and develop the thesis statement. Each paragraph presents one aspect of the topic, usually announced in its *topic sentence*. Because the paragraph includes a series of related sentences on one topic, it has *unity, coherence,* and *development*.

### The Topic Sentence

Every good paragraph deals with a single topic or aspect of a topic. The sentence that states the paragraph's subjects is the *topic sentence*. The topic sentence is usually the most general sentence in the paragraph; it is developed and supported by the specifics in the sentences that follow. In a sense, the topic sentence has the same relationship to the paragraph as the thesis statement has to the essay.

Experienced writers do not include a topic sentence in every paragraph. But until you become an adept writer and are certain that your paragraphs stick to one idea, you should provide every paragraph with a topic sentence. Most topic sentences are placed at the beginning of a paragraph, although they can appear in other parts of the paragraph.

Individual paragraphs in the body of an essay usually treat one part of the central idea of the essay. The topic sentence alerts readers to the central idea and to the writer's attitude toward it. Topic sentences, therefore, elaborate on the ideas that support and develop the central idea of the essay.

The first sentence in the following paragraph is the topic sentence, and it announces the main idea of the paragraph in a general way: "The explosion in publishing books on how to raise children is of little surprise." The remaining sentences present several specific reasons that illustrate and support the topic sentence's ideas. Like most well-written paragraphs, this one begins with a general point and then supports it with several specific details.

> *The explosion in publishing books on how to raise children is of little surprise.* First, most young parents do not live with their own parents. In the past, grandparents could be relied upon to supply much instruction and help in raising children, but now they are in different homes, different cities, or even different parts of the country. Another reason is that different books apply different approaches, appealing to different types of parents. One book may emphasize a naturalistic approach to child rearing, another may be written by a doctor with a more scientific approach, while others have a sort of homey feeling, recreating the flavor of a grandmother's advice. Finally, books tend to give readers a feeling of certainty, that the answer to their baby's crying lies somewhere within the pages of a book.

The topic sentence is clear. It tells the reader what to expect in the sentences that follow, and reminds the writer what the central idea of the paragraph is, so he or she is unlikely to include sentences that wander off the topic.

A topic sentence can also be placed in the *middle* of the paragraph. This position is effective when the writer wants to begin with one or two details to lead up to the topic sentence, and then follow it with more support. In the next paragraph, notice how the topic sentence is preceded and followed by sentences that provide specific details and support. The topic sentence is italicized.

> The wilderness areas of the United States are being trampled upon by more and more hikers, backpackers, fishermen, and hunters every year. While these are the people most enthusiastic about safeguarding the wilderness, they may not realize that their very presence disrupts the lives of the plants and animals they

wish to protect. *The United States needs to place more areas of wilderness in reserve as strictly off limits to humans.* Only by removing all human involvement can plants and animals have the chance to regain and maintain their natural order, in which no creatures are frightened or hunted out of their natural habitat, no plants are crushed underfoot, no waters are polluted, and no sounds and smells of humans make birds and animals jittery and nervous. A strict off-limits policy would give Nature a chance to rejuvenate herself.

The topic sentence sometimes appears at the *end* of a paragraph. This position is particularly effective in building up to a controversial or unexpected conclusion. The writer first provides a number of facts and details and then tops them off with a sentence that serves as a conclusion or summary. In the following paragraph notice that the writer offers a number of facts and then offers the topic sentence.

In ancient Greece, slaves were used to perform tasks that the free classes felt were beneath them. Aristotle himself argued that most people lacked the superior qualities of the soul, and determined therefore that not everyone was fit to be free. He felt the practice was fundamentally natural and good. Even the Cynics and Stoics, who argued that slavery was contrary to nature, did not actively oppose the practice. Slaves were bought and sold, excluded from military and naval service except in moments of great crisis, and held no power in political life. *Thus, while the Western world may look upon Ancient Greece as the mother of democracy, slavery was an integral and accepted part of life there.*

One common weakness of topic sentences is that they try to cover too much territory. If your topic sentence is vague or very broad, you will have trouble writing a paragraph that develops it fully. "Something needs to be done to help the environment" is not as good a topic sentence as "Recycling is an excellent way to help preserve natural resources." A good topic sentence must be precise so it can be developed in a paragraph and can control the other sentences in the paragraph.

## E X E R C I S E 1

Which of these sentences are narrow enough to serve as topic sentences of paragraphs?

1. Several factors are holding back the attempt to unify Europe.
2. Football is a better sport than baseball.

3. Carla knew that if she made this sale, the promotion would be hers.

4. India, like the United States, is populated by many ethnic groups.

5. Psychologist Abraham H. Maslow identified five different types of human needs.

6. Educators are constantly rethinking how the classroom environment affects students.

7. Recent sensational cases of serial murderers such as Jeffery Dahmer and John Wayne Gacy have caused many people to become more intrigued with the criminal mind.

8. Japanese high-school students have better math test scores than American high-school students.

9. The alternative music scene owes its roots to punk rockers like the Sex Pistols.

10. There are many reasons why high-school students should be required to take a course in computers.

11. Use of lysergic acid diethylamide, or LSD, has increased in recent years for several reasons.

12. Elvis Presley has been spotted in innumerable places since his death in 1977.

13. Cars painted in certain colors seem to attract police more than other cars.

14. By studying Rapid Eye Movement (REM), psychologists and physiologists have come to an important conclusion about the meaning of dreams.

15. As we traveled across the country by train last summer, we were impressed by the diversity of this nation and its people.

---

## E X E R C I S E 2

Each group of sentences below can be rearranged as a paragraph. Select the topic sentence in each group and arrange the remaining sentences in the order that seems most logical. Remember: The topic sentence is the most general sentence in the paragraph because it states the main idea of the entire paragraph and includes all the ideas in the body.

1. a. The future for existentialists is wide open to all possibilities.
   b. Jean-Paul Sartre and Martin Heidegger can both be considered existentialists.
   c. Existentialists basically interpret the world in a way that emphasizes its concreteness and problems.
   d. Existentialism is a philosophy that has helped to shape twentieth-century thinking.

    e. Humans are free to make their own choices, according to existentialists.

2. a. Until 1922, Dublin was the seat of British authority in Ireland.
   b. Vikings invaded and settled the Dublin area during the ninth century, and in the twelfth century, the English claimed sovereignty over Ireland.
   c. Dublin is the most important city in Ireland, site of its violent past and hopeful future.
   d. Today, Dublin remains the commercial and social hub of a free and independent Ireland.
   e. Dublin first appeared in Ptolemy's *Guide to Geography* in A.D. 140 and probably had been inhabited since prehistoric times.

3. a. Alcoholics will lie, cheat, or steal to maintain their ability to drink.
   b. Unless they stop drinking completely, alcoholics may lose their jobs, their friends, and their families.
   c. Alcoholics lose the ability to control their drinking over time.
   d. Alcoholism can be a devastating problem.
   e. Although scientists still disagree over the precise causes of alcoholism, the effects of alcoholism are well-known.

4. a. Moving back home with his parents would save him quite a bit of money.
   b. He was glad that he no longer had to work full-time while going to school.
   c. His income tax refund was enough to cover his expenses for the rest of the semester.
   d. The dean's office approved his student loan, and he could cut his working hours.
   e. He finally paid off his car.
   f. Things were beginning to look up.

5. a. Computers speed up registration by providing up-to-date information on open classes.
   b. They assist instructors by grading multiple-choice tests.
   c. Computers now perform many tasks on my campus.
   d. Computers can supply advisors with instant and complete information on requirements, career information, and personal data while they are talking to a student.
   e. Computers keep records for the bookstore, library, cafeteria, and maintenance department.

## E X E R C I S E 3

Here are some groups of sentences that need a topic sentence to tie them together. For each set, write a topic sentence for the paragraph.

1. (*Your topic sentence*)
   First, a janitor has to make sure that he has all of his equipment ready: mops, brooms, rags, cleaners, waxes, polishers, plastic trash can liners. Typically, a janitor will try not to do all jobs every day. Usually trash is picked up every day, so that must be done quickly. Next, the floors need attention. Most days floors are only mopped or vacuumed, depending on what is appropriate. However, occasionally tile floors will need waxing and buffing, and this will probably consume a great deal of time for the janitor. In addition, bathrooms must be cleaned every day.

2. (*Your topic sentence*)
   The first moment I knew we were having an earthquake was when I woke up, half out of bed. There was a loud rumbling that sounded like a train was about to come through my bedroom. I heard several crashes that I later discovered were glasses I had left on the kitchen counter to dry overnight. All I could do was hold on to the side of the bed and just pray that the shaking would end soon. When it did, I got out of bed and ran outside. All over my neighborhood, cars parked on the street had been pushed around, some away from the curb, some over the curb. I was stunned.

3. (*Your topic sentence*)
   Ralph Waldo Emerson was the son of a Unitarian minister. He first went to Boston Public Latin School and then to Harvard College. He was ordained as a Unitarian minister in 1829, but he ultimately resigned from the ministry. He wrote several influential works, including "The American Scholar," "Address at Divinity College," "Uriel," and *The Conduct of Life*. He died in 1882.

4. (*Your topic sentence*)
   One item I bought was a money belt. It wrapped around my waist under my shirt. Outside of actually stripping me, no pickpocket was getting into that, but it did make me look ten pounds heavier than I actually was. I also wore a shoulder holster under my shirt in which I placed our passports and travelers checks. Finally, I used a cheap, flat wallet that I slid only into my front pockets, and I only put small amounts of money in that for convenience. I had decided that if a pickpocket did pick me, he was going to be disappointed.

5. (*Your topic sentence*)
   This pigment is called melanin. People who can form a little melanin are yellow-haired and blue-eyed. People who can form a fair amount of melanin have brown hair (or even black hair) and brown eyes. There is enough melanin in the skin to give them a swarthy complexion. If the amount of melanin is high enough, the skin itself is distinctly brown, sometimes quite brown.

# E X E R C I S E 4

Develop each of the following subjects into a topic sentence. Remember that a good topic sentence is narrow enough to be covered in a paragraph.

| | |
|---|---|
| Lawyers | Flowers |
| Family | Ocean pollution |
| England | Computers |
| Electronic gear | Motherhood |
| Airplanes | Furniture |

## The Unified Paragraph

Every paragraph should be *unified*—that is, the topic sentence and every other sentence in the body should relate to one main idea. The best way to be certain that your paragraphs have *unity* is to construct a specific focused topic sentence and then develop it through the entire paragraph. If the paragraph sticks to what is promised in the topic sentence, it has unity. Any sentence that does not develop the topic violates the unity of the paragraph and should be omitted.

In the following paragraph, notice how the italicized sentence introduces another idea into the paragraph and violates the unity of the paragraph:

> Edgar Allan Poe (1809–1849) made several outstanding contributions to nineteenth-century American literature. With his short story "The Purloined Letter," which was to be the model for Sherlock Holmes stories, he helped to create the modern detective story. He also wrote important literary criticism in which he strove to emphasize the proper use of language, correct meter and structure in poetry, and adherence to the ancient unities. *Writing can be a long and difficult process.* However, Poe is probably best known as a writer of the macabre because of his fascination with death, as exhibited in stories such as "The Fall of the House of Usher," "The Tell-Tale Heart," and "The Cask of Amontillado."

The topic sentence announced the main idea of the paragraph: Edgar Allan Poe is a major American writer of the nineteenth century. The fact that writing is a long and difficult process is irrelevant—the writer has introduced a sentence that does not contribute to the development of the topic sentence.

Some paragraphs lack unity because they are only a collection of unrelated ideas; they look like paragraphs because the first line is indented, but they do not develop one single topic. In the paragraph below, notice how the writer discusses a number of topics, all of which are abandoned:

> I went golfing the other day with Rich, Mark, and Scott. The golf course was in great condition. Rich didn't play too well. Mark's wife is working as a model right now. She's making a ton of money. I played pretty well. It was hot though. I think if I just got out and practiced a bit more, I could really improve my game and finally beat these guys.

As you can see, this paragraph is chaotic. It goes nowhere because it never started out to say anything. It is a hodgepodge of miscellaneous thoughts. The writer could salvage some of the sentences and rework them into topic sentences for separate paragraphs, but as the paragraph stands now, the impression is of bouncing from one thought to another.

One of the best ways to test the unity of a paragraph is to analyze how the sentences support the topic sentence. This is particularly effective when the topic sentence comes at the beginning of the paragraph. This kind of paragraph will usually fall into one of two patterns. In the first pattern, all of the sentences are *coordinate*; that is, they are equal to each other, and each is a comment on the topic sentence. The Edgar Allan Poe paragraph is an example of this pattern; the sentence that violated the unity of the paragraph has been deleted.

> Edgar Allan Poe (1809-1849) made several outstanding contributions to 19th American literature.
> With his short story "The Purloined Letter," he helped to create the modern detective story that was to be the model for Aurthur Conan Doyle's Sherlock Holmes stories.
> He also wrote important literary criticism in which he strove to emphasize the proper use of language, correct meter and structure in poetry, and adherence to the ancient unities.
> However, Poe is probably best known as a writer of the macabre because of his fascination with death exhibited in stories like "The Fall of the House of Usher," "The Tell-Tale Heart" and "The Cask of Amontillado."

In this pattern, all of the supporting sentences are equal, and each is a comment on the topic sentence. As a result, the paragraph has unity.

In the second pattern, the first sentence of the paragraph is a topic sentence and the second is a development of it. The third sentence is either another comment on the topic sentence or a comment on the sentence immediately before it. In other words, paragraphs that follow this pattern will consist of two kinds of sentences: coordinate sentences that are equal to each other and that make a comment on the topic sentence, and subordinate sentences that make comments on the sentences they follow. Any sentence that fails to comment on the topic sentence destroys the unity of the paragraph and should be deleted.

Here is an example of a unified paragraph written in this pattern. The topic sentence and supporting sentences are arranged below it so that you can see their relationship.

> Technology has changed the way that workplaces operate, even in areas that would not occur to many people. White-collar workers use computers in some of the more obvious ways. They employ computers as word processors and data crunchers, for billing and watching inventories, for making projections for the next business quarter, or even for filing tax returns with the IRS. However, blue-collar workers have also seen computers enter their workplaces, sometimes at the cost of their jobs. Computers run the robotics in super-modern factories; they can eliminate the need for secretarial help; and they can perform quality checks that used to be done manually. Even service industries rely heavily on computers. In some fast food establishments, computers record orders and cash flow, or tell a low-paid laborer when to turn a hamburger patty on the grill.

Technology has changed the way that work places operate even in areas that would not occur to many people.

White collar workers use computers in some of the more obvious ways.

They employ computers as word processors and data crunchers, for billing and watching inventories, making projections for the next business quarter or even filing tax returns with the IRS.

However, blue collar workers have seen computers enter their world, sometimes at the cost of their jobs.

Computers run the robotics in super-modern factories, they can eliminate the need for secretarial help, and they can perform quality checks that used to be done manually.

Even service industries rely heavily on computers.

In some fast food establishments, computers record orders and cash flow, or tell a low-paid laborer when to turn a hamburger patty on the grill.

In this paragraph the topic sentence is supported directly by three sentences ("Supporting sentences 1, 2, and 3") illustrating the use of computers in the workplace. Each of these sentences in turn, is followed by a sentence that makes a comment on it.

By studying the pattern of support—by noticing whether every sentence in a paragraph makes a comment about either the topic sentence or the sentence it follows—you can easily tell whether a paragraph is unified.

---

# E X E R C I S E 5

Each of the paragraphs below contains a sentence that destroys the unity of the paragraph. Underline that sentence. Then, for each paragraph, prepare a diagram similar to the one constructed for the technology in the workplace paragraph.

1. The role of religion in education in this country has changed over time, but it has nevertheless remained a powerful force. Among the earliest English colonies were Puritans fleeing religious persecution. For the Puritans, learning to read was important so that people could read the Bible, and the task of teaching children to read first fell to the parents. Over time though, education started to come into conflict with religious beliefs, especially when science began to propose ways of looking at the world that ran contrary to a literal interpretation of the Bible. One such case is the famous Scopes Trial of 1925. No one has the right to tell people what their religion should be. In 1963, the Supreme Court ruled that mandatory prayer in public schools was unconstitutional. Even today there is conflict in many school districts over how parents' religious beliefs should or should not be reflected in the instruction children receive in public schools.

2. Uganda is a country with a troubled past. First, it was subject to colonial rule by Britain until it gained its independence in 1962. Uganda is a landlocked East African country with a population of over 14 million people. In 1971, Major General Idi Amin Dada took over Uganda in a military coup and began a reign of terror. In 1978, Amin had his military forces invade Tanzania. This turned out to be a mistake because Tanzanian forces retaliated a year later and removed Amin from power.

3. Americans seem to have lost their sense of responsibility. Everyone else is at fault. If a criminal is caught, he blames his parents who abused or neglected him, schools that didn't educate him, or a society that doesn't accept him. Nothing is said to be wrong; all actions are viewed from different perspectives, and, according to this philosophy, no one perspective is

superior to another. Liberal judges let criminals go free on technicalities. Underlying this intellectual exercise seems to be the idea that we are only victims of our environment, without any ability to think or act for ourselves. Ultimately, the criminal is seen as acting in ways that are inevitable based on his circumstances.

4. One of the most remarkable mammals in the world is the wolf. Wolves are highly intelligent and social animals that live in packs of several to two dozen or more. Wolves are believed to mate for life. While many people think of wolves as dangerous, their chief sources of food are deer, moose, and caribou, not humans. In fact, people are the greatest threat to wolves. Many human cultures have incorporated wolves into their mythology. The wolf has been hunted to such a great extent that his range, which once spread throughout North America and Eurasia, has been greatly reduced.

5. The controversy over the death of Bessie Smith, the great blues singer, has never ended. On September 26, 1937, Bessie was killed in an automobile accident on a Mississippi road. One account holds that she bled to death on the road while waiting for medical attention. Supposedly an ambulance arrived, but its driver picked up a less seriously injured white woman first, then came back for Bessie. Other sources claim that Bessie Smith died in the back of an ambulance on the way to a black hospital after she had been refused admittance to a white hospital. Columbia Records has released over 150 of her recordings in recent years.

---

## E X E R C I S E 6

Developed two topic sentences from the subjects in Exercise 4; for one of them, write a paragraph organized like the model on page 35; for the other, write a paragraph organized like the model on page 36.

---

## Coherence in the Paragraph

You have seen that when a paragraph is unified, all the other sentences support or develop the topic sentence. But the unity alone is not enough to make a paragraph clear. It must also have coherence. Coherence means "sticking together," and in a coherent paragraph, all the ideas stick together. A coherent paragraph is one in which the ideas are put in the right order with the right connecting words so that the reader is never confused. This makes the writer's thought easy to follow from sentence to sentence and from paragraph to paragraph.

Good writers rely on two ways of making their paragraphs coherent: arranging their ideas in a logical order, and using linking words or phrases between sentences to help the reader understand how the ideas are related.

## Coherence Through Order

The best way to make the middle or supporting paragraphs of your essay coherent is also the most obvious way: by arranging their ideas in a pattern that makes sense to your reader. After jotting down your ideas, but before writing the paragraph, you should decide which ideas to discuss first, which to discuss second, and so on, according to a logical order. The purpose or content of the paragraph will usually suggest an appropriate arrangement.

To explain an idea or defend an opinion—the purposes of expository and persuasive writing—you would probably arrange your ideas in one of the following patterns: *order of importance, general-to-specific* (sometimes called *deductive*), and *specific-to-general* (or *inductive*). When you wish to narrate an experience or present the steps in a process, you would normally arrange your details in *chronological order*, the sequence in which they happened. When you wish to describe a person or a scene, you will organize the details in a *spatial order*. (For a detailed discussion of chronological and spatial order, see pages 87–93 in Chapter 5.)

*Order of Importance.* One of the most useful ways of arranging ideas in a paragraph is *in order of importance.* Technically speaking, such a paragraph can be arranged in two ways: by beginning with the most important idea and proceeding to the least important, or by beginning with the least important and building up to the most important. The disadvantage of the first pattern—from most important to least—is that it is anticlimactic. There is a letdown after the opening sentence or two, and the paragraph dwindles away. The advantages of building up to the most important ideas stem from the suspense involved and the tendency for readers to remember best what they read last. The paragraph that concludes with a surprise, a clever comment, an appeal for action, or some other strong ending is more likely to be successful.

To organize the ideas in a paragraph according to their order of importance, you should first make a list of the ideas supporting your topic sentence. The most important ideas should come first, then the next most important, and so on. In writing the paragraph, take your ideas from the list in reverse order. Not every paragraph can be constructed in this pattern, of course, but it can be an emphatic way to arrange ideas.

In the paragraph below, notice how the writer introduces his least important ideas first, then presents his most important idea in the last sentence:

> My friend Paul has created enormous problems for himself. First, he neglected to study for a test because he was afraid of failure, thereby ensuring that he would not pass. Since Paul was already on academic probation, this failing grade was the final straw and he was dismissed from school. Because he had borrowed money to pay for school, he now had to find work with no degree. All he could find were low-paying, low-skills jobs that were very tiring and somewhat demeaning. Depressed, he began to drink heavily and injured himself by falling off a ladder at work. However, because he had been drunk at work when he injured himself, he received no worker's compensation and was fired instead. The last I heard, Paul was seen downtown walking with a limp, a bottle of fortified wine in hand, accosting women and yelling obscenities at passersby.

In the preceding paragraph, the writer presents a series of unfortunate incidents that happened to Paul because of his failure to study for a test. The paragraph builds to its sad and unfortunate conclusion.

In the next paragraph, also written by a student, notice a similar structure: a series of facts about the waste of newspapers in the world leads to the important fact at the conclusion of the paragraph.

> Paper is one substance that Americans can do a lot more to recycle, and the effect of doing so could be enormous. About 62 million newspapers are purchased daily in the United States, but only 26 million wind up being recycled. This means that over 500,000 newspapers wind up in landfills each and every week. In newsprint alone, Americans discard over 30 million trees yearly. If Americans could increase the number of newspapers they recycle, we could reduce the waste of trees, lessen the bulk of materials that are clogging our landfills, and even reduce air pollution caused by the garbage trucks that haul newspaper to the landfills.

*General-to-Specific.* The *general-to-specific* (or *deductive*) pattern is the most common type of paragraph order. This arrangement begins with a topic sentence that makes a general statement followed by a series of supporting sentences that supply specifics: details, examples, and facts. Because the reader knows what the main point is, he can follow the development of the thought more easily. For this reason, the deductive pattern minimizes the chances for reader misunderstanding and is particularly effective for informing and clarifying.

Notice how the following paragraphs begin with a general statement (the topic sentence) and then proceed to specifics that support the generalization.

> The advent of television almost certainly brought with it effects its inventors neither anticipated nor necessarily wanted. Families may stay together in the home more, but they are watching a program together, zombie-like, not interacting. Graphic violence and sex without consequences have worked like a corrosive on American middle-class values. The network news broadcasts, which once were sober and serious, have gradually become another vehicle for entertainment, hyping shock and sleaze like the worst tabloid. New shows are simply the old ones with new faces, and comedies require laugh tracks so viewers can determine what's supposed to be funny. The only redeeming factor television has maintained since its earliest days is the "off" button.

> An entire industry has grown around the act of getting married. There is, of course, the wedding gown, which can be bought off the rack or ordered through a catalogue at a boutique, and may range from a few hundred dollars to several thousand after accessories are included. Bridesmaids will require dresses, hose, shoes, perhaps even hats and gloves. Men may rent tuxedos, a considerably cheaper venture. Flowers are considered mandatory in most weddings, both to decorate the building and the people in the wedding; the costs can again easily run into hundreds of dollars. A church may charge rent, a minister or priest may require some payment, and there will be lots of silence if some musicians have not been hired. Naturally, a photographer will be happy to record all this, for a fee.

*Specific-to-General.* In the general-to-specific pattern, the opening topic is followed by supporting sentences that are more specific. The *specific-to-general* (or *inductive*) pattern reverses this order. It presents a series of individual, specific facts, details, impressions or observations, and ends with a generalization or conclusion, usually the topic sentence.

This pattern is less common than the general-to-specific because it is more difficult for the reader to follow. On the other hand, it is useful in holding in suspense an opinion or conclusion that might be contrary to what the reader believes or expects. For this reason, it is especially appropriate in persuasive writing.

Notice the pattern of the following paragraph: the author presents a series of facts and then presents her conclusion, which serves as the topic sentence.

The uninitiated view the Bible as a religious tract, a boring book of rules. Nothing could be further from the truth. In large part, the Bible is a collection of stories. In them, we find the kinds of people we know and relate to even today, such as Cain and Abel, and the jealously that led to murder; or Ruth, who lost her husband and found herself in a foreign land; or David, a figure of triumph but also of human weakness. A reader will find stories of love, war, lust, anger, greed, sorrow, loneliness, and virtue. In short, the Bible is filled with many tales that expose all sides of human existence.

Below is another example of a paragraph that follows the *specific-to-general* pattern. It, too, presents a series of facts and concludes with a general statement.

Because money was tight after the widespread bank failures that followed the crash of the stock market in 1929, new laws governing bankruptcy were passed in the 1930s, most importantly the Chandler Act of 1938. The effect of the laws was to make borrowing easier and to lessen the penalties for those who could no longer repay. Owners of failed businesses were allowed to try to settle their debts without facing imprisonment. Honest debtors were able to have part of their debt discharged, so that they could get a new start on life. As a result of the loosening of credit and the decrease in the penalties for failure to repay debt, more people were encouraged to start their own small businesses.

*Chronological Order.* In paragraphs organized *chronologically*, events and details are arranged in the order in which they occurred, usually moving from the first or earliest to the last or latest. Not all paragraphs arranged chronologically tell stories. Some give directions or explain a process; others summarize historical events; and still others report on the steps or actions taken by an individual or an organization. Nevertheless, they all share an underlying similarity: they present their ideas in the order in which they happened.

In the following paragraph notice that all of the details are presented in the order in which they happened:

The collapse of the Berlin Wall virtually overnight was one of the most important and unanticipated events in recent memory. The fall of the wall that had long separated the German city, as well as a nation, really began with the advent of Mikhail Gorbachev's policies of *glasnost* and *perestroika*. Gorbachev visited East Germany, and eleven days later, Egon Krenz was named as party chief, ending decades of tyrannical rule by Erich Honecker, who was too ill to rule. Soon, East Germans began sneaking across the border to Hungary and Czechoslovakia, eventually making their way into West Germany. When it became clear that the Hungarians and Czechs felt no desire to stop the East Germans, what started as a stream threatened to turn into a flood. Krenz gambled that if the government opened the way directly to West Germany, the long suppressed East Germans would feel less compelled to leave East Germany permanently, would visit the West, and then willingly return. That opening was all the East Berliners needed. On November 9, 1989, Berliners from both sides met at the wall, and in a dramatic scene, they embraced each other, climbed on top of the wall, danced and celebrated, and even began tearing the wall down. This was a day to remember, a day many never expected to live to see.

When you use chronological order, it is important that you relate the events in the order in which they occurred. The paragraph above would have been confusing to readers if the writer had started with the celebration, then discussed the ascension of Egon Krenz, and so on. You can avoid such confusion by including all points or incidents as they happened.

*Spatial Order.* If the purpose of your paragraph is to tell how something looks, the most effective organization pattern is usually *spatial*. If you write a description of your neighborhood, your room, or the view from the top of the Empire State Building, you will want your readers to have a mental picture of what you are describing. Like a movie photographer with a hand-held camera, you may choose to focus the scene from your vantage point and then move outward, from left to right, from right to left, or from near to far. In describing a house or a building, you would probably first describe the exterior and then the interior. By moving systematically rather than haphazardly over the scene, you convey to the viewer the overall plan or arrangement of the scene.

A description of a person also makes use of the spatial pattern. If you were writing a description of your father, for instance, you would bewilder your reader if you were to describe his shoes, then his hair, and then his eyes. But following closely the order in which eyes see (or movie cameras move), spatial order gives the reader a clear picture of the object being described.

Below is a paragraph based on spatial organization. Notice that the details are not presented in a hit-or-miss fashion; instead, they follow a pattern that lets us visualize the subject.

My first job was at a restaurant washing dishes with a man named Zachary. As I look back now, I realize that Zachary must have only been in his forties, but he looked older because his hair was speckled with gray. He had a wispy mustache that grew down over his upper lip. His skin was marred by deep lines that cut through his face, all coming from his eyes as if he were perpetually squinting, probably the result of spending too much time in the sun. His body was thin but tightly muscled, and he could move large crates of vegetables that larger men refused to budge without a hand cart. He moved in quick, jerky fashion, like a man who'd drunk a pot of coffee. He always wore a dirty white T-shirt and blue jeans with big hobnail boots. Those boots would thump when he walked, announcing his presence before he was anywhere to be seen.

In the next paragraph notice how the details are arranged in a spatial pattern: from the left, ahead of us, and to the right of us, as if caught by a movie camera being swung in an arc.

> The inside of the cathedral took our breath away. Inside, to the left, was a side chapel to the Virgin Mary, a large statue placed behind rows of candles. Further along that side were several paintings, each depicting one of the stations of the cross, and above them were tall stained glass windows, one for each of the twelve apostles. Walking up the center aisle, we saw in front of us the altar, with an ornate, gold-inlaid wall behind it, featuring at least half a dozen statues to Mary, Jesus, and other saints. The wall on the other side was partially covered; it appeared to be undergoing repairs. On the far right next to us was a baptismal font that appeared to be of white marble. The stained glass windows, the gold altar, and the beautiful paintings made it seem for a moment as if we were truly back in the Middle Ages.

Spatial order creates a visual effect. In order for your reader to see your subject, you have to select details that make the subject clear, and you have to present those details in a pattern that your reader can follow.

There are other ways of arranging your ideas in a logical order so that your paragraphs will be coherent. The patterns described here, however, are used most often. The material itself will usually determine the best order to follow. In an ordered paragraph, the thoughts follow naturally from sentence to sentence.

## E X E R C I S E 7

Following the directions given, write paragraphs arranged in each of the specified patterns.

1. Arranging your ideas *in order of importance*, write a paragraph of at least 100 words on one of the following topics:
   A day worth remembering
   The problems with college
   Reasons for violence in society
   The effects of technology

The duties of a citizen
The advantages of a liberal arts education
The disadvantages of a liberal arts education
Family

2. Arranging your ideas in either *general-to-specific* or *specific-to-general order*, write a paragraph of at least 100 words on one of the following topics:
   Advantages of living alone
   Racial discrimination
   Problems with landfills
   Criminal computer hackers
   Hazards of being a fire fighter
   America's obsession with sports
   Benefits of family planning
   The dangers of car phones
   Responsibilities of being a parent
   Problems of being from a non–English-speaking family

3. Arranging your ideas in *chronological order*, write a paragraph of at least 100 words on one of the following topics:
   The first day of college
   A fishing or hunting trip
   Asking someone out for the first time
   Using a fax machine
   Selecting music for a party
   An automobile accident
   A playground during recess
   A wedding

4. Arranging your ideas in *spatial order*, write a paragraph of at least 100 words on one of the following topics:
   A beautiful park
   My ideal boyfriend's or girlfriend's appearance
   The bathroom counter
   The library study area
   The interior of my car
   The view from the highest point in town
   The campus hangout

---

## Coherence Through Linking Devices

In addition to arranging ideas in a logical order, you can make paragraphs coherent by linking one sentence to the next using *transitional words and phrases and other linking devices*. These devices signal the curve and directions of the thought as you read through the paragraph. With them, the reader is prepared for each new idea and can relate each new statement to the last. Without them, a paragraph can sound like a list of unrelated ideas.

Notice how each sentence is isolated from the next in this paragraph, making it sound wooden:

> Morning people and night people often clash. Morning people function best in the early hours of the day. Night people work better during the evening hours. Morning people are up at dawn, getting ready for a new day. Night people see the sunset as only the beginning of their day. Morning people have almost a puritanical sense of the rightness of their way of living. The world is set up for morning people. Most workplaces require employees to come into work in the morning and leave in the late afternoon. Night people have to adjust to this. They suffer low productivity during the morning hours when they would rather be asleep. Night people are seen as lazy, or worse, as moral degenerates.

Notice how much smoother this paragraph becomes when transitional words, phrases, and other linking devices are used to make the paragraph more coherent.

> Morning people and night people often clash. Morning people function best in the early hours of the day *while* night people work better during the evening hours. Morning people are up at dawn, getting ready for a new day, *but* night people see the sunset as only the beginning of their day. Morning people have almost a puritanical sense of the rightness of their way of living. *After all,* the world is set up for morning people. Most workplaces require employees to come into work in the morning and leave in the late afternoon. Night people have to adjust to this. *Consequently,* they suffer low productivity during the morning hours when they would rather be asleep. *Therefore,* night people are seen by morning people as lazy, or worse, as moral degenerates.

Transitional words and phrases show the relationship between sentences. In some ways they are like traffic signs. They tell the reader what is ahead, warning of a turn or curve, advising when to slow down, and so on.

Examine the following sentences for their use of transitions:

> The golf pro spent extra time working on her putting stroke. *As a result,* she made several crucial putts during the tournament. (*"As a result"* suggests that the second sentence is the effect or consequence of the first.)

> My aunt Betty was looking forward to being a grandmother. However, she did not intend to become a full-time nanny for my cousin. (*"However"* alerts the reader to a contrasting idea aloud.)

Here is a list of some of the most common transitional words that connect sentences, making them more coherent:

| also | however | next |
| although | in addition | on the contrary |

| | | |
|---|---|---|
| and | in conclusion | second |
| as a result | in fact | similarly |
| besides | later | still |
| but | likewise | that is |
| consequently | meanwhile | therefore |
| finally | moreover | though |
| for example | nevertheless | whereas |
| furthermore | on the other hand | yet |

# E X E R C I S E 8

In the following sentences, supply the most fitting transition. Try to avoid using the same transition twice.

1. Roger told me that organic chemistry was a difficult course; _____, his warning did not prepare me for the many hours of study and lab work that were required.

2. Most of the rock stars today are actually cynically constructed, slick rip-offs of past popular bands; ____ my favorite band is totally original.

3. Britt looked like a million bucks at the party; ____, Randall decided he would ask her for forgiveness.

4. American car companies are back in the business of making smaller cars; ____, Geos and Saturns are especially popular with young people on budgets.

5. The entire world has a stake in seeing that the republics of the former Soviet Union can become peaceful, productive nations; _____, many nations favor giving generous amounts of aid to these new countries.

6. ____ he claimed that he had not committed the murders, the evidence was stacked against him; ____, he entered a plea of "not guilty."

7. Jerry was on the phone setting up a golf game; ____, his wife was packing her bags to leave him.

8. The shrinking of the defense budgets has caused many private companies to lay off employees; ____, electrical engineering majors are no longer guaranteed jobs out of college.

9. ____ Scott owned his own business, his parents wanted him to finish his college degree.

10. LaCrisha enrolled at Howard University; ____, she knew she would miss California.

Another device to link sentences in the paragraph is the *pronoun*, particularly when it refers to the subject of a previous sentence.

> *Lacrosse* is growing in popularity throughout the United States. *It* demands as much running as soccer, requires hand-eye coordination, and allows for some physical contact.

The use of *It* makes clear that the demands of lacrosse are being discussed.

By *repeating key words*, you can also connect your sentences more smoothly:

> *English* soccer teams are often supported by some of the most violent and unruly fans in the world. *English* hooligans travel in large numbers to other countries to get drunk and pick fights with locals in a perverse attempt to gain a psychological edge over their team's opponents.

If *English* were not repeated, the relationship between the two sentences would not be clear.

The *repetition of sentence structure* is another way of establishing a connection between two sentences:

> In Italy, parents introduce their children to alcohol consumption without emotional overtones, yet frown on drunkenness. In France, parents are more emotional about favoring or opposing alcohol consumption, yet they have a greater acceptance of drunkenness.

By repeating the structure of the first sentence, the writer has smoothly connected the second sentence.

## Developing Paragraphs

A common weakness in college writing is thin and underdeveloped paragraphs. While there is no exact rule about the minimum number of sentences required in a paragraph, a short paragraph is often a sign that the writer did not follow through in her thinking about the topic. As a result, many weak paragraphs consist of little more than a topic sentence and one or two generalities, as if the writer hoped the reader would complete the thought for her.

You will often encounter brief paragraphs in newspaper writing, where the narrow column of the page requires shorter paragraphs for the readers' convenience. Brief paragraphs are also used to show a division or shift in the section of an essay or to draw attention to a startling fact or an important statement. In general, however, it is a good rule to examine carefully any paragraphs you have written that contain only one, two, or three sentences. The chances are good that they are underdeveloped.

The length of a paragraph depends on the topic. The best measuring stick is your topic sentence: what promise did you make in it to your reader? Are a series of examples anticipated as a result of your topic sentence? Is a definition of a term used in the topic sentence promised, or do you imply that you will present a comparison or contrast between two objects or people? The expectations raised by your topic sentence determine, to a great degree, the length and development of your paragraph.

→ Here is a student-written paragraph describing happy hour on a Friday at a bar where she works as a waitress. The paragraph is underdeveloped because the writer makes a few vague observations, but nothing that we can see or hear—nothing that makes the topic sentence come alive.

> When happy hour at the Ancient Bull finally starts, the scene is basically one of chaos. The place gets real crowded, everyone wants to be served at once, and the bartenders are confused. It's truly a madhouse, but somehow it all works out. I make a lot of money during happy hour, but I've really earned it.

Notice how vague the paragraph is: ". . . scene is basically one of chaos," and "it's truly a madhouse." What does the author mean by chaos? What are the bartenders confused about? What qualities are similar to those of a madhouse? We do not know the answers to these questions; as a result, the paragraph is blurred and indistinct.

Here is a revised version of the same paragraph. Notice how the writer has developed the topic sentence with details that make the scene more vivid.

> When happy hour at the Ancient Bull finally starts on Fridays, the bar changes from being nearly empty to being a virtual battlefield. Men come in singly or in pairs, loosening their ties and calling to us waitresses before they've even had a seat. Women enter, almost always in groups, laughing. By this time, Greg, the manager, has usually turned up the volume on the loudspeakers a notch on the rock and roll oldies station. Men usually want beer or hard drinks, the women usually want white wine or vodka gimlets. The orders come so quickly that the bartenders get confused as to who ordered what and how much different drinks cost. Gretchen, Lisa, and I are usually on together, and we've gotten good at dividing up the tables and getting to people standing around, but with noise from the music and talking, sometimes we can't even hear each other talk, which can lead to tables being missed. Thank goodness Tori usually covers all requests for food. She winds up being as busy as anyone, whirling through crowds with baskets of hot wings or fried zucchini strips. Eventually, the floor becomes slippery from spilled beer, and the lines outside the

bathrooms start to back up into the tables, so I'm always asking people to move out of my way. By the end of the shift, I'm worn out, but when I look in my pockets, I may have as much as a hundred dollars.

As you can easily see, the revised paragraph is fully developed. It offers the sights and sounds of happy hour, helping us to see and hear the confusion mentioned in the topic sentence. By comparing the two versions you can appreciate the difference between an undeveloped and a developed paragraph.

### Strategies for Developing Paragraphs

The strategies or patterns for developing paragraphs are similar to those discussed in Chapter 6, "Developing the Essay: Six Patterns." An individual paragraph can be developed by example, comparison and contrast, and so on. Like essays, some paragraphs may combine patterns in their development; a definition paragraph, for example, may combine examples with divisions and classification.

You may find it helpful to refer to the six developmental patterns on pages 99–139 as you study this section.

### EXEMPLIFICATION

Remember, a paragraph developed by *exemplification* begins with a generalization, which it then supports with specific cases or examples. The examples should be typical, to the point, and supportive of the generalization.

Much of America's greatness stems from the variety of ethnic groups that have settled here over the centuries, bringing with them their own languages, religions, customs, and cuisines. Many cultures feature special meals for certain celebrations. Many African Americans celebrate *Kwanzaa* with dishes such as Spicy Pea Soup, Kwanzaa Fried Chicken, and Sweet Potato Pie. Italian Americans celebrate the Festival of San Gennaro with pizzas, calzones, and zeppole. Swedish Americans may celebrate Christmas with Gravlax with Dill, Pork Brawn, and Herring and Potato Casserole. A Jewish Seder may feature roasted shank of lamb, matzo, bitter herbs, charoset, parsley, hard-boiled eggs, and saltwater. Chinese New Year may be celebrated with "Long Life" noodles, Dragon Fish, and Spring Rolls. The variety of tastes, textures, and presentations can keep even the most adventurous taste buds excited all year round in America.

## E X E R C I S E 9

Write a paragraph of at least six sentences on one of the topics below, using examples to develop your paragraph. Begin by writing your topic sentence and listing at least three specific examples that make the topic sentence clear. Then write your paragraph.

The benefits of learning first aid
Women who have overcome obstacles
The cyclical nature of fashion
People who are heroes
What makes for a strong marriage
Pesky door-to-door salespeople
Inexpensive gifts for the family
Commercials that are enjoyable
Fears that people have about technology
Corruption in public office

## CLASSIFICATION

To *classify* is to show how parts of a whole are related; a paragraph developed by *classification* divides a topic into ideas or parts according to their similarities.

### Classification

The dramatic works of William Shakespeare have typically been divided into three groupings: histories, comedies, and tragedies. The histories dramatize important people and events from English history, although Shakespeare was not overly concerned with factual accuracy. The histories include such plays as *Richard II, Henry IV Pats 1 and 2,* and *Richard III.* The comedies were greatly influenced by comedic conventions from France and Italy, and include such favorites as *Much Ado about Nothing, As You Like It,* and *Measure for Measure.* The tragedies are often considered Shakespeare's greatest works and include *Othello, Macbeth, Lear,* and *Hamlet, Prince of Denmark.*

## E X E R C I S E 10

Select one of the following topics and develop it into a paragraph based on classification:

Good household pets
Tutoring services available on campus

The people involved in staging a play
Cable television stations
Flowers in your garden
Books you like to read
Churches in your city
Ancient mythological traditions

---

## COMPARISON AND CONTRAST

Comparison and contrast paragraphs present the similarities and differences between items. Paragraphs using the block method first present all of the relevant details or aspects of one object, then all of the corresponding qualities of the other. Paragraphs developed point-by-point alternate the points of comparison, presenting the differences or similarities of each object in turn.

### Block Method

Chipping and putting are two different strokes used around the green to try to get the ball as close to the hole as possible. Chipping resembles putting, only with a lofted club, such as a wedge, nine, eight, or even seven iron. The key is to line the shot up like a putt, keeping your wrist stiff throughout the stroke. The stroke is very nearly level, as in a putt, and you should practice using the same stroke every time. Use a different club to achieve different distances; the higher lofted the club, the shorter the distance. The object is to carry the fringe and get the ball rolling as quickly as possible. Pitching is done with a wedge, and resembles a full swing with an iron. With a pitch, the object is to get the ball in the air, landing it softly on the green, with less roll than a chip. With the ball aligned with your right foot, you should shift your weight slightly forward in a moderately open stance. The amount of swing you take will determine the distance the ball carries in the air. This is an excellent shot for carrying traps or thick rough. You may wish to choke down on the wedge for shorter shots.

### Point-by-Point

New scientific studies suggest that men and women may think differently, not from social conditioning, but from physical differences in the brain. So when a man who gets lost tries to read a map, and a woman simply asks a stranger for directions, they're just doing what comes naturally. According to these new studies, men may have more specialized brains, and women have better interconnections between the brain's two hemispheres, the result of the sexes' differing levels of testosterone in the womb during gestation. These brain structures lead to different capabilities. As a result, men excel at being mathematicians, athletes, or construction workers; women are innately equipped to be our top doctors, diplomats, and politicians. One note of caution: These studies are only preliminary, and differences within each gender still far outweigh differences between the genders.

## E X E R C I S E 11

Select one of the following pairs and write a paragraph developed by comparison and contrast using either the block or point-by-point arrangement.

Winners and losers
Rap and rock
Street smarts and school smarts
A book and a movie based on the book
Owning a home and renting a home
Two vacation spots
Martin Luther King and Malcolm X
Two Native American tribes

## PROCESS AND ANALYSIS

Paragraphs developed by process and analysis are usually organized chronologically as the steps in the process occur. Some process analyses explain how to do something; other process analyses explain how something happens in nature.

### How to Do Something

Learning how to paint a room can save you money and improve the look of your home. First, you must decide on a color. Go to a local paint store, which will have plenty of color samples you can take home. Once you pick one out, the store employees will happily sell you the type and quantity that you need for your walls. Be sure to pick up all of the necessary accessories, including rollers, brushes, pans, drop cloths, and paint thinner. It's a good idea to have a painter's hat and some disposable gloves. Remember to prepare the room properly, removing or covering all objects, cleaning the walls of dirt and grime, and removing all outlet covers. Lay drop cloths wherever spills are possible. When you paint, apply the paint liberally, but not excessively. Rollers will work well for most stretches of the wall; use brushes for the corners and edges a roller can't properly cover. You will probably need to do at least two coats, so be sure to allot a day for each coat. With the right equipment and little experience, you can give your room a whole new look.

### How a Process Occurs

The formation of stars is relatively simple. Vast dense clouds of interstellar hydrogen and dust collapse due to their massive gravity. As the cloud condenses, the particles heat up until they begin to glow red. The cloud continues to condense and heat until it reaches a level at which thermonuclear reactions occur. These reactions are either proton–proton or carbon-cycle reactions. At this point, the cloud ceases to condense and maintains its shape, like our sun. The star will stay at this stage, referred to as the main sequence, for much of its life. Only after all the hydrogen inside the star has been converted into helium will the process of the star's decay begin.

## E X E R C I S E 12

Select one of the subjects below and write a paragraph explaining how to do something, or how something happened or came about. Write at least 125 words.

How to cook with a wok
How to organize a Neighborhood Watch group
How to prepare for a job interview
How to impress boyfriend's or girlfriend's parents
How to study for a final exam
How to print a file from the computer
How immigration laws have changed
How the Great Depression started
How the first atomic bomb was made
How teenage suicides can be prevented
How Bill Clinton won the presidency
How 12-step programs help addicts

## CAUSE AND EFFECT

A paragraph that is developed by cause and effect will answer one of the following questions: "Why did this happen?" or "What will happen because of this?" That is, it will either begin with an *effect* and then examine or speculate on its causes, or, reversing the order, present a series of *causes* and speculate on their probable effect.

### Cause to Effect

A recent study done by Dr. Daniel M. Sosin and Dr. Jeffrey J. Sacks sought to determine whether states with helmet laws consistently had lower rates of head injury-associated death from motorcycle accidents. Differences in regions around the United States, including riding patterns, population distribution, weather, and so forth, were accounted for in the study. The scientists claim that helmet laws reduce the number of deaths from head injury associated with motorcycle accidents by 50 percent. No matter what factors are considered, states with mandatory helmet laws have lower rates of death by head injury in motorcycle accidents. Thus, helmet laws have proven to be an effective way to promote public safety by reducing unnecessary head injuries.

### Effect to Cause

Arizona and Florida are popular getaway spots for snowbirds from the North and Midwest. After the holiday season is over, the snow on the ground no longer seems quaint; it's cold, dirty, and slushy. People have trouble remembering the last time they saw blue sky, and kitchen knives need to be carefully hidden away. January and February pass by like time on death row. By late March or early April, people are ready to do almost anything to get away. Anywhere there is heat and sun seems like a good idea. So the snowbirds head off, knowing that they will pay inflated hotel rates, restaurant bills, and plane fares. Without question, they will say, it's worth it.

## E X E R C I S E 13

Select one of the following topics and write a paragraph developed by cause or effect.

The influence of fundamentalist Christians on national politics
Population growth and living standards
The value of the dollar and international trade
Terrorism in America
Universal health care
Talk shows
The decline of labor unions
High technology
Single-parent families
Advertising and the car buyer

## DEFINITION

A paragraph developed by definition tells what something is and what it is not. It usually accomplishes this by presenting the general category something belongs to and then showing how it is different from other items in that category.

One of the prime directives for the young is to be cool. But what is cool? For one thing, cool is not "hot," which has a quality of intense emotion or an up-to-the-minute awareness of the latest pop culture trend. But hot burns out—fashion and fan magazines chart what's in and what's out each month. Cool is something more sustainable. Cool is low-key, but self-assured. Cool is the confidence of knowing who you are and what you are about, without having to be showy. Cool may draw attention to itself, but only on its own terms. Cool is the fashion that never goes out of style, like Coco Chanel's simple, black evening dress, a night spent listening to live jazz, or Humphrey Bogart in *Casablanca*. Cool is effortless style.

## E X E R C I S E 14

Select one of the following terms and define it in a paragraph of at least 125 words.

| | |
|---|---|
| Justice | Fashionable |
| Patriotism | The phrase "real life" |
| Faith | A slang term you often use |
| Liberalism | A technical term you are familiar with |
| Art | A term from a science book |
| Modern | A term from one of your history or political science textbooks |

## C O M P U T E R  E X E R C I S E

Your instructor will prepare a list of topic sentences, or you may use some of the topic sentences from Exercise 1. In groups of two or three students, work on a topic sentence. Your group should choose the method of development that will work best for your topic sentence; then write a paragraph to support the topic sentence using whatever method of development you choose. Be creative with facts if necessary. The purpose of this exercise is for your group to build well-constructed paragraphs.

Once your group has completed its paragraph writings, share them with other groups either by broadcasting the groups' screens around the room, or by using an overhead projection system. Your entire class can read and critique each of the paragraphs to see if your group chose the best possible method of development, and if indeed the paragraph followed that method.

# *Introductory* and *Concluding* *Paragraphs*

The introductory and concluding paragraphs are important parts of the essay. The introduction creates the first impression and therefore must be effective. The conclusion is the writer's last chance to influence or impress readers, while leaving them with a sense of completion.

Some writers write the introduction first, but others prefer to write it after the rest of the essay has been written. Some write the conclusion first, using it as a kind of final destination point to aim for as they write. Regardless of when the introduction and conclusion are written, they are vital parts of the essay.

## *Introductions*

A good introduction to an essay performs several jobs. The most obvious is to introduce the subject that you will develop and to pave the way for the thesis statement or controlling idea of the essay. The introduction should also catch the readers' interest, making them want to read on. A good introduction informs readers of the writer's intention and suggests the tone of the essay, indicating whether it will be humorous, angry, or serious.

Some suggestions for writing introductions, with examples from student papers, follow.

*Begin with a Direct Statement of Your Topic and Thesis.* Many male workers still hold to the view that women are less valued in the workplace and belong in the home. Because of this, the American workplace continues to be plagued with the problem of sexual harassment. Sexual harassment on the job erodes productivity, is degrading to a woman's self-esteem, and creates a stressful work environment.

*Begin with a Personal Anecdote.* I could not have been happier when my best friend Debby married her boyfriend, Al. Debby and Al had not been dating for long, but they had seemed so happy. After the wedding, I did not see her for about three months. Finally, I dropped by her apartment unannounced. When she opened the door, I was shocked to see that her face was bruised. She tried to laugh off the bruise, and told me that she had fallen in the shower. But that bruise was just the beginning, and over time I discovered that Al was beating her. Still, Debby maintained that even when he did hurt her, he was very sorry and besides, she had done something to provoke his violence. Only after she would up in the hospital did her parents insist on getting her out of the apartment and into counseling. From this experience I discovered that a psychology of victimization and dependency keeps many women from leaving their husbands, even in some of the worst circumstances.

*Begin with a Scene or Narrative.* The man looks haggard, with dirty clothes, a blackened face, and gloves with holes in the fingers. He stands at an intersection holding a sign that says "Will Work for Food." Drivers stream by, mostly ignoring him, but once in a while someone stops and hands him some change or a dollar bill. He barely seems to move the entire time. This scene is played out daily by thousands of homeless people in America's cities and towns. Most people feel compassion for those who are less fortunate, but their compassion has worn thin for a homeless population that never seems to go away. Some feel that money given to homeless people does no good, only paying for drugs or alcohol, and that the homeless will *not* work for food even if work is offered. Indeed, drug and alcohol abuse among the homeless is prevalent; no significant solution can be found that does not first address their substance abuse problems.

*Begin with a Question.* How is the world going to provide food, clothing, shelter, and jobs as we head toward having five billion people? Can we somehow manage our world's resources to avoid the widespread famine, wars, environmental devastation, and human suffering that overpopulation has brought in the past? Until the answers to these questions can be found, we must somehow find a way to encourage family planning with the goal of having zero population growth.

*Begin with Statistics.* One out of every three children in America is born out of wedlock, and those unwed mothers who receive welfare receive it for an average of eight years. Each year, teenage mothers receive $34 billion in welfare benefits. Clearly, one path to welfare reform must be to reduce the number of children born to women who cannot support them.

*Begin with a Quotation.* "Ask not what your country can do for you, ask what you can do for your country," said John F. Kennedy in his inaugural address to the nation in 1961. Cynics today find that statement trite and naive. Still, many people, with little recognition or credit, keep the spirit of JFK alive through volunteer work in their communities, VISTA work in our own country, or Peace Corps work abroad.

*Begin with an Imaginary Scene or "What If" Situation.* Imagine that private ownership of guns has ceased. Only police and the military are allowed guns, and the only other people who have are criminals. Now, what if you hear a criminal breaking into your house, and police help is at best ten minutes away? What will you do to protect your family and yourself? Private gun ownership is necessary for personal protection because no police force can protect citizens from all possible criminal acts.

*Begin with a Surprising Statement.* While most traditional and established Christian churches oppose homosexual marriage, there is evidence that suggests the Church in the Middle Ages at least tacitly acknowledged and perhaps even endorsed homosexual marriage. This evidence may help lead some of today's Christian churches to endorse homosexual marriage. Homosexual marriage is a commitment and a bond between two adults who love and care for each other, just as heterosexual marriage is, and should receive the blessings of the church.

## Some introductions to avoid.

> *Don't begin with an apology:* "Although I don't know very much about the topic, I will try to discuss . . ."
>
> *Don't begin with a cliché or trite opening:* "According to Webster's dictionary, . . ."
>
> *Don't begin with platitudes and sweeping generalizations:* "Honesty is the best policy."
>
> *Don't begin with an opening that restates or defines the title of the essay:* For an essay titled "Mutations and Their Causes," "This refers to the process that sometimes occurs during cell division" is not a strong beginning.

## Conclusions

The conclusion of your essay, like its introduction, can fulfill several purposes. It can summarize your main points or restate your thesis, avoiding the same words and expressions that were used throughout the essay. It can suggest a sense of closure by referring to a quotation or fact used in the introduction. Some conclusions ask the read to do something—to take action, consider another alternative, or think more deeply about an issue or problem. Other conclusions speculate on the future by predicting what will happen as a result of the situation described in the essay.

Your conclusion should be in proportion to the length of the body of the essay. For a short paper, a few sentences are enough. For longer papers, one or two paragraphs would be appropriate. Regardless of length, your conclusion should convey a sense of completion.

Some suggestions for writing conclusions, with examples from student papers, follow.

*End with a Summary of Your Main Points.* **The** reasons for opposing the death penalty are clear and convincing. First of all, innocent people have been executed in the past and undoubtedly will be in the future, no matter that precautions are taken. Next, the death penalty is cruel since there is no way to execute a person without inflicting pain and terror. Also, the death penalty turns the government of the people into the moral equivalent of a murderer. For these reasons, the death penalty should not be used and should be declared permanently unconstitutional.

*End with a Restatement of Your Thesis.* **The** greenhouse effect is as yet an unproven phenomenon. Changes in the weather should only be regarded as temporary, not as changes to climate, since climate can only be measured over decades. Until decades have passed and the greenhouse effect can actually be proven, prudent environmental protections need to be followed, but alarmists and radical environmentalists should not dictate policies that could be devastating to the economy.

*End with a Fact or Quotation Used in the Introduction.* "Am I my brother's keeper?" asked Cain. In short, the answer is yes, and this means that we as a society have a duty to care for the mentally ill who cannot care for themselves. We need to establish comprehensive health care reform that will aid the mentally ill, not brush over their problems with inadequate outpatient care, leaving them to fend for themselves on the streets where they suffer and eventually die.

*End by Asking Your Audience to Do Something.* The only way the United States will be able to preserve the world's environment is by consuming less and recycling more, and this must happen at the level of the individual. Recycle all aluminum, plastic, and paper goods either through participating in curbside recycling or taking them to collection centers. Use less water by shutting water off when not in use, planting gardens that require less water, and using brown or dirty water for plants when possible. Moderate your use of electricity and gasoline. By changing our behavior on an individual basis, we can lessen the demands on our resources as a nation.

*End with a Prediction.* Strict guidelines must be imposed to ensure that genetic engineering research only produces cures to genetic diseases. Otherwise, if scientists are left alone in their labs to manipulate genes as they see fit, inevitably some ambitious and unethical scientists will develop the genetic equivalent of the atomic bomb, either through human cloning or the development of a new superhuman. Humanity does not need that.

## Some conclusions to avoid.

*Don't apologize for what you have written or for the way you have written it:* "I realize more could have been presented about this topic, but I was unable to get much information . . ."

*Don't use clichés to introduce your conclusion:* "Last but not least . . ."

*Don't raise ideas that contradict your thesis, or ideas that belong in the body of your essay:* "Some people would argue that hitchhiking should not be prohibited in our city. They point out that our public transportation system is inadequate and that many students do not own cars. Nevertheless, I believe that hitchhiking should be prohibited on the streets of this city."

*Don't introduce new ideas that are unrelated to your thesis:* "Taking a year off after graduation from high school, therefore, allows the young person time to plan his or her future and to choose, without the pressure of the college environment, the most satisfying and rewarding course of action. Graduates of vocational trade schools often receive excellent starting salaries . . ."

*Don't make the conclusion abrupt.* The following sentence would be too abrupt if it comprised the entire conclusion: "These are my reasons for allowing prayer in the public schools."

# COMPUTER EXERCISE

Using either the list of topic ideas from Appendix B or ideas from the instructor, write introductions that catch the reader's attention. Write at least three different introductions for the same topic using the different techniques described on pages 57–59. Then, using either the broadcast function or the overhead, share your introductions with the class and have classmates critique them. This same exercise can also be used with conclusions.

4

# Planning
# the Essay

An essay can be thought of as a series of paragraphs about one main idea. The main idea of the essay is usually expressed in a *thesis statement*, a sentence that tells the reader what the essay will cover. In other words, the thesis statement summarizes, usually in one sentence, the controlling or main idea of the essay. If there is no thesis statement, or if it is difficult to locate, the paper will probably be a collection of unrelated ideas without focus. The result will be confusion for the reader, and the writer will have failed in conveying his or her ideas.

## An Overview of the Essay

The typical essay contains three parts: an *introduction*, a *body*, and a *conclusion*. The *introduction* presents the thesis statement and catches the reader's interest so that he or she will read on. Introductions can vary in length, depending on the length of the essay. For a brief essay of 300 to 500 words, a paragraph will usually be enough. Longer essays sometimes contain introductions of two or more paragraphs.

The *body* is the longest part of the essay. It usually consists of several paragraphs, and its purpose is to develop and expand on the thesis statement. Each paragraph in the body of the essay treats a different aspect or division of the thesis statement. An indentation in the first line of the new paragraph is a signal to the reader that a new thought is being introduced.

The *conclusion* of the essay is usually stated in the last paragraph, although, as in the case of introductions, it may require several paragraphs in a long essay. The purpose of the conclusion is to signal that the essay is coming to an end. It reminds the reader of the major points, restates the thesis, or urges the reader to take a certain course of action.

The following diagram illustrates the main parts of the essay. Notice that the thesis statement is placed at the end of the introductory paragraph. Although it is acceptable to place it in other locations, many writers recommend that the thesis statement conclude the introductory paragraph so that it can lead in naturally to the body of the essay.

In reading magazines and books you will occasionally find an essay that departs slightly from this three-part structure. For example, an introduction may consist of only one sentence that is absorbed into the body of the essay, or it may run several paragraphs; the body may contain a dozen major points presented in a dozen paragraphs; and the conclusion may be a single sentence or several paragraphs. You may even find essays in which the thesis statement is strongly implied rather than directly stated. In any case, you will still be able to recognize the basic three-part structure in such essays.

# TITLE

## INRODUCTION WITH THESIS STATEMENT

## BODY

## CONCLUSION

The following essay was written by a student. Notice the three-part structure: the first paragraph concludes with the *thesis statement,* the next three paragraphs make up the *body* and support the thesis statement, and the *conclusion* ties the essay together.

---

### How to Choose a Major

*Introduction with thesis statement*
Almost as soon as a high school student picks a college or university, she hears the familiar question, "What's your major?" The question can be daunting and frustrating for students because many seventeen, eighteen, or nineteen year olds are not yet ready to commit their lives to the study of one particular subject. Yet, the question will not go away, and before the start of their junior year, all students must declare a major. Choosing the wrong major could lead to wasted time and money, or worse, a lifetime spent doing something the student does not like. *Despite the challenge of choosing something so important at such a young age, picking the right major can be done if students follow a few simple steps.*

*Body*
Before beginning the search, students need to clarify for themselves just what exactly they want out of life. Most colleges and universities have career centers where students can go to take a test to see which professions they are best suited to enter. Often, these tests center more on values, trying to assess what kind of life the students enjoy. Students must be honest when they answer questions such as "How important is money to me?" or "Am I willing to put in long hours with little pay for a job that gives mostly non-tangible rewards?" The tests will also ask what type of activities students prefer, whether they like to work alone or in groups, and whether they value professional life more than personal or family life. There are no right answers to these questions. What students may find from these tests are areas or types of occupations that best suit their values and goals.

While the career center may help students focus on long-term goals, students should consult working professionals to determine how they like their jobs and what they studied to get those jobs. All professions have advantages and drawbacks. Students should try to learn what they are. They need to ask questions about education, time commitments, ability to advance, financial rewards and responsibilities, how the job impinges on family life, what the social status is, and the prospects for employment in that field. A student may feel she wishes to be an architect until she speaks to a few and discovers that the job is not as glamorous for them as she had imagined. Another student may discover that being a physician involves far more of a time commitment than he had originally imagined, but that the nontangible benefits were more rewarding as well. Students should keep in mind that what worked for others may not work for them; they should try to speak to as many professionals in their field of interest as possible.

Finally, students should examine the lists of majors available to them at their chosen college or university. Some professions have majors that tie in quite closely; for instance, electrical engineers usually major in electrical engineering. However, other career choices are not so limited. Students wishing to pursue a degree in law may major in English, political science, philosophy, or history, among others. Not all students who eventually wish to get an M.B.A. degree use business as their undergraduate degree. Some use economics, English, or perhaps even engineering or computer science. Minors can also be helpful, if the college offers them, because they can give students extra background in an unrelated subject. Pairing biology with a minor in philosophy might be quite attractive to medical schools.

*Conclusion*   Students can choose majors if they are willing to honestly ask themselves a lot of questions and explore many alternatives. In the end, students should keep in mind that many students change majors, and often students wind up working in fields unrelated to their major, yet enjoying both experiences. Still, students are usually better off if they can develop some sort of long-range goals that their major will fit, even if those goals are subject to change.

## Starting the Essay

When faced with writing an essay, some students sit down and write a first sentence, then chew their pencils for a while, hoping that a second sentence will follow, and then a third, and so on. It is possible to write a paper like this, of course, but it is a painful method, and the results are usually dismal.

Most experienced writers, on the other hand, realize that the act of writing follows a certain *process*, a series of steps that begins with a blank page and ends with an organized, unified, and coherent presentation of their ideas. Here are the steps in the process of writing an essay, which will be explained in this and the following chapters.

1. *Choosing and Limiting a Topic*

2. *Determining Your Purpose and Audience*

3. *Gathering Material*

4. *Writing a Thesis Statement*

5. *Organizing and Outlining Your Essay*

6. *Writing the First Draft*

7. *Revising and Editing Your Essay*

As you write your essays you will often find yourself repeating some of these steps. For example, after arranging your material into a pattern, you may decide that you need more ideas. You may find after outlining your paper that your subject is still too broad and that you will have to narrow it some more, or you may complete the first draft only to realize that you have abandoned your thesis and actually developed another one. In any case, you will find that writing an essay consists of a series of continuous and overlapping actions and steps. By following the process, you will overcome your fear of writing and become a more confident and effective writer.

## 1. Choosing and Limiting a Topic

Many of the topics you will write about in college will be assigned by your instructors. In such cases, make certain that you know exactly what the subject or question demands. Many student papers fail because the writers did not understand the assignment clearly. If your instructor asks for a paper explaining the importance of the Black Plague on European society, for example, he will not appreciate a paper discussing Chaucer's *Canterbury Tales*.

If you are allowed to choose the topic for your paper, the following section will help you avoid several pitfalls that students often encounter as they try to select a topic.

## Choosing a Topic

When you have to choose a topic, your first reaction might be that you don't have anything interesting to say. This is not true, of course—you are a unique individual with unique experiences, interests, hobbies, opinions, and abilities. Therefore, the first step toward selecting a topic might be a self-inventory.

What experiences have you had that others would like to read about? Where did you grow up? Where did you go to school before attending college? Describe your family. What are your parents' occupations? What ethnic, religious, or cultural customs does your family observe? What languages are spoken at home? What kinds of work experience have you had? What was the worst job you ever had? The best? What are your plans for a job and family? Who has influenced you? What subjects would you like to learn about?

The point is clear: one of the best sources for an essay topic is yourself. You are a treasure-house of ideas that others would like to read about.

In addition to the inventory described above, use the prewriting techniques suggested in Chapter 2 to explore potential topics. By freewriting, brainstorming, asking questions, and referring to your journal, you will make the pleasant discovery that as you write, you will have many things to write about that others will want to read.

If allowed to choose your topic, keep these guidelines in mind:

Choose a topic that interests you and about which you either have some knowledge or can acquire without much trouble.

Choose a topic that is small enough to handle in the usual essay of 500 to 700 words. Broad topics such as "love," "war," "happiness," and "religion" would have to be narrowed and restricted to be discussed adequately in a theme of this length.

Choose a topic that will be interesting to your readers. An elaborate description of your dog, while fascinating to you, might not hold your readers' attention.

Try to avoid topics that have been exhausted: arguments for and against capital punishment, the legalization of marijuana, abortion, and so on. Write about them if you have something fresh and new to say; it is unlikely, however, that you can add anything interesting to the millions of words your instructor has had to read on these topics.

## E X E R C I S E 1

Now it is *your* turn to select a subject that could develop into an essay of 500 to 700 words. Using the suggestions in the preceding pages and in Chapter 2, choose a subject that you are interested in and know something about. If you need help in triggering ideas for possible topics, look at the list below; if you still don't see a suitable topic; turn to the list in Appendix B ("300 Writing Topics"). Select your topic carefully because you will be asked to develop it into a complete essay.

The fitness craze
Second-hand smoke
Women in the military
Illegal aliens
Political correctness
Physician-assisted suicide
The ozone layer
Israel–PLO relations
The working student
Cultural diversity
Hip-hop
Alternative wedding ceremonies
Credit cards
Welfare reform
The New World Order
Contemporary art

## Limiting a Topic

After you have decided on a subject, your next job is to trim it to manageable proportions. Think of your subject as a pie: you are going to offer your reader one narrow slice. Many beginning writers make the mistake of being too vague or general; they offer their reader the whole pie. They confuse the *subject* with a *specific topic*. A few examples will illustrate the difference.

"Television" is too broad a topic to be treated adequately in a typical college essay, but "The viewing patterns of preschool-age children" is a topic that could be handled in a relatively short essay. Likewise, "sports" is beyond the ability of any writer to discuss in a few pages, but "The difference between college and minor league baseball" is narrow enough to be covered in 750 words. Similarly, "reading" is too shadowy and vague as a topic; "the intellectual and emotional benefits of reading," however, could be treated in an essay.

The subjects in the left column are general; the narrowed topics in the right column are more specific and therefore more manageable for a short essay.

| Subject | Narrowed Topic |
|---|---|
| History | The Treaty of Guadalupe Hidalgo |
| Death | The death of my grandfather |
| Literature | The appeal of horror fiction |
| Television | A scapegoat for society's ills |
| Food | American kitchens are becoming increasingly cosmopolitan |
| Morals | The case for abstinence |
| Education | Why college is not for everyone |
| Religion | Should religion have a role in public education? |
| Technology | Why newer isn't always better |
| Holidays | Celebrating the Vietnamese New Year in an Anglo neighborhood |

## E X E R C I S E 2

In Exercise 1 you were asked to choose a subject that you could develop into an essay of approximately 500 to 750 words. Using the techniques of freewriting, brainstorming, and asking questions, narrow your subject until you are certain that you could adequately cover it in the prescribed limit. Your instructor may ask you to discuss your topic with other students in your class to help you focus it.

## 2. Determining Your Purpose and Audience

After you have narrowed your subject, your next job is to decide your purpose and to identify your intended audience. Every piece of writing has a purpose and an audience. You may be writing to borrow money (purpose) from your parents (audience). You may wish to change the physical education requirements at your college (purpose) by writing a letter to the dean (audience). Or you may simply wish to send birthday greetings (purpose) to a friend (audience). In each case, knowing your purpose and your audience will help you devise a plan for making your meaning clear and will put you firmly in control of your letter or essay from the start.

## *Purpose*

In a sense, every kind of writing has a purpose, even if it is to express the writer's emotions as he or she writes a private diary entry. But most composition teachers agree that the purposes of writing for others can be reduced to these three: (1) to *entertain or please* the reader by making the subject enjoyable (the *aesthetic aim*); (2) to *inform or instruct* the reader by conveying or explaining the meaning of certain information (the *informative aim*); (3) to *persuade* the reader by convincing him or her to follow a certain course of action (the *persuasive aim*).

Scientists and engineers who write on the job are aware of the importance of determining the purpose of a particular piece of writing. When they write proposals and recommendations to a client, their purpose is largely persuasive; when they write technical memos and progress reports, their purpose is largely informative. In many cases they have to juggle or combine purposes; a persuasive recommendation report might have sections that inform, and a proposal whose larger purpose is to persuade will also try to please its reader.

In your own writing, both in and out of class, you will find that these purposes often overlap, with the result that you will sometimes entertain your reader as you inform, or inform as you try to persuade. Nevertheless, each piece of effective writing has a *main* or *dominant* purpose. If it does not, it will be like a boat without a rudder, drifting without direction.

As you prepare to write, you must decide on your purpose. Suppose that you have to write an essay on AIDS research. As you acquire information about the topic, you are faced with decisions:

Do you want to explain to your readers what type of research is being done, and the directions for the future?

Do you want to convince your readers that more resources need to be devoted to AIDS research? Or fewer?

Do you want to convince your readers that AIDS research is currently showing little promise of finding a cure and that preventative measures are the only hope?

Do you want to show your readers that AIDS research is still being conducted in ways that duplicate research yet leave other avenues unexplored?

Each of these purposes is related to the topic, yet each differs from the others. If you decide that your purpose is to write an informative essay in which you explain the current state of AIDS research, you will have to forgo any lengthy development of the topics suggested by the other questions. If, on the other hand, you decide that the purpose of your paper is to persuade readers that AIDS research is currently underfunded given the enormity of its task, you would probably need to include information about the current state of AIDS research. In this case your overall purpose is to *persuade*, but to support your argument you will find it necessary to *inform*. If, however, your essay wavers between explaining what AIDS research has learned and urging your readers to donate more money, you may fail to either inform clearly or persuade convincingly. A paper that shifts its purpose succeeds only in losing readers.

## Writing a Statement of Purpose

The best way to avoid confusion of purpose is to formulate a *statement of purpose* before writing. This is a sentence that states your purpose in relation to your audience and your subject. It helps you keep in mind your central idea and the response you want from your reader.

Imagine that you want to convince your city council to ban smoking in all public areas. Keeping in mind your purpose, your subject, and your audience, you might write a statement of purpose like this:

My purpose is to convince the city council that all public areas should be declared "Smoke Free" zones.

Writing a statement of purpose will help you keep your audience and purpose in sight. As you will see in Chapter 5, it will also help you select the most effective strategies for developing your ideas. Here are some examples of statements of purpose. Notice that they connect the subject, the purpose, and the reader.

My purpose is to encourage the reader to buy only tuna that is labeled "Dolphin safe."
My purpose is to inform the reader about the dangerously high levels of bacteria that appear in our local drinking water.
My purpose is to persuade the reader to back a new local initiative to renovate the downtown business district.
My purpose is to get other students to listen to and appreciate classical music.

### E  X  E  R  C  I  S  E  3

Reread several essays or papers that you have written this or last semester. For each one, formulate a statement of purpose. Here is an example: "My purpose was to convince the reader that the space program is still vital to the United States and should once again be made a high priority item in our federal budget."

### E  X  E  R  C  I  S  E  4

Write a statement of purpose for the topic selected in Exercise 1. Be sure that it combines the subject and your purpose.

## Audience

As noted, every piece of writing—unless it is a private diary—is intended for an audience. If the writing is a college essay, the audience is the writer's instructor and fellow students. If the writing is an application for a job, it is the writer's prospective employer; if it is a request for a raise or promotion, the audience is the writer's supervisor. Unless the words have the right effect on the audience, the writer won't get the grade, the job, or the raise.

We have all heard about the professor who knew his subject but could not explain it to his students. He, too, had a problem with his audience. Knowing the audience you are writing for is important because that knowledge determines to a great extent, *what* you say, *how* you say it, and the tone or approach you take to the subject and to your reader. After all, what works with one group of readers will not necessarily work with another.

The following letters demonstrate that their writer is aware of this principle. In the first letter, Chandler is writing to his buddy to explain why he is giving up a job that his parents got for him to devote more of his time to writing poetry. In the second letter, he is writing to his parents to inform them of this same decision. Notice that although both letters convey essentially the same information and discuss the same subject, their language, tone, purpose, details, and attitude of the writer toward the reader differ greatly.

Pat,
What's up? You know, I've been chillin, trying to figure a way out of this mess. My old man pulled some strings to get me that job, and

I've been afraid that if I bail, they'll think I'm dissing them. But I gotta follow my heart, you know what I mean? I've decided that I've got to give this poetry gig a real shot. I'd be seriously bumming sitting in an office with a bunch of yuppies. Forget it. I ain't no suit. Instead I'm gonna hang with the vampires at the Cup, spilling java and watching the Bettys. Bukoski would be proud.

See ya,

Chan the Man

---

Dear Mom and Dad,

I want you both to know how appreciative I am that you found me such a good job working as a technical writer for Scottsglen Engineering. I know that you, Dad, used your friendship with Mr. Scott to get me in. However, you must know that technical writing is not my life's ambition, and that if you remember, both of you always told me to follow my heart, and that personal satisfaction is much more important than money. Therefore, I have decided to devote myself to writing poetry this summer. Only if I spend long hours of hard work writing will I stand a chance of becoming the kind of poet I aspire to be. Of course, I will be working during the summer. I've lined up a job at a popular coffee house where they have late night poetry readings. They don't pay much there, though, so if you could lend me some money (which I'll pay back as soon as a I can) I would greatly appreciate it.

Love from your son,

Chandler

---

You probably noticed several differences between these letters by Chandler. His letter to his friend Pat is filled with slang and colloquialisms: "chillin," "dissing," "yuppies," "Bettys" and so on. In fact, many people regard "Bettys" as a blatantly sexist term for women. This informality is intensified by the allusion to the good time he plans on having working at the coffee house instead of working at an engineering firm. The overall impression is of a young man who is looking forward to a carefree summer and has little worry about his finances or his future. The second letter is more deferential and formal than the letter to Pat. He chooses more formal words that make his refusal of the technical writing job sound like the only honorable thing to do in the face of his life's goals. He reminds his parents of their advice to him, and how he is only following that advice. He avoids slang, and his sentences are longer and more complex. He also sets the context of his summer job within the long range goal of becoming a writer, and appears to make reasonable his request for money. He even signs the letter with the longer version of his name. All in all, the two letters show clearly that Chandler had each reader in mind, and that he adjusted his purpose, content, and language accordingly.

## E X E R C I S E 5

Each of the following passages was written with a particular audience in mind. Who is the audience in each case? Describe the intended reader as clearly as you can. Are you included in that audience? Why or why not?

1. Light is electromagnetic radiation that can be perceived by the human eye. Electromagnetic radiation wavelengths occur over a range of thirty orders of magnitude. The waves measure from as small as $3 \times 10^{-22}$ centimeters to as long as millions of kilometers. Wavelengths that are perceptible to the human eye range from $7 \times 10^{-5}$ centimeters to $4 \times 10^{-5}$ centimeters. The ranges immediately adjacent to these wavelengths are also referred to as light, with infrared at just off longer wavelength range and ultraviolet at the shorter one.

2. Hey dude, chill out. Ain't no big deal.

3. Law school can change your life! The Lucas State University College of Law will host a law school information seminar in your area. Questions will be answered regarding such important issues as requirements for admission, the Law School Admission Test (LSAT), Career Planning and Placement, and scholarships. Seating is limited. Call to register.

4. No, Spot, no! Use the newspaper, Spot!

5. Turning to Docket item 2349–8, I think you will find that the ad hoc conference committee reporting to the standing committee has found that without further investigation no new actions can be taken. The committee recommends that this item be tabled until such time as action can be taken, which is most likely to fall in the next calendar year, after the next election has been held and new officers have been installed.

6. Are you lonely? My friends and I are waiting by the phone for your call. Don't be shy. Pick up the phone, and we'll have a real good time. Call 1–900–555–2317. All major credit cards accepted. No minors allowed.

7. Hay una variedad de países que componen el mundo hispánico y existen diferencias entre ellos. La naturaleza en España y especialmente en Hispanoamérica es muy variada. Las diferencias y los contrastes entre las cuidades y los pueblos son enormes. Existen varias razas y grupos étnicos en el mundo hispánico.

8. Thank you for the wonderful housewarming present. I have always wanted a hand-woven toaster oven cover. How

thoughtful! Now I won't have to clean the outside of the toaster oven nearly so often.

## Identifying Your Audience

As you prepare to write, you must ask yourself several questions about your audience:

Who is going to read this?

What do I know about my readers? What are their ages, sex, educational backgrounds, and occupations? What are their attitudes, values, beliefs, and prejudices?

How much do my readers already know about the subject?

Are they experts on it? Reasonably informed? Or is my subject likely to be completely unfamiliar to them? Can I assume they understand the basic concepts of my subject, or should I explain them?

How can I keep my readers' attention and make them want to read?

If they already know much about my subject, what can I do to make it interesting to them? If they are hostile toward the subject, how can I make sure that they will read the paper with an open mind? Do my readers expect to be entertained, informed, or persuaded?

What can I do to help my readers understand my writing?

What will be the best way to organize and develop my ideas?

What kinds of examples should I use? Is a formal, reserved style better, or should I use a more relaxed, personal style?

When you have answered these questions and identified your audience, you will be better able to choose the kinds of information—the facts, arguments, and examples—that will work best for your purpose and audience. You will also be able to select the appropriate tone and level of language and the best way to organize your material. In short, by picturing your audience in your mind before you write, you can determine the best way to satisfy their expectations.

## E  X  E  R  C  I  S  E        6

One of the best ways to study the importance of audience is to examine magazines. If the following magazines are available on your local magazine racks or in your college library, study their contents and advertisements. Notice the subjects of the articles, the level of the vocabulary, and the point of view, approach, and tone of the articles. Then try to describe the audience or reader that the publishers and advertisers had in mind for that particular magazine.

| | |
|---|---|
| *The New Republic* | *Jet* |
| *Road and Track* | *Mother Jones* |
| *Architectural Digest* | *Cosmopolitan* |
| *Seventeen* | *Foreign Affairs* |
| *Fortune* | *Playboy* |
| *Ms.* | *The Atlantic* |

In a sense there is no such thing as *the* audience—there are only *audiences.* A stockbroker who owns a motorcycle might be an avid reader of *Motorcycle World,* and a surgeon who surfs might subscribe to *Surfer.* In fact, all of us change our "masks" or identities as we go from one magazine or article to another. We are baseball fans as we read the sports page, amateur gourmets when we read the food section, and movie critics as we compare our reactions to a film with those of a reviewer.

Faced with such a various audience, then, what are you to do? Simply this: recognize that your reader exists only as long as he or she reads your essay. That is, you should avoid falsely stereotyping any social, economic, political, or religious group by assuming that they all share the same reading tastes. The readers you are writing for often share only one thing: an interest in your subject. If you are enthusiastic, knowledgeable, and interesting, you will capture your readers.

But what about the audience for your essays in college? For such an audience, a natural, informal tone is most effective. You can assume that you are writing for readers who are educated, intelligent, and curious about the world. They have a variety of backgrounds and interests, and they are serious and thoughtful. They want to read an essay that is interesting, clear, and informative. If you meet their expectations, you can count on their attention.

## E X E R C I S E 7

Imagine that you have just been placed in charge of the new cafe on campus, specializing in coffee, soda, and sandwiches. In order to encourage business, you want to appeal to both students and faculty. Write two letters to be distributed, one amongst students, the other amongst the faculty. In each letter point out the advantages to that group of eating at the new cafe.

## E X E R C I S E 8

Imagine that your younger sister is a freshman at your college. Because a foreign language is required, she enrolled in Russian, but the course was canceled due to low enrollment. Now she wants to quit college altogether. Write a letter encouraging her to remain in college. Then write a letter to the dean or president of the college asking that classes that fulfill requirements not be canceled due to low enrollment.

---

## 3. Gathering Material

Having selected a topic, determined your purpose, and identified your audience, you are now ready to take the next step in the process of writing your essay: gathering material.

To develop your topic, you need to gather ideas, facts, examples, and details. If your topic is based on a personal experience, the ideas will probably come tumbling forth. If your topic is on a subject other than yourself, however, you will have to set aside time for acquiring material to support your topic.

"Gathering material" does not necessarily mean a trip to the library. You have several techniques for collecting ideas about a topic at your command. You can begin by brainstorming and freewriting. Jot ideas down as they come to you, without worrying about their order or relationship to each other. List anything about the topic that comes to mind; eventually you will find a focus or central point for your essay.

By asking questions, a technique discussed in Chapter 2, you can shake loose many additional ideas. Many writers base their questions on the six journalistic questions: *who, what, when, why, where,* and *how.* By asking *who* is connected with your topic, *what* it means, *why* it is important, and so on, you will generate more ideas than you thought were possible.

If you are having trouble coming up with ideas, talk to someone knowledgeable about the topic. Friends, relatives, and faculty members are often able to give you additional ideas or leads. If you have been assigned a topic that you don't know anything about, read some articles about it. Look in the *Readers' Guide* in your college library for articles that might contain helpful information. If you quote directly or paraphrase from an article, consult with your English instructor or look on pages 266–269 for the correct way to acknowledge your sources.

Students who complain that they can't think of anything to write about usually wait until the last minute before they begin the assignment. By giving yourself enough time to consider the topic and think it through, you will soon accumulate a list of ideas. Then you will be ready for the next step: developing your thesis statement.

## 4. Writing a Thesis Statement

After looking over your list of ideas, ask yourself what you want to say about them. What are you really trying to tell your reader about the topic? The answer to that question is expressed in the *thesis statement*, a sentence containing the main idea and purpose of the essay. Put another way, the thesis statement is an announcement of what the author intends to do in the essay—what he will prove, demonstrate, illustrate, or clarify. The thesis statement helps the reader know what to expect. Here are three thesis statements taken from different essays:

---

There is no issue more important than the avoidance of nuclear war.

Carl Saigon, *To Preserve a World Graced by Life*

---

That astrology is preposterous is, of course, obvious to everyone except people with stupendous capacities for the willful suspension of disbelief.

George F. Will, *The Astrological Impulse*

---

Modern English, especially written English, is full of bad habits which spread by limitation and which can be avoided if one is willing to take the necessary trouble.

George Orwell, *Politics and the English Language*

---

In the first essay we expect to learn why the avoidance of nuclear war is more important than any other issue of our day. In the second, we expect Will to show that astrology is preposterous and to explain why those who believe in it are gullible. In the third essay we expect to be given examples of the "bad habits" that have crept into modern written English, along with suggestions for avoiding them.

Not every piece of writing contains an explicit, directly stated thesis statement. In personal essays, poems, plays, and novels the author may not offer a thesis statement. She depends, instead, on the reader to infer or deduce the main idea or purpose of the selection. In essays, reports, and other kinds of functional writing, however, most writers tell the reader directly what the main idea is and why the piece should be read.

The thesis statement contains two parts: the *topic* and your *assertion* or view of the topic—what you intend to say *about* the topic. Thus, "skiing" is a *topic*; "Cross-country skiing is the best way to enjoy the outdoors" is a *thesis statement*. "The college cafeteria" is a *topic*; "Although many students complain, the college cafeteria serves food that is tasty, nutritious, and economical" is a *thesis statement*. A paper about "skiing" or "the college cafeteria" would be a rambling, directionless collection of ideas. With a specific thesis statement as a guideline, however, an organized and coherent essay could be written about either topic.

Below are several topics with sample thesis statements:

| | |
|---|---|
| *Topic:* | The effect of a new downtown renovation project |
| *Thesis Statement:* | The new downtown renovation project has brought new life to a part of the city that had been given up for lost. |
| *Topic:* | rap music |
| *Thesis Statement:* | Rap or hip-hop music, once seen as the music of black inner city youths, is increasingly popular among white male teenagers from the suburbs. |
| *Topic:* | Role models |
| *Thesis Statement:* | While the media makes heroes out of popular athletes and movie stars, the proper role models for teenagers are best found in the home, at school, or at work. |
| *Topic:* | return to college in mid-life |
| *Thesis Statement:* | Older students usually do well in college because they are often more motivated, disciplined, and eager to learn. |
| *Topic:* | sharks |

| *Thesis Statement:* | The growing popularity of shark meat has led to such overfishing of sharks that they may face extinction in the near future. |
|---|---|

A well-stated thesis gives your paper a sense of purpose and direction. It answers the reader's question, "What's the point?" In a very real sense, a thesis statement is a commitment or promise by the writer to the reader. It tells the reader what to expect, and it offers a hint of the overall plan of the paper.

When should you develop your thesis statement? Should it be immediately after you have worked out your specific topic, or after you have accumulated your ideas and thought about them? Most experienced writers would probably agree that there is no magic moment for hatching the thesis statement. At times, you will know your purpose and main idea early in the writing process. At other times, you may find that you have started to write with one thesis statement in mind only to discover as you write that you actually were committed to another statement. The best advice, then, is that working out your thesis statement early gives you a plan and a goal and will keep you from expending wasted effort.

At the beginning of this chapter you were told that many writers prefer to place the thesis statement at the end of the first paragraph in a short article or essay before proceeding to develop and support it in the following paragraphs. For longer essays with introductions consisting of several paragraphs, the thesis statement can be placed at the beginning or at the end of the introduction. Your thesis statement might even be found in the concluding paragraph of the essay; this is effective in essays presenting arguments for and against a proposition, culminating in your own view at the end of the essay. The *exact* location is not important. What you should be certain to do is formulate a statement that clearly and succinctly announces to your reader the main or controlling idea that you intend to present.

## Some Reminders When Writing Your Thesis Statement

A thesis statement should be stated in the form of a *sentence;* otherwise, it is just a topic. "Alcohol abuse" is a *topic,* but "Alcohol awareness programs need to be introduced at the junior-high and high-school levels to counteract the growing tendency among teenagers to drink heavily" is a *thesis statement.* Incidentally, longer papers sometimes require more than one sentence to express the thesis statement.

The thesis statement should not be expressed as a question. "Do you know if your tax money is being used wisely?" fails to state clearly the writer's position on the topic. "Tax dollars are too often wasted on frivolous spending or outright fraud" is a thesis statement because it presents the writer's point of view.

Don't state the obvious as your thesis statement. "Alaska is the largest state in the Union" is a fact, but it is not a thesis statement because it leaves you no room for developing an essay. Similarly, "Divorce is one of the major threats to the family" is so obvious that your reader may yawn, "So what else is new?"

Your thesis statement should be manageable enough for the typical college essay of 500 to 750 words. "The effects of the Cold War on the American economy" is worthy of a book, or at least a long chapter. "The maintenance of a large military-industrial complex during the Cold War shaped the American economy" would be better but would still require extensive development. "The emphasis on the development of highly sophisticated technologies during the Cold War led to civilian applications that improved Americans' standard of living" is more limited and manageable and could be developed adequately in an essay.

Avoid a thesis statement that leads to a laundry list without proving anything. A thesis such as "There were a lot of great rock and roll bands in the 1960s" will lend itself to a series of names, dates, songs, and album titles. Such a paper is generally too broad, proves little, and quite often will bore the reader. Instead, narrow your focus with a thesis such as "The Grateful Dead's popularity has endured since the 1960s because of the simplicity and sincerity of their music, the fanatical loyalty of their supporters, known as Dead Heads, and the charm and genius of their live performances."

Your thesis statement should not be too narrow. A paper that proposed to explain how to tie a tie, for example, would be too limited and boring. A paper claiming that the choice of a tie is often a cue to the wearer's personality, however, would be substantial and interesting.

The thesis statement in a first draft will often lack focus or will need additional revision. By asking the following questions, you can improve weak thesis statements:

1. Is the thesis statement clearly presented? Will the reader know exactly where I stand on the topic?
2. Is the thesis statement narrow enough to cover in a 500–750 word essay? Have I tried to cover too much territory?
3. Have I avoided making an obvious statement that cannot be debated or discussed? If so, can I reword the statement so that it has an argumentative edge?
4. Is my statement worded so that readers will want to read further? Have I caught their interest enough to make them curious about my view of the subject?

# E X E R C I S E 9

Read the following thesis statements and decide whether each is specific and narrow enough. Rewrite any that are not.

1. Many different types of music are called rock and roll.
2. Television has been made a scapegoat for society's problems.
3. Generation X has been unfairly characterized as lazy, whining slackers.
4. Contrary to popular belief, women are better drivers than men.
5. No one cares about common courtesy anymore.
6. Fly fishing is the most challenging type of fishing.
7. Grading in college should be abolished and replaced by written evaluations.
8. Senior citizens today make up the wealthiest generation this country has ever seen.
9. Study of the sciences develops a way of thinking that is quite different from that developed by a liberal arts education.
10. The local newspaper consistently downplays crime and violence in favor of soft news about charity balls and crafts festivals.

# E X E R C I S E 10

Write an original thesis statement for the following subjects. Each thesis should express the purpose stated in parentheses.

1. Your choice of major (*expressing yourself*)
2. the advantages of learning how to use computers (*persuasion*)
3. how to find an article in the campus library (*inform*)
4. the worst date you ever had (*expressing yourself* or *entertaining*)
5. why the administration should (or should not) have rules governing acceptable expressions of speech on campus (*persuasion*)
6. your roommate's quirks (*entertaining*)
7. a law that does not work (*informing* or *persuading*)
8. why drug abuse remains a problem in society (*informing* or *persuading*)
9. the advantages of living in a city (*persuading*)
10. why love and sex are sometimes confused (*informing*)

## E X E R C I S E 11 ✓

Now it is time to write a thesis statement for the topic you selected in Exercise 1. Look over the ideas you have collected and ask yourself, "What is the point? What do I want to tell my reader?" The answer to those questions will be your thesis statement. Don't try to cover too much ground, but don't be too narrow or obvious. Your thesis statement should be stated as a sentence. And remember: It is a promise to your reader.

## C O M P U T E R   E X E R C I S E

Send a copy of each thesis statement done in Exercise 10 to your instructor. Your instructor will compile each of the thesis statements by sentence number, for example, putting all the thesis statements for item #1 together, and so on. Then, your instructor will broadcast each of the items, listing the students' thesis statements, to the class. Critique the statements, discussing relative strengths and weaknesses, and how each of the statements would be developed as an essay. Many statements will be similar, some may even be identical, so look to see how each can be altered to be more distinctive.

# 5

# *Shaping the Essay: Organizing Your Ideas*

# 5. Organizing and Outlining Your Essay

Organizing and arranging your ideas in an essay is like pushing furniture around in a new apartment. You try to achieve the most logical and attractive effect, yet you must recognize the boundaries you have to work within. The most interesting and exciting ideas in the world will not be worth much in an essay if your reader can't follow them. This means that all of your facts, details, impressions, and examples have to be organized in a plan that will make sense to your reader.

## Organizing Your Essay

The nature of some topics suggests the best organizational pattern. For example, narratives relating events that occurred in a particular time sequence are organized most effectively in *chronological order*, and descriptions of objects and people usually lend themselves to *spatial ordering*. Some topics, however, cannot be organized in a time or space order. Instead, the writer must impose an order on them and create a pattern of organization that will make sense to the reader. The most effective arrangements are *in order of importance, from general to specific,* and *from specific to general.*

After you have planned your essay as described in Chapter 4, you are ready to begin organizing your essay. The first step is to make a list of all your ideas. This step is similar to brainstorming as described in Chapter 2, except that your task now is to list all the main and lesser ideas that you believe should go into your essay. Do not worry if there do not seem to be strong connections between all the items on your list; you will work through that problem later.

## Outlining Your Essay

An outline is a plan for your essay, and it is a helpful tool for organizing and shaping your ideas. Preparing an outline will help you test your essay for *unity* and *coherence*. Although both of these qualities of good writing were discussed at greater length in Chapter 3, we should review them briefly now.

Your essay has *unity* when all of its ideas support the thesis statement. When you finish your outline, check it be sure that each major section relates to the thesis statement. Within each major section, make certain that each example and supporting detail supports the main idea of that section. In particular, check to see that you have not retained ideas that are unrelated to your thesis statement and its major subdivisions. Chapter 3 presents several ways to test your writing for unity.

Your essay has *coherence* if there are connections between your ideas. You must move logically and orderly from one sentence to another and from one paragraph to another. If you detect abrupt shifts and gaps in your ideas, be sure that those ideas are in the right place in your paper. One way of showing the relationship between ideas is to use expressions such as *furthermore, however, although,* and *in addition* to connect sentences and paragraphs. Chapter 3 offers other methods for making your writing coherent.

Keep in mind that the outline is a tool for organizing your essay—it is never the end product. It is not a sacred document that should never be changed. But whether it is a rough outline like those in this chapter or a formal outline like the one on page 276, an outline is invaluable for giving your essay direction—it helps you see the structure of your essay at a glance.

### Chronological Order

Ann Dozier, a returning student, was given an essay assignment in which she was asked to narrate an incident. Here is a list of ideas that she prepared after she thought about the day of her wedding.

Thesis statement: "While the day of your wedding may or may not be the happiest day of your life, it almost certainly will be the most chaotic and exhausting one."

1. Everyone seems to want to talk to me at once
2. There was a mix-up with the rings
3. Many friends were there on both sides
4. My parents both cried
5. Getting up early in the morning with little sleep
6. Going to the hairdresser and finding my future sister-in-law already there so I had to wait.
7. Weddings are expensive
8. Rushing to get ready
9. I had to walk back to the hotel room from the hairdresser
10. The church looked beautiful
11. Aunt Susan and Uncle Michael came all the way from Omaha—my favorite relatives—so I spent a lot of time with them.
12. The music started—it was finally happening!

13. John looked nervous in his tuxedo
14. The ceremony went by so quickly–after all that planning!
15. Staying late for photos; last ones at our reception
16. Our colors were purple and white
17. Some people still don't believe in marriage—like Vic and Janelle
18. Alcohol in the afternoon made me tipsy, then tired
19. The wedding dance—a wonderful break
20. Trying to spend ten minutes with everyone was exhausting
21. The photographer took so many pictures!
22. Many people were friends of our parents that I didn't even know
23. We left early to the hotel—for a nap. Honest!
24. A day we'll remember forever

    As you can see, Ann's thesis suggests that she wants to write an essay in which she conveys to her reader her sense of the reality of a wedding day as a chaotic and tiring experience. Her list of ideas is filled with incidents and impressions from her own wedding day. However, she has two problems: several of the ideas on the list are not related to her thesis, and those that are on the subject are not in the order in which they happened. Her job now is to look over her list and decide what should be cut and how to arrange the remaining ideas.

    The ideas numbered 7, 10, 16, 17 do not have anything to do with her purpose or thesis. Item 7 deals with a separate aspect of weddings, the cost, and 10 is an observation that does little to advance the thesis. Item 16 also deals with the aesthetics of the wedding, but not the confusion or exhaustion. Item 17 is a separate issue dealing with the value of marriage itself.

    Having removed the irrelevant items, she puts the remaining ideas in the order in which they happened, or *chronological order*. Here is her reorganized list; notice that she has renumbered the items and changed the wording of a few.

1. Getting up early in the morning with little sleep
2. Going to the hairdresser and finding my future sister-in-law already there, so I had to wait
3. I had to walk back to the hotel room from the hairdresser
4. Rushing to get ready; speeding in the car with my maid of honor
5. The wedding started—it was finally happening!

6. Walking down the aisle I could see many friends were there on both sides
7. John looked nervous in his tuxedo
8. There was a mix-up with the readings—Mark read the wrong Shakespearean sonnet
9. My parents both cried
10. The ceremony went by so quickly—after all that planning!
11. The photographer was a little annoying with all of her photo taking
12. Staying late for even more photos; we were the last ones at our reception
13. Everyone seemed to want to talk to me at once
14. Many people were friends of our parents that I didn't even know.
15. Trying to spend ten minutes with everyone was exhausting
16. Aunt Susan and Uncle Michael came all the from Omaha—my favorite relatives—so I spent a lot of time with them
17. The wedding dance—a wonderful break
18. Alcohol in the afternoon made me tipsy, then tired
19. We left early to go to the hotel—for a nap. Honest!
20. A day we'll remember forever

This list is much easier to follow; the reader gets the overall plan of the proposed essay, and senses the general direction of the thought. But a problem still remains before Ann can use her list as a guide to the writing of her essay: the list presents all of the ideas as if they were co-ordinate, or equal in importance. As we look at her list, we are not sure which incidents are important and which are less important—there is no subordination or grouping of ideas according to their importance.

Ann now takes the final step in organizing her essay. She decides which ideas are important and therefore deserve a separate paragraph, and which are less important, and will serve as supporting details. She puts her less important ideas under the main ones, continuing to cross out, change, narrow, and expand her ideas as she revises and rearranges.

Here is Ann's scratch outline, based on her revised list:

*Thesis:* "While the day of your wedding may or may not be the happiest day of your life, it almost certainly will be the most chaotic and exhausting one."

1. Preparation for the wedding
   Getting up early in the morning with little sleep
   Going to the hairdresser and finding my future sister-in-law already there, so I had to wait
   Walking back to the hotel room from the hairdresser

> Rushing to get ready; speeding in the car with my maid of honor
>  2. The wedding itself—it was finally happening!
>     Walking down the aisle I could see many friends were there on both sides
>     John looked nervous in his tuxedo
>     There was a mix-up with the readings—Mark read the wrong Shakespearean sonnet
>     My parents both cried
>     The ceremony went by so quickly—after all that planning!
>  3. The photo shoot
>     The photographer wanted to reinact some crucial missed shots
>     Family shots of all permutations
>     Staying late for even more photos alone; we were the last ones at our reception
>  4. The Reception
>     Everyone seemed to want to talk to me at once
>     Many people were friends of our parents that I didn't even know.
>     Trying to spend ten minutes with everyone was exhausting
>     Aunt Susan and Uncle Michael came all the way from Omaha—my favorite relatives—so I spent a lot of time with them
>     The wedding dance—a wonderful break
>  5. The Getaway
>     Alcohol in the afternoon made me tipsy, then tired
>     The garter and bouquet tosses
>     We left early to go to the hotel—for a nap. Honest!
>     A day we'll remember forever

Ann's outline suggests that her essay will have five paragraphs and that each will present, in chronological order, the sequence of events that happened on the day she and John got married. Not every detail that will be in her essay is included in her outline. Nevertheless, by making an outline she has given herself a compass to follow as she begins to write.

Notice that Ann's outline is not polished, and that it consists, for the most part, only of phrases. This kind of outline (a "scratch" or rough outline) is satisfactory for a short essay, but for longer papers you will want to write a more detailed outline like the one on page 276.

## Spatial Order

As Ann's outline demonstrates, a thesis statement will often suggest the best way to organize an essay. Her paper followed chronological

order. But if your essay is primarily a description of someone or something rather than a narration, *spatial order* is probably the best pattern
to follow.

Spatial order is based on the order in which our eyes see and
movie cameras move: from top to bottom, left to right, near to far, and
so on. A description of a scene from the top of a tall building would be
based on the selection of details that would help the reader visualize
the scene. But instead of flinging the details at the reader in random order, we have to present those details in a pattern that will make sense
to the reader.

Here are some notes written by Mai Nguyen for an essay in which
she describes her experiences as a first-time visitor to Manhattan.

> *Thesis statement:* "Manhattan's wealth of civic, cultural, and
> human attractions makes it a great urban vacation spot."

1. The city was supposed to be unfriendly, unyielding, and ugly
2. big buildings and noise on the streets were true
3. people were friendlier than I expected
4. it rained the first two days there
5. the Empire State building experience; a beautiful sight
6. Broadway: the theaters were smaller than I expected inside
7. The ice rink at Rockefeller center was also smaller than expected
8. walking around was easy and fun
9. Greenwich Village a disappointment: like too many other
   places
10. Coney Island was fun; Aquarium; Beach in Brooklyn
11. Queens as a large area of varied neighborhoods
12. a little like going back in time
13. LOVE the sidewalk hot dog stands
14. getting lost
15. Yankee stadium—history right in front of me (my father's fa-
    vorite team)
16. Ellis Island and Statue of Liberty—tourist attractions with
    meaning
17. Museums: Met and MOMA. Wow!
18. Jamaal the friendly cab driver; really helped us out
19. people in Central Park, very nice; directions to Strawberry
    Fields
20. A wonderful place to visit; would I live here?
21. St. Patrick's Cathedral—seems almost odd; out of place.
22. Hard to walk around without thinking about all the history
23. Last night spent at great aunt's on Staten Island
24. So many different people; a very different way of living—very
    old fashioned in some ways, and very new in other ways
25. Dutch were the first European settlers

As you can see, Mai jotted down notes in a dizzying blur. Now she has to go back through them, discard the irrelevant details and place the rest in an order that will make sense to her reader. This means that items 10, 11, 15, and 21 will be deleted because they concern boroughs other than Manhattan. Items 4, 20, 21, 22, and 25 can all be deleted as well since they will not help develop her thesis. Because Mai wants to give the reader a sense of actually being in Manhattan as a visitor, she knows that she will have to arrange her details in spatial order. Otherwise, she risks losing the reader with a confusing barrage of places, names, and details that may occur at several different locations.

Since the island of Manhattan runs roughly north and south, Mai decides to start at the southern tip of the island and work her way northward. She will first begin with the trips to Ellis Island and the Statue of Liberty, then move on to the island at Battery Park, catch a cab with the friendly driver Jamaal and describe the scene until she gets to Greenwich Village. From there she can hop on the subway and head up to midtown, go to a Broadway play, head up to the top of the Empire State Building, visit her favorite museums, maybe even eat a sidewalk hot dog to catch a little local flavor. Then she can go northward to Central Park, see Strawberry Fields, and then head even farther north to see Harlem. Her essay should move smoothly and methodically, just as though the reader were right alongside her for the entire journey.

Arranging her notes, Mai eliminates those details that seem trivial or unimportant to her thesis statement. She groups ideas according to their relative importance so that each main idea is followed by its supporting details. Because she wants to emphasize the historical, civic, and cultural importance of what she sees rather than any ability to find rest and relaxation in New York, she changes her thesis statement. Her outline, like Ann Dozier's, does not contain every detail that will eventually find its way into her essay, but it is enough to keep her on course. Now that she has imposed some order on her material, she is ready to write.

*Thesis statement:* "Manhattan's picturesque landscape of urban life provides a wealth of civic, cultural and historical attractions."

1. The southern tip of the island and Greenwich Village
   Ellis Island and Statue of Liberty—tourist attractions with meaning
   The big buildings of Wall Street and noises on the streets
   Greenwich Village a disappointment: juggler, musicians, and other sidewalk artists remind me of acts I've seen in my hometown's park
2. Midtown—from High Above and Inside
   The view from the top of the Empire State Building

What the inside of a Broadway theater looks like
3. The 50's
   How Rockefeller center's ice rink seems smaller live than on TV
   The architecture of St. Patrick's Cathedral seems out of place and time
4. Central Park
   The park as a jungle in the midst of the city
   Strawberry Fields was a small, somewhat sad corner
   Beautiful Metropolitan Museum of Art
5. Uptown and Harlem
   The ivy league university on the hill over Harlem
   Busy, multi-ethnic variety of 125th St.?
6. Conclusion: Huge variety of the old, the beautiful, the important, and the mundane.

Ann Dozier's essay narrating her wedding day follows chronological order, and Mai Nguyen's description of Manhattan is arranged in spatial order. But effective writing often combines both patterns. If you were writing about the first fish you ever caught, you might tell, in chronological order, the steps you took on that unforgettable day: picking up your fishing buddy, selecting a fly rod, driving to the lake, learning to bait a hook, and finally, after hours of frustration, catching a bass. But while relating these incidents chronologically, you might also include some details organized spatially: a description of the beautiful sunrise as you left your home, the calm surface of the lake, and the flash of the fish as it leaped above the water, for example. Good writing, then, often uses elements of both patterns.

## *Logical Order*

Some topics cannot be arranged in terms of time or space. Instead, the writer has to impose a logical order on them, creating a pattern that will make the most sense to the reader. Several possibilities exist for this kind of order.

*Order of Importance.* One effective system of arrangement is *in order of importance.* Essays arranged in this pattern usually begin with the *least* important ideas and build up to the *most* important or dramatic ideas. If done well, this arrangement creates mounting interest and suspense.

Pamela Steindahl write the following preliminary list of ideas for an essay explaining why she is majoring in English.

*Thesis statement:* "I have decided to major in English because it offers several advantages."

1. Flexibility
2. I already love to read books
3. I want a job that uses writing somehow
4. Good pre-law degree if that's what I choose
5. Mary Laine majored in English and really liked it
6. Develops your ability to think well
7. good degree to combine with a second degree like economics if I want to get an MBA
8. Many Humanities-school majors make good money in the long run
9. I can keep the books I buy and read them again in the future because I enjoy them
10. The classes are often small and intimate with lots of in-class discussion, which I like
11. A good degree to have if I decide to go into advertising
12. As a kid, I always wanted to read—it's been a lifelong passion
13. I read that the heads of several Fortune 500 companies actually had their undergraduate degrees in English
14. Maybe I'll finally write the great American novel
15. There's a lot of history in the study of English too, which I like
16. I'm already starting to look at things, not just books, but also movies, TV shows, art, and people, more critically.

As you can see, Pamela's ideas are not in any particular sequence or order. Because they are not connected in a time sequence and do not describe anything, she cannot use a chronological or spatial order.

After studying her list, she decides to present her ideas *in their order of importance,* beginning with the least important and building up to the most important. Her most important reason for majoring in English she decided, was for the flexibility the degree offered for her future plans to work or attend graduate school. Therefore, she saves this for the end of her paper. The *least* important reason is that the major will develop her critical thinking skills. If your major is English also, you may disagree with her thinking. In that case, your outline would be different from hers.

Here is Pamela's scratch outline. Notice that she has combined items 2 and 12, and 8 and 13, because they repeat essentially the same ideas. She has deleted item 5 because it is not pertinent to her thesis statement. Her outline is not elaborate or formal, but it is adequate to serve as a guide for a 500–750 word essay.

*Thesis statement:* "I have decided to major in English because it offers several advantages."

1. Critical thinking skills
   learning how to think well
   already seeing the results in terms of approaching books, movies, TV, art, and people differently

2. I enjoy the activities of this major
   I have always loved to read books
   I can keep the books I buy and read them again
   The classes are often small and intimate with lots of in-class discussion, which I like.
   There's a lot of history in the study of English, too, which I like
   I want a job that uses writing somehow; maybe someday I'll write the great American novel
3. The flexibility of this major
   Good pre-law degree if that's what I choose
   Good degree to combine with a second degree like economics if I want to get an MBA
   I read that the heads of several Fortune 500 companies actually had their undergraduate degrees in English
   A good degree to have if I decide to go into advertising

*From General to Specific and From Specific to General.* Two other patterns often used for arranging ideas in expository and persuasive writing are moving *from general to specific* and *from specific to general.* When you arrange your ideas from the general to the specific, you introduce your reader first to the "big picture": you begin with a generalization or overall view of your topic which is then clarified or substantiated in the body of the essay by a series of specific examples.

Suppose you were writing about the effect of diet on longevity and overall health. You might begin with a generalization: societies whose members live the longest avoid those foods most likely to block arteries or contribute to high blood pressure and strokes. The rest of your paper would examine, in a series of specific instances, the typical diets of those groups or cultures whose members are known for their long lives. Additional details on the findings of physicians and scientists on the effects of popular American foods such as french fries and Twinkies would serve to support the opening generalization.

A paper on the same topic moving from the specific to the general might begin with an examination of specific foods and their effect on cholesterol, blood pressure, and heart disease. You might then examine the diets of several societies known for their longevity and show that they avoid harmful foods. After accumulating and presenting a series of specific instances, you would conclude with a generalization: societies whose members live the longest avoid those foods most likely to clog arteries or contribute to high blood pressure and strokes.

Here is an outline for an essay on another topic that moves from the *general to the specific.* Notice that the writer begins with a generalization in the first section and then illustrates it with specific details.

*Opening generalization:* The United States is a nation living on credit, which does not bode well for its future stability.

I. The psychology of debt
   A. Numbers are so large as to be meaningless
   B. Growing acceptance of high debt at all levels of society
   C. The "Let my grandchildren pay for me" attitude
II. The effect of the national debt on interest rates
   A. Greater the debt, higher interest we must pay to get people to buy up the debt
   B. Higher rates means greater pressure on future budgets
   C. Higher federal rates force up other rates for consumer debtors on mortgages and credit cards
III. The effect of national debt on the federal budget
   A. Increase in percentage of budget to pay interest
   B. Decrease in discretionary spending
   C. A vicious cycle of carrying over interest payments from previous debt makes each year increasingly difficult
IV. The national debt is steadily increasing
   A. Yearly totals
   B. Congress's inability to cut spending
   C. Public's refusal to pay higher taxes or see middle-class entitlements cut

The same ideas could be arranged in a *specific to general pattern*. Notice that the following outline begins with a series of particulars that leads to the generalization.

I. The national debt is steadily increasing
   A. Yearly totals keep going up
   B. Congress's ability to cut spending
   C. Public's refusal to pay higher taxes or see middle-class entitlements cut
II. The effect of national debt on the federal budget
   A. Increase in percentage of budget to pay interest
   B. Decrease in discretionary spending
   C. A vicious cycle of carrying over interest payments from previous debt makes each year increasingly difficult
III. The effect of the national debt on interest rates
   A. Greater the debt, higher interest we must pay to get people to buy up the debt
   B. Higher rates means greater pressure on future budgets
   C. Higher federal rates force up other rates for consumer debtors on mortgages and credit cards
IV. The psychology of debt
   A. Numbers are so large as to be meaningless
   B. Growing acceptance of high debt at all levels of society
   C. The "Let my grandchildren pay for me" attitude

*Concluding generalization:* The United States is a nation living on credit, which does not bode well for its future stability.

Which organizational pattern—from general to specific or from specific to general—should you use? The choice depends to a great extent on your topic and your thesis statement. If your thesis is likely to meet resistance, you might first offer a series of particulars and specific examples that leads to your generalization or thesis. On the other hand, the advantage of leading with the generalization is that the reader knows exactly where you are going; you have told her what you want to convey, and she fills in the argument with the details you supply. These patterns, often called *deductive* and *inductive,* are discussed in greater detail in Chapter 10 ("Writing the Persuasive Essay").

## A Review of Steps to Follow in Organizing and Outlining Your Essay

Jot down all of the components you can think of that might belong in your essay: statistics, examples, facts, details, reasons. Do not worry about their order; you will take care of that later. Test each idea on your list in terms of your thesis statement: does it belong in your essay, or is it off the subject? If it is irrelevant, cut it. Be ruthless!

Look over your topic and thesis statement again to see if their wording suggests the best way to organize your essay. For instance, an essay that explains how to do something is best arranged *chronologically,* and a topic that implies a visual impression would normally require a *spatial order.* On the other hand, content that does not lend itself to either a time or space pattern could be arranged in a *logical* order: *in order of importance, from general to specific,* or *from specific to general.* The ideas on your list will often suggest a suitable arrangement.

Group related ideas. Make separate "stacks" or "piles" of ideas, either on paper or in your head. In each group, select the main idea that includes all the others. Arrange the major groups according to the pattern you have selected. Make a scratch outline and order these groups, testing each item for its relevance to your thesis statement.

## E X E R C I S E 1

List at least five main ideas to support five of the topics below. Arrange the ideas in the organizational pattern specified in parentheses.

The benefits of a college education (*general to specific*)
A teacher you learned a lot from (*general to specific*)
Your neighborhood (*spatial*)
The benefits of owning your own car (*order of importance*)
A work of art (*spatial*)
Your first impressions of your college or university (*specific to general*)
How to play your favorite sport (*specific to general*)
Why I am (or am not) politically active (*order of importance*)
How to do one of the following: barter in a foreign city, change an infant's diapers, cook homemade spaghetti with meat sauce, install a new garbage disposal, play the guitar, prepare to move to a new home (*chronological*)

## E X E R C I S E   2

List the ideas for the thesis statement that you wrote (page 84) for your essay and then apply the steps discussed on page 97. After selecting the organizational pattern most suitable for your essay, write a scratch outline.

## C O M P U T E R   E X E R C I S E

As in Exercise 2, make a list of ideas for a thesis statement. Then, working with a partner, determine how each of your ideas would best be organized: by chronological order, by spatial order, by order of importance, from specific to general, or from general to specific. Note the items that have been duplicated or need to be left out. Then, rearrange your own items into an informal outline to fit that order. This will work best if you can use a copy function to preserve your original list and make the outline from the copy of the list. Finally, have your partner check your outline to see if it uses the correct order and incorporates all relevant ideas.

# 6

# Drafting the Essay: Six Patterns

## 6. Writing the First Draft

Writing an essay forces you to make a number of decisions. You must select a topic, formulate a thesis statement, identify your purpose and audience, and determine the organizational plan you will follow. One of the most essential steps as you prepare to write your first draft is to selecting the most suitable mode or pattern for developing your essay.

### Selecting a Pattern

The pattern you will use depends on your purpose and your thesis statement. If you want to show your reader how something words or how it came about, you would recreate the *process*. If you want your reader to see the similarities or differences between two things or ideas, you would use *comparison and contrast*. And if you are trying to show your reader what something is by giving illustrations, you would develop your essay by *exemplification*.

The wording of your thesis statement will also point toward the most appropriate pattern of development. For instance, "There are three kinds of people who drive sports cars" suggests an essay developed by *classification*. "Most hunting accidents are caused by carelessness" will probably be developed by *cause and effect*. "'Feminism' is a concept that has several meanings, depending on the person or group that uses it" will probably require an extended *definition*. If you consider your thesis statement carefully, you should have little trouble selecting the right pattern.

Although your purpose and thesis statement will largely determine the method of development you use, your paper will probably not be restricted to *one* method. Instead, you will often combine methods: *comparison and contrast* with *exemplification, definition* with *exemplification* or *classification,* and so on. Nevertheless, each essay will be developed chiefly by one method. By choosing this primary method, you are providing a plan for your paper so that the reader can follow your thoughts.

Fortunately, the patterns used to develop an essay are similar to our normal thought processes. We tend to think of examples to illustrate a point, we classify and divide groups into categories, we compare and contrast things and ideas, we determine how things work and what they are made of, we look for the causes of events and their effects, and we try to explain what things are. By using these patterns in your writing, then, you are following paths that are familiar to your reader.

Here are the most common patterns of development:

Exemplification
Classification
Comparison and Contrast
Process and Analysis
Cause and Effect
Definition

To select the best pattern, ask yourself the questions your reader might ask. The kinds of questions you ask will suggest the method best suited for developing the thesis statement, as the following examples demonstrate.

| | |
|---|---|
| *Thesis Statement:* | Many athletes who achieve phenomenal success in their sports are actually poor role models for children. |
| *Questions:* | Who are the athletes that you have in mind? In what ways were they successful in their sports? Why are they poor role models for children? |
| *Method:* | Exemplification |
| *Thesis Statement:* | The population of a county jail at any one time includes different types of people facing vastly different futures. |
| *Questions:* | What different types of people are likely to be in jail at any one time? What different types of offenses will cause a person to wind up in jail? How are these people alike, and how are they different? What kind of future does each face? |
| *Method:* | Classification |
| *Thesis Statement:* | The difference in laws governing the purchase and consumption of alcohol in United States and Sweden represent fundamentally different approaches and attitudes toward drinking. |
| *Questions:* | How are the laws governing the purchase and consumption of alcohol in the United States and Sweden different? Are the laws uniform throughout Sweden, or do they vary as they do in the United States from state to state? What attitudes are reflected in these laws? Are the rates of alcoholism in the two countries the same or different? Are drunk driving rates similar or different? |
| *Method:* | Comparison and Contrast |
| *Thesis Statement:* | Setting up and running a small business can be difficult and time-consuming, but also quite rewarding. |
| *Questions:* | How does a person set up and run a small business? What steps are involved? |

*Method:*  Process and Analysis

*Thesis Statement:*  Many people believe that the moon and the stars have the power to directly influence human behavior.

*Questions:*  How could the moon and stars cause changes in human behavior? What effect do some people believe the moon and stars have? Who is affected? Is there any empirical evidence to back up such assertions?

*Method:*  Cause and Effect

*Thesis Statement:*  Most people's understanding of the word *poor* seems to incorporate some measure of low income and small material wealth while ignoring the spiritual and emotional aspects.

*Questions:*  What is *poor*? What distinctions can be made between material and nonmaterial considerations? How can spiritual and emotional aspects be calculated, quantified, or judged?

*Method:*  Definition

## E X E R C I S E  1

For each of the following thesis statements, list the *questions* likely to be asked by the reader. Then select the *method of development* most appropriate for answering the questions.

1. The study of botany involves the ability to observe fine details and record them accurately.
2. Sigmund Freud's name is better known, but Carl Jung may have provided more helpful insights into our understanding of the human mind.
3. Many women today have to battle the ghosts of their grandmothers as they struggle to be good wives and mothers while establishing careers for themselves.
4. The story of Prince Charles and Princess Diana reveals the clash between fantasy and reality in our understanding of royalty.
5. The effort to label albums as obscene has only made those albums more attractive to teenagers looking to rebel.
6. During my high-school years, I had several teachers who should have been fired for incompetence.
7. Everyone seems to want to pursue *happiness,* but few even know what the word means to them.
8. Study habits and attitudes toward school are often determined by a student's cultural background.

9. Some zealous parents of Little Leaguers display behavior that borders on child abuse.

10. The withholding tax on tips has caused many hardships for waiters.

---

## Developing an Essay by Exemplification

Many of the papers you write in college will be developed by exemplification. For making a statement clear and supporting a generalization, examples are powerful tools. If you give your reader examples, he or she has a good idea of your point. If you do not supply examples, the reader will probably have only a hazy notion of what you are trying to say.

Even individual paragraphs suffer when they consist only of general statements:

> My girlfriend Carolyn is so wonderful. She's so nice to me, and she really knows how to make me feel good when I'm down. I also like the way she dresses. She has a lot of style. She's pretty interesting, too. The things she talks about definitely make me look at the world differently.

This paragraph is vague. Do you have any idea what Carolyn is actually like? All we have is a series of unsupported general statements that leave us with unanswered questions: What does she do to make the speaker feel good? How does she dress? What fashions or style does she prefer? What makes her interesting? What topics does she like to talk about, and what is her attitude about them?

In the revision below, notice how much more specific the paragraph becomes, chiefly because the writer has added examples:

> My girlfriend Carolyn is so wonderful. Whenever I'm feeling down, she suggests we go for a long walk along the shore. She knows this will make me happy again. I also like the way she dresses, with her ripped blue jeans, tank top, and dreadlocks. She likes to wear a lot of jewelry too, most of it handmade, which she buys at craft shows. She's always talking about the possibilities in the world, and how people hold themselves back mentally. She believes that psychic power is one of the great untapped resources of humanity, and so much of what is ill and wrong with the world could be changed if we were only more aware of ourselves and our true nature.

### Organizing the Essay Developed by Exemplification

After you have listed examples that illustrate and clarify your thesis statement, you are faced with a question: In what order should you present your examples? If the examples occur chronologically, the obvious arrangement is in the order in which they happened. But if they do not have a sequential relationship, the best arrangement is usually *in their order of importance*, beginning with the least important and ending with the most dramatic example. In this way, you conclude your essay forcefully.

The organization of an essay developed by example is relatively straightforward. Your introduction usually contains your thesis statement, and the body of the essay presents a series of examples to support it. The conclusion reinforces the thesis. A typical essay might look like this:

*Paragraph 1:*  *Introduction* (with thesis statement)
*Paragraph 2:*  *First example*
*Paragraph 3:*  *Second example*
*Paragraph 4:*  *Third example*
*Paragraph 5:*  *Conclusion*

(*Note:* The outlines in this chapter illustrating the organization of essays usually consist of five or six paragraphs. This structure is for *illustrative purposes only;* as noted in Chapter 4, an introduction may consist of several paragraphs, the body might include a dozen or more paragraphs, and some conclusions require several paragraphs.)

The five-paragraph pattern illustrated above could be used for developing the following thesis statement: "Much of what we think is true—scientific 'facts,' episodes in history, anecdotes about famous people—turns out to be false." An outline for an essay developing this thesis statement might look like this:

*Paragraph 1:*  *Introduction,* with thesis statement: "Much of what we think is true—scientific 'facts,' episodes in history, anecdotes about famous people—turns out to be false."
*Paragraph 2:*  Examples of myths and mistaken scientific notions about physical phenomena and occurrences
*Paragraph 3:*  Examples of commonly confused events (battles, elections, geographical discoveries)
*Paragraph 4:*  Examples of legends, mistaken accomplishments and identities, exaggerated reputations
*Paragraph 5:*  *Conclusion*

An alternate organizational pattern for the essay developed by exemplification is sometimes effective. In this method the writer begins his essay with one or more startling examples to catch his reader's interest, delaying the introduction of his thesis statement, which is then presented in the second paragraph. The rest of the paper presents more examples to support the thesis. A typical paper arranged in this pattern would look like this:

*Paragraph 1:*   *One or more startling examples*
*Paragraph 2:*   *Introduction* (with thesis statement)
*Paragraph 3:*   *Second example*
*Paragraph 4:*   *Third example*
*Paragraph 5:*   *Fourth example*
*Paragraph 6:*   *Conclusion*

An outline of an essay that follows this pattern based on the above thesis statement might look like this:

*Paragraph 1:*   Series of surprising "facts" (Columbus did not discover America; Leif Ericson did. A compass doesn't point to the North magnetic pole *or* to the North geographic pole. The Declaration of Independence wasn't signed on July 4th, etc.)

*Paragraph 2:*   Delayed introduction, with thesis statement: "Much of what we think is true—scientific 'facts,' episodes in history, anecdotes about famous people—turns out to be false."

*Paragraph 3:*   Examples of myths and mistaken scientific notions about physical phenomena and occurrences.

*Paragraph 4:*   Examples of commonly confused events (battles, elections, geographical discoveries)

*Paragraph 5:*   Examples of legends, mistaken accomplishments and identities, exaggerated reputations

*Paragraph 6:*   *Conclusion*

## Guidelines for Writing an Essay Developed by Exemplification

An essay developed by exemplification may be based on one detailed example, or it may be developed by a series of examples that support the thesis statement. In either case, the writer must follow certain guidelines:

*Examples should be related to the point being made, and they should be typical and representative of the type under discussion.* This means that you should not cite exceptions or rare instances as examples to prove your point. A thesis claiming that formal education in our society is not necessary for success would not be convincing just because Jesus Christ, Abraham Lincoln, and Socrates were cited as examples of those who did not graduate from college.

*The best examples are often taken from your own experience.* Personal examples are not always available, of course, but when they are, they have an impact. They have the ring of truth and conviction about them, and as a result are usually convincing. An essay that argues that a vegetarian diet leads to improved health and peace of mind would be much more convincing if you gave examples from your own life instead of anecdotes you have read.

*Don't present your examples in a haphazard, random order.* Follow a plan.

### A Student-Written Essay Developed by Exemplification

Here is a student-written essay developed by exemplification. Notice how it is organized: The introductory paragraph presents the thesis statement, and the body of the essay (paragraphs two through four) presents a series of examples, all illustrative of the thesis statement. The conclusion wraps up the paper by relating additional examples to the thesis statement. As a result, we have a sense of closure or completion as we finish the paper.

---

The Nobel Peace Prize: The Ultimate Political Statement

First awarded in 1901, the Nobel Prizes were begun under directions from the will of Alfred Nobel, the inventor of dynamite. Awards are given annually in physics, chemistry, physiology or medicine, literature, economics, and peace. The Nobel prizes are to go to individuals or groups that have made outstanding contributions to their field. Although any award given could be considered controversial based on disagreements over standards, the awards in most categories are given based on measurable achievements that can reasonably be defended. The exception to this is the Peace prize. The Nobel Peace Prize has often been given as a way to reward political dissidents and humiliate repressive regimes rather than to acknowledge any true measure of peace; in other words, the Peace prize is often a measure of political correctness, not accomplishment.

Look, for example, at the 1973 recipients of the Nobel Peace price, Henry Kissinger of the United States and Le Duc Tho of North Vietnam. They received the Peace prize for the signing of the Paris Accords, which were to put an end to the war in Vietnam. The accords did not end the war; they simply ended U.S. involvement in the war. The end of the war came when the North Vietnamese and the Viet Cong conquered the South in 1975. Even without this kind of hindsight, the committee should have looked at who they were rewarding: Kissinger expanded the war into Cambodia and Laos, contributing to enormous amounts of killing and misery, and Tho represented a North that had been unremittingly hostile in its efforts to unify the two Vietnams. The award was made in the flush of the rhetoric and propaganda surrounding the Accords, and now stands as a bad joke in the history of the prize.

An entire category of the Peace Prize is devoted to leaders of oppressed groups; the actual achievements of the recipients lie more in their symbolic importance than in any accomplishments. Among these recipients are the Dali Lama, the religious leader of the Tibetans who have been under Chinese rule since the 1950s; Archbishop Desmond Tutu of South Africa, an outspoken critic of apartheid; and Rigoberta Menchu, an advocate for the indigenous peoples of Guatemala. While people throughout the world may sympathize with their causes, the Nobel Prize committee is also using the prize as a slap in the face to those governments, such as in China, South Africa, and Guatemala, whose policies they abhor. The Dali Lama and Menchu still speak out; Tutu lives in post-apartheid South Africa thanks to the efforts of two Peace Prize recipients who really did deserve the prize, Nelson Mandela and F. W. de Klerk.

A special look should be taken at the prize awarded to Mikhail Gorbachev in 1990. Gorbachev was and still is the darling of the West, a "good" Soviet leader. The Peace Prize was a pat on the back to help his policies of *perestroika* gain greater acceptance at home. However, as long as the Cold War was on, Gorbachev did little except what he was forced to do in terms of nuclear arms control. Gorbachev intended economic changes; he wanted peace only so far as to lessen the costs of sustaining a large military force. Gorbachev's peace was really an absence of aggressiveness, which encouraged a coup attempt that led to the demise of the Soviet Union. Only after Boris Yeltsin took the reins did the world feel safer as he allowed the Baltic states to leave the Soviet Union. The subsequent partitioning of the Soviet Union into the present-day republics came about after Gorbachev was gone from power. In some ways, Gorbachev was not so much a peacemaker as a man trying to cope with the economic realities of the Soviet Union's final years.

Certainly all attempts to lessen conflict, war, and aggression in the world are to be applauded. However, the Nobel Peace Prize has too often been used as a political carrot to reward symbolic figures rather than actual peacemakers. Mother Teresa, Andrei Sakharov, and Lech Walesa—these are all undeniably noble people with causes that have much worldwide sympathy. But should they have been Nobel?

## E X E R C I S E 2

After reading the essay carefully, answer the following questions.

1. What is the thesis statement of this essay? Why is it best developed by examples?

2. How are paragraphs two through four related? What is their function?
3. How does the last paragraph "tie up" the preceding examples in the essay?

---

# E X E R C I S E 3

Make a list of examples that illustrate one of the following thesis statements. Your examples may come from your reading, your conversations with friends, personal experience, or from current events. Next, arrange the examples in the most effective order, following the suggestions in this section. Then write an essay developing the thesis statement with your examples.

1. Movies are worse than ever.
2. American automobile manufacturers are trying to beat the competition with better-made, less expensive cars.
3. Many people are turning to fundamentalist religions to find answers to life's difficult questions.
4. Some of the craziest, kookiest lifestyle ideas have originated in California.
5. How people dress can say a lot about how they feel about themselves.
6. Several new rock bands have reinvigorated the local music scene.
7. Young children should be encouraged to play sports that emphasize running and coordination and avoid violent contact.
8. A hobby can turn into a profitable business.
9. Old age is not a barrier to accomplishment.
10. Some laws are unfair.

---

## Developing an Essay by Classification

*Classification* is a method you may use for developing a subject when you wish to sort things or ideas according to similar characteristics. It provides one way of answering the question "What (or who) is it and where does it belong?" The simplest scheme of classification is to split your subject into a two-part system. Page 109 shows an example using campus organizations as the topic.

These classifications are not exhaustive. They may need to be explained or analyzed in further detail, but by using a simple system of grouping into categories, you can create a working outline before you

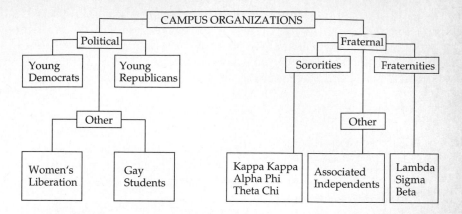

begin to write your essay. Classification should be easy for you as long as you remember to put things in like classes.

Classification usually proceeds from the general to the specific, major to minor, or from categories that include the most of some characteristics to those that include the least. How could you classify "Campus Organizations" further? You could determine which ones are composed of men and which of women; which have members predominantly in the 18–21 age group; which have most of their members in the over 25 age group; and which are politically active and which are not. Finally, you could determine the relation between a campus chapter and its national affiliate.

When classifying, you must remember to take care that your subclasses are of the same rank. In the "Campus Organization" chart, you would not equate the classes Fraternal, Young Republicans, and Theta Chi. They are different levels. However, you *can* discuss two fraternities in equal terms: you may evaluate the service projects of the two groups, for instance, or compare the cost of joining these two organizations, or discuss the relative effects they might have on the student government.

You can approach classification in two ways: horizontally or vertically. All of the major divisions may be discussed together and then the subcategories considered. This would be a horizontal organization. Or, one major division at a time may be taken and all of its subdivisions discussed before considering the next major division. This would be vertical organization.

Classification works well in developing essays that clarify or explain. In writing a paper about soap operas, for example, you might begin by breaking up a typical "soap" into its parts in terms of the people involved: the producer, director, writer, and the actors, explaining the responsibilities and contributions of each to the show. You could then develop your paper by putting the audience into categories:

women who work at home, senior citizens, college students, and the unemployed, for instance, and explain the interest and motivation each group has for viewing the programs. Or you might classify the soap operas on the basis of their main characters, the villains and heroes, the crises, and the similarities and differences among the plots.

## Organizing the Essay Developed by Classification

Classification essays are organized by categories. The introduction normally states the thesis and tells the reader the categories or classes by which the subject is classified. The paragraphs that make up the body of the essay present each category or class in turn, and the conclusion reinforces the thesis statement.

Here is an outline for such a paper.

*Paragraph 1:* Introduction with thesis statement indicating basis of classification
*Paragraph 2:* First category
*Paragraph 3:* Second category
*Paragraph 4:* Third category
*Paragraph 5:* Conclusion

An outline for an essay developed by *classification* might look like the following:

*Paragraph 1:* *Introduction with thesis statement:* "Many people speak of pollution as if there were only one type, but the alarming fact is that there is water, air, and soil pollution."
*Paragraph 2:* Water pollution; sewage, industrial wastes, fertilizer contamination.
*Paragraph 3:* Air pollution; electrical power plants and motor vehicles, smoke and exhausts.
*Paragraph 4:* Soil pollution; hazardous waste sites; city dumps.
*Paragraph 5:* *Conclusion*

## Guidelines for Writing an Essay Developed by Classification

When using the pattern of classification, you should follow these important guidelines:

*There must be a unifying principle or purpose for your classification.* Merely listing parts and objects is not enough. Explain to your reader in your introduction why you are breaking things down into various categories. For example, an essay that merely divided the colleges and universities in your state into two- and four-year institutions would have little point. But an essay that pointed out the advantages and disadvantages, the available majors, and the expenses for attending each kind of college would have a direction and purpose.

*Be certain that your categories are logical and do not overlap.* Dividing the student body into "men, women, and athletes," for instance, would be inaccurate because "athletes" obviously includes individuals from the first two groups.

*When classifying, be certain that the parts account for all elements of the subject.* A division of the federal government into the judicial and legislative branches would be incomplete because the executive branch is omitted.

## E X E R C I S E 4

Using *classification*, place the following items into categories or logical groups. Be ready to explain the basis of your classification. You should discover at least three categories.

| | |
|---|---|
| The Beatles | Willie Nelson |
| Beethoven | Charlie Parker |
| Alabama | U2 |
| Chopin | Elvis Presley |
| Hank Williams | Duke Ellington |
| Miles Davis | Mozart |

*A Student-Written Essay Developed by Classification*

Here is a student-written essay that uses classification in its approach to the subject of barbecue.

### What Is Real Barbecue?

The aroma of the Old West's open ranges comes wafting into your nostrils as you step into the barbecue restaurant. You look left and right and see families and couples tasting, smelling, and devouring slabs of beef or pork, smothered in thick, tomato-based sauce. Beer is sure to be close at hand, as are cole slaw, corn on the cob, french fries, or perhaps barbecued beans. But among true barbecue aficionados, distinctions between type, flavor, presentation, and effect must be made, for not all barbecue is the same. Among the many styles are Texas barbecue, East St. Louis barbecue, North Carolina barbecue, and the little-known but much loved Memphis barbecue. Each of these has its own qualities that make its fans rabid for more.

For the true devotees of Texas barbecue, there is no other form of cooking that can go by the name barbecue. Indeed, Texas barbecue is what comes to mind when the nation thinks of "barbecue." Ribs of beef or pork are cooked over an open fire or smoked using hickory, mesquite, alder, or cherry. The ribs are slathered in a rich sauce made primarily of tomato, vinegar, and chilies or peppers. The specific recipe, of course, varies from cook to cook, but the final product is usually a thick, hearty sauce. Be sure not to make the mistake of putting the barbecue on before the meat is cooked. This is a virtual sacrilege to the barbecue connoisseur. Some folks prefer to cook chicken or even steaks for their barbecue, but the true Texas barbecue chef will only cook ribs, served with cole slaw, potato salad, and plenty of Lone Star beer.

In East St. Louis, they won't hear of barbecuing anything except pork. Only hickory wood can be used in the cooking process. No mesquite, no cherry, no alder. As for the sauce, if it does not begin with red pepper pods, no reputable chef in the state of Illinois will lay claim to it. East St. Louis barbecue is for purists.

North Carolina barbecue is a lighter, tangier barbecue. The pork is cooked until the meat is practically falling off the bone. Then, the meat is removed from the bone and shredded. In North Carolina, there is a preference for using oak wood for these fires. The sauces vary, but generally tend to be lighter than the Texas or East St. Louis variety. In North Carolina, hush puppies are likely to be served with the barbecue. Hush puppies are made from corn meal and are deep fried. North Carolinians consider hush puppies and barbecue a legendary combination.

Memphis barbecue may be the least well-known, but it has fanatical adherents who will touch no other barbecue. Throughout the city of Memphis are small barbecue restaurants that smoke pork on the premises. The older the restaurant, the better and more esteemed the barbecue since age only helps the smoking process. Memphis barbecue is served sandwich style. As in North Carolina, the pork is first shredded off the bone. The meat is then placed on the heel of a hamburger bun. Sauce is applied to the pork. Then, on top of this is placed a generous helping of cole slaw (each restaurant has its own recipe for this as well), and the crown of the bun is placed on top, usually after being dabbed with more sauce. Memphis is so proud of its unique approach to barbecue that every May there is a cook-off to determine the city's best barbecue.

A great deal of the charm and enjoyment of barbecue comes from the variety of meats, cooking methods, sauces, and serving methods. Residents of every region in the United States have come up with their own variation of barbecue, from Louisiana to Maine, from the Carolinas to California. The true lover of cooking and eating will simply have to try them all, perhaps several times, before deciding on any favorites.

# E X E R C I S E 5

After reading the above essay carefully, answer the following questions.

1. How does the writer's first paragraph suggest the method of development and organization that she will follow?
2. What is the basis of the classification in this essay—what is being classified?
3. What are the categories listed by the writer? In what paragraphs do they appear?
4. How are paragraphs two through six developed? What other method of development is used?
5. How does the last paragraph reinforce the thesis of the essay?

# E X E R C I S E 6

Using classification as your basic method of development, select one of the following topics and sort it into categories. Write an essay developing your categories, making certain that you explain to your reader your purpose in classifying the thing, and the basis or plan for your classification.

1. Methods of cooking eggs
2. Academic divisions at your college or university
3. Annoying personalities
4. Popular magazines
5. Computers
6. Ways to exercise
7. Parents
8. Stock-car drivers
9. Ways to attract the opposite sex
10. Recreational vehicles

## Developing an Essay by Comparison and Contrast

One of the most common writing assignments in college is the paper organized by comparison and contrast. Its popularity derives, in part, from the fact that it is one of the most common ways our minds organize information. We spend much of our day comparing and contrasting: selecting clothes to wear to school and work, deciding what to order from a menu, examining cuts of meat at the store, choosing a television program to watch, or picking a book to read. In your college assignments you are often asked to point out the similarities and differences between forms of government, between characters in a novel, or theories on the origin of the earth.

In each of these instances you are analyzing two or more items and noting their similarities *(comparisons)* and differences *(contrasts)*. Technically speaking, comparisons reveal similarities *and* differences, and contrasts are concerned only with differences. In practice, however, comparisons suggest likenesses, and contrasts point out differences.

The purpose of comparison and contrast essays is to explain and evaluate material. We can explain something as exotic as the marriage customs of the Bushmen of the Kalahari by contrasting them with the marriage customs of Americans, or we can explain something as commonplace as a favorite pen by comparing it with one that is familiar to our reader. Usually, however, we compare and contrast for the purpose of evaluating: we want to show that one book or movie is superior to another, or that a particular instructor or make of car is better than another.

When organized and developed carefully, a comparison and contrast essay has a unity and logic that helps the reader understand our ideas. If an essay, however, is only a series of scrambled likenesses or differences that lead nowhere, the result will be chaos. To be certain that your comparison and contrast essays have clarity and coherence, read the guidelines on page 118 carefully.

### Organizing the Essay Developed by Comparison and Contrast

Your first job in organizing your comparison and contrast essay is to decide what you intend to emphasize: the differences or the similarities between the two subjects. This can best be done by making two lists—one for the differences, and the other for the similarities—and choosing the most appropriate angle. Your next job is to list the differences or similarities in their order of importance, beginning with the least significant and building up to the most dramatic and important.

The organizational patterns most often used for developing a comparison and contrast essay are *object-by-object* and *point-by-point*. Each has its own strengths as well as weaknesses; the complexity of your material and the length of your paper will determine the best method for you.

An essay using the *object-by-object* pattern of organization first presents all of the relevant details or aspects of one object, and then all of the corresponding qualities of the other. A concluding paragraph usually follows, summarizing the likenesses or differences or expressing an opinion. If you wished to contrast city living with country life using this pattern, you might first list all of the advantages of city living, then present the advantages of living in the country. Your concluding paragraph would then express a preference based on the differences enumerated.

Because your reader might have a short memory, you should use the object-by-object pattern only when there are few points to be cited or when your essay is relatively short. The standard college essay of 500–750 words is short enough to consider using the object-by-object pattern. Further, you must be certain that you do not allow digressions to destroy the design of your paper. Be sure, for example, that you give the same treatment to both items being compared or contrasted.

The *point-by-point* pattern is particularly helpful for complex comparisons and for longer papers. An essay using this plan alternates the points of comparison between two objects. In a detailed comparison of American and English high schools, for instance, you might explain how the American school is organized, then do the same for the English school; a discussion of graduation requirements for the typical American school might be followed by the same information for the English school. The organization of such a paper resembles a ping-pong game, as the differences or similarities of each object are presented in turn.

Because it helps the reader keep in mind the two things being compared or contrasted in their being frequently mentioned, the point-by-point approach gives unity and coherence to complex topics. An entire essay developed in this pattern often profits by a closing paragraph that presents a conclusion based on the differences or likenesses established.

Here is an outline for a paper following the *object-by-object* pattern. Notice that it is organized one object at a time: the first paragraph contains the introduction and thesis statement, and the second paragraph discusses only Object A. The next paragraph is devoted only to Object B, and the last paragraph serves as a conclusion.

*Paragraph 1:* Introduction and thesis statement
*Paragraph 2:* Object A
• Point 1
• Point 2
• Point 3

*Paragraph 3:*   Object B
                 • Point 1
                 • Point 2
                 • Point 3
*Paragraph 4:*   Conclusion

Here is an outline for a paper following the *point-by-point* pattern. Notice that unlike the object-by-object pattern, this method organizes the paper around points: either similarities or differences. Each paragraph or section of the paper discusses a single point shared by both objects.

*Paragraph 1:*   Introduction and thesis statement
*Paragraph 2:*   Point 1 of Object A
                 Point 1 of Object B
*Paragraph 3:*   Point 2 of Object A
                 Point 2 of Object B
*Paragraph 4:*   Point 3 of Object A
                 Point 3 of Object B
*Paragraph 5:*   Conclusion

Which pattern is better: *object-by-object* or *point-by-point?* Many instructors prefer the point-by-point pattern because it allows the writer to cover more details without confusing the reader, particularly with complex or involved subjects. The reader sometimes has the feeling, after reading an essay organized object-by-object, that he has read two separate essays only thinly connected. On the other hand, it is a convenient pattern for allowing the writer to deal with one item at a time. The advantage of the point-by-point pattern, with its interlocked network of ideas, is that it continuously reminds the reader of the two objects and the point being made about them.

Using transitions in the comparison and contrast paper will help your reader follow your ideas, regardless of the method of organization you use. Words such as *however, too, alike, in common, moreover, on the other hand, but, similarly, instead, both,* and so on show relationships between ideas.

Here are outlines for two comparisons and contrast papers. The first is based on the object-by-object pattern, and the second follows the point-by-point pattern.

## *Object-by-Object*

*Paragraph 1:*   *Introduction and thesis statement:* "Having lived at home for a semester and in a dormitory for a semester, I believe that there are more advantages to living in a dormitory."

*Paragraph 2:*  **Object A:** Living at home
  *Point 1:* Cut off from the social life of college
  *Point 2:* Parents expect me to participate in home life when I'm too busy
  *Point 3:* Sense of dependency; still relying on parents for food and shelter
  *Point 4:* Lack of privacy; parents see every time I arrive and leave the house

*Paragraph 3:*  **Object B:** Dormitory life
  *Point 1:* Living at the center of campus life; getting the full college experience
  *Point 2:* Focused in on college exclusively
  *Point 3:* Sense of independence; cut the apron strings
  *Point 4:* Greater privacy; able to come and go as I please; no one to answer to except myself

*Conclusion:*  I found that living in the dormitory afforded greater independence, better social opportunities, and increased my concentration on my studies.

## Point-by-Point

*Paragraph 1:*  *Introduction and thesis statement:* "An examination of the different attitudes among youths in the 1960s and youths in the 1990s reveals profound changes that have occurred in this country, mostly for the worse."

*Paragraph 2:*  *Point 1 of Object A (1960s youths):* Youths were more altruistic, embracing programs such as the Peace Corps.
  *Point 1 of Object B (1990s youths):* Youths are more materialistic, concerned with getting their piece of the action.

*Paragraph 3:*  *Point 2 of Object A (1960s youth):* Youths were willing to explore things and ideas that were new or foreign.
  *Point 2 of Object B (1990s youth):* Youths are less willing to explore the new and instead are more interested in nostalgia, exploring the familiar.

*Paragraph 4:*  *Point 3 of Object A (1960s youth):* Youths believed that the world could be changed for the better.
  *Point 3 of Object B (1990s youth):* Youths believe that the world cannot be changed for the better.

*Paragraph 5:*  *Point 4 of Object A (1960s youth):* Youths were more confident about their futures professionally and personally.

Point 4 of Object B (1990s youth): Youths are uncertain
about their futures professionally and personally.

*Paragraph 6:* *Conclusion:* Perhaps the increase in materialism and
uncertainty about the future in today's youths reflects
America's slide from uncontested economic domina-
tion in the 1960s to the more unstable economic conditions of the 1990s.

## E X E R C I S E 7

Using either the object-by-object or point-by-point pattern, write
an outline for a paper in which you show the differences or similarities between two objects that you are familiar with: two movie
stars that you like, two restaurants you have been to, two careers
or lifestyles, two teachers, two types of cars, or two other objects of
the same class.

### Guidelines for Writing an Essay Developed by Comparison and Contrast

*Be certain that you are comparing items of the same general class, even though
they differ in their qualities.* You can compare the Baptist faith with the
Methodist, because they are both Protestant denominations, and you
can compare Baptist doctrine with Roman Catholic teaching because
both groups are Christian. You can even compare Baptist and Jewish
beliefs, because both groups are religions. But you could not compare
Baptists with policemen, because there is no category that encompasses both—there is no logical basis for a comparison and contrast.

*Do not try to compare more than two things in a short paper.* A chapter in a
book can compare and contrast three or four (or more) objects, but an
essay of 500–750 words should be limited to two.

*Before writing your paper, decide what your main idea or purpose is.* A comparison and contrast paper makes a point and is more than a list of
likenesses and differences. It should lead to a conclusion.

*Be fair; if you are trying to show the superiority of one object over another,
give equal space to both objects being contrasted.*

*Give your reader several examples to make clear the differences and similari-
ties between the subjects of your paper.*

# E X E R C I S E 8

Which of the following pairs of subjects could be developed into a comparison and contrast essay? Which could not?

1. Immigrants from the past and immigrants today
2. Albert Einstein and atheism
3. The ancient Roman Empire and the United States
4. Tall and short people
5. George Washington and Simon Bolivar
6. Olympic athletes and wealthy heiresses
7. Lincoln Continentals and Abraham Lincoln
8. Chicago and Boston
9. Lightning and the lightning bug
10. The community college and the four-year university

## A Student-Written Essay Developed by Comparison and Contrast

The student-written essay that follows is developed by comparison and contrast. Because there are not a great number of differences being contrasted and because neither subject is treated extensively or in depth, the writer has used the *object-by-object pattern.*

### Video versus Theaters

Want to avoid high ticket prices, long lines for popcorn, and strangers talking during the best parts of a movie? Rent a home video. Thanks to the plummeting prices of video technology, VCRs are almost as ubiquitous as the home television, and the two in combination can form an inexpensive alternative to going to movie theaters. However, the experience of the movie theater is not actually duplicated by watching videos at home. While watching movies at home is less expensive, watching movies at the theater still offers a better entertainment experience.

Watching videos at home can make for an inexpensive and cozy evening. Video rentals are usually quite inexpensive, ranging from $1 to $3 per night. At these prices, someone could rent two videos for less than the cost of one theater ticket. Particularly for parents, the savings can be significant. Since popcorn and sodas are enormously overpriced at the theaters, sodas and popcorn can be had at home for a fraction of the cost. Many families will watch videos while enjoying their dinner, or perhaps just dessert. As for comfort, people can lie down on the floor, lounge on sofas, or prop themselves up on pillows if they wish during the movie. Should anyone need to go to the rest room, the movie can be stopped—no need to miss anything! Home videos are very viewer friendly.

While the costs and convenience of the home video are attractive, the true experience of movie-going is lost unless one goes to the theater. Movies were designed and made for the large screens, and no home television can duplicate that effect. The darkness all around and the large screen in front focus the viewers' attention and energies on the movie alone. Many scenes would appear diminished on the small screen at home. Also, attending the theater is a community experience; one shares with others the same movie at the same time, not isolated at home. The very act of leaving the home itself for a brief while can be a refreshing experience, too. There is something special about the neon lights, the titles of movies and stars in large block letters, the overpriced popcorn, and the murmuring crowds that reminds viewers that they are taking part in a communal ritual descended from the ancient Greek theaters.

For those who can afford the cost, the experience of viewing movies in a theater is preferable to viewing the movies at home. For those who cannot afford the theaters, the home video alternative is attractive. Neither one is likely to force the other out of business anytime soon. The two, while superficially similar, are fundamentally different experiences. There is room enough for both in America's culture of leisure.

## E X E R C I S E 9

These questions are based on the essay above.

1. How does the opening paragraph of the essay prepare the reader for the organization of the essay?
2. Where is the thesis statement?
3. The second paragraph deals with watching videos at home, and third discusses going to movie theaters. Is there an abrupt shift from one to the other, or does the writer provide a transition? If so, what is it?
4. How does the concluding paragraph tie the essay together?
5. Would the essay have been more effective if it had been organized in the point-by-point pattern? Explain.

## E X E R C I S E 10

Using either a point-by-point or an object-by-object pattern, select one of the following pairs of objects and develop it into an essay using comparison and contrast. If you prefer, use one of the topics suggested in Exercise 7 (page 118).

A place you used to live as you remember it then and as it was when you revisited it when you were older

Travel by train versus travel by car

The East Coast and the West Coast

Two movies of the same type

Two cultures you are familiar with (Chicano and Anglo, black and white, etc.)

• The qualities males and females look for in a mate

Two homes you have lived in

• Living together and getting married

Using credit cards and living on a cash-only basis

## Developing an Essay by Process and Analysis

"How is it done?" "How did it happen?" These are the questions answered by essays developed by *process and analysis.* Some process papers tell the reader how to do or make something: change a tire, train a puppy, mix concrete, or plant a tree. Others explain how something happened or how it takes place: how the pyramids of Egypt were built, how the blood circulates through the body, or how the Roman Catholic Church elects a Pope. In all cases the purpose is to provide information to the reader as clearly and directly as possible.

Because all process essays essentially explain how an act is done or a process happens, their ideas are presented chronologically. Every idea follows the previous one in a *time sequence.* If the ideas are presented out of order, the results will be chaotic. Imagine trying to put together a transistor radio from a kit whose instructions began, "After receiving a radio signal, adjust the aerial to improve reception." Or imagine an essay explaining how Jonas Salk discovered the polio vaccine in which the writer first discusses the controversy over the vaccine and the tragic deaths that were caused by insufficiently tested vaccine samples, followed by an account of Salk's early experiments with polio viruses and antibodies, concluding with earlier attempts to find a cure for a virus. The reader would be justifiably bewildered in following such an account. The first requirement, then, is to make certain that all the steps are presented in a clear sequence.

When writing the process paper, you should make it more than a list of steps. Such a paper would be technically correct but would have all the excitement of a set of directions for assembling a bicycle. Give your paper direction by giving it a thesis statement. For instance, instead of just listing in order the steps in taking a blood sample, write a thesis that lets the reader see an overall pattern. "Taking a blood sample is more painful for the nurse than for the patient" is more inviting as a thesis than "There are three steps to follow in taking a blood sample." In this way your paper has a point of view; it is leading somewhere.

## Organizing the Essay Developed by Process and Analysis

Because the purpose of the process and analysis paper is to explain how a procedure is done or how it occurs, the introduction should contain a thesis statement that gives the reader an overview of the process, as well as your approach to it. The process should be divided into steps, usually in a time (chronological) sequence. Each major step of the procedure normally is treated in a separate paragraph. The conclusion reviews the procedure and reinforces your thesis statement.

The outline below is for a typical process and analysis paper. Keep in mind that the outline is for illustrative purposes only. The first paragraph does not always contain the thesis statement, and the number of steps in a process and analysis paper may vary, depending on the topic.

*Paragraph 1:* Introduction and thesis statement: announcement of the purpose or overall view
*Paragraph 2:* Step 1 or Stage 1
*Paragraph 3:* Step 2 or Stage 2
*Paragraph 4:* Step 3 or Stage 3
*Paragraph 5:* Step 4 or Stage 4
*Paragraph 6:* Conclusion

The following outline is for a process essay in which the writer wants to tell the reader how to do something: how to write a term paper.

*Paragraph 1:* *Introduction and thesis statement:* "Writing a term paper doesn't have to be a traumatic experience if you follow six easy steps."
*Paragraph 2:* *Step 1:* Selecting and narrowing your topic
*Paragraph 3:* *Step 2:* Formulating a thesis
*Paragraph 4:* *Step 3:* Finding your information
*Paragraph 5:* *Step 4:* Taking notes
*Paragraph 6:* *Step 5:* Writing the first draft

*Paragraph 7:*   *Step 6:* Revising and polishing
*Paragraph 8:*   *Conclusion*

The next outline is for an essay in which the writer wants to tell the reader how a process happens: the major stages in a child's intellectual development. Like the outline for an essay explaining how to do something, this outline is arranged chronologically.

*Paragraph 1:*   *Introduction and thesis statement:* "According to the Swiss psychologist Jean Piaget, there are four major stages in a child's intellectual development."
*Paragraph 2:*   *Stage 1:* The sensory-motor stage (from birth to age two)
*Paragraph 3:*   *Stage 2:* The preoperational stage (from the second to seventh years)
*Paragraph 4:*   *Stage 3:* The concrete operations stage (from the seventh to the eleventh years)
*Paragraph 5:*   *Stage 4:* The formal operations stage (from about the twelfth to the fifteenth years)
*Paragraph 6:*   *Conclusion*

## Guidelines for Writing an Essay Developed by Process and Analysis

*Do not try to explain something you do not understand.* Choose a subject that you know something about and can explain clearly.

*Being by breaking the subject into its basic steps.* Make certain that you have not omitted any important steps, then write a brief introduction telling your reader what you are going to explain or tell.

*Define any technical or abstract terms early in the paper.* You don't want to confuse your reader with unfamiliar terms.

*Present the steps of the process or analysis chronologically.* Use words such as "first," "next," and "finally." These will keep you on track and will help your reader follow your paper without any problems.

*When you have finished your paper, check it over.* Make sure you haven't omitted any steps.

## A Student-Written Essay Developed by Process and Analysis

In the essay below, the student wants to tell the reader how to prepare to run a marathon. Notice that the first paragraph concludes with the thesis statement ("Nevertheless, runners who already train twenty to twenty-five miles a week can successfully complete a marathon if they follow certain important steps.") Paragraphs two through six present the steps, and the last paragraph offers a concluding idea.

How to Train for a Marathon

The human imagination and will is drawn to big feats, such as scaling Mount Everett or reaching the North Pole. But only a select few ever have a realistic chance of experiencing such an achievement. Thousands, maybe millions, of people have the capability, if they also have the will, to run a marathon. The marathon stands as the ultimate running event; its origins stretch back to ancient Greece when the Athenian Pheidippides ran from Marathon to Athens to announce the defeat of the Persians in battle. Legend has it, however, that he collapsed and died immediately afterwards. Since then, the marathon has had the aura of a terrifically difficult event. Nevertheless, runners who already train twenty to twenty-five miles a week can successfully complete a marathon if they follow certain important steps.

A long run once each week is an important start for the beginning marathon runner. Serious training should start about four to five months before the scheduled race. During this time, the runner should schedule one run each week that is perhaps twice as long as any other run. If a runner is averaging three miles each day, he or she should start with a long run of six miles once a week. The runner should add one mile to that long run each week, but every third week, he or she should cut back a bit on the long run to give the body a rest. Over the course of several months, the runner should get that long run up to twenty miles, but there is no need to go full marathon distance in training. The weekly long runs will help give the runner the endurance needed to last the full marathon distance.

During the rest of the week, the runner must put in easy to medium difficulty runs, gradually increasing their distance, too. For the beginning marathoner, about three days of the week should be spent on these runs. If a runner starts off averaging three miles a day, he or she should increase the mileage about one mile each month. The runner should not be afraid to scale back occasionally on these runs, too, if the workouts seem too difficult.

An important part of these shorter runs is pacing. The runner should carry a stopwatch and try to learn what pace is most comfortable. A beginning runner may want to try a 10-minute mile, for instance. A beginner should remember that the objective is to complete the marathon, not to set any records. When the runner wants a more vigorous workout, he or she can up the tempo of the run for a few miles in the middle, but not throughout the entire run. Pace training is critical if the runner expects to complete twenty-six miles.

Next, a runner should schedule rest days. A beginning runner should take two nonconsecutive days off each week. While some runners feel that off-days just delay their training, the truth is the body needs time to recuperate. The runner should schedule one off-day the day after the long run. The second off-day could follow three days of training.

Finally, the runner should devote one day each week to cross-training. Cross-training will help the runner continue aerobic exercises without putting as much strain on the body. Bicycle riding or swimming are excellent cross-training activities for a runner as they exercise the leg muscles while avoiding undue stress. Also, cross-training adds some variety to the runner's regimen. This will help ease boredom or mental fatigue.

All runners must keep in mind not to overtrain. A runner should take an extra day off or lessen the difficulty of the training if necessary. The runner who overtrains is more susceptible to injury. As the day of the marathon approaches, the runner should ease back on the training. Approximately three weeks before the marathon, the runner should begin scaling back the distance of the long run and the difficulty of the shorter runs. The runner should take several days off the week of the marathon, and just do an easy, short run the day before the marathon.

Ultimately, the runner's commitment to the goal of completing a marathon matters as much as or more than any training strategy. Not everyone is capable of following a training regimen over the course of four to five months. Without desire, a runner will slack off in training and will lack the preparation needed. But the runner who does want this badly enough can experience the joy and pain of completing a marathon.

## E X E R C I S E 11

Using the outline on page 122 as a model, write an outline for "How to Train for a Marathon."

## E X E R C I S E 12

Select one of the following topics and write an essay in which you explain how to do or make something. Divide the process into steps, following the suggestions and the outline on page 122.

How to refinish a piece of wooden furniture
How to get credit
How to apply for a job
How to change the oil in your car
How to resolve a dispute with your roommate
How to select the right wine with a meal
How to decorate on a budget
How to become rich
How to grow your own vegetables
How to improve your appearance

## E X E R C I S E  13

Select one of the following topics and write an essay in which you explain to your reader how a certain process or event occurs or takes place. Follow the suggestions and the outline on page 122.

How a bill becomes law in the federal government
How the birthing process occurs
How carbon dating works
How to start your own business
How people get on TV game shows
How butterfly wing patterns are determined
How sausages are made
How photosynthesis occurs
How the process of aging among males or females takes place
How news is gathered for television

## Developing an Essay by Cause and Effect

"Why did this happen?" "What will happen because of this?" Every time we ask questions like these, we are thinking in terms of *cause and effect*. The driver who wants to know why his engine keeps dying in traffic, the scientists who ponder the effects of genetic engineering, and the cook who wonders why the soufflé collapsed are all following a familiar way of thinking: leaping back and forth from effect to cause and from cause to effect.

When writing a cause and effect essay, you emphasize cause or effect depending on your purpose. Most essays follow one of these plans:

They begin with a result (the *effect*) and then examine the probable *cause;*

or
They begin with the *cause* and then speculate on its likely *effect*.

In the first plan you are searching for causes in the past; in the second you are looking ahead, considering possible consequences. Many topics can be approached from either direction. Using the first plan you could, for instance, begin your essay by discussing today's economy in terms of unemployment figures, the prices of food and automobiles, the cost of housing, and so on. These *effects* could then be traced to their causes: high interest rates, foreign imports, wage increases, and the price of oil.

If you start with the cause, you could speculate on how it will in turn lead to future effects: a possible depression, political unrest, an increase in welfare, a ban on foreign cars, and a decline in the housing industry, for example.

## E X E R C I S E 14

Select three of the following topics. Then, following the two plans as explained above, list as many *causes* and *effects* as you can think of. Here is an example:

*topic:* Cheating in college

| *Causes* | *Effects* |
|---|---|
| Fear of failure | Students do not learn the material |
| Heavy workloads impinge on time | Lowers respect for education |
| Pressure to succeed | Teachers act like cops |
| Laziness | Plagiarism policies on all campuses |
| Peer pressure | Students believe they can bluff or cheat their way through life |
| Low probability of getting caught | No sense of accomplishment for the student |
| Part of a culture that emphasizes easy solutions to difficult problems | |

*Topics*

1. Adult illiteracy
2. The Persian Gulf War
3. Working mothers
4. Serial killers
5. Grade inflation

6. Child labor laws
7. Alcoholism
8. The interest in alternative medicine
9. Violence at abortion clinics
10. The trade deficit with Japan

---

## *Organizing the Essay Developed by Cause and Effect*

Whether your essay moves from an effect to a cause or from a cause to an effect, its organization will be similar. Your introduction should contain a thesis statement that identifies the cause and alludes to its effect, or specifies an effect and refers to its cause. The paragraphs in the body of the essay present the causes or the effects, and the conclusion reinforces the thesis.

Here is an outline for an essay that moves from *cause to effect*:

*Paragraph 1:*  *Introduction, thesis:* "As people find that the materialism is a hollow and shallow pursuit, they are turning to more spiritual ways of understanding their world." (*Cause*)

*Paragraph 2:*  *Effect 1:* Many traditional churches and synagogues are experiencing the return of the people who left the churches during the radical movements of 1960s.

*Paragraph 3:*  *Effect 2:* Evangelical and fundamentalist Christian churches, formerly seen as fringe aspects of religious life in America, are attracting new adherents in record numbers.

*Paragraph 4:*  *Effect 3:* Interest in alternative spiritual understandings, as found in New Age thinking, meditation, or Far Eastern religions, pulls in many young people.

*Paragraph 5:*  *Effect 4:* Islam, once thought to be alien to this country, is today one of the fastest growing religions in the United States.

*Paragraph 6:*  *Conclusion*

Here is an outline for an essay that moves from *effect to cause*:

*Paragraph 1:*  *Introduction, thesis:* "The world's stock of fish is dwindling rapidly as fleets of ships scour the ocean to meet the increased demand for fish." (*Effect*)

*Paragraph 2:*  *Cause 1:* The demand for fish has increased with the world's population explosion and the change in eating habits in the Western world.

*Paragraph 3:*  *Cause 2:* The increasing sophistication of commercial fishing techniques has meant increased efficiency at finding the fish.

*Paragraph 4:*   *Cause 3:* The ships today are capable of taking in far greater loads of fish each day than in the past.

*Paragraph 5:*   *Cause 4:* The illusion has existed that the ocean's resources are inexhaustible, leading to underregulation and weak enforcement of open ocean fishing.

*Paragraph 6:*   *Conclusion*

## Guidelines for Writing an Essay Developed by Cause and Effect

Much bad writing stems from careless cause and effect reasoning. Simply saying that something is the cause of something else, or that *this* will cause *that*, will persuade no one. You can avoid the common pitfalls when writing the cause and effect essay if you follow these suggestions:

*If your topic is controversial, it is important to examine and present evidence, cite statistics, and look for more than one possible cause.* More often than not, there is more than one cause for a given effect.

*Keep in mind that the fact that something happened before something else occurred is not proof of a cause-and-effect relationship.* If you have a pain in your neck and take a pill, the fact that the pain disappeared is not sufficient proof that the pill was the cause of the pain's disappearance. It may be that the pain would have disappeared even if you had not taken the pill. If you failed a math test, it is probably because you did not study, rather than because you didn't take your rabbit's foot to class. See pages 225–227 for a discussion of errors in reasoning, particularly in cause-and-effect relationships.

## Two Student-Written Essays Developed by Cause and Effect

Here is an essay that moves from an *effect* (stated in the first paragraph) to a series of *causes* (listed in paragraphs three through five), with a conclusion that reinforces the thesis stated in the first paragraph. The second paragraph disputes one commonly believed *cause* of the *effect*.

---

Sometimes a Cigar Is Just a Cigar: A Examination of
Why We Dream

In the Old Testament, Pharaoh called for the Hebrew prisoner Joseph to interpret his dreams. Today, psychologists interpret our dreams. Because of the pioneering work of Sigmund Freud and Carl Jung, the interpretation of dreams has focused on the idea that dreams are our unconscious's way of communicating with us, mostly through symbolism. Thus, a woman dreaming of wearing tattered blue jeans is actually anxious about getting pregnant because she fears she has bad genes. The symbols have come to be seen as set, no matter who the dreamer is; thus, a snake in a dream is really a penis. However, today dream interpreters reject such ready-made interpretations of symbols and emphasize that we dream for a variety of reasons, employing symbols that frequently arise from our individual circumstances.

It is a myth that eating certain foods will cause bad or unpleasant dreams. According to psychologists who study dreams, food does not actually affect our dreams. We will not have a nightmare if we indulge in pickles and pizza just before bed, although a stomachache is still a possibility.

One reason for what we dream is that we may be working out problems from our daily lives. Stress, anxiety, and frustration during the day may well find that their way into our dream life. In fact, experts say that two-thirds of our dreams are unpleasant. So, if we have trouble with our boss or experience stress at home, it is likely to appear somehow in our dreams. We may dream that our mother is Saddam Hussein or that we work in a slaughterhouse. Essentially, our unpleasant dreams are an attempt to rework the problems in our life.

There are some common themes in dreams that may reflect our current state of mind. Many people experience flying in their dreams. This is usually associated with good feelings, happiness, and freedom. Falling in dreams is scary, and so are chase dreams. These types of dreams reflect some inner anxiety. Another type of dream is the examination dream, in which we must accomplish some sort of task and usually fail. Nevertheless, experts caution that no two people's dreams, even when they share a common theme, are exactly alike, so they need to be looked at individually.

Sexual dreams, astonishingly enough, are not just bold attempts by our subconscious to inform us of our secret desires. We may have sex with someone in a dream simply because something about that person reminds us of our lover. Experts note that dreaming about having sex with someone we do not like in real life may mean that we like only certain qualities about that person, or that we want more attention from that person. In other words, there is no need to wake up in the morning in fear that we actually are in love with some horrible person simply because we dreamed about having sex with him or her.

Why we dream is still the subject of much study and debate, but since the days of Freud and Jung, we have come to see that no simple patterns or explanations can be placed on dreams. Books that purport to include lists of dream symbols cannot be taken too seriously since an individual's circumstances have much to do with what is dreamed. What is still true, however, is that dreams are interesting, important, and deserving of our attention.

---

Here is an essay that moves from one *cause* (stated in the first paragraph) to a series of *effects*.

---

Not Fit for Human Consumption: Why Suburbs Mean the
Death of Civilization as We Know It

Once upon a time in a land not far away at all, American families lived in single-family detached houses that came equipped with front porches, garages in the rear, and yards for playing in. These neighborhoods can still be found today, but in a state of disrepair; the typical middle-class family has fled the once friendly streets of the city for the distant, safer, newer suburbs. However, in doing so, these families find themselves in neighborhoods designed for automobiles, not people, with massive garages dominating the fronts, sidewalks unused by pedestrians, and serviced by strip malls several miles away. The flight to the suburbs has alienated people from city life, encouraged an automobile culture that has little to do with humanity, and isolated families from one another.

One result of the flight to the suburbs is an increasing alienation of the middle class from the urban lower class and the inner city in general. The typical suburb was formed around some large city, but is populated by people who may rarely venture into the central part of the city at all. Others will travel into the city to work. They drive on superhighways, park their cars in their building's underground garages, and never need to venture onto the city's sidewalks for more than a few moments. A typical worker's only contact with the downtown locals may be with harassing beggars or inebriated winos. One effect is that the middle class no longer has much sympathy for the poor, many of whom are actually working hard at low-paying jobs, not begging for money. The money and the people with money flee the inner cities, leaving behind those least able to revitalize the cities.

The leaving and the arriving are intrinsic to suburban life because the suburbs do not exist without the freeways, and it is on the freeways that many people spend two or three hours each day commuting. If people have errands to run, the commute will be even longer. Gone are the days of living over one's shop; instead, living and working ten, twenty, or even thirty miles apart is not uncommon. One glance at the freeway during rush hour confirms that most cars have just one person, the driver, and besides the obvious environmental consequences of this, the freeway commute has psychological consequences. Freeway commuters are loners, in competition with other cars for space and right of way. Some combat this by listening to talk radio, a phenomenon that in some way addresses people's need to feel connected to one another. Stuck alone on the freeway for hours each day, people cannot help but become more distant, impersonal.

Once home, the driver is greeted by garage doors, from one end of the suburb to the other. No front porch swings, few folks walking on the sidewalks, just row after row of garage doors and tiny lots of sheltered, isolated families. Neighborliness is truly an effort where the homes are designed to keep people away from each other. The modern suburban house is on a small lot, bounded by fences. Children home from the day care center play in backyards, away from each other. They are cautioned to stay away from the streets because of the danger from cars, so if children congregate, it must be by prior arrangement. Spontaneity is difficult even for children when fences and garages keep people from one another. The answer is the neighborhood park, just a short drive away, but that is usually empty.

Perhaps the designers of suburban neighborhoods did not intend for them to destroy the human spirit. Certainly their advertising brochures at newly open housing tracts try to promote the qualities of family and neighborhood. But the truth is, the suburbs have been disastrous to cities and families. The only beneficiaries have been automobile manufacturers and strip mall operators. Suburbs need to be designed that help people live a better life, not avoid life altogether.

# EXERCISE 15

1. Using the outline on page 128 as a model, write an outline for "Sometimes a Cigar Is Just a Cigar: An Examination of Why We Dream."
2. Using the outline on page 128 as a model, write an outline for "Not Fit for Human Consumption: Why the Suburbs Mean the Death of Civilization as We Know It."

# E X E R C I S E    16

Select one of the following topics and develop it into an essay moving from causes to effects or effects to causes.

The high rate of divorce
Illegal immigration
The information superhighway
The growing use of social security numbers for identification purposes as a threat to privacy
The decline of the single-family farm
Wildlife conservation efforts
Cheating on income-tax returns
The conservative movement
Growing demand for the death penalty

## Developing an Essay by Definition

"What is it?" "What does it mean" Whether asked on an examination or in a conversation, these questions call for a definition, one of the most common kinds of writing assignments. Disagreements between couples, companies, and countries often occur because of confusion over the exact meaning of words. A husband and wife might differ over what constitutes "punishment" for their child, an employee and a manager might disagree over "generous salary," and the Japanese and the Americans disagree over "fair trade."

When we define, we are trying to clear up confusion. Surprisingly, it isn't always the esoteric or difficult word that needs to be clarified; often it is the familiar word or phrase whose meaning defies agreement.

# E X E R C I S E    17

Familiar words often prove to be the most difficult to define. Select five of the following items and write a precise definition of each. Compare your definitions with those of others in your class. How similar were your definitions? What do the differences suggest?

| | |
|---|---|
| patriotism | silence |
| femininity | work |
| good food | decent |
| happiness | sin |
| success | beauty |

Words can be defined in three ways: by a *synonym* (substituting a familiar word for the word to be defined), by a *formal definition* (the kind often used in the dictionary), and by an *extended definition*, which develops the meaning of the word in a paragraph or essay.

Definition by synonym is the most concise way to define: a *melee* is defined as "a fight," a *maxillary* as "a jawbone," and *jejune* as "immature." The advantage of a definition by synonym is brevity. The danger occurs when the synonym is as confusing as the word being defined. To define "redundancy" as a "tautology," for example, is not very helpful.

The *formal definition* can often be expressed in one sentence. It consists of three parts: the term to be defined, the general class it belongs to, and the way it differs from all other members of that class. Here, in chart form, are some formal definitions:

| term | general class | differentiation |
|---|---|---|
| A *violin* | is a *string instrument* | that *is held under the neck* and *is usually played with a bow.* |
| A *gaffer* | is the *member of a film crew* | who *sets up the lighting.* |
| A *trapezoid* | is a *quadrilateral* | that has *only two parallel sides.* |

The formal definition can be very helpful because of its exactness, and for that reason is often used by dictionary makers.

## E X E R C I S E   18

Write formal definitions of the following items:

| | |
|---|---|
| fountain pen | aunt |
| staple | floppy disk |
| bathroom | fork |
| eyeliner | pants |

As helpful as synonyms and logical definitions are, it is sometimes necessary to extend a definition if the term being defined is complex, or if we want to say something interesting or significant about it. In these instances we write *extended definitions*, often as long as an entire essay.

# Organizing the Essay Developed by an Extended Definition

Unlike essays developed by the previous patterns in this chapter, the essay based on an extended definition follows no customary pattern. Its organization depends, in great part, on what is being defined and what the writer intends to say about it.

Here are some of the questions you might ask about your subject before writing a definition essay:

What are some examples of it? (*example*)
How many kinds are there? (*classification*)
What is it similar to or different from? (*comparison and contrast*)
How is it done? How does it work? (*process*)
What causes it? What are its results or effects? (*cause and effect*)

In addition to applying these questions, you can sometimes make a definition clear to your reader by describing the subject physically: for example, its size, color, weight, and height. If the object or term evokes personal memories or associations that are helpful in explaining the term to your reader, include those as well.

To see how this technique for defining a term works, let us examine the possible ways to develop an essay defining "socialization." Sociologists and psychologists use this concept to describe the process by which children develop behavior patterns that fit in with the standards of their culture.

What are some examples of socialization in our culture? (*example*)
What are some examples of behavior that is *not* acquired by socialization? (*example*)
How many kinds of socialization processes are there? (*classification*)
How is the socialization process similar to other human behaviors or processes? (*comparison*)
How is the socialization process different from other human behaviors or processes? (*contrast*)
How does the socialization process start? (*process*)
How does it work? What are its stages? (*process*)
What causes it? What are its effects? (*cause and effect*)

As you can see, merely answering these questions would provide an abundance of material for an essay defining the term. And as this list of questions also demonstrates, it is usually possible (and advisable) to use more than one method of development when defining a term. By doing so, you present the term in all its aspects, and you help your reader to understand it more readily.

## E X E R C I S E  19

By using the approach outline above, show how one of the following terms could be defined by a variety of developmental patterns. Do not write an essay; simply list the kinds of questions that would suggest the development of the definition.

Initiation
Nuptials
Bar mitzvah
Homecoming
Recognition
Rejection
Punishment
Falling in (or out of) love

### Guidelines for Writing an Essay Developed by Definition

*Begin your essay with a formal definition.* This tells your reader the boundaries or limits of your definition.

*Tell your reader why you are defining the term.* Perhaps you want to show how it is confused with another term, or maybe you want to present some interesting examples and facts associated with the concept.

*Use several examples to make certain that your reader knows what you mean when you use the term.*

*Avoid using the old cliché, "According to Webster. . . ."*

### A Student-Written Essay Developed by Definition

Here is a student-written essay defining the "Heisenberg Uncertainty Principle." Notice how the writer uses a variety of developmental patterns to make the meaning clear.

The Heisenberg Uncertainty Principle

In the twentieth century, many great discoveries have been made that have turned our understanding of science on its head. These discoveries have called into question the assumptions of hundreds of years of scientific inquiry. For instance, Newton's laws were found to be no longer applicable at both terrifically fast speeds or at the level of quantum physics. But one of the discoveries that has cast a shadow over much of scientific research through its implications is Heisenberg's uncertainty principle. Understanding this principle and its consequent implications for all research is crucial for any student of science today.

Werner Heisenberg, a German physicist, stated that it is impossible to measure with absolute certainty both the exact position and the exact velocity of an object at the same time. This principle was derived after observing difficulties that scientists had at determining position and velocity at the subatomic level. He reasoned that these difficulties arose not out of any defect or inadequacies in the instruments used to measure position and velocity; rather, the nature of the connection between particles and waves at the subatomic level brought this about.

A simple example can be seen with an electron that orbits the nucleus of an atom. An electron is actually smaller than a wavelength of light; therefore, it cannot be seen by any light wave–based instrument. Instead, shorter gamma rays are used. The trouble is that the gamma ray has so much energy that when it strikes an electron, it knocks that electron out of its path, changing its direction and velocity in an unpredictable way. Thus, the use of the gamma ray causes an undeterminable change in the electron's velocity and direction. In other words, the attempt to observe the electron affects the electron.

If the observer is able to fix position, then velocity is uncertain. If the observer is able to determine velocity, then the position is uncertain. Each factor is related inversely. The greater the certainty of one factor, the higher the uncertainty of the other factor. Only one factor, position or velocity, can be known with certainty at any point in time. This forms the core of Heisenberg's principle.

However, there is an even greater significance to this principle. As noted earlier, the very attempt to observe the electron changed the electron. This led to the understanding that we cannot observe something without changing or affecting it in some way, however small. This is what called into question one of the basic assumptions that scientists had been making for centuries: that they could somehow objectively observe nature. Now, according to Heisenberg's principle, science is no longer exact, but dependent on the way in which observations are made. There is no independent reality, only reality as we observe it.

The result is that scientists can no longer separate themselves and the scientific method from the phenomena they observe. There will always be an uncertainty in those observations, not because of our equipment or techniques, but because of the way nature actually is. In some ways, this is refreshing. After all, Heisenberg is pointing out, we are a crucial part of the world we observe, not outside of it.

## E X E R C I S E 20

1. What is the main developmental pattern used in the first paragraph of this essay?
2. Paragraphs three and four combine cause and effect with definition. Point to specific examples of each pattern.
3. What pattern is used chiefly in the fifth paragraph?
4. Comment on the concluding paragraph: Is it effective? Does it bring the essay to a close, or does it leave you anticipating more?
5. How many developmental patterns were used in this selection? What does this tell you about the strategies or patterns used to develop an essay that defines a term?

## E X E R C I S E 21

Select one of the following terms and write an extended definition. Keep in mind that you will probably use more than one developmental pattern in writing your definition.

| | |
|---|---|
| Motherhood | Pornography |
| Progress | Relaxation |
| Hip | Liberal |
| Civilization | Intelligence |
| Satisfaction | Adventure |
| A radical | A bargain |
| Home | Sexy |
| Sportsmanship | Nature |

## C O M P U T E R   E X E R C I S E

Your instructor may have assigned one or more of the patterns in this chapter to be developed into essays. If so, write the essay on the computer. Some students find that writing a rough draft by hand first is easier, but you should attempt to compose the first draft on the computer. Doing so will save time.

The purpose of this exercise is to become more aware of the structure in your essays. In order to do this, highlight or underline your thesis sentence and each topic sentence in your essay. Also highlight or underline the sentence in your conclusion that restates the thesis.

Now, exchange essays with either your partner or a peer editing group in the class via the computer network. Go over the section in this chapter for the development pattern that has been selected. You should be able to see that the essay you are examining follows the appropriate guidelines. Pay close attention to the thesis and topic sentences. Is the thesis concise and clear, and does it indicate implicitly the organizational pattern of the essay? Do the topic sentences present the main point of the paragraphs they are in, and are they logically connected to the thesis? Make any suggestions or comments in all capital letters or in brackets [] so that the writer can distinguish your comments from the original text. Avoid commenting too much on matters of style and language since you will look at those matters at greater length in Chapter 7. Return the essays and consider the comments made on your essay. Make any changes necessary.

# 7

# *Revising and Editing the Essay*

# 7. Revising and Editing Your Essay

Some people are willing to settle for the second-best in life. Refusing to expend the effort and concentration necessary to complete any worthwhile job, they prefer to take the easy way out. As a consequence, they rarely produce anything that is distinguished, and they let opportunities for excellence slip through their fingers.

People with this attitude usually take the same approach to their writing. They write in a hurry, rarely looking back to revise or edit their material. If they are students, they often turn in the first draft of an essay full of rambling, undeveloped ideas and careless mistakes. They ignore the fact that every piece of writing can be improved by careful revision and editing, and that all writers—especially professionals—find it necessary to revise their work.

These writers fail to give their work the final polishing it deserves because they think that revision means at most only a search for mistakes in spelling, grammar, and punctuation. While it is true that *editing* includes the correction of such errors, *revision* involves much more. It includes (but is not restricted to) rearranging and reorganizing ideas, rewording sentences, adding of new material, and deleting unnecessary material. It is, in other words, an examination of the draft from the ground up.

Revising and editing are overlapping but different tasks. When you *revise,* you examine your thesis statement or main idea, your supporting evidence or details, their arrangement, your sentence structure, and your word choice—in other words, the overall effectiveness and clarity of your paper. Keep in mind that "revision" comes from two Latin words meaning "to see again"; if you can stand back and look at your essay as if you were an outsider reading it for the first time, you will save yourself disappointment later. When you *edit,* you consider such matters as grammar, punctuation, usage, and spelling. The editing stage is usually done last—after the revising stage. After all, you don't want to interrupt the flow of ideas to look up the spelling of a word or the rule for the placement of a comma.

The revising and editing methods in this chapter take you through your essay several times as you look (and listen) for ways to improve your paper. The first step in revision is to *hear* your essay so that you can get an overall impression of its impact. The second step in revision is to *read* it carefully as you consider the Revision Checklist on page 144. This step focuses your attention on content and organization, the development of ideas, and style, especially sentence structure and word choice. The editing stage, as mentioned, is last; this is the time to check for mistakes in grammar, punctuation, and spelling.

## Hearing Your Essay

One of the best ways to begin the revision of a piece of writing is to hear it. Seeing your writing is usually not enough; as you read it silently, you unconsciously fill in missing punctuation marks, letters, and even words, and you may not catch rough sentences or awkward transitions. When you *hear* the essay, however, you use different cognitive and critical skills that will expose the errors that might escape a silent reading.

Some instructors like to arrange peer editing groups for their students. If this is the case, you will find yourself asking and answering questions about your essay and those of other students. Your instructor will give you a set of questions or areas of concern to address for each essay. However, many instructors do not use peer editing groups in the classroom. You should still seek to work with another student, preferably a classmate, to read your essays to each other and help each other with the revision process. You can use the questions in this chapter to guide your revision.

One note of caution: Proper revision takes time. This includes time between writing the first draft and initiating the revision process. Time away from your essay helps you to see your words and ideas more clearly, with a fresher perspective. If you attempt to write first drafts and revisions in the same evening the day before the essay is due, you are likely to repeat mistakes. Your perspective will not have changed, and you will not have had time to contemplate what you have written and how you could have written it better. Plan your schedule to have a first draft ready several days before the final draft is due to allow sufficient time to set the essay aside for a while before beginning the revision process. Procrastination is the enemy of successful revisions.

Begin by asking a friend or fellow student to read your essay aloud to you. If you prefer, read it yourself using a cassette recorder and play it back. In either case, follow along with a copy of the essay and a pen. As you listen, mark anything that bothers you. Do not try to make corrections as you listen; instead, concentrate on the following questions:

Does this essay sound like *me?*
Does it have an overall design and flow?
Is the paper smooth? Are there any words or sentences that stick out or jar?
Is it interesting? Or dull? Does the beginning draw the reader in effectively? Would the reader want to know and read more?
What is my purpose? What point am I trying to make to my audience?

Do I talk down to my reader? Do I say the obvious? Do I sound too formal?

Is the essay clear? Is there enough information? Are there any sudden jumps?

Does the paper end abruptly?

What have I not included? Should I find a way to include it or is it better left out?

You will probably notice that your reactions range from the less important ("Should I use a different word here?") to the more fundamental ("I wonder whether I ought to cut out this section"). You will also discover that revision is not just a cleaning-up operation but a process that usually triggers new ideas as you examine the structure and organization of your paper. Keep in mind that as you revise, you are *rethinking;* as a result, you are likely to change anything in your paper.

An analogy might be helpful here. When you buy a house you often need to do some remodeling. Sometimes you have only to apply a fresh coat of paint or replace some broken window panes. After living in the house a while you may find that you want to move a door or a window. You may decide to add on a room or tear down a wall. If the foundation is cracked or if the supporting beams are weak, you may have to replace the joists or shore up the footing. Only rarely can you assume that you will not have to make any repairs or modifications.

This is also the case when writing an essay. You may discover that your first draft needs only minor remodeling: a few words changed here, a sentence or two there, and perhaps some additional bracing and support in sections that sag. A closer examination, however, may reveal some shaky premises, windy passages, or an entire section that needs to be renovated. Rarely will you find that your first draft cannot be improved.

After you have listened to your essay and satisfied yourself on the points you have noted, you are ready to read it, emphasizing its content and organization.

## Revising for Content and Organization

The content and organization of an essay—its ideas and design—are as related as the two sides of a coin. It is virtually impossible to isolate one from the other. As you revise your first draft, you will move back and forth from its content to its organization. The revision checklist below will help you as you go over your paper.

# REVISION CHECKLIST

## First Reading

1. *Is your thesis statement focused so that the reader knows exactly what your controlling idea is? (See pages 79–82.)*
2. *Does the introduction catch the reader's interest and lead naturally into the thesis statement? (See pages 57–59.)*
3. *Do you have enough information to support your thesis statement? (See pages 78–79.)*
4. *Can the reader sense a direction or movement of the ideas through the essay? (See pages 86–97.)*
5. *Are all of the ideas on one subject and in the right order? Do they advance the thesis without wandering off? (See pages 67–70.)*
6. *Does each middle (body) paragraph deal with one point or aspect of the topic? Does each sentence in each body paragraph deal with that point? (See pages 34–37.)*
7. *Does each paragraph have enough development so that its topic sentence is supported? (See pages 48–56.)*
8. *Does the conclusion express a sense of finality without seeming abrupt? (See pages 59–61.)*

---

## Revision Case Study: A Student Essay

To help you see how the revision process works, a first draft by J. R. Salazar, a freshman, is included in this section. Read his first draft carefully. Later, you will reread it to check for content and organization. Use the checklist above as a guide. You should use this checklist to go over all of your own writing as well.

---

J. R. Salazar
Professor Hoffman
English 101
6 March 1995

They Blinded Me from Science

English, math, and history are considered the most important subjects by public high school. A minimum course requirement is designed to give students a healthy intake of these subjects. Trying to provide students with a well-rounded education is a worthy cause, but science is put low on the priority scale in doing so. Approximately one year of a science course is required to graduate. Compared to the three and four year requirements of other courses, this seems minimal. The problem is that science has been lumped together with electives like woodshop, office service, and physical education. Students do not have to take much science, but they have to take at least two years of P.E. The system needs to rethink the logic behind its programs. They need to push science up to the same priority level as the other three core subjects and make the other three more interesting for the students to study.

In a world becoming more dependent on science and technology, it should be mandatory for students to take science no matter what field they want to get into. In elementary school, one teacher taught all subjects including science. Everybody was exposed to it. Upon entering junior high, students were slowly allowed to pick their own courses. That is where the break started to occur. If they had made science a mandatory class they could not have opted not to take it. Somehow kids started to dislike science and decided to avoid the subject altogether. Many kids get the mistaken impression that science is difficult, boring, and irrelevant to their daily lives. So year after year, the number of students interested in science declines. If science were mandatory, then students would have a continuous learning experience with it all the way through high school. Then they would have a good background for it and may have even developed a liking for it. Besides, the excuse that the subject is difficult, boring, and irrelevant can be used as an excuse for any other subject, not just science.

One of the biggest problems in the world today is finding a good job. That's where science can come in. Students today seem to graduate and then not have any options. A high school diploma doesn't count as much as it used to. One reason is that if a student has a diploma, that doesn't mean he knows very much about science. So he really can't get a job in science, and probably isn't very interested in getting one anyway. But if a student take more science he might have enough to get a job or at least be enthusiastic enough to go to college and major in science and get a job. But there are a lot of jobs in science, more than in English, math, and history, and students need to realize it.

Making science a mandatory subject will not solve all the problems. There is still the problem of other methods in which the three subjects are taught. Although they are considered the most important subjects by the schools, they are the least liked by students. Often the association of boring lectures, monotonous teachers, and endless lectures comes with these classes. On the other hand, these subjects are pretty straightforward, not allowing much room for creative teaching. However, that does not mean it is impossible. If individual teachers could find a way to grasp the students' interest, through interesting lectures, fun activities, and more interaction, there might be a better attention span and learning capacity. It seems much easier to do that with science, which is just another reason why it should be emphasized more.

There will always be a place for students interested in English, history, and math. They could go on to be the next generation of English, history, and math teachers. However, if the interest in science education continues to diminish, there will be a great void that will be hard to fill. It is great that the education system is preparing students for their roles in life, but they need to enforce the importance of the role of science. America today is a far cry from the leaders of the world in science back in the 1950s and 1960s. The education system needs to push science more if we want to regain that level of excellence.

---

As you read the following discussion, you will notice that some of the questions from the revision checklist have been combined. This reflects the way you will revise your paper as you look for several things at the same time.

---

*1. Is your thesis statement focused so that the reader knows exactly what your controlling ideas is?*

---

The place to begin a revision is with its backbone: the thesis statement. On a separate sheet of paper, write down the main idea of your essay. If you can't, your paper lacks a focus and you need to step back and reconsider what it is that you want to tell your reader. Ask a friend to read your paper and identify the main idea. If you don't agree, you need to work on making the thesis statement more specific.

J.R. Salazar's thesis statement is reasonably clear, but it needs to be more focused. He states, "They need to push science up to the same priority level as the other three core subjects and make the other three more interesting for the students to study." Confusion stems from several problems. First, who "they" refers to is unclear.

Would this be the school administrators, the board of education, or the state legislature? The phrase "priority level" is also vague. A greater problem is that J.R. is essentially tackling two different ideas: the first is that students need to take more science courses, and the second, unrelated idea is that instruction in English, math, and history needs to be made more interesting. The first idea is stronger; the second would be difficult to develop because "more interesting" may be too subjective to define. In either case, he must limit himself to one controlling idea.

---

*2. Does the introduction catch the reader's interest and lead into the thesis statement? Does the conclusion express a sense of finality without seeming abrupt?*

---

Look over your opening paragraph. Did you begin with a "hook" that would catch your reader's interest and make him want to read on? Does your introduction suggest the tone and organization of your essay? Did you avoid beginning with a cliché or platitude?

J.R.'s opening paragraph needs rewriting because it is vague, lacks focus, and is trying to do too much. As noted above, he essentially is dealing with two paper topics, the need for more science instruction and the need to make instruction more interesting in English, math, and history. He has not developed an interesting opening to grab the reader's attention. He describes the numbers of courses required for a diploma, but not in a way that clearly presents a problem. The need for more science appears to be assumed rather than proven. Much of the proof should be developed in the main body of the paper, not in the introduction. However, the paper does at least have the sketchy beginnings of an argument. J.R. clearly feels that high school students need to study more science, and that science is more valuable than electives such as woodshop, office service, and physical education. Nevertheless, he cannot assume that his reader will agree that these classes are of lesser importance.

J.R.'s concluding paragraph is marred by what appears to be a gratuitous jab at the study of English, math, and history. After conceding in the introduction that these are serious subjects on par with science, he should avoid implying that students who major in these subjects can only go on to become teachers in those subjects. Even the statement "It is great that the education system is preparing students for their roles in life . . ." seems to contradict the opening to his conclusion. Also, J.R. is still assuming the importance of science. He does at least refer to the past when the United States appeared to place a greater emphasis on the study of science, but why the educational system of the past is appropriate for the present is not clear. His concluding sentence only vaguely restates the thesis from the introduction.

---

### 3. Does the body of your essay support your thesis? Do you have enough ideas, facts, and information?

---

After you have sharpened your thesis statement and are satisfied with it, look at your middle paragraphs to see if they contain enough support. On a separate sheet of paper, jot down the ideas in each paragraph that support your thesis statement. Are you satisfied that you have developed enough material, or should you add supporting information? Have you supplied convincing examples, facts, and reasons that make your thesis clear to the reader?

Paragraph two of J.R.'s paper explains that all students have equal exposure to science in elementary school, but that exposure begins to decline once students are allowed to choose their own courses in junior and senior high school. But his explanation of why students do not pick science courses voluntarily seems weak, which he implicitly acknowledges in the paragraph's closing sentence. Because any subject can be labeled as difficult, boring, and irrelevant, the burden remains on J.R. to explain why science in particular is described this way.

Paragraph three tries to advance the case for increasing the science requirement by appealing to the need for jobs. While this may be a valid idea, J.R.'s method for developing the paragraph is weak. He only generalizes about the job market in science, and even tacitly admits that a high school diploma may not be enough for a job in science by suggesting that students major in the sciences in college.

Paragraph four presents even bigger problems. This paragraph deals with teaching techniques and how they may be to blame for students' lack of interest, not only in science, but also in English, math, and history. This is a fundamentally different topic of discussion. If J.R.'s thesis is that high school students should take more science courses, even limiting himself to a discussion of how the teaching techniques of science teachers bore students or make the subject more difficult to grasp will not help to prove his thesis. Only if J.R. chooses to write about the second idea in his original thesis would he be able to salvage this paragraph.

Clearly, J.R.'s essay lacks sufficient proof. This is partially a result of his poor thesis statement, but it is also a result of his tendency to use generalizations. Also, he assumes too much on the part of the reader, mostly that the reader will agree with everything he says. He needs to develop more specifically the reasons that education in science is a good idea for all American high school students.

Before trying to revise J.R.'s middle paragraphs, however, we should note that the thesis will have to be rewritten in order to determine what changes can be made.

---

*4. Does each paragraph deal with one point or aspect of the thesis statement, and is that point expressed in a topic sentence? Are there ideas that need to be expanded? Are there any ideas that are irrelevant and unrelated to the thesis statement? Are the paragraphs in the right order?*

---

This is one of the most important phases of your revision. You are looking at each paragraph as a mini-essay, testing it for its unity and development, as well as for its support of the thesis statement.

As we look again at J.R. Salazar's essay, we can note ideas that need to be expanded, moved, or eliminated. We can also make recommendations for improving the relationships of the paragraphs in the essay to strengthen the movement of ideas.

First, J.R. needs a new thesis statement. J.R. should consider his two controlling ideas and settle on one. In this instance, J.R. probably should decide to write exclusively on proving that the requirement of one year of science for a high school diploma should be raised to three years. This would enable him to narrow the scope of his essay, dropping the teaching techniques idea. Now he could drive home his point about the importance of an education in science for all students without being distracted by irrelevant concerns. Because J.R.'s original middle paragraphs were too short on ideas to completely support his new thesis, J.R. would have to brainstorm or freewrite on his topic to discover new ideas. He should write a new, informal outline setting his new ideas into the organizational pattern that will be most effective. J.R. might come up with three main topics such as the importance of science in daily life, the prevalence of science-related jobs, and the understanding of the world that science can give students. A suggested revision of paragraph two might look like this:

> Science can impact the daily lives of individuals in ways many people do not recognize. Our daily transportation, whether by automobile, train, plain, or bicycle, employs physics and sometimes chemistry. All responsible citizens need some knowledge of biology and chemistry to be able to respond intelligently to public health issues such as pollution and AIDS. The medicine that people use is the result of biology, chemistry, and physics; a better understanding of how medicine interacts with the human body will make people better, healthier patients. Even matters as simple as

diet and nutrition have their basis in biology and chemistry. While the average high school student cannot and should not be expected to understand the intimate details of sophisticated technology, he or she should have a grasp of the basic principles underlying that technology. Otherwise, the world appears to be run by magic. A student who cannot explain why a light turns on and off with the flip of a switch is as ignorant as one who cannot read.

Notice that the revision sharpens the focus of the paragraph and supports the thesis by emphasizing through details the presence of science in daily life. Since J.R.'s essay will be developed by order of importance, this is the least important point of support. Nevertheless, it establishes the principle that knowledge of basic science is as important as basic English skills.

The third paragraph of the first draft should be revised to develop J.R.'s second most important point: There are many science-related jobs in the marketplace. His paragraph maintains that because students are not exposed to science in school they do not realize the potential for getting a job in science. But the development is weak because the paragraph lacks specifics, and only seems to advance when he argues that enthusiastic high school students will major in the sciences in college. A stronger topic sentence is also necessary, one that limits the topic to the thesis. A revision of this paragraph might be:

> Increasing the science requirement may actually help students find good jobs. Many high school graduates have difficulty finding a job, and that's where science can come in. A student with a background in biology, chemistry, or physics is more likely to be taken on in a company specializing in one of these fields. Although the knowledge gained in a high school class might not cover everything the student needs to know, a student who is familiar with the subject can be trained for the job. Another possibility is that students will major in science in college because of their exposure in high school, and that will lead to a job. Because this country is constantly advancing in technology, there are many jobs in science-related industries, more than in English, math, or history. If students have little exposure to science, they may never learn this.

Paragraph four of the first draft deals with teaching techniques. While the case can be made that some students are turned off to science by boring instructors, that does not advance the revision. Since the revised thesis would only focus on reasons for increasing the science requirement for high school students, the existing paragraph should be deleted in its entirety. Instead, J.R. should use paragraph four to develop the most important topic in support of his thesis, that the study of science helps students to understand their world in a whole new way. Precisely what this new understanding is needs to be specified, and the importance of this understanding also needs to be made clear. Here is a suggested revision:

The study of science will help students to understand their physical world through the use of scientific method. Students will learn about the processes of observation and analysis, about learning to formulate theorems and proofs, and how to conduct experiments to test hypotheses. Students will discover how biologists classify plants and animals, how chemists are able to predict and analyze chemical interactions, and how physicists explore worlds as large as galaxies and as small as atoms. There is reason, structure, and order in the scientific method, and if students can learn how, they too can think in a clearer, more orderly fashion. When errors appear, the scientist learns to recognize and correct them. Simply put, the study of science gives students a leg up on the study of life itself, in all its variety and possibilities.

Now we can return to the introduction and conclusion of J.R.'s essay. If we had tried to revise them earlier, the proposed paragraphs might not have accurately introduced or concluded the revised body of the essay. Now, however, we can see the movement of the thesis statement and the middle paragraphs, and we can revise the introduction and conclusion. Here is a suggested revised introductory paragraph:

Many school administrators seem to regard English, math, and history as the most important subjects in public high schools. After all, students are required to take three or four years of these courses to obtain a high school diploma. Trying to provide students with a well-rounded education is great, however science is being ignored. In many schools, only one year of a science course is required for graduation. The problem is that sciences such as biology, chemistry, and physics, have not been seen as basics, but as electives or specialties, like woodshop, office service, or physical education. School administrators need to rethink the logic behind this and give science the same importance as the other three core subjects. High school students should be required to study three years of science to obtain a diploma.

The concluding paragraph, as we already noted, seems overly defensive and even a little bitter toward students who study English, math, and history. The reference to the 1950s and 1960s only works if the reader is convinced that education needs are the same now as they were then. Instead, this suggested revision tries to look toward the future:

Increasing the number of required science courses will benefit all high school students, whether they eventually work in science-related jobs or not. The world of tomorrow is going to be a sophisticated, technology-based world. Only by recognizing that science is the key to the future will students be prepared. High school students without any knowledge of the basics of science will be as handcuffed as those who cannot read, write, or do simple arithmetic are today. The educational system cannot allow this to happen.

## The Title of Your Essay

A good title, like a good introduction, suggests the contents of the essay. J.R.'s title is an attempt at an allusion to an old song, "They Blinded Me with Science," but the result is more confusing than enlightening since no one is actually preventing students from taking science courses. A better title might be "Science Education: Not a Luxury But a Necessity," which would reflect the idea behind the thesis.

Your title does not have to specify the exact scope of the contents of your essay; on the other hand, it should give at least a hint of what the reader will find. Do not use a general title that promises more than you intend to deliver. "New Orleans Jazz," for example, is hardly an accurate title for an essay that is restricted to a discussion of Louis Armstrong. Nor should you use a title that is too vague or ordinary: "The Importance of Education," "An Interesting Day," or "A Surprise Party."

The best titles are relatively brief, direct, and exact—and they catch the reader's interest. Note these titles:

"American Fat" (an article about wordiness)
*Custer Died for Your Sins* (a study of the American Indian)
"Who's Afraid of Math, and Why?" (an analysis of the fear that math induces)
*Zen and the Art of Motorcycle Maintenance* (an autobiographical study of Eastern philosophy)
"Four-Letter Words Can Hurt You" (an article about obscenities)
"Clothes Make the Man—Uneasy" (an article about changing styles)

## E X E R C I S E 1

Improve the following titles:

| | |
|---|---|
| A Fun Thing | My First Job |
| Kindergarten | My Favorite Dog |
| China | Laughter |
| Woodwork | Why I Vote Libertarian |

## Revising for Style

In our health-conscious society with its emphasis on fitness, it would appear that few people are satisfied with their bodies. Everyone seems to be either too heavy or too skinny. So it is with writers. They seem to either overwrite or underwrite—to either be wordy, drowning their ideas in excess verbiage, or too lean and spare or vague, starving their ideas by failing to supply enough information. As you revise your essay for style, ask yourself whether you are an overwriter or an underwriter: whether you have written too much and therefore need to trim your verbal fat, or whether you have starved your sentences and readers and need to nourish them with more ideas.

When we discuss the style of an essay, we are usually referring to its sentences and word choice. If you read your paper aloud (or listened to it as someone else read it), perhaps you noted on your paper those sentences that were difficult to read or that caused the reader to stumble. Examine those sentences to locate the source of the problem. Similarly, look at the words that the reader stumbled over or that were incorrectly emphasized. Try to analyze what went wrong.

The revision of J.R. Salazar's essay emphasized its content and organization. During that revision many sentences and individual words were changed. Listed below are some of them; see if you can detect others. In each case, why were the words or sentences changed?

*Paragraph 1:* This paragraph contains a comma splice; can you find it:? Is the word "great" appropriate and accurate? What might be better?

*Paragraph 2:* Should "impact" be used as a verb in this sentence? Notice the sentence structure; are the sentences smooth? Are they connected with transitions? Is the analogy at the end of the paragraph overdone?

*Paragraph 3:* Is the transition from paragraph 2 clear? Can you improve on the phrase "constantly advancing in technology"?

*Paragraph 4:* Can you change the second sentence to give it parallel structure? Improve the transition between the third and fourth sentences. Is the concluding sentence logical? Why or why not?

*Paragraph 5:* Does the first sentence adequately serve to restate the thesis? Are phrases such as "world of tomorrow" and "key to the future" acceptable, or are they vague abstractions? Does the conclusion provide a good sense of closure to the essay?

## REVISION CHECKLIST

*Second Reading*

*1. Are your sentences tight and concise rather than padded and lumpy? Look carefully at each sentence for redundancies, repetition, and fillers. Make sure that every sentence says as much as* possible in as few words as possible without sacrificing your meaning. *(See pages 161–163.)*

**2.** *Do your sentences vary in length? Count the words in ten sentences and determine your average sentence length. If you average only ten to fifteen words, your sentences are probably too short. On the other hand, if you average more than about 25 or 30 words, they are probably too long. (See pages 165–167.)*

**3.** *Are your sentences varied in structure? If most of your sentences follow the subject-verb pattern, rearrange some of them. Use a variety of strategies, including loose and periodic sentences and parallel structure. Examine every verb in the passive voice; try to replace it with a verb in the active voice. (See pages 168–180.)*

**4.** *Are the tone and level of your word choice appropriate to your topic? Do you move back and forth from slang to Standard English? Select the level of language and the tone that is best for your audience and subject and stick to it. (See pages 203–205.)*

**5.** *Do you use words that are concise and exact, avoiding triteness and clichés? Make certain that every word in your essay means exactly what you mean. Be sure that you have avoided tired language, pretentious words, and other language that masks your meaning. (See pages 200–203.)*

---

# E X E R C I S E 2

Revise the following sentences eliminating wordiness, choppy or excessively long sentences, clichés, unnecessary passive voice constructions, and inappropriate diction.

1. In my opinion, it may be possible that under certain circumstances such an act could conceivably be considered wrong by some.
2. We will have to toe the line on spending, tighten our belts, and whistle past the graveyard until we get our next paycheck.
3. According to all the newspapers, O.J. Simpson is an American hero because of his heroic deeds on the football field.
4. Vincent Van Gogh really kicks butt on Pablo Picasso.
5. The author came to the bookstore. She is famous. She is from New York. She came to sign autographs.
6. It is clear that the original *Star Trek* series was run on the cheap compared to *Star Trek: The Next Generation*.
7. There is no cause for concern by the farmers about the price of corn dropping because there is a government subsidy program that was designed to help in such a circumstance.

8. That Supreme Court justice is one swinging dude!
9. Jessie's failing marks really left her over the barrel, but if she can keep her head above water this semester, she should be back in the saddle.
10. Kay told me a sad tale of woe about having to read for two hours a day, but I told her that that's par for the course when you're a college student, and it's no big deal.

## Editing Your Essay

The purpose of editing your paper is to get rid of its warts and blemishes: to correct any mistakes in grammar, spelling, and punctuation. The editing stage is important because the kinds of errors you look for in the editing process can create the impression that you are careless and sloppy in your approach not only to writing, but to logic and problem solving as well. These mistakes can create the impression in your reader's mind that you should not be trusted or believed.

After revising your essay as suggested in the preceding pages, retype the revision, leaving plenty of room for corrections and changes. One excellent way to detect errors is to read the paper aloud, just as you did when you began your revision. This time, however, you will be looking for (and listening to) errors in grammar, missing transitions, misspelled words, and all of the other errors that distract your reader.

Your voice will usually catch errors in usage; if you stumble over a sentence, mark it and go on. After you have read the entire essay, return to the marked passages and work on them until they sound right. Refer to the handbook section in this book (pages 320–353) if you are not certain about the kind of mistake involved.

As you look over your paper, carefully examine all punctuation marks, especially the comma. The comma gives writers more problems than any other punctuation mark. Be sure that you use quotation marks in pairs, and that you can substitute a period for every semicolon that separates two independent elements in a sentence. Review pages 339–348 for any punctuation rules you'd like to check.

Your mind can play tricks on you when you look for spelling errors. You think you see letters that are not there, and you ignore those that are there. Reading each line of your essay backwards will help you because it forces you to read each word singly, in isolation, instead of in a phrase. Look for words that have given you trouble in past papers. Circle any words that do not look correct; use your dictionary to verify your correctness. Do not trust your intuition—use the dictionary for all words you're not sure of. Misspelled words irritate readers and make them wonder about the accuracy of your ideas.

After you have edited your paper and are positive that you have made all the necessary corrections, you are ready to prepare the final copy of your essay. Use the editing checklist below as you go over your revised paper.

## Editing Checklist

1. Are your sentences grammatical? Have you avoided sentence fragments, comma splices, and run-on sentences? (See pages 321–325.) Have you avoided errors in subject-verb agreement (pages 326–329) and mistakes in pronoun reference and case (pages 331–333)?
2. Are your sentences clear? Have you avoided misplaced and dangling modifiers (pages 330–331) and unnecessary shifts in voice, tense, or person (pages 334–337)?
3. Are your sentences effective? Have you used coordination and subordination when appropriate (pages 174–175)? Are your sentences concise and varied (pages 162–167)?
4. Are your sentences punctuated and capitalized correctly, particularly in the use of commas, semicolons, and periods (pages 339–348)?
5. Have you used a dictionary to check the spelling of all troublesome words, rather than just guessing?

## Manuscript Form and Proofreading

You would not think of wrapping an expensive gift in torn or soiled paper. Nor would you show up for a job interview in a soup-stained shirt or tattered trousers. The same principle applies when you turn in written work to your instructors—you do not want your effort and ideas to be overshadowed by a sloppy or careless manuscript. Check your paper carefully to be sure that it represents your best work. If your instructor has not given you directions for preparing your manuscript, follow these suggestions as a guide.

If you type, use white unlined paper of standard size (8 1/2 by 11 inches). Type with a clean black ribbon, double-spacing, on one side of the paper. If you write, use standard size lined white paper (*not* the kind ripped out of a spiral notebook) and black ink. Whether typing or writing, leave margins on all four sides. The first line of each paragraph should be indented about five spaces.

If you use a title page, type or write the title of your essay, your name, the instructor's name, the name of the class, and the date. Center the title about four inches from the top of the page; capitalize the first word and all other important words. Do not use a period after the title.

Drop down about four or five spaces and type or write your name; about two spaces below your name, type or write the name of your class. See page 275 for a sample title page. If you do not use a title page, place the title on the first line of your essay and place your name, the instructor's name, the name of the class, and the date in the upper left-hand corner of the first page. Place your last name and the page number, beginning with page one, in the upper right corner.

Your last job before submitting your paper is to proofread the manuscript carefully. During this stage you are looking for any errors in your essay: misspelled words, punctuation and typographical errors, and other mistakes that would distract your reader. Proofreading requires that you change the focus of your attention. You are no longer looking beneath the surface of your paper for such weaknesses as lapses in logic, undeveloped paragraphs, or irrelevant details. Now you are examining the surface structure of your essay—you are, in effect, examining the wrapping and the ribbon.

The first requirement in proofreading is to give yourself enough time. You can't spot all of your mistakes if you have to rush through the paper. As you read your final copy, look first for misspelled words. Be sure that you have correctly hyphenated words; use the dictionary if you are not certain. Draw a line neatly through all words that you wish to omit. If you want to add material, uses a caret ($\wedge$).

If you have several erasures, changes, and corrections on a page, recopy it. Messiness can detract from the effectiveness and impact of your writing. When you are satisfied that you have made all necessary corrections, staple or clip the pages together. Never turn in unbound sheets of paper to your instructor.

# E X E R C I S E  3

Using the Editing Checklist on page 156 as your guide, correct any errors in grammar, punctuation, spelling, or clarity that you can find in the following essay.

### Television Ethics

The purpose of television is to entertain, yet there seems to be a farely large segment of society that believe television should also educate. Not just *Sesame Street*-style shows either. A number of people from former Vice President Dan Quayle, priests and ministers, and newspaper columnists arround the world, think that TV is to blame for the decline of moral standards in this country television, according to them, should teach us how to behave in proper Fashion. But this ain't so. The television reflects society it does not create society.

While many have complained about the alleged preponderance of sex and violence on the screen, TV actually is rather tame. As far as sex goes, almost all of it is suggested. True pornography can only be found on special cable channels. What happens on most television shows is an opening kiss, a dimming of the lights, and then a morningafter shot of two people waking up in a bed together. Nudity in fact very tight controlled. Societies standards for TV are far stricter than for movies. A child at a Pg-thirteen movie could be exposed to much more explicit nudity and sexual acts than a child watching television.

The violence on TV is more explicit than the sex—but even so, the violence on the newsshows and newspapers may be even worse. When viewers watched a madman in Waco burn down his own home, killing dozens including helpless children, they were watching the news, not fiction; only after that happened did TV networks run copycat docudramas that could not approach the horror of the real thing. Two brothers murder their parents: Is it revenge or greed? A man shoots up a subway shouting racist epithets. A famous football star is accused of murdering his wife and a young, handsome waiter. Are these ideas pitched for the Movie of the Week? Only after they happened in real life first.

Shows do not really have the power to change how people behave, to suggest otherwise implies that people have no will power of his own, no self-control. Millions of people watch *Murder, She Wrote* every week and no matter where Angela Landsbury goes, someone gets killed. Does that mean we have a greater acceptance of murder? That we are more likely to commit murder? Anyone who commits a murder must pay the price, not act like the TV made her do it. The same goes for sex. People have to live their own lives, not act out what they see on TV.

TV does have many family-oriented shows on TV and if people watch them, they can stay on the air for a long time like *The Waltons* and *The Wonder Years*. TV executives are at heart greedy not lusty and violent. They want shoes that people will watch so *Barney* come in the morning because kids will watching it *Melrose Place* in the evening because it gets a big audience. TV is not the great teacher, its the greater entertainer, parents, brothers and sisters, teachers, and friends as the ones who show us how to live.

# COMPUTER EXERCISE

Take an essay that you have been asked to rewrite. Be sure the essay is double-spaced. With either your partner or a small group, read through each other's essays. Using the computer, comment on the text in the computer file itself. You may set off your remarks by using brackets [] or using all capital letters. Be sure to answer all the questions asked on pages 142–143. Save this marked up file under a new file name, so that you have your original essay and at least one marked version of it. Consult this marked version when rewriting your essay for your instructor.

One useful variation of this is to only look at a specific aspect of your essays. For instance, you may simply wish to focus on the introductions. You may wish to group all the introductions together into a single file. This will enable you to analyze the comparative strengths and weaknesses of each other's writing more closely. Remember, though, that there is no single way to write a good introduction, so avoid slavishly imitating what you think is the best introduction in your group. This variation can work for any part of the essay.

When you think that you are done revising your essay, run your essay through a spell check on the computer. Then, print out your essay. Set your essay aside for a day, and then proofread the printed copy. Check for usage errors that the computer did not catch. Most spell-check programs will not distinguish between proper and improper uses of words such as "then" and "than." You must always remember to proofread the final printed copy of your essay no matter how often you have run your essay through a spell checker.

# 8

# *Writing*

# *Effective*

# *Sentences*

What are effective sentences? Most experienced writers would agree that they are *concise, varied,* and *emphatic.* Effective sentences say as much as possible as economically as possible without sacrificing clarity. They use a variety of structures and are different lengths. They emphasize the important ideas so that the reader can recognize the writer's intentions.

## Conciseness

The best sentences contain no flab or unnecessary words. Compare the following sentences:

> *Wordy:* Someone whom I know pretty well is considering acquiring a vehicle in order to travel to and from her place of employment so that she can maximize the cost efficiency of the fuel consumed along said route. (37 words)
>
> *Concise:* My girlfriend is considering buying an economy car for her daily commute to work. (14 words)

By cutting the verbiage in half, we have made the sentence clearer and stripped it of its pomposity. This does not mean that all sentences must be brief or "bare bones." When you want to emphasize certain words or ideas, concrete, specific details may be necessary to make the meaning clear. But empty phrases, padding, and unnecessary repetition add nothing to the meaning of a sentence and create barriers between you and your reader.

When you write a first draft, you will probably be wordy. As you revise, you should look for padding and unnecessary words. In particular, watch for the following constructions.

### Redundancies

A redundant phrase is one that contains unnecessary repetition; it says the same things twice. Here are some common examples: *blue in color, cooperate together, few in number, fundamental principles, smaller in size,* and so on. Compare the two versions of the following sentences:

> *Redundant:* She will speak to the forum at 7 P.M. in the evening.
> *Concise:* She will speak to the forum at 7 P.M.
> *Redundant:* The same identical essay was turned in by two students for the assignment.
> *Concise:* The same essay was turned in by two students.
> *Redundant:* The major league baseball owners, after much debate, finally reached a consensus of opinion.
> *Concise:* The major league baseball owners, after much debate, finally reached a consensus.

You will occasionally want to repeat an idea in different words to emphasize a particular point. Except in those instances, cut out any repetitive words or phrases that do not emphasize or clarify your point.

### Unnecessary Words

Unnecessary words clutter up a sentence because they add nothing to its meaning. Like redundancies, they are no more than padding. Compare the following sentences:

> *Wordy:* In view of the fact that the rain forests are being burned down and destroyed, the nations of the world need to propose and enact acceptable solutions that will really work to stop this problem which affects everyone everywhere.
>
> *Concise:* Because the rain forests are being destroyed, the world must work to find an acceptable solution.

The left column below contains typical wordy expressions; the right column contains concise phrases.

| Wordy | Concise |
|---|---|
| Make inquiry regarding | Inquire, ask |
| At this point in time | Now |
| Have under consideration | Are considering |
| In view of the fact that | Because, since |
| For the purpose of | For, to |
| Of an indefinite nature | Indefinite |
| At the present time | Now |
| In order to | To |
| For the reason that | Because |
| In the final analysis | Finally |
| In the case that | If |

This is not an exhaustive list, but it suggests how familiar and subtle wordy expressions can be. As you revise your writing, delete any unnecessary words.

*All-purpose Nouns.* Words such as "aspect," "factor," "field," "kind," "thing," "element," and "situation" are overused. Writers who cannot think of a more precise word often resort to them; they can usually be deleted by rewording the sentence.

> *Wordy:* Having entered the field of X-ray technology as my major, I have become personally aware of factors that can contribute to overexposure to X rays.
>
> *Concise:* Since majoring in X-ray technology, I have learned how overexposure to X rays occurs.

Sentences that begin with "It is" and "There is" (and the plural, "There are") are usually weaker and less assertive than sentences that begin with the real subject.

> *Wordy:* There were gang members involved in the robbery.
> *Concise:* Gang members were involved in the robbery.
> *Wordy:* It is a fact that American business executives care more about quarterly profits than about long-term gains.
> *Concise:* American business executives think more about quarterly profits than about long-term gains.

Phrases such as "in my opinion," "it seems," "I believe," and "I think" can usually be cut from a sentence without damaging it; the result is usually a more forceful sentence.

> *Wordy:* In my opinion, the culture of materialism is responsible for the decay of the family.
> *Concise:* The culture of materialism is responsible for the decay of the family.
> *Wordy:* I believe that the acceptance of alternative medicine into the nation's health-care plans will significantly lower costs.
> *Concise:* The acceptance of alternative medicine into the nation's health-care plans will significantly lower costs.

## E X E R C I S E 1

Revise the following sentences, making them as concise as possible without changing their meaning.

1. Queen Elizabeth II, who is the mother of Prince Charles, cannot be happy with him or his wife, who is Princess Diana, because of the disgrace their troubled marriage has brought upon the monarchy of England.
2. There is a clear feeling that John Wayne was the greatest film cowboy out of all of them.
3. As an immigrant coming from South Korea, Kim intended to hold on to his native Korean culture as well as adapt to his new country, the United States.
4. The horrible treatment of the Native Americans or Indians by the United States and its representatives during the nineteenth century is surely one of the most abominable chapters in the long history of the United States.
5. She would not help anybody with any assistance whatsoever.

6. I believe that the President should be elected by direct election of the voters in which everyone has one vote and that the candidate with the most votes wins, not by the current Electoral College system.

7. At the present moment in time it is useless to predict or speculate on what will happen to the nation's health-care system.

8. The reporters and journalists who cover and report on the story are beginning to sound biased or prejudiced about this story.

9. The pursuit or quest for gold has been a central, fundamental, principal action of human history since the beginning of time.

10. The ballgame went into extra additional innings and did not end until late at night at 1 A.M.

11. We enjoyed listening to the soft musical ballad which told a story.

12. The contemporary student of today needs to have her mandatory word processor.

13. When Julie returned to her old childhood neighborhood in which she grew up, she was shocked at how small and tiny everything seemed compared to what she remembered as a child.

14. The self-inflicted gunshot wound of suicide victim Kurt Cobain depressed and upset many of his supportive fans.

15. When Yvonne received the scholarship as a gift from the local Women's Club, she vigorously thanked the group of women profusely.

16. Luke has been assigned the responsibility of collecting, maintaining, and supervising records that deal with the utilization of the coffee-making machine on a per diem or daily basis.

17. Insofar as learning to play a musical instrument is concerned, the harp, in my own personal opinion, would be in the category of the kind that is difficult to learn to play.

18. Although they were few in number, the early settlers who came to this country brought with them strong and devout religious faith and beliefs.

19. In view of the fact that the job market is constantly changing and being modified, the counselor urged each and every student to plan alternative plans for the future.

20. It is a fact that there are many individuals who do not vote in elections.

# E X E R C I S E    2

Revise the following paragraph, making it as concise as possible without changing its meaning.

Over the course of time including now, Italy has remained a popular tourist spot for people to go to on vacation. With its many great, historical, and important old cities, Italy has many attractions for visitors from all over. To begin with, I believe that Rome has the most to offer. For starters, Catholics around the world will want to visit the Vatican in Vatican City in Rome. This is where the Pope lives, and there are many beautiful, important sights to see including the works of Michelangelo who painted the Sistine Chapel which has recently been restored and returned to its original condition. Another city of great historic and artistic importance is the city of Florence which is where many historically and artistically important people used to live. The Italian Renaissance, which was historically and artistically important, found full flower and prospered in Florence. Next to the great cities of Italy is Venice which is famous for its water canals. Venice itself is a relatively small city which is interspersed with canals on which you can take trips in a gondola which is guided by a person called a gondolier. Venice is a different contrast to Rome and Florence because of its history in the past as an empire that controlled large amounts of territory including Cyprus, Crete, Constantinople, and other areas in the eastern Mediterranean region. These are only three of the many historic and artistically important cities of Italy which many visitors like to travel to on their vacations.

## Sentence Variety

Good writers include a variety of sentence types in their essays. They mix shorter with longer sentences and employ a variety of sentence patterns. The relationship between the ideas is clear, and the reader can follow the writer's thought without any problems. Weak writers, by contrast, often produce choppy, repetitious, and monotonous sentences. In this section we will look at several ways to write varied sentences that are smooth and mature.

### Sentence Length

Good writers use sentences of different lengths. A paragraph filled with sentences of the same length is monotonous. A series of short sentences sounds immature, as the following paragraph demonstrates.

Stephen Crane was an American writer. He wrote short stories, novels, and poetry. He was born in Newark, New Jersey. He was the fourteenth child in his family. He was the son of a Methodist minister. His mother was the daughter of a Methodist minister. He rebelled against the teachings of his parents. He took on vices. These vices included reading novels, going to the theater, playing baseball, smoking tobacco, and drinking alcohol. He attended a military school. There he came under the influence of a Civil War

enthusiast. That man's name was the Rev. Gen. John Bullock Van
Petten. He later became the model for the character of Jim Conklin
in *The Red Badge of Courage.* Crane flunked out of Lafayette College. Then, Crane attended Syracuse University for one semester.
That was in 1891. He mostly played baseball there. It was at Syracuse that he began writing *Maggie: A Girl of the Streets.* This novel
helped start Crane's career. He wrote *The Red Badge of Courage* in
1895. He wrote a number of well-known short stories too. He died
in Germany. He had tuberculosis and malaria. It was 1900. He was
only 28 years old.

The above paragraph suffers from monotonous sentence structure. By
combining some of the shorter sentences, you can avoid the boring
style:

> Stephen Crane was an American writer of short stories, novels,
> and poetry. Born in Newark, New Jersey, he was the fourteenth
> child in his family. He was the son of a Methodist minister, and his
> mother was the daughter of a Methodist minister. He rebelled
> against the teachings of his parents. He took on vices, including
> reading novels, going to the theater, playing baseball, smoking to-
> bacco, and drinking alcohol. Crane attended a military school
> where he came under the influence of a Civil War enthusiast, the
> Rev. Gen. John Bullock Van Petten. Van Petten later became the
> model for the character of Jim Conklin in *The Red Badge of Courage.*
> After military school, Crane flunked out of Lafayette College.
> Then, Crane attended Syracuse University for one semester in
> 1891, but he mostly played baseball there. However, at Syracuse
> he began writing *Maggie: A Girl of the Streets.* This novel helped
> start Crane's career, which eventually included *The Red Badge of
> Courage* in 1895 and a number of well-known short stories. He
> died in Germany in 1900 of tuberculosis and malaria. He was only
> 28 years old.

Do not, however, get the idea that short sentences should always
be avoided. They can be effective for summing up a point or for making the reader stop abruptly to consider a key comment, observation,
or conclusion.

A short sentence can be effective at the beginning of a paragraph:

> Consider this. For years now we have witnessed the agony of
> refugees from Asia, starving Cambodian men, women, and chil-
> dren, fleeing Vietnamese, struggling ashore on Malaysia from
> some leaky boat after a horrid passage across the South China Sea.
> Some of these boats make it; many do not. But all of these boats, as
> has been written, carry on them the same inscription: "This is what
> happens to friends of the United States."

A short sentence can also be effective at the end of a paragraph:

> Some naysayers believe that this country's best days are gone. They cite the increased economic competition with Japan and Germany, the inability to control world events in the post-Cold War era, the rise of immigration both legal and illegal, the growing psychological malaise on the part of the American public. The naysayers look at the past as America's glory days and see the future only as a place of diminished opportunities and negligible rewards. But the naysayers are wrong.

In both passages, a short sentence is contrasted with a series of longer sentences. As a result, the short sentences catch the reader's attention.

## E X E R C I S E 3

The following groups of sentences are from the first drafts of student papers. Revise each paragraph by varying the length of the sentences.

1.  Needle exchange programs as a subject of great controversy. The controversy is over whether exchanging needles is a good idea. On one side, people argue that exchanging needles will help stop the spread of AIDS and other infectious diseases. On the other side, people argue that exchanging needles will encourage drug abuse and put local governments in the business of supporting illegal activities. Some medical professionals believe needle exchange programs work. Other medical professionals do not believe that needle exchange programs work. Most police departments oppose needle exchange programs as well.

2.  Small public libraries are an endangered species. Small public libraries serve local communities. By themselves, those communities lack political power. They are seen as easy targets when local municipalities face budget cuts. They find that their hours are cut. They may be closed for several days of the week. They may be shut down permanently. They may be consolidated with larger libraries. The local communities must band together to keep their local libraries from having their budgets cut.

3.  The basic problem in our schools is obvious. It is the practice of giving credit where none has been earned. This has gone on for years. Students have been passed rather than flunked. As a result, illiteracy among high-school graduates is growing. The solution is equally obvious. It is the widespread giving of F's.

# E X E R C I S E 4

Revise the following paragraph by varying the length of the sentences:

The Spanish Armada set sail from Lisbon. The time was May 1588. Spain was looking to invade England. They had a fleet of about 130 ships and 8,000 sailors and 19,000 infantry. They were to help a Spanish invasion force coming from the Netherlands. The English had 197 ships and 16,000 men. The difference was that most of the English men were sailors. They were not infantry troops like the Spanish had who were unused to sailing. The Spanish ships were slow and designed for close combat. The English ships were smaller, lighter, and more maneuverable. Another thing was that the Spanish commander, Duque de Medina-Sidonia, was inexperienced. The English had more experienced commanders in Sir Francis Drake and Sir John Hawkins. The combination of these factors, plus poor weather conditions, led to the decisive defeat of the Spanish fleet. After that, Spain began to decline as a world power. England's rise to power began.

## Word Order

Inexperienced writers tend to begin every sentence with the subject. This is natural, because the subject-verb pattern is the most common arrangement in English sentences. A series of such sentences, however, can be boring and monotonous. By beginning some of your sentences with something other than the subject you can make them more interesting. There are two methods for doing this: placing modifiers before the subject, and inverting the normal word order.

*Normal order:* Spain is Europe's third largest country in land size, and it covers 194,885 square miles.

*Appositive first:* Europe's third largest country in land size, Spain covers 194,885 square miles.

*Normal order:* Wayne stepped back to look at his first painting, satisfied and proud.

*Participles first:* Satisfied and proud, Wayne stepped back to look at his first painting.

*Normal order:* Scott swung his fists at his opponent blindly.

*Adverb first:* Blindly, Scott swung his fists at his opponent.

*Normal order:* I found a ten-dollar bill in my pocket.

*Prepositional phrase first:* In my pocket I found a ten-dollar bill.

*Normal order:* A stranger appeared from behind the bushes.

*Object first:* From behind the bushes appeared a stranger.

*Normal order:*   Sean ran across the playground.
  *Subject-verb*
   *inversion:*   Across the playground ran Sean.

Additional suggestions for varying sentence patterns and for combining shorter sentences are on pages 180–189, "Sentence Combining."

## E X E R C I S E 5

Each of the following sentences follows the subject-verb pattern. Rewrite the sentences, following the suggestions given above.

1. Paris is a city of great romance for many visitors.
2. The football coaches stopped practice early after the temperature rose to over 100 degrees.
3. Niagara Falls is still one of the most popular honeymoon spots in the United States.
4. Jack Nicholson was a regular fixture at Los Angeles Lakers home games during the Magic Johnson era.
5. The former Soviet republics need foreign investment to become prosperous.
6. The opera diva stormed off the stage, stunning the audience.
7. Some people believe that God created the world in seven days.
8. A cry came from behind the curtain.
9. Marcel Proust wrote *A Remembrance of Things Past* without much concern for its length.
10. My mother hates spiders.
11. Brazil is the largest country in South America, and its coffee helps the entire world start the day.
12. My friend Juan is a faithful fan of the Florida Marlins, and he rarely misses a home game.
13. Harold did not get his security deposit back because he did not take good care of the apartment.
14. The thief crept across the floor soundlessly.
15. Michaela found a large tip under the empty beer mug.
16. Michael Jordan tried his hand at playing professional baseball after an unparalleled career in basketball.
17. Professor Stallings uses the King James translation for her course on the Bible as literature.
18. Doctor Samuel Mudd was a physician in Maryland who was falsely accused of conspiring to assassinate Abraham Lincoln.
19. Alice Walker is one of the most talented American novelists.
20. Women need the cooperation of their husbands and children so that they can pursue careers, according to my sociology professor.
21. The Internal Revenue Service has audited Mr. Steilen's tax returns every year for the past decade because of his carelessness in filling out his tax forms.

## Loose and Periodic Sentences

Another technique for achieving sentence variety is to use a mixture of *loose* and *periodic* sentences. In a *loose* sentence, the main idea comes first, and less important ideas follow. In the *periodic* sentence, the main idea comes at the end of the sentence.

> *Loose:* I found a note pinned to my door when I came home this afternoon.
>
> *Periodic:* When I came home this afternoon, I found a note pinned to my door.
>
> *Loose:* Farmers have to supply food for this country and others despite unpredictable weather, hostility from environmentalists over the use of pesticides, and the physical dangers of farm work.
>
> *Periodic:* Despite unpredictable weather, hostility from environmentalists over the use of pesticides, and the physical dangers of farm work, farmers have to supply food for this country and others.

As you can see, the loose sentence is built in stages. It completes the main statement and then explains or amplifies it. Most of our conversations and writing consist of loose sentences, as we pile details on details as we think of them. For this reason the loose sentence is sometimes called a *cumulative* sentence. The loose sentence actually lacks the suspense of the periodic sentence because the details and qualifiers that follow its main idea weaken its impact. The periodic sentence, on the other hand, holds the reader in suspense because it holds the main statement until the end. Everything that precedes it builds up the idea in the main clause at the conclusion. The periodic sentence is more emphatic, therefore, because it creates more suspense—the reader (or listener) has to pay attention to the very end.

A word of caution: Don't overdo periodic sentences. The suspense that they generate can be overdone, and they can become just as monotonous as any other structure that you rely on heavily. But used occasionally to break up the sameness of loose sentences, they will improve your style.

## E X E R C I S E 6

Change the loose sentences to periodic sentences, and the periodic sentences to loose sentences.

1. Because of his gambling troubles, Pete Rose was banned from consideration for the Hall of Fame.

2. She would have been better prepared for the fashion business if she had known how to sew.
3. By the time you read this, I will be on a plane to South America.
4. The best thing about owning your own house is not having to share a wall with neighbors.
5. Tom Stoppard wrote the play *Rosencrantz & Guildenstern Are Dead* based on two minor characters in Shakespeare's *Hamlet*.
6. The price of long distance phone calls has gone down since AT&T was broken up.
7. After Columbus discovered the Americas, Europe was changed forever.
8. Some comics get their jokes from genuine humor while others rely on crude and vulgar behavior to get laughs.
9. To a man, they were ready to die for their country.
10. You may be able to purchase a ticket from a scalper if the stadium has been sold out.
11. If the cost of insurance goes up much higher, I may have to sell my car.
12. Cockroaches are still plentiful in New York City despite all attempts to eradicate the pests.
13. Ted Kennedy has little chance to become President because of what happened at Chappaquiddick.
14. Computers have achieved ubiquity in the daily life of Americans with little trauma or controversy.
15. Roger Staubach was one of the greatest quarterbacks in the history of the National Football League.
16. Directly ahead of them, standing in the middle of the road casually munching on a mouthful of hay, was a large cow.
17. The Spanish invaders murdered or raped many of the Indians they met despite the fact that the vast majority of the Indians were friendly.
18. Many college seniors are uneasy because they are uncertain that they will be able to find a satisfactory job upon graduation.
19. Geoffrey Chaucer was the first poet to be buried in the Poets' Corner of Westminster Abbey.
20. According to many movie critics, the best film ever made was *Citizen Kane*.

## Sentence Imitation

Sentence imitation is an excellent way to improve your own sentence construction. The process is simple: copy several sentences that you like by writers you admire. Analyze the structure of the sentences, noticing, for example, where the subject and verb are, where the main idea is placed, where the modifiers and unimportant parts are located, and so on. Then write an original sentence, following as closely as possible the same pattern. It isn't necessary to have the exact number of words as the model sentence; the object is to write a sentence that follows the same pattern.

You will notice several things happening in your own writing after you practice sentence imitation. You will discover why some sentences work and others don't, and by paying close attention to how professional writers put words together, you will be using patterns in your own writing that might never have occurred to you. A side benefit to this exercise is that you will add new words to your vocabulary.

Study these model sentences and their imitations, written by students. You will notice that most of the model sentences, as well as those in the exercise below, are loose or cumulative sentences.

| | |
|---|---|
| *Model:* | To err is human, to forgive, divine. (*Alexander Pope*) |
| *Imitation:* | To work is exhausting, to loaf, refreshing. (*Student*) |
| *ANALYSIS:* | The writer of this example has tried to imitate Pope closely. Notice that Pope's sentence links pairs of words opposite in meaning: *err, forgive; human, divine.* The student's version attempts this same contrast: *work, loaf; exhausting, refreshing.* |
| *Model:* | Ask not what your country can do for you, but what you can do for your country. (*John F. Kennedy*) |
| *Imitation:* | Do not ask what your fraternity can do for you, but what you can do for your fraternity. (*Student*) |
| *Model:* | A lot of bad luck fell on our wedding day, even though the matchmaker had chosen a lucky day, the fifteenth day of the eighth moon, when the moon is perfectly round and bigger than any other time of the year. (*Amy Tan*) |
| *Imitation:* | There was a great deal of trouble on the day of my confirmation, even though the bishop had chosen a feast day, the Feast of the Immaculate Conception, when Our Lady was conceived without sin. (*Student*) |
| *Model:* | The dim roar of London was like the bourdon note of a distant organ. (*Oscar Wilde*) |
| *Imitation:* | The far-off rumble of the L.A. freeways was like the low hum of a piano's bottom note. (*Student*) |
| *Model:* | Calico-coated, small-bodied, with delicate legs and pink faces in which their mismatched eyes rolled wild and subdued, they huddled, gaudy motionless and alert, wild as deer, deadly as rattlesnakes, quiet as doves. (*William Faulkner*) |
| *Imitation:* | Deeply tanned, bikini clad, with hopeful eyes and flirtatious smiles and lean bodies that swung smooth and practiced, they walked, giggling loudly and nervously, coy like a breeze, rushing like a wind, waiting like a storm. (*Student*) |

*Model:* Women don't want to exchange places with men. (*Gloria Steinem*)

*Imitation:* Teenagers don't want to go to parties with their parents. (*Student*)

## E X E R C I S E 7

Write original sentences, imitating the structure of the following sentences.

1. Never complain and never explain. (*Benjamin Disraeli*)
2. In a culture like ours, long accustomed to splitting and dividing all things as a means of control, it is sometimes a bit of a shock to be reminded that, in operational and practical fact, the medium is the message. (*Marshall McLuhan*)
3. For fools rush in where angels fear to tread. (*Alexander Pope*)
4. To every thing there is a season, and a time to every purpose under heaven: a time to be born, a time to die, a time to plant, and a time to pluck up that which is planted, a time to kill, and a time to heal. . . . (*Ecclesiastes*)
5. The mass of men lead lives of quiet desperation. (*Henry David Thoreau*)
6. Up the road, in his shack, the old man was sleeping again. He was still sleeping on his face and the boy was sitting by him watching him. The old man was dreaming about lions. (*Ernest Hemingway*)
7. She ran the whole gamut of emotions from A to B. (*Dorothy Parker*)
8. Rage cannot be hidden; it can only be dissembled. (*James Baldwin*)
9. For masterpieces are not single and solitary births; they are the outcome of many years of thinking in common, of thinking by the body of the people, so that the experience of the mass is behind the single voice. (*Virginia Woolf*)
10. The quality of strength lined with tenderness is an unbeatable combination, as are intelligence and necessity when unblunted by formal education. (*Maya Angelou*)

## Emphasis

Effective sentences emphasize their main ideas, keeping related but less important ideas in the background. *Coordination, subordination, parallelism,* and *the use of the active voice* are techniques that will make your sentences more emphatic and your ideas more forceful.

## Coordination

To show the relative importance of two or more ideas in a sentence, you can connect them by means of *coordination* or *subordination*. You *coordinate* two or more ideas that are equally important. Ideas that deserve equal emphasis can be linked in several ways: by coordinating conjunctions (usually *and, but, or,* and *nor*) and by conjunctive adverbs such as *however* and *therefore.*

Here are two examples of coordination:

| | |
|---|---|
| *Two simple sentences:* | Marina worked at the front desk during the mornings. During the afternoons she worked in the billing office. |
| *Coordinated with a conjunction:* | Marina worked at the front desk during the mornings, but during the afternoons she worked in the billing office. |
| *Coordinated with a conjunctive adverb:* | Marina worked at the front desk during the mornings; however, during the afternoons she worked in the billing office. |

When combining ideas, be careful that you do not end up merely stringing them together with a series of *ands* and *buts*. Excessive coordination is just as ineffective as a series of choppy simple sentences.

| | |
|---|---|
| *Excessive coordination:* | Del was crying, and Heather was laughing, and the casket was lowered into the ground. |
| *Revised:* | While Del was crying and Heather was laughing, the casket was lowered into the ground. |

*Faulty coordination* occurs when there seems to be no logical connection between two coordinated statements. In such cases, you can show the relationship between the clauses by subordinating one idea.

| | |
|---|---|
| *Faulty coordination:* | Ben asked for the check, but the job had not been completed. |
| *Revised:* | Ben asked for the check even though the job had not been completed. |

## Subordination

To subordinate is to show that one idea is less important than another in a sentence by putting it in a subordinate structure. The task in subordinating, therefore, is to identify the main idea and place it in a main clause and then place the less important material in a dependent or subordinate construction.

The writer and reader can usually agree on which idea in a sentence is more important:

*The program began as I was answering the phone.* (Most readers would agree that the less important idea is what the writer was doing when the program began. *As I was answering the phone* is a subordinate clause.)

At times, however, only the context can suggest which idea should be emphasized:

> When Mozart was five, he wrote his first composition for the piano.
> When he wrote his first composition for the piano, Mozart was five.

The first version emphasizes that Mozart wrote a composition for the piano; note that this information is in the coordinate or main clause. In the second sentence, the emphasis is on the fact that Mozart was five, as stated in the main clause. These sentences illustrate the principle that the main idea should normally be placed in the main clause, with supporting information in subordinate elements.

*Excessive subordination* occurs when a writer crams too many loosely connected details and subordinate structures into one sentence, as in the following:

> The lion hunter, who had taken a large rifle out of his truck, started to step carefully toward the bush into which the lion had stumbled, because of the wound to his hindquarter, which Barasa said was not fatal.

The best way to revise such a sentence is to break it up into two or more sentences, putting the main ideas in main clauses:

> The hunter took a large rifle out of his truck. Because Barasa said the wound to the lion's hindquarter was not fatal, the hunter stepped carefully toward the bush into which the lion had stumbled.

*Faulty subordination* (or "upside-down" subordination) occurs when the logically important idea is placed in a subordinate position:

> Hein had been in this country for only two years, although he can speak English almost flawlessly.

This sentence suggests that the main idea is that Hein has been in this country for only two years; it is likely, however, that the idea to be emphasized is that he can speak English almost flawlessly. By putting the main idea in the main clause, we can make the sentence more emphatic:

> Although Hein has been in this country for only two years, he can speak English almost flawlessly.

# E  X  E  R  C  I  S  E     8

Rewrite the following sentences by subordinating less important ideas to more important ones.

1. Paula wrote her teacher a note to complain about her grade, and she felt she had been dealt with unfairly.
2. Team U.S.A.'s victory over Canada in World Cup competition was a major advance for soccer in this country although many onlookers still say the sport will never gain the wide popularity of baseball or football.
3. Isaac lost his hearing as a result of a childhood accident, and he can use American Sign Language.
4. Although Lara was admitted to graduate school in Texas, she had applied to about a dozen schools across the nation.
5. Months ago no one had ever heard of Nicole Brown Simpson and now everyone in the country does.
6. He has made several bombs although Arnold Schwarzenegger is one of Hollywood's biggest box office stars.
7. Gertrude Stein is as well-known for the company she kept as for what she did herself, and she had an interesting personal life.
8. Scott's golf game started to deteriorate, and he steadfastly refused to take any lessons to fix it.
9. Air Force Captain Charles Yeager flew the Bell X-1, and he exceeded the speed of sound, and therefore he became the world's first supersonic flyer.
10. At one time condors were prevalent in the western half of the United States although they are an endangered species today.

# E  X  E  R  C  I  S  E     9

Rewrite the following paragraph, subordinating less important ideas to more important ones.

Mothers are certainly well-recognized in our society. Society accepts the idea that mothers require special time off to be with their infants. Many employers give maternity leave for women. They bond with and care for their babies during this time. Fathers typically do not. Most employers do not recognize the need for paternity leave. Fathers are forced to take sick leave to be with their child. Similarly, the publishing industry pours out dozens of books on parenting. The vast majority of them are directed toward mothers. Fathers appear to be tacitly discouraged from being a part of the early lives of their children. At best they are encouraged to help the mothers with their tasks. Importantly, the tasks are still considered the mothers', not a shared responsibility. Small wonder that fathers do not feel responsible for young infants. The world around men tells them that caring for infants is strictly mothers' work.

---

## *Parallelism*

Parallelism is the use of similar grammatical forms in a sentence to express ideas of similar importance. Parallel structure can make sentences smoother and can make clear the connection between the ideas in those sentences.

Compare the following sentences:

> *Faulty:*   I like to walk, to run, and swimming.
> *Parallel:*   I like walking, running, and swimming.

Read the following pairs of sentences carefully; try to determine which sentence in each pair is smoother and more emphatic because of parallelism

> He began his life in poverty; he was wealthy when he died.
> He began his life in poverty; he died rich.

> Because the snow was cold, the sidewalks were icy, and also because she noticed that the wind was gusting in from the north, Hope decided to stay indoors.

> Because the snow was cold, the sidewalks were icy, and the wind was gusting in from the north, Hope decided to stay indoors.

The second sentence in each pair uses parallelism, and therefore is smoother and more emphatic.

As you probably noticed from the preceding examples, parallel structure can employ single words, phrases, or whole clauses:

> The vacation was *short, stressful* and *expensive.* (adjectives)

> He was unable to speak without stuttering *in front of an audience, with women, and over the phone.*

> *Where she lives, how she dresses, and who she knows* can be found on the information sheet of the Lonely Hearts Club.

## E X E R C I S E    10

Improve the following sentences by using parallel structure.

1. At the 1992 Special Olympics in Barcelona, my friend Ben took a silver medal in the swimming competition, and the bronze medal in the long jump was won by Ben's brother, Nathan.
2. In the morning, she felt stiff, dehydrated, and she was still feeling exhausted.

3. Dr. Cobble's office has contemporary artwork, large book-cases, and he is located in a corner of the top floor of the administration building.
4. The game requires a pad of paper, and you also need a water glass.
5. The police officer decided that the child was either lost or that his mother had abandoned him.
6. He was always eating pop-tarts in the morning, peanut butter sandwiches at lunch, and every evening he ate a hot dog with a soda.
7. The newspapers reported that the flooding in the farmlands was causing great damage to crops, and also the equipment was all ruined.
8. Some professional athletes ruin their public image by being arrogant, greedy, and they get involved in drug abuse.
9. When we visited Memphis, we walked around the Beale Street district, saw the famous ducks at the Peabody Hotel, and we went on a tour of Elvis's home, Graceland.
10. This method of capital punishment is used in Florida, Texas, and they apply it in California, too.
11. Despite the closed windows, locked doors, and the fact that the heater was going full blast, she felt a cold draft come through the room.
12. My job consisted of sweeping the floor, opening up in the morning, and customers had to be waited on when the owners were at lunch.
13. They vowed never to return, and they would always remember.
14. The congregation decided that the new pastor's sermons were boring and contained little humor.
15. Because the weather was mild, and also we were able to take a few days off, we decided to hike in the Blue Ridge Mountains.

---

### Active and Passive Voice

You will often be able to choose between active and passive voice when composing sentences. The active voice is usually more direct. For this reason you should use active verbs except in cases when you have good reason to use passive ones.

In a sentence built on an *active* verb, the subject performs the action:

José threw the ball.

The *passive* voice turns the sentence around. The doer remains the same but is placed in a less important position, and the object becomes the subject:

*Passive:* The ball was thrown by José.

As you can see, active voice emphasizes the *doer* of the action, and passive voice emphasizes the *object* or *receiver* of the action. Therefore, the choice of active or passive voice depends on the relative importance of the doer and the recipient of the action. Compare these sentences:

> Amnesty International protested the execution of the minor.
> The execution of the minor was protested by Amnesty International.

In the first sentence the verb (*protested*) is active and stresses the *doer* of the action (*Amnesty International*). In the second sentence the verb (*was protested*) is passive and stresses the *recipient* of the action (*the execution of the minor*). When the result of the action is more important than the performer, use the passive voice. Passive voice is also acceptable when the doer of the action is unknown:

> *Passive:* Tabitha, the cat, *was captured* inside the cargo hold of a 747. (In this case, the *doer* is unimportant.)

In general, however, avoid the passive voice because it is wordy and less direct. Notice the difference between these sentences:

> *Passive:* It was understood by the soldiers that their duty would be to feed and protect innocent civilians. (*17 words*)
> *Active:* The soldiers understood that their duty was to feed and protect innocent civilians. (*13 words*).

Another consequence of the passive voice is that it obscures the performer or doer of the action:

> *Passive:* A suggestion was made to cut the school budget by eliminating the counseling department. (*Suggested by whom?*)
> *Passive:* It is recommended that the mess in this room be cleaned up. (*Who is making the recommendation? Who is to clean up the mess in the room?*)

## E X E R C I S E   11

Change the following sentences from passive to active voice to make them more emphatic.

1. The large population in prison of repeat offenders was cited by the commission as one reason for the need to find alternative sentencing for first-time, nonviolent offenders.
2. The prize was won by the team from Central High School for best marching band at the Christmas parade.

3. The window was broken by Tommy with one mighty swing of his bat.
4. A state of emergency was declared by the governor after the water swept over the banks of the river.
5. It was said by the townspeople that the woods were still inhabited by Reed's spirit.
6. It was clear that the trust that had once existed between the two of them had been broken beyond repair.
7. The silken fiber that is spun by orb spiders is twisted into an endless variety of patterns.
8. The auto wreck was witnessed by Lucilla as she was driving to work.
9. New evidence that brain damage can be caused by boxing was cited by a panel of physicians last week.
10. New safeguards were approved by the hospital administrator so that the chance of an incorrect dosage given by a nurse would be eliminated.

## E X E R C I S E    12

Rewrite the following paragraph, making the sentences more emphatic by using active voice where appropriate.

It has been decided by the members of the committee on water apportionment that water would be apportioned to the new High Tide development according to occupancy expectations. The expectations have been charted by Shale and Sand developers. It was further decided that the water apportioned would be paid for up to and including date of sale by the management coalition, which is referred to as Bronze Age Ltd. Exceptions may be granted by the committee after a hearing is held at a date to be determined later by the committee.

## *Sentence Combining*

Sentence combining is an important and effective way to improve your writing. By learning how to combine short sentences into longer, smoother, and more interesting sentences, you can develop your writing style in a variety of ways. Because sentence combining uses most of the techniques already discussed in this chapter, it is introduced in this concluding section. Sentence combining employs a series of steps that we will follow, beginning with the most obvious and progressing to more subtle patterns.

## *Using Coordination to Combine Sentences*

The most obvious (though not always the best) way to combine two or more short sentences is with a *coordinating conjunction (and, but, or, for, nor, yet, so)*, preceded by a comma or with a *semicolon.* This will produce a compound sentence.

| | |
|---|---|
| *Simple sentences:* | Randall bought a bicycle with his earnings. Doug bought a backpack. |
| *Combined:* | Randall bought a bicycle with his earnings, *and* Doug bought a backpack. |
| *Combined:* | Randall bought a bicycle with his earnings; Doug bought a backpack. |
| *Simple sentences:* | During the past semester, Khan worked hard in the tutoring labs. She still had trouble with her grades. |
| *Combined:* | During the past semester, Khan worked hard in the tutoring labs, *but* she still had trouble with her grades. |

By using coordinating conjunctions you will often be able to combine short sentences into single sentences containing one main clause. Sentences can be combined this way when both the original sentences have the same subject or the same verb. The conjunction is not preceded by a comma in sentences constructed this way.

| | |
|---|---|
| *Same subject:* | Suzanne ran cross-country. She played basketball. |
| *Combined:* | Suzanne ran cross-country *and* played basketball. |
| *Same verb:* | Leroy spoke about life in New Mexico. Ramon spoke about life in New Mexico. |
| *Combined:* | Leroy *and* Ramon spoke about life in New Mexico. |

## E  X  E  R  C  I  S  E      13

Using the preceding examples as a guide, combine the following pairs of sentences in the most appropriate way, using either a coordinating conjunction or a semicolon.

1. The vegetables at the supermarket are usually fresh. The fruit is often not ripe yet.
2. She will wait until she hears from him. She will leave now.
3. The demand for fish is as high as it has ever been. The ocean's supplies are becoming depleted.
4. Bob's application to the seminary was rejected. He did not give up hope of becoming a minister.

5. You should check to make sure your attic is properly insulated. You should also check the attic for any signs of water damage.
6. The people on the other side of the tracks are rich. We are poor.
7. Our society appears to value winning at all costs. Losing honorably has its merits.
8. The sergeant ordered the private to report for K.P. duty. The private refused.
9. The tax bill will be approved by the budget committee. It will probably be vetoed by the governor.
10. In last night's movie I loved the character of the old woman. Her husband irritated me.

### Using Subordination to Combine Sentences

Another way to combine shorter sentences is by using *subordination*, or making a single complex sentence out of two simple sentences. A complex sentence consists of an independent clause and a dependent clause. Dependent clauses begin with *connecting words* that indicate that the clauses are incomplete or dependent thoughts. By placing a connecting word in front of a simple sentence, you change it into a dependent clause. By attaching the dependent clause to a simple sentence, you create a complex sentence. The two kinds of connecting words you can put in front of dependent clauses are *relatives* and *subordinating conjunctions*.

When a relative (*who, which, that, whom, whose*) begins a clause, the result is a *dependent clause*. Notice what happens to the following sentences when they are combined by changing one of them to a dependent clause:

> *Simple*   J. Edgar Hoover was head of the FBI for 48 years. He
> *sentences:*  died in 1972.
> *Combined:*  J. Edgar Hoover, *who died in 1972,* was head of the FBI for 48 years. (*Or:* J. Edgar Hoover, *who was head of the FBI for 48 years,* died in 1972.)

In general, the idea that you want to emphasize should be placed in the independent clause.

Notice how the following pairs of sentences have been effectively combined by using relatives:

> *Simple*   Charles Proteus Steinmetz was an important pioneer
> *sentences:*  in the understanding of alternating current systems. He promoted educational opportunity for the handicapped.
> *Combined*  Charles Proteus Steinmetz, who was an important pio-

| | |
|---|---|
| *using* who: | neer in the understanding of alternating current systems, promoted educational opportunity for the handicapped. |
| *Simple sentences:* | The art of basket weaving dates back thousands of years. The art is still practiced in many cultures today. |
| *Combined using* which: | The art of basket weaving, which dates back thousands of years, is still practiced in many cultures today. |
| *Simple sentences:* | Eddie carried in the vacuum cleaner. He had borrowed it from his mother. |
| *Combined using* that: | Eddie carried in the vacuum cleaner that he had borrowed from his mother. |
| *Simple sentences:* | Many people once saw Elvis as a dangerous rebel. Later, he developed a calculated, commercial Las Vegas persona. |
| *Combined using* whom: | Elvis, whom many people had once seen as a dangerous rebel, developed a calculated, commercial Las Vegas persona. |
| *Simple sentences:* | Dana's ability to control her temper worsened in high school. She eventually was expelled during her junior year. |
| *Combined using* whose: | Dana, whose ability to control her temper worsened in high school, was eventually expelled during her junior year. |

Notice that some dependent clauses are set off by commas. For a discussion of the use of commas with essential and nonessential clauses, see pages 340–342.

## E X E R C I S E 14

Combine the shorter sentences in each section below according to the directions, supplying commas when necessary.

1. Combine the following pairs of sentences by changing one of the sentences to a *who* clause.
   a. Pat Mulligan was one of the best local musicians I ever heard. He never was signed by a record company.
   b. Roger became interested in playing tennis only after reaching his sixties. He is competing in a national seniors tournament.
   c. Ray Kroc was the founder of McDonald's. He served as an ambulance driver in World War I, was a jazz pianist, and sold blenders in his younger days.

2. Combine the following pairs of sentences by changing one of the sentences to a *which* clause.
   a. From 1901 to 1950 Connie Mack was the sole manager of the Philadelphia Athletics. The team went to the World Series nine times during that span.
   b. Many critics consider the best movie of the 1970s to be *The Deer Hunter*. It starred Robert DeNiro and Meryl Streep.
   c. Honey contains an enzyme. The enzyme prevents it from molding.
3. Combine the following pairs of sentences by changing one of the sentences to a *that* clause.
   a. Jim had to turn back and watch the ship. The ship was moving slowly out of the harbor, his wife still standing on the deck, waving.
   b. Janis raised the camera to her eye to focus the lens on the cathedral. She had borrowed it from her uncle.
   c. The physician discussed the patient's ailment. His explanation was in confusing and technical language.
4. Combine the following pairs of sentences by changing one of the sentences to a *whom* clause.
   a. Dennis read a poem at our wedding. We dearly miss him.
   b. The caller left a threatening message on the machine. Jackie hated him.
   c. We will meet a man at the box office. He will have our tickets.
5. Combine the following pairs of sentences by changing one of the sentences to a *whose* clause:
   a. Desiree left a message for the treasurer. His car's headlights were on.
   b. Henri Matisse was perhaps the most important French painter of the twentieth century. His works featured expressiveness of color.
   c. Sally Ride was the first American female astronaut. Her home is in Encino, California.

*Combining with Subordinating Conjunctions.* Sometimes you can improve your sentences by combining them through the use of *subordinating conjunctions*. Here are some of the most common: *after, although, as, as soon as, because, before, if, since, unless, until, while,* and *when*. This is not a complete list, but it suggests the kinds of words you can put before short sentences to combine them with other sentences, thereby creating longer, smoother sentences.

Notice how each of the following pairs of sentences is combined into a smoother sentence by the use of a subordinating conjunction.

| | |
|---|---|
| *Simple sentences:* | Hurricane Andrew approached the Atlantic coast. The Red Cross was already mobilizing their people. |
| *Combined* | As Hurricane Andrew approached the Atlantic coast, |

| | |
|---|---|
| *using* as: | the Red Cross was already mobilizing their people. |
| *Simple sentences:* | Change your oil every 3000 miles. Your car's engine will last longer. |
| *Combined using* if: | If you change your oil every 3000 miles, your car's engine will last longer. |
| *Simple sentences:* | The Israelis still control most of the occupied territories. The Palestinians have limited self-rule in Jericho and Gaza. |
| *Combined using although:* | Although the Palestinians have limited self-rule in Jericho and Gaza, the Israelis still control most of the occupied territories. |
| *Simple sentences:* | The National League broke the American League's string of six consecutive wins in the All-Star game. Tony Gwynn scored the winning run in the tenth inning. |
| *Combined using* when: | When Tony Gwynn scored the winning run in the tenth inning, the National League broke the American League's string of six consecutive wins in the All-Star game. |
| *Simple sentences:* | The plane was forced to make an emergency landing in a corn field. Three of its engines had shut down. |
| *Combined using* because: | Because three of its engines had shut down, the plane was forced to make an emergency landing in a corn field. |
| *Simple sentences:* | Richard Nixon resigned from office in disgrace in 1974. He rehabilitated his image by writing several books, giving speeches, and advising other presidents on foreign policy. |
| *Combined using* after: | After Richard Nixon resigned from office in disgrace in 1974, he rehabilitated his image by writing several books, giving speeches, and advising other presidents on foreign policy. |

Each of the introductory clauses in the above sentences was followed by a comma. Introductory words, phrases, or clauses should be separated from the main (independent) clause by a comma in order to make the sentence easier to read and to prevent misreading. Consider the possible confusion in the following sentence: *After we had eaten the dog was fed.* When a comma is inserted after the introductory clause, the sentence is easier to read: *After we had eaten, the dog was fed.*

Combine each of the following pairs of sentences by using one of the following subordinating conjunctions: *after, although, as, as soon as, because, before, if, since, unless, until, while,* and *when.*

1. The drought had gone on for six years. Golf courses and business parks with large stretches of lawn continued to be built.
2. Beth completed her program in CPR. She was ready to help anyone with breathing trouble or a heart attack.
3. Harry Truman was expected to lose the election in 1948. He won.
4. My first attempt at a model aircraft was a disaster. The wings were out of line and I got glue all over the pilot's windshield.
5. Virtual reality seems to be taking the place of real reality. Appearances seem to matter more than substance.
6. The power in the house went out. An accident down the street had knocked out a transformer.
7. Marsha appeared on stage. I had wondered if she would ever conquer her fear of singing in public.
8. The firefighters heard about the blaze in the downtown hotel from a man in a car. They took off immediately without waiting for a phone call.
9. The writer James Thurber revised his short stories many times. He was never satisfied with the first draft.
10. The idea of Atlantis has fascinated mankind. Plato first wrote about it in 335 B.C.

---

*Using Phrases to Combine Sentences.* The third way to combine your sentences is to reduce or condense a simple sentence into a phrase and combine it with another simple sentence. The most commonly used phrases are *appositives, participial phrases, prepositional phrases, infinitives,* and *gerunds.* An *appositive* is a noun phrase that is set beside another noun and identifies or explains it. When two related sentences describe or identify the same subject, one of the sentences can usually be made into an appositive.

| | |
|---|---|
| *Simple sentences:* | Greg Norman is one of the world's best golfers. He is also known as "The Shark." |
| *Combined using appositive:* | Greg Norman, one of the world's best golfers, is known as "The Shark." |

Two sentences can sometimes be combined by changing one of them into an adjective phrase by using an *-ing* or *-ed* word, or *participial phrase.*

| | |
|---|---|
| *Simple sentences:* | Robert E. Lee led his troops into battle at Gettysburg. He was trying to break the fighting spirit of the North. |
| *Combined using -ing:* | Trying to break the fighting spirit of the North, Robert E. Lee led his troops into battle at Gettysburg. |
| *Simple* | Habitual offenders are now faced the possibility of |

*sentences:* lifetime sentences. Perhaps they will mend their ways.
*Combined* Faced with the possibility of lifetime sentences, per-
*using -ed:* haps habitual offenders will change their ways.

You can sometimes combine choppy sentences by using a *prepositional phrase.*

*Simple* The children looked for Easter eggs under the sofa.
*sentences:* They looked on top of the book case. They looked inside the TV cabinet.
*Combined using*
*a prepositional* The children looked for Easter eggs under the sofa, on
*phrase:* top of the book case, and inside the TV cabinet

By changing one of the verbs to the *infinitive* (the "to" form of the verb), you can often combine shorter sentences.

*Simple* Home buyers want all aspects of a property inspected.
*sentences:* They may hire a private inspector.
*Combined using* To inspect all aspects of a property, home buyers may
*the infinitive:* hire a private inspector.

Verbs ending in *-ing* are called *gerunds.* You can often combine sentences by adding *-ing* to a verb so that it can function as a noun.

*Simple* Monique worked the pottery wheel with her feet. Her
*sentences:* hands moistened the clay. She started to shape a bowl.
*Combined using* Working the pottery wheel with her feet and moisten-
*a gerund:* ing the clay with her hands, Monique started to shape
a bowl.

## E X E R C I S E 16

Combine or rearrange each of the following groups of sentences into a single, smoother sentence by condensing one of the sentences into a phrase.

1. Chicago is known as the Windy City. Chicago can have particularly rough weather despite the mitigating presence of Lake Michigan.
2. The pilot called in to the control tower for clearance to land. The pilot was trying to make an emergency landing.
3. Bastille Day is celebrated on July 14. It commemorates the storming of the Bastille prison at the start of the French Revolution.
4. Our golf clubs are in bags. The bags are at the side of the garage. The bags are underneath the rafters.

5. The politician did not speak without notes. She wanted to avoid errors.

6. Enrico Caruso made millions of dollars in the early part of this century. He was one of the greatest tenors ever.

7. During the track and field season, Travis felt the pressure of being a student-athlete. He tried to train hard enough to compete and study enough to get good grades for medical school.

8. Jay needs to lose some weight. He needs to improve his image in front of the camera.

9. The elderly lady was fascinated by the car's capabilities. She asked the salesperson numerous questions about acceleration, the turning radius, and maximum speed.

10. The class was outraged. They were upset. They refused to believe that their class had been cancelled.

11. I tried to find Grandma's ceramic water pitcher under the sink. I looked on top of the refrigerator. I looked inside the cabinets.

12. Alfred Nobel was the Swedish inventor of dynamite. He established the Nobel Prizes with a bequest of nine million dollars.

13. The first recipient of an "Oscar" for acting was Janet Gaynor. She was only twenty-one when she received the trophy.

14. New Orleans is an exciting city. It has many beautiful neighborhoods and also has many tourist attractions.

15. The advertisement featured fresh peaches and plums. The advertisement caught my eye.

---

## Evaluating Your Sentence Combinations

By this time you have discovered and practiced many techniques for combining sentences. You have probably also noticed that there are several ways to combine even the simplest set of sentences. Perhaps you are wondering whether there is a "right" way to combine each particular set of sentences. And maybe you are wondering whether longer sentences are always better than shorter sentences. This is a good time to consider these questions.

No particular method of sentence combining is better than the others. In particular situations, however, some sentence combinations are, in fact, better than others. The most effective sentences are those that are the most direct in meaning, the smoothest in rhythm, and the most appropriate in emphasis. No sentence can be effective if its meaning is not clear, if more than one meaning can be construed from it, or if it is difficult to understand. The first requirement, then, is clarity of meaning. But a sentence should not only clearly convey an idea. It should also please the reader by its rhythm, its balanced parts, and the arrangement of its ideas. Finally, an effective sentence directs the reader's attention to the point that the writer wants to emphasize, rather than to an irrelevant or trivial detail.

Is a longer sentence always better than a short one? It depends. It depends on the purpose of the sentence, its location in the paragraph, and its relation to other sentences in the paragraph. In the section on sentence length you saw that a short sentence can be more effective than a longer one, for example, because it can abruptly interrupt the flow of a paragraph and force the reader to stop and consider a particular point. On the other hand, you should remember that the sentences of professional writers are, in general, longer than those of beginning writers. Only by experimenting with the vast number of sentence-combining strategies available and by trying them out in your own writing will you become confident at selecting the most appropriate sentences to fit the situation.

## E X E R C I S E 17

Read the lists of sentences that follow. For each group of sentences, determine what the central idea or topic sentence of the paragraph is. Then combine the sentences in the most appropriate order, using the sentence-combining techniques you think are most effective for developing the topic.

1. Brazil won the 1994 World Cup.
   It became the first country to win four World Cups.
   Its team was led by the great duo of Bebeto and Romario.
   The World Cup was held in the United States in 1994.
   The World Cup is held every four years.
   The team Brazil defeated was Italy.
   Italy has won three World Cups.
   The final game ended 0–0.
   The teams played 30 minutes of scoreless overtime.
   Penalty kicks after the overtime period decided the winner.
2. Beatrix Potter was an heir to a cotton fortune.
   Her childhood was lonely and dull.
   She developed a great love of animals.
   She painted watercolors of animals.
   She made up stories with these animals to send to a sick child.
   The stories proved to be well received.
   Her stories were published.
   Her stories were translated into French, Spanish, and Welsh.
   She created such characters as Peter Rabbit, Jeremy Fisher, Jemima Puddle-Duck and Mrs. Tiggy-Winkle.
   She died in 1943.
   Her stories are still popular today.

3. The Seven Wonders of the ancient world were designated by Alexander the Great.
   He was a military strategist.
   He came to the Macedonian throne in 336 B.C.
   From age 13 to 16, he was taught by the philosopher Aristotle.
   The Seven Wonders were a way of emphasizing the extent and glory of his empire.
   His greatest military victory was storming the city of Tyre in 332 B.C.
   He subdued Egypt and occupied Babylon after his victory in Tyre.
   He invaded India in 326 B.C.
   He consolidated his empire.
   He died ten days after being taken ill, in 332 B.C.
   He became ill after a prolonged banquet and drinking bout.

## E X E R C I S E 18

Rewrite the following paragraphs so that their sentences are smoother and the relationship between their ideas is clearer. Use the sentence-combining techniques that seem most appropriate.

1. Kurt tried to relax. He was standing offstage. His entrance was about to come. He felt like he was sweating. The water drops seemed to slide slowly down his cheeks, ruining his stage makeup. He asked one of the stage crew if his makeup was fine. She grunted. He took that for a "yes." He kept thinking of his line. He repeated it over in his head. He wondered where his parents were in the audience. He knew his friends were in the audience. He stepped quietly to the back of the set's doorway. He heard his cue. He opened the door. He was blinded by the stage lights. He looked to the actress on his left. She was holding an unlit cigarette. "Phone call for Mrs. Morris," he said.

2. *Aladdin* is a big moneymaker. It is one of the biggest money-makers of all time. *Aladdin* is a tale for young children. Many have seen the movie several times. The story is a typical story of frustrated romance. The romance is between a young man who lives by his wits on the streets and a beautiful princess who has everything except freedom. The songs are wonderful. The animation is stunning. Most people love the movie because of the character of the genie. Popular actor Robin Williams is the voice of the genie. The genie captures the best of Williams' qualities of imitation and improvisation. Virtually every moment the genie is on screen, he is doing something interesting. He steals the show. The plot of this boy-meets-girl tale is predictable. The genie's antics are not.

# COMPUTER EXERCISE

Rewrite the simple sentences in Exercise 17. Try combining them in several different ways. Your computer's copy function will aid in this. You should see that there is not just one way to write a passage. Each decision you make to combine or not to combine groups of words affects the meaning and nuance of the final product.

You can then share these results with other members of your class or your instructor using a broadcast function or an overhead projection system.

# 9

## *Using the Right Word*

Choosing the right words to express ideas is a troublesome task for all writers and speakers. Part of the problem stems from the vast array of available words. The English language includes over a half-million words, and thousands of new ones are added every year. Of course, no one can master more than a small portion of the English vocabulary. But by reading widely, being curious about words, and carefully choosing the words that we use, we can communicate our ideas precisely and effectively.

What are the right words? They are the ones that keep the reader's interest; the wrong words distract or confuse. The right words are exact, fresh, vivid, and appropriate to the situation and audience. The wrong words are vague, inaccurate, stale, insincere, and inappropriate.

In this chapter we will look at some of the problems writers face when searching for the rights words and consider some of the ways to find them. In addition to this chapter, you should consult *Appendix A: A Glossary of Usage* at the back of this book and a good college-level dictionary for advice on word choice.

## Abstract Words and Concrete Words

Much weak writing is caused by the overuse of abstract words when concrete words would be more appropriate. Abstract words refer to concepts and ideas. *Education, tool,* and *transportation,* for example, are abstract terms. Concrete words name observable things or properties: *lecture hall, screwdriver,* and *1989 Honda* are concrete terms. Some words, of course, are relatively more or less specific than others. *Dog* is more specific than *animal,* but more abstract than *Jim's French poodle.*

The specificity of your word choice—how general or specific you need to be—depends on the audience and the subject. When discussing complex ideas in philosophy or political science with an audience that routinely uses them, abstract words are appropriate. But to support or explain a generalization and to give your reader a precise idea of what you have in mind, you should use specific, concrete words. Compare the following:

| Abstract | Concrete |
|---|---|
| The chef impressed her audience with her cooking expertise. | Julia Child showed how to make a simple but tasty Vichyssoise using homegrown leeks and potatoes, and combining them with cream and chicken stock. |
| Measures to protect our microchip industry from foreign competition are needed. | Congress should pass laws that place quotas and levy excise taxes on imported microchips whose sales are hurting American microchips. |

Readers of the revised versions of these abstract sentences would have a good idea of Julia Child's cooking lesson and the steps necessary to protect our microchip industry. Even single words can be made more specific, as the two lists below make clear. Notice the difference in meaning between the words in the left column and those in the right column.

| **Abstract** | **Concrete** |
| --- | --- |
| poet | Maya Angelou |
| success | getting admitted to graduate school |
| rock band | Pearl Jam |
| model | Cindy Crawford |

As you revise your writing, examine carefully the words that are abstract and general, asking yourself whether you can find more specific and exact words to use. By doing this you will help your readers visualize your ideas more clearly.

## E X E R C I S E 1

Make a list of more specific words for each of the following general terms. For example, for *walk*, you could list *strut, wiggle, trudge, slouch, slink, bounce, crawl, saunter*, and so on. Use your dictionary or thesaurus if necessary.

| | |
| --- | --- |
| fine | sweet |
| hot | bad |
| food | talk |

Writing that is full of vague or general expressions is useless. It leaves too many unanswered questions in the reader's mind. Consider the following sentence:

Hope's desk is a real sight.

Were you able to see or imagine Hope's desk? What is "a real sight"? Here is a more concrete vision:

Hope's desk looks like the city dump.

This sentence is focused more sharply, but it can be improved by adding specific details:

Hope's desk is a jumble of old magazines, soda bottles, makeup, old love letters, and the remnants of several pizzas.

Now we have a better chance of imagining Hope's desk. The word choice is more exact, and we don't have to rely totally on our imaginations.

Consider the following pair of sentences. Notice how the first sentence has been improved by the use of specific words and details.

> *Vague:* He wished for many new things to happen in his new country.
>
> *Specific:* Now that he was in the United States, he wished that he would have the opportunity to work hard and be paid a fair wage; that his children would have the chance to grow up in peace and not experience war; and that they would go to school, attend college and make better lives for themselves than they ever could have in Vietnam.

## E X E R C I S E 2

Rewrite the following sentences, adding specific details and substituting exact words for any that are too vague.

1. The game was very exciting.
2. Mr. Simmons did not like to do certain chores inside the house.
3. Julie was stunning in her new outfit.
4. The director pioneered some unusual techniques in filmmaking.
5. After checking the house, Mrs. Cobble decided that everything was fine.
6. The reviewer wrote bad comments about the new shop's controversial subject matter.
7. The car did not seem to be operating properly.
8. The physical therapist told the professional athlete to do certain exercises to help her recover from her injury.
9. Roberta's trip to Chicago was memorable for its many interesting events.
10. Several aspects of the president's tax program were regarded as inequitable by the opposition.

## Denotation and Connotation

To use the right word, you must be aware of denotation and connotation. The *denotation* of a word is its dictionary meaning—the literal meaning that most readers would agree on. According to *The Random House Dictionary*, a "home" is "a house, apartment, or other place of residence." But "home" has other meanings, as well. Those meanings or associations are a word's *connotation*: what it suggests or implies in the reader's mind. "Home," for instance, may suggest childhood, family memories, a sense of belonging, and other comforting thoughts.

The meaning of a word is affected by its connotations and by its context—the way it is used in a particular passage. Consider, for instance, the following: *teacher, educator, professor, pundit*. They all mean essentially the same thing, but each word has a special connotation and therefore a different meaning:

*teacher*—This is a general word that can be applied to virtually all levels of schooling.

*educator*—The connotation is more formal and may include school administrators as well as teachers.

*professor*—This word is applied to college and university faculty of the highest rank and implies someone with great expertise in his or her field.

*pundit*—This refers to a learned teacher but carries a derogatory connotation of someone who gives opinions in an authoritative or critical manner.

To speak of your instructors as "professors," therefore, would be to suggest that they are acknowledged experts; "pundits," on the other hand, would imply that they simply offer a lot of unsubstantiated opinion in class.

Another series of examples will help to clarify the meaning and importance of knowing the connotation of a word. A "clunker" and a "hot rod" denote the same thing: automobile. But "clunker" suggests an older car badly in need of repair, while "hot rod" evokes a picture of a "souped up" or modified car that has been maintained by its youthful owner. Similarly, "children" and "offspring" have essentially the same denotation, but differ in their connotations. "Children" is more personal, and perhaps suggests more affection; "offspring" is neutral and carries a biological nuance.

To make matters more confusing, words can be correct in one situation but inappropriate in another. A well-known sequence of sentences makes this point clear:

I am determined.
You are stubborn.
He is pig-headed.

Each means essentially the same thing, but most of us would probably prefer to be known as "determined" rather than "stubborn" or "pig-headed."

As the preceding examples demonstrate, words sharing the same denotation can have distinct connotations. Unfortunately, the dictionary doesn't furnish the connotations of most words; you have to learn them by paying attention to the way they are used in conversations and in writing. Because the connotations of words can create unintended impressions, be sure that those secondary meanings fulfill your purposes.

## E X E R C I S E 3

Explain the difference in meaning in the following pairs of sentences.

1. The McLaughlins like to throw a big party on St. Patrick's Day.
   The McLauglins like to have a bacchanal on St. Patrick's Day.

2. The baseball team owner was well-known for being frugal.
   The baseball team owner was well-known for being cheap.

3. The senator was regarded as an excellent public speaker.
   The senator was regarded as a big talker.

4. The widow's behavior at the funeral was mournful.
   The widow's behavior at the funeral was lugubrious.

5. Janelle's boyfriend thought that her new diet made her gaunt.
   Janelle's boyfriend thought that her new diet made her svelte.

## E X E R C I S E 4

Find the inappropriate word in each of the following sentences and replace it with a word with the right denotation.

1. The behavior of animals in nature is completely immoral.
2. At the end of the period, the students were banished from the classroom.
3. The weatherman prophesied low clouds with afternoon sunshine for the next few days.
4. This restaurant is infamous for its tasty food, prompt service, and reasonable prices.
5. Mother Theresa is notorious for her work with the poor and the sick in India.

# E X E R C I S E 5

Each of the words below has a standard denotation as well as a common connotation. Using your dictionary when necessary, explain the denotation and connotation of each.

| | |
|---|---|
| twisted | baby |
| excuse | chauvinism |
| girl | blue |
| rendezvous | stiff |
| gay | cold |

## Sexist Language

In recent years, people's awareness of how sexism has permeated the language that we use has increased. To combat blatant sexism, many writers try to find gender-neutral terms whenever possible. Some substitutions have been relatively painless, such as "journalist" or "reporter" for "newspaperman," "firefighter" for "fireman," "police officer" for "policeman." Other substitutions have been more awkward, such as "freshperson" and have not achieved full acceptance. Nevertheless, you should make a conscious attempt to avoid language that only refers to the male gender and find gender-neutral substitutes.

There are several ways to avoid sexist language when using pronouns. One easy fix is to use the plural form of words, so that a sentence that reads "A student at Central College must find his own housing" can be changed to "Students at Central College must find their own housing." This fix avoids the awkwardness of "he/she" or "his or her" constructions. Such constructions are occasionally unavoidable, but if used excessively they can make your writing cumbersome. Alternatively, many professional writers use female gender pronouns throughout an essay or chapter.

Avoid stereotypical expressions or derogatory terms. Using "girls" or other slang expressions to refer to women is offensive to many people of both genders and should be avoided completely. Sensitivity to the issue of gender discrimination, as with the issue of racial discrimination, is the key to keeping your writing free of offensive language.

## Clichés

Good writing uses lively and original words and phrases. It avoids *clichés*—worn out, tired expressions that have lost their impact through overuse.

The first person who wrote or said "This is a tempest in a teapot" or "That's water under the bridge" was using his or her imagination. But having been repeated millions of times, both expressions have lost their original punch and now suggest only that their users are too lazy to find fresh ways to express their thoughts.

See if you recognize any of your favorites in this list of clichés.

acid test
a crying shame
after all is said and done
all work and no play
as luck would have it
at a loss for words
a barrel of laughs
beating around the bush
better late than never
the bitter end
blushing bride
bored to death
the bottom line
in broad daylight
burn the midnight oil
busy as a bee
by leaps and bounds
by the seat of your pants
cold as ice
cool as a cucumber
at the crack of dawn
dog-eat-dog world
doing your own thing
down and out
easier said than done
fit to be tied
for better or worse
ghost of a chance
green with envy
hard as a rock
heartfelt thanks
heaven-sent
high as a kite
in all its glory
in this day and age
last but not least
light as a feather
the long and short of it
middle of the road
mother nature

neat as a pin
needless to say
not a prayer
in the nick of time
in a nut shell
on the ball
one in a million
out of sight
pave the way
picture of health
point with pride
the powers that be
pretty as a picture
pride and joy
quick as a flash
raining cats and dogs
rat race
ripe old age
sadder but wiser
sharp as a tack
short and sweet
six of one, half a dozen of the
    other
slept like a log
slow but sure
tell it like it is
tried and true
under the weather
uphill battle
view with alarm
water over the dam
water under the bridge
wend our way
where it's at
white as snow
without further ado
work like a horse
worth its weight in gold
young in spirit

As you can see, clichés are everywhere—we are all guilty of using them. You cannot purge them completely from all speech or writing, but you can reduce your reliance on them. First, be suspicious of phrases that come to mind too quickly—expressions such as "straight from the shoulder," "beat a hasty retreat," and so on. Second, search for original phrases and words to express *your* ideas instead of relying on those that were coined years ago. By becoming aware of clichés and how easy it is to use them, you can reduce your reliance on them.

## E X E R C I S E    6

Rewrite each of the following sentences, using specific and fresh language to replace any clichés.

1. Barbara said it was just a case of rotten apples because Karen turns into a pumpkin at midnight.
2. If you buy that cheap table set, you're being penny-wise but pound foolish.
3. The undervalued stock is just sitting out there for the picking.
4. Jeff arrived at the dance already three sheets to the wind.
5. When his girlfriend gave him his walking papers, Joshua said she had a heart of stone.
6. The clerk acted as dumb as a stump when I asked to see the sale items.
7. Rod informed the IRS that they cannot get blood from a turnip.
8. The pay she receives is a mere drop in the bucket.
9. After his date with Helen, he avoided her like the plague.
10. He boasted that he tells it like it is without beating around the bush.

## Euphemisms and Pretentious Writing

One of the deadly enemies of clear writing is insincerity and phoniness. Euphemisms and pretentious word choice contribute to these vices. A *euphemism* is a word or expression used to avoid a word with unpleasant or painful associations. Some euphemisms are acceptable; just think what "to make love" or "to go to the bathroom" spares us. But euphemisms can be used to mislead or to magnify. Thus, janitors are sometimes called "sanitary engineers" and used-car salesmen become "transportation counselors."

Pretentious writing makes something trivial or plain seem very important or complicated. The result is often a series of hollow words or sentences that disguise commonplace ideas. Here is a typical example of pretentious writing, by Talcott Parsons, a famous American sociologist:

> The problem of order, and thus of the nature of the integration of stable systems of social interaction, that is, of social structure, thus focuses on the integration of the motivation of actors with the normative cultural standards which integrate the action system, in our context interpersonally. These standards are, in the terms used in the preceding chapter, patterns of value-orientation, and as such are a particularly crucial part of the cultural tradition of the social system.

This passage is pretentious because it disguises a somewhat obvious idea. Parsons is attempting to say that people who share standards expect one another to stick to them; to the extent they do, their society will be orderly.

But scholars are not the only one who abuse the English language; politicians and other public figures have contributed shameful examples in recent years. The National Aeronautics and Space Administration's press releases referred to the tragedy of the shuttle *Challenger* as "an anomaly" and the astronauts' coffins as "crew transfer containers." During the Iran-Contra hearings, Lieutenant Col. Oliver North contended that the purpose of the committee's investigation was "to criminalize policy differences between co-equal branches of government." A savings bank facing bankruptcy was described as having a "substantial negative net worth," and another company referred to demotions of its employees as "negative advancement."

The problem with euphemisms and pretentious writing is that they mislead the reader by masking the writer's real meaning and intention. Euphemisms and pretentious writing are used in advertising, bureaucratic publications, and statements by politicians when the writer or speaker wants to gloss over an unpleasant truth or magnify something unimportant. As in the case of clichés, everyone occasionally uses them because of their availability.

The following list contains some examples of euphemisms and pretentious phrases. The meaning of each term follows in parentheses. See if you can add examples to the list.

adult entertainment (dirty movies)
orderly withdrawal (retreat)
facial blemishes (pimples)
the disadvantaged (the poor)
custodian (janitor)
viable alternative (choice)
modification (change)
dentures (false teeth)
correctional officer (prison guard)

prioritize (arrange)
reprioritize (rearrange)
sanitation engineer (garbage collector)
domestic (maid or butler)
passed on, laid to rest, met his or her Maker (died)
detention center (jail)
culturally deprived environment (slum)
members of a career offender cartel (gangsters)
counterfactual propositions (lies)
misspeak (lie)
fair trade (price fixing)
economy car (small car)
bathroom tissue (toilet paper)
to suffer irregularity (to be constipated)
radiation enhancement device (neutron bomb)
preowned (used)
pacification of the enemy infrastructure (attacking an enemy
    village)
a combat emplacement evacuator (shovel)
aerodynamic personnel decelerator (parachute)
antipersonnel detonating devices (bombs)
revenue enhancement (a tax increase)
engage in the decision-making process (decide)
parameters (limits)
interface (meet)
at this point in time (now)

## E X E R C I S E 7

Here are some sentences containing euphemisms and pretentious
writing. Reward them, using direct and clear language.

1. "We believe it is in the interest of international stability and
   the American people to avoid the tendency that we have experienced on occasions in the past to rush to summitry for summitry's sake and to bring about euphoric expectations and
   then to dash that euphoria against the rocks of ill-prepared
   summitry." (*From a statement by former Secretary of State
   Alexander Haig*)
2. "To draw a link from cost-effectiveness studies to realized human potential is a payoff for internal business management
   just as important as the impact such cost savings studies and
   their results have on the taxpaying clientele of the District. The
   single endeavor, in this case a cost-effectiveness improvement

project, realizes both an internal necessity for responsible management viz-à-viz evaluation and an external necessity for accountability." (*From a letter written by a school administrator*)

3.  "Stamps in this book have been gummed with a matte finish adhesive which permits the elimination of the separation tissues." (*From a publication of the U.S. Postal Service*)

4.  "The findings of ongoing research have shown that a number of physiological effects occur under conditions of noise exposure. These studies demonstrate that noise exposure does influence bodily changes, such as the so-called vegetative functions, by inhibition of gastric juices, lowered skin resistance, modified pulse rate and increased metabolism." (*From a document published by the Federal Aviation Administration*)

5.  "We were not micromanaging Grenada intelligencewise until about that time frame." (*From a statement by Admiral Wesley L. McDonald, United States Navy*)

## Levels of Usage

As noted in Chapter 2, we have different "voices," which can range from the intimate and slangy to the highly impersonal and formal. Your word choice should reflect the voice you have chosen for a particular writing situation, just as your choice of clothing suggests the way you want to be viewed in a particular social situation. The dictionary can suggest the status or level of many words, but in most cases, you will have to decide on the correct word.

Your attitude toward your audience and your subject will also determine the level of your diction or word choice. If you have ever told a traffic judge how you were driving and then retold the story to your friends, you already understand the importance of the audience, the situation, and the subject in your selection of words.

When writing or speaking to your superiors or to public figures or in formal situations, a formal tone and diction is appropriate. However, in essays and other college writing, an informal level of diction is best. When talking to close friends in informal social situations, a mixture of informal diction and slang can be suitable. The following sequence, which ranges from the most formal to the most informal, illustrates the range of options available to you and suggests how an idea can be modified according to the audience and situation.

The occasion was most delightful.
The evening was enjoyable.
We had a good time.
We had a fantastic time!
We had a ball!

## Slang

Everybody uses slang. It adds a dash of humor and "hipness" to speech and gives its user a chance to be different. Slang is also a symbol of being a member of an "in group." But there are two problems with slang. First, it usually doesn't last long, becoming outdated within a few weeks or months. Words such as *chick* and *heavy*, for example, were once popular but now seem headed for oblivion. The other problem with slang is that it quickly loses any precise meaning. Ask several friends what "bad" or "cool" means *exactly*, and you will see that slang terms are usually vague and general. For these reasons it is best to limit slang to informal conversation and to avoid it in serious writing.

When you forget or ignore the audience or situation, you can make inappropriate word choices. Notice how jarring the conclusion of the following sentence sounds because the writer used inconsistent diction.

> The trustees of the National Gallery of Art announced reluctantly that electronic-monitoring devices will be installed at all exists of the museum because a painting by the Dutch artist Rembrandt was ripped off.

## Informal English

Informal English is the level of language used in most college writing. It is more casual than Standard English but more precise and formal than slang. It is the language of magazine articles and newspaper and television stories, as well as most classroom lectures. It uses slang to achieve a humorous or ironic tone, but never at the risk of destroying the overall tone of the sentence or passage.

Informal English often uses contractions but avoids an excessively conversational tone. As you can tell, Informal English is hard to define precisely. It uses a variety of expressions and words to achieve its effect. It strives for a middle level of diction, the normal level for most college writing.

## Standard English

At the other end of the spectrum from slang in terms of formality is Standard English. One student described the relationship between Standard English and slang as similar to that of formal tuxedo and blue jeans. Standard English is more dignified and serious; it avoids slang and uses contractions (*it's, doesn't* and so on) sparingly. This does not mean that Standard English is stiff, wooden, or pretentious. It *does* mean that it is used on those occasions when precision, accuracy, and a formal tone are required. Although it doesn't have to use long words,

Standard English uses more words of Greek and Latin origin than slang or Informal English does.

As in the case of slang, Standard English can sound ridiculous when it is inappropriate for the situation or audience. Notice, for example, how pompous the following excerpt sounds:

> Summoning his courage and clearing his throat, Ralph said nervously, "Gee, Wanda, I'd sure like to osculate you. If that offends you, I'd settle for some interdigitation."

If you were Wanda, how would you respond?

The following pairs of words suggest the difference between Standard and Informal English.

| Standard | Informal |
|----------|----------|
| prevaricate | lie |
| instruct | teach |
| consume | use |
| locate | find |
| range | stove |
| nude | naked |

## E X E R C I S E 8

Read the following three paragraphs carefully. Which one is written in slang, which in Informal English, and which in Standard English? Notice the differences in word choice, particularly in the use of personal pronouns, contractions, passive voice, and level of diction. Which one is more specific? Which one is easier to read? What would be the proper situation for each paragraph? For example, would the first one be suitable for reading to a convention of psychiatrists?

1. Flying scares the heck out of me. You're up there, spam in a can, just waiting to drop. How can they keep a big hunk of metal up in the air? It makes no sense to me. The bigger they are, the harder they fall. Falling from six miles up would be a hard fall—you'd be as flat as a pancake. Honestly, dude, I've got to admit, if I have to fly, I'll do it because I don't want nobody seeing what a chicken I am about it. I just hope to God those fly boys in the cockpit know what they're doing, and that the beast they stick us in won't just fall apart. Then I look for the stewardess to bring me drinks, fast.

2. Man's ability to fly in airplanes still astonishes me. That these machines of steel and aluminum, weighing tons, can somehow manage to become airborne is fundamentally a matter of

physics and engineering, this my brain knows and accepts. However, the fear in my body does not and cannot accept this knowledge. My body responds to a simpler, more primal understanding: that which goes up must come down. However, my fear of public humiliation is greater than my fear of dying in a fiery crash since I do fly when I must. I simply take my seat, strap on the seat belt, say a prayer, and try to convince myself that the pilot is well trained, the plane is in excellent condition, and that the flight attendants have plenty of beer on board.

3. The principles of aerodynamics are constant, but human-kind's understanding of these principles is changing. Contemporary commercial aircraft have been designed to maximize the understanding based on experience of said principles, including such principles as the circulation theory of lift of an airfoil of infinite span and the vortex theory of lift of a wing of finite span. The application of such theories allows the passenger a reasonable probability of safely concluding any given flight. Hesitancy based on unpredictable variables may inhibit confidence in safety, but the social ramifications of a refusal to participate in all transportation by air would be severe. The passenger on a commercial flight should be advised that all personnel are properly trained, vehicles are maintained at peak safety and efficiency standards, and that the imbibing of alcoholic beverages is permitted by passengers of legal age.

## E X E R C I S E 9

Using your dictionary if necessary, arrange the expressions in each of the following groups in order from the most informal to the most formal.

1. clean; immaculate; spick-and-span
2. nuptials; tying the knot; wedding
3. domestic; servant; maid
4. cop; peace officer; patrolman
5. woman; chick; lady
6. smart; erudite; sharp
7. father; dad; sire
8. affluent; rich; loaded
9. drunk; inebriated; loaded
10. pooped; exhausted; tired

## E X E R C I S E     10

Rewrite the following sentences, replacing any words that are not appropriate.

1. At the graduation ceremonies, the valedictorian's speech to her fellow students, their parents, and the faculty, was totally cool.
2. The city council's decision to allow the last remaining parcels of undeveloped land to be turned over to MegaBucks Company for development into a toxic waste treatment facility is messed up.
3. As Roger and Alicia chatted together in front of the high school gym, Alicia's boyfriend Tony became jaundiced.
4. Prince Charles cannot become the King of England until Queen Elizabeth II kicks the bucket.
5. We rented a summer cottage for the entire family. It was near the lake, clean, inexpensive, and roomy. My husband complained that it was not properly fenestrated, however.

## E X E R C I S E     11

Select one of the situations below and write it in three different versions: first, in slang; next, in Informal English; finally, in Standard English. Write about five or six sentences for each version.

1. a description of meeting a person you are attracted to
2. eating the food in the school cafeteria
3. a visit to an amusement park or zoo
4. how to study in a college environment
5. welcoming remarks to three groups of visitors to your campus: the Governor of your state and his aides; students from another college; a group of jazz musicians

## Using Figures of Speech

In your writing you will occasionally want to compare one thing to another by using a figure of speech. Such a comparison—often between an abstract idea and something concrete—can add clarity and uniqueness to writing when used judiciously.

Two closely related figures of speech are *metaphors* and *similes*. A *metaphor* makes an implied comparison between two things:

Cindy's ornithic singing was perfectly matched to the music. (*Ornithic* means relating to birds; thus, Cindy's singing is compared to that of a bird.)

A *simile* also compares two things, but usually uses *like* or *as:*

Cindy sang like a bird. (Cindy's singing is explicitly compared to that of a bird.)

Figures of speech can enliven writing, but they must be consistent. If the pictures they create are not logical or do not fit, their meaning will be confusing or ridiculous. Consider the following:

We will march down the stream to victory together.

Unless the stream is only a few inches deep, we will need to wear hip boots. Such a figure of speech is called a *mixed metaphor* because its images clash.

## E X E R C I S E   12

Revise the following sentences which contain ineffective figures of speech.

1. He took on a second job to try to get his head above water, but he still seemed to live hand-to-mouth.
2. The economics class was deadly dull and time passed by as slow as molasses until all the students were bored stiff.
3. To today's nuclear physicists, splitting the atom is as simple as child's play, but they still are in the dark about how to fuse atoms.
4. The whale rose out of the water like a volcano erupting out of the ocean, spouting water from its blowhole like a fire hydrant that had been busted off its moorings.
5. Flapping her arms and stampeding down the aisle, Miss Perez circled the room.

## C O M P U T E R   E X E R C I S E

Make a list of slang terms that you are familiar with. Then, *translate* these terms into Informal English, and then into Formal

English. What happens each time? Is slang more general or more specific than other forms of English? How clear would the meaning of your slang expressions be to people unfamiliar with you and your way of expressing things? Is Formal English more comfortable or uncomfortable for you? Do you find that your vocabulary is limited once you try to translate into Formal English?

Share your list with others in the class either by broadcasting or by using an overhead projector. Do any of your classmates use slang expressions that you have never heard or that you don't understand? What does this tell you about the use of slang versus the use of Informal and Formal English?

# *Writing the Persuasive Essay*

We have already discussed expository essays, in which the writer's purpose is to inform the reader. Much college writing, however, requires you to *persuade* your reader to take a specific course of action or to accept a particular point of view. This chapter will consider the problems that are unique to persuasive writing, including its intention, its relationship to the audience, and the special kinds of support or evidence it requires. Despite these differences, you will see that persuasive essays can follow the same patterns that you learned in Chapter 6 ("Drafting the Essay: Six Patterns") for developing expository essays. For example, when writing a persuasive essay you may support your argument by exemplification, by comparison and contrast, or by cause and effect.

In a sense, every essay is persuasive because you are trying to convince your reader that you are trustworthy. But what we call persuasive essays are often based on controversial topics: Should the theory of evolution and the biblical account of creation both be taught in the public schools? Should the death penalty be abolished? Should the military draft be reinstated? Topics such as these often face hostile audiences, and the writer of a persuasive essay has to work hard to win their agreement.

There are two ways to approach a controversial topic. The first is to set out to win at any cost by proving that you are right and your opponent is wrong. Those who write essays this way are not trying to change their readers' minds. All they want to do is score points, and they will generally use any technique to do it: personal attacks and sarcasm, purely emotional appeals, quoting out of context, or evading the issue. This approach succeeds only in antagonizing the critical reader.

The other way to approach a controversial topic is to try to change the reader's mind by playing fair: by looking at the same issue from the reader's point of view, using logical arguments, citing evidence, and being rational. This does not mean that you will not appeal to your reader's emotions. It does mean, however, that you will adopt a reasonable tone and be tactful and honest.

## The Assertion and the Persuasive Essay

As with the expository essay, the first step in writing a persuasive essay is to formulate your assertion in a thesis statement. If the thesis has been supplied by your instructor, your position in the paper has been decided for you. But if you have been given a topic on which to base your assertion, you should first list your ideas on the topic. This stage is similar to prewriting when writing an expository essay. You can explore your own thoughts by freewriting and brainstorming. You can talk to friends about the topic, test your ideas and get others' views.

After surveying the ideas you have developed, you can write your the sis statement or assertion.

Though you may find that your thesis statement will be softened or modified in the finished essay, a working thesis might be bold, as in the following:

> The only thing worse than a lawyer is a lawyer who advertises on television and such advertising should be banned.

The problem with this assertion is that while it may express the writer's feelings, it is far too aggressive to be accepted by an open-minded reader.

By giving more thought to the topic and revising the first thesis, the writer might end up with a more convincing assertion:

> Advertising on television lowers the dignity of all lawyers and should be banned.

This revised assertion is calmer and more likely to encourage the reader to accept it.

The thesis statement in a persuasive essay must not be a statement of fact; it must be an assertion over which people can differ. You could not, for example, write a persuasive essay based on the following thesis: "Wetlands in the United States have decreased in size by five percent in the last ten years." Assuming this is a statement of fact, there is nothing to dispute. But you *can* argue the following assertion: "Wetlands in the United States have decreased in size by five percent in the last ten years due to neglect by the federal government to enforce environmental standards." Such a statement is subject to challenge and could provide the basis of a lively persuasive essay.

After you have written your thesis statement, apply three tests to find out whether you can use it. First, is it a question? If so, reword it, because a question does not contain an assertion. Do not write, "Should leaf blowers be banned in our city?" Instead, write "A ban on leaf blowers should be enacted by our city council."

The second test of your thesis statement: Is it one that everybody would agree with? If so, rule it out. A thesis statement such as "The President has an important job" is so bland that few would disagree. As a result, your paper would never get off the ground. But if you said, "The President's job is actually unimportant since most decisions that truly affect people's lives are made in the business community," you would elicit a response from your readers, and you would spark controversy.

The third test of your thesis statement is the one first mentioned: Does it merely state a fact? If so, it offers nothing to debate, and therefore it is unsuitable as the assertion for a persuasive essay. But if your thesis statement takes sides in a genuine controversy about which people can differ, you are ready for the next step.

## E X E R C I S E 1

Which of the following statements could serve as the thesis for a persuasive essay? Reword any unsuitable statements so that they can serve as acceptable assertions.

1. The technology behind guided missiles, advanced combat aircraft, and other sophisticated weaponry has removed the horror of killing from war.
2. Because of the danger posed by high voltage power lines, homes should be built no closer than one hundred yards from the nearest power lines.
3. The "proof" of the existence of extraterrestrials is unconvincing.
4. Why is it that short people face discrimination?
5. The typical college student today is looking for a vocational education more than a liberal arts education.
6. I prefer fly fishing to deep sea fishing.
7. The insularity of the suburbs gives people a woefully incorrect understanding of the lives of less fortunate people.
8. Statistics show that Asian Americans are one of the fastest growing ethnics groups in the United States.
9. The reunification of Germany has led to new dangers for the rest of Europe.
10. My favorite movie of last year was *Philadelphia*.

## E X E R C I S E 2

Below are some topics that generate controversy. For each, write an arguable assertion that could be developed into a persuasive essay.

1. TV evangelists
2. Drunk drivers
3. Preserving local environments
4. Corruption in college athletics
5. Gun control
6. The fall of the Soviet Union
7. Mental Illness
8. Surrogate mothers

9. The trade deficit
10. A national health insurance plan

---

## COMPUTER EXERCISE

Focus freewrite for five minutes on a topic of your choice or on an assigned topic. Then, perform a loop as described on page 16, and write for five more minutes. Then, write down ten thesis sentences based on the topic. The thesis sentences can be contradictory, but each one should be specific and arguable.

Share your topic sentences with the class using either the broadcast function or an overhead projection system. How many students wrote identical or quite similar thesis statement? Which thesis statements seem commonplace? Which seem original and perceptive?

---

## The Audience for the Persuasive Essay

In Chapter 4 you learned the importance of keeping your audience in mind as you write an expository paper. The audience in that case wanted to learn or to be informed. The audience for a persuasive paper, on the other hand, is more difficult to please: Either they are undecided, or they disagree with your thesis statement. In other words, they are either hesitant or hostile. You can assume that they are interested in the subject. You can also assume that they know some of the arguments on both sides of the issue. If they are neutral, they are waiting for you to convince them that you are right. If they are hostile, they will be looking for weaknesses in your argument. In both cases it is important that you know something about their interests, background, and knowledge of the issues.

Your readers have a right to demand proof and valid reasons for agreeing with you. Your job, therefore, is to convince them by the soundness of your arguments. It is equally important to create an impression that suggests that you understand their point of view, having examined it carefully, and that you respect their beliefs. You will not be able to do this if you adopt a tone that offends them. Above all, you should avoid personally attacking them or sounding condescending. By taking a conciliatory and fair stance, you will invite their respect and encourage them to consider your arguments.

After you identify your audience, you can determine the best approach, the appropriate level of diction, and the most effective kinds of arguments for your paper.

# E X E R C I S E 3

Your audience will affect the kinds of arguments you offer. Consider each of the following situations.

1. Imagine that you have to deliver a speech to a gathering of military leaders in which you defend the abilities of women to participate in combat. Write a list of arguments for such a position.
2. Imagine that you are giving a speech before the National Organization for Women in which you argue that women should be excluded from roles in the military that may put them in combat situations. Write a list of arguments for such a position.
3. What arguments would you give to a meeting of the American Civil Liberties Union to support the rights of states to try children accused of serious crimes as adults?
4. What argument would you present in favor of teaching creationism in public schools to a local board of education?
5. What argument would you present against teaching creationism in public schools to a group of ministers and parents who support the teaching of creationism?

## Supporting Your Assertion

Having settled on your thesis statement (which contains your assertion and identifies your audience) you should now make a list of your supporting arguments as well as those that oppose your assertion. By anticipating the arguments of your opponents, you will convince your readers that you are knowledgeable and fair. More important, you will strengthen your own position by refuting those arguments as you begin to present your own view.

Most effective persuasive essays rely on three kinds of appeals to support their assertions: *rational appeals, ethical appeals,* and *emotional appeals.* The rational appeal is the most important, but the others, when used with discretion, can be very effective.

### Rational Appeals

Mere opinion will not be enough to support an argument or persuade your readers—they demand and deserve *evidence.* Therefore, you will have to offer them proof. *Facts and statistics* are among the most impressive kinds of rational proof and should therefore be used in abundance to support your assertion. They suggest objectivity and finality, and they can often convince a skeptical reader. For example, in a letter to your college newspaper arguing for the construction of additional handball courts, you could strengthen your case by furnishing such facts and statistics as the number of students who use the courts each day, the number who can't get on the crowded courts, the percentage of students by comparison who have no other opportunity to participate in organized physical activity, or the benefits of playing handball. Such evidence would be much more convincing than mere pleading or irate demands.

Or suppose that you believe that our criminal justice system has been too lenient. In your opinion, current sentencing practices have encouraged, rather than discouraged, violent crime. Suppose that you happened to read a magazine article that contained the following facts:

1. In 1955, 46 robberies occurred annually per 100,000 in the population: today the rate is more than 270—a sixfold increase.
2. Rape rates have more than tripled.
3. Murder per capita has more than doubled.
4. The aggravated-assault rate has increased more than sixfold.
5. Overall, taking into account both urban and rural areas, the major-crime rate is more than four times what it was four decades ago.*

Such a parade of facts and statistics, when added to other evidence, would strengthen a controversial thesis statement and help to sway the undecided reader. Keep in mind, however, that although facts are indisputable, they can be subject to contradictory interpretation. When the United States Marines landed on the Caribbean island of Grenada, they found huge warehouses of munitions and a nearly finished landing strip, which the American government cited as evidence that Cuba planned to use the island as a military outpost. Cuba, while not disputing the facts, argued that the munitions belonged to the Grenadan army and that the landing strip was to encourage tourism.

Statistics, like facts, can also be manipulated. Suppose that a wealthy industrialist with an annual income of $1,000,000 a year lives on a street with only one other occupant, an impoverished widow with an annual income of $2,000. The average income on that street is $500,000—at least, mathematically. But such an interpretation of the statistics would create a distorted impression of the facts and the neighborhood. If used fairly, however, facts and statistics can form a sturdy underpinning for your argument.

*Examples* are another effective kind of rational proof. Although by themselves they do not prove the truth of an assertion, their impact and the attention they attract can be convincing. In arguing for government aid to public television broadcasting, for instance, you might give examples of programs such as "Romper Room," "Sesame Street," concerts, documentaries, and plays that are made available to viewers

*Information is from Paul H. Robinson, *Atlantic Monthly*, March 1995, pp. 72–78.

who might not otherwise see them. Such examples would be far more effective than lofty appeals to the citizens' right to the airwaves and the need for an enlightened public.

Examples make the abstract and general more specific, thereby strengthening your argument. Be certain, however, that your examples are typical, not exceptions to the rule. Careful readers will detect examples that are not representative of your assertion.

*Personal experience* that supports your argument can be convincing because it has the qualities of urgency and relevance. Your own experience brings a controversy to the level of the concrete, the specific, and the personal. If you are arguing for bilingual education, for example, your own experience learning English in a bilingual program would be of interest to your reader. Or suppose that you are arguing for mandatory safety inspections for automobiles and buses in your state. Suppose, too, that you describe an accident in your neighborhood in which a school bus careened down a hill out of control because of faulty brakes, resulting in injuries to several students. Evidence based on such firsthand knowledge often has more impact on a reader than any other kind of support.

When offering personal experiences as support for your thesis, be careful to select those that are not merely emotional anecdotes. Personal tales of woe usually offend readers who are looking for solid proof. Also, avoid personal experiences that are too unusual or atypical. A story of how your great-aunt Mildred worked as a surgeon in the 1930s does not prove that discrimination against women did not exist in the past, but rather than some women were able to succeed in spite of such discrimination. Also, telling about mistreatment at the hands of your college's bureaucrats does not by itself prove the general incompetence of the college's staff. Be careful not to make a hasty generalization (see page 225 for an explanation) based on your personal experience.

The *testimony of experts* is another effective way to support your argument. By quoting respected authorities you lend credibility to your assertion. Be sure that your authority is recognized as knowledgeable on your topic. The testimony of your cousin Raul on the advance of African killer bees into this country would not be as impressive as testimony from a biologist or scientist—unless Raul were working for the Department of Agriculture.

### Ethical Appeals

Logic, as powerful as it is, often needs to be supplemented by other kinds of appeals. The *ethical appeal* is based on *you*, the writer. This appeal gets its impact from the impression you create of yourself, the writer of the essay.

You want to be respected and trusted by the audience; you want your readers to feel that you are honest and reliable. There are three ways to accomplish this. The first is to write in a rational and informed style and avoid name-calling, personal attacks, and wild exaggerations. The second is to write straightforward, clear prose that shows you have nothing to conceal. The third is to be in command of your evidence. By quoting authorities, presenting facts, and arguing logically, you will create the impression of a fair and informed writer.

The ultimate effect of the ethical appeal is to say to your reader, "You can believe me. I am a fair, objective, and informed person who has thoroughly investigated this controversy. The assertion that I offer you, therefore, is reliable because I am trustworthy."

### Emotional Appeals

Emotions are never a substitute for logic and solid evidence. But when the facts are not in question, and action is desired, an emotional appeal is appropriate, perhaps indispensable. An emotional appeal can help stir your audience's feelings and predispose them to take a particular course of action. It can take advantage of their sense of dignity or their sense of justice.

Advertisers are well aware of the powerful tug of the emotions on our purse strings. The American flag, laughing children, puppies, vibrant young people, and saintly, elderly faces are commonly used to sell everything from cars to corn flakes. When used to "sell" an idea, however, emotional appeals should be used with caution. Readers are usually quickly to detect appeals that are offering emotions rather than evidence.

In the critical days during the "Battle of Britain" in World War II, Prime Minister Winston Churchill made his great "blood, toil, tears and sweat" speech. He inspired the British people, spurring them to heroic efforts. In more recent years the late Martin Luther King, Jr., used emotional appeals to great effect in many of his speeches and essays in order to persuade Americans to support the civil rights movement.

Not only speeches but individual words or terms can carry emotional appeal. By calling industrialists "rapers of the earth" or environmentalists "barriers to progress," a writer appeals to readers' emotions. You should use such terms with caution; if not chosen carefully, you can make an audience hostile toward your argument. But when used with discretion, the emotional appeal can be an effective method for persuading your reader.

How much support in the form of rational, ethical, and emotional appeals is needed in a persuasive essay? It depends on your topic and your audience. An essay arguing against the increased use of nuclear energy in the United States would require a great deal of complex evidence, including statistics, examples, facts, and testimonials. If such an essay were addressed to an audience of executives of power companies, it would require special tact and delicacy to present the evidence. On the other hand, if the audience were a group of homeowners who live near a nuclear plant and have petitioned for the closing of the plant, the evidence could be presented more forcefully, since the audience would not be hostile.

By presenting rational, accurate proof and by convincing your readers that you are fair and objective, you will encourage them to examine the evidence from your point of view. Then, and only then, can you count on them to support your assertion.

## *Moving from Evidence to Conclusion: Inductive and Deductive Reasoning*

Having offered your evidence, you have laid the groundwork for your conclusions. There are two ways to move from your evidence to your conclusions: *induction* and *deduction*. In *inductive reasoning*, a large number of individual cases or experiences are listed and on the basis of these cases, a probable generalization or *conclusion* is drawn. *Deductive reasoning* works from the opposite direction. It moves from a general premise or generalization (called the *major premise*) and a particular fact or instance (the *minor premise*) to a *conclusion*.

Let's assume you want to buy a new car. As you ponder the decision, you follow a series of steps in reasoning. You talk to friends who have new cars. One complains that her Alpha breaks down often and is usually in the shop for repairs. Another says that the performance of his Beta has been disappointing. Still another says that his Gamma is difficult to shift into gear and has too small a trunk. Then you talk to the instructor of the automotive class at your college who tells you that her students have been working on Delta cars in both day and evening classes, and that she and the students are pleased with them. Your conclusion is that the Delta is the best car. Up to this point your reasoning has been *inductive*: you have made a series of observations about the quality of different cars and you have arrived at a generalization that Delta is the best car. You then make an *inductive leap*: you assume that the generalization arrived at on the basis of your friends' and instructor's experiences applies in your case. Having arrived at your generalization by inductive reasoning, you now use *deductive reasoning*: you move from the generalization to individual cases. You apply a premise (you want to buy the best car) to a generalization (Delta is the best car) and you arrive at a conclusion (you want to buy a Delta).

The following steps illustrate how inductive and deductive reasoning were combined in the example above:

### Inductive Reasoning

You made a *series of observations* about individual cars.
Alpha
Beta
Gamma
Delta
On the basis of these observations you reached *a conclusion* or *generalization*:
"Delta is the best car."

### Deductive Reasoning

You began with *a major premise* based on your generalization:
*Major premise*: "Delta is the best car."
Then you applied a particular case as your *minor premise: Minor premise*: "I want to buy the best car."
You then reached a conclusion:
*Conclusion*: "I want to buy a Delta."

You move constantly from induction to deduction in your daily life. In fact, these reasoning processes are natural ways of thinking as you evaluate evidence and apply generalizations to even the most insignificant situations. But when reasoning about complex issues and when trying to persuade others to accept your views, you use inductive and deductive reasoning more carefully and consciously. In the following pages we will examine both kinds of reasoning and their relationship to persuasive writing.

### *Inductive Reasoning*

Most of what we know has been learned through inductive reasoning. As we saw in the car example, induction moves from individual instances and observations to a generalization or conclusion. Observing sumo wrestlers offers another example. All of the sumo wrestlers that I have seen on television are huge and must weigh at least 300 pounds. All of the sumo wrestlers that my friends have seen in Japan were huge men. And all of the pictures of sumo wrestlers in sports magazines and newspapers that I read are of large men. I therefore conclude that all sumo wrestlers are large men. Of course, I have not seen *all* of the sumo wrestlers in the world, but I base my generalization on a fair sampling.

To reach my generalization I have taken an *inductive leap*, a jump from the evidence (sumo wrestlers that my friends and I have seen or heard about) to a generalization (all sumo wrestlers are large men).

The safest inductive leap—and therefore the most reliable generalization—is based on the largest number of typical examples. If the only wrestling match I ever witnessed features midget wrestlers, and if I concluded that all wrestlers are midgets, I would be guilty of a *hasty generalization* (see pages 225–227 for an explanation of this and other errors in logic).

Most inductive arguments are more complicated than the sumo wrestlers example above. Regardless of their complexity, however, they require you to make connections between particulars or samples in order to come to a generalization about an entire class of particulars or samples.

All inductive arguments must be based on two principles: the generalization must be based on a sufficient number of samples, and the samples must be typical and reliable. In discussions of certain racial groups, religions, or nationalities, we often encounter generalizations that ignore these principles: "Jaycees are corrupt. The treasurer of our chapter was indicted for bribery." "Don't tell me about Episcopalians. We lived next door to an Episcopalian family for two months." "Professor Mobley is a terrible instructor. My friend worked very hard in his chemistry class and received a D." "Teenagers are terrible drivers."

When hearing or reading such generalizations, ask yourself whether there is sufficient evidence to justify such sweeping statements. In your own writing (and in your reading), be wary of words such as *none, all, never,* or *every* when they are applied to generalizations. It is safer (and more likely correct) to substitute such terms as *some, many, often,* or *probably*.

## Inductive Reasoning and the Persuasive Essay

Because the process of inductive reasoning begins with numerous facts, examples, instances, and observations and then leads to a conclusion or generalization, it is often an effective way to organize a persuasive essay. Many readers can be convinced or persuaded if they are first provided the evidence. For instance, if you are arguing against student evaluation of the faculty at your college, you might enlist your readers' support if you show them that students are inconsistent when they evaluate their instructors. Some students want to "get even" because they received an *F*; others rate a teacher highly because he or she gave them an *A* or told jokes; still others judge the instructors on the basis of their dress or accent or ethnic background. After presenting the information you have compiled, you can lead your readers to your concluding generalization: student evaluation is inconsistent and should be abolished. Of course, the more evidence you can present, the more likely it is that your generalization will be sound and will be accepted by your reader. If you were to cite only one student who had evaluated an instructor infairly, your argument would not be convincing. It is not only the number of examples or the amount of evidence that is important; the particulars that you offer to support your generalization must be representative so that your inductive leap is justified.

### *Deductive Reasoning*

The opposite of inductive reasoning is *deductive reasoning*. It is the process of arriving at a conclusion by starting with a generalization or assumption instead of with a specific instance. For example, if you know that all of the theater arts majors at your college are working on a production of *Hello, Dolly!* and that Sandy is a theater arts major at your college, then you may conclude that Sandy is working on *Hello, Dolly!* These three statements comprise a *syllogism,* a three-part argument consisting of a generalization that has been arrived at by deduction (the *major premise*), a specific case of the generalization (the *minor premise*), and a *conclusion.*

> All of the theater arts majors at your college are working on a
>     production of *Hello, Dolly!*
> Sandy is a theater arts major at your college.
> Sandy is working on a production of *Hello, Dolly!*

If both premises in a syllogism are true and if the reasoning process from one part of the syllogism to the other is valid, the conclusion is true. An inductive leap is not necessary, as it is with inductive reasoning, because the conclusion is inescapable. In this syllogism, only one conclusion can be reached. You can't say that Sandy is not working on the production of *Hello, Dolly!* because that contradicts the premises; nor can you say that Sandy is shy, because that goes beyond the premises.

If one of the premises is false, the conclusion will be false, even if the syllogism follows the correct form. Consider the following:

*Major premise:*  All Chinese food uses ginger.
*Minor premise:*  My cousin always cooks with ginger.
*Conclusion:*  My cousin only cooks Chinese food.

But my cousin is not limited to cooking Chinese food. The conclusion is false because the major premise is false: All Chinese food does *not* use ginger. If my cousin made a Chinese dinner one evening, the conclusion would have been reached by chance, not by logic. To repeat, then: a deductive argument can be considered reliable only if the premises are true and if its form is valid.

Most of us do not employ the full-fledged syllogism when we speak. Instead, we usually present our propositions as *enthymemes*, which are compressed syllogisms. Notice the following:

Of course my Volkswagen is well built; it's made by Germans.

If this enthymeme were expanded into a complete syllogism, it would look like this:

*Major premise:*   German cars are well built.
*Minor premise:*   Volkswagens are German cars.
*Conclusion:*   My Volkswagen is well built.

By using an enthymeme, the speaker assumes that his listener or reader accepts the implied premise (in this case, that Germans build good cars).

Using enthymemes can be risky because they ask the listener or reader to follow an argument without seeing all of the premises laid out. For premises that are not controversial ("Honesty is the best policy," "An education is important today"), this is not a problem. But if the premises are controversial, the writer or speaker will have to show their validity before proceeding further. The following sentences illustrate the problem.

His word can't be trusted; he's a politician. [The first statement is the conclusion and the second statement is the minor premise of a syllogism whose major, unstated premise is something like "All politicians are untrustworthy."]

I doubt that Sharon's marriage will last; her parents were divorced. [Like the preceding example, the first statement is the conclusion and the second statement is the minor premise of a syllogism; in this case, the major premise is something like "All children of divorced parents will have marriage problems."]

In both examples the unstated but implied premise is too shaky and controversial to be accepted without evidence. Any paragraph or essay based on such a premise would have to be supported to be convincing.

### *Deductive Reasoning and the Persuasive Essay*

Using the principles of deduction to organize a persuasive essay can be very effective. The conclusion of the syllogism (which is the thesis of the essay) usually appears in the opening paragraph. The subsequent paragraphs support the truth of the conclusion. If the premises are reliable and if the conclusion follows logically from them, such a pattern is convincing.

In actual practice most writers do not base deductive essays on pure syllogisms, particularly when writing on controversial topics. It is difficult to state a meaningful or significant major premise that encompasses "all" or "none" in social sciences, politics, and related fields, areas in which controversy often arises. A generalization or major premise that is true for "all" members of a group is usually self-evident and therefore likely to be bland or noncontroversial. Most writers settle for a generalization based on convincing evidence. Writers usually employ enthymemes—incompletely stated syllogisms that contain an implied premise the writer assumes readers will accept—rather than formal syllogisms.

Essays based on deduction often use a series of informally stated syllogisms. In such an essay the initial thesis statement is derived from the conclusion of the first syllogism; the essay can then move to a defense of each premise in separate paragraphs and return to an expanded explanation of the conclusion. Because the major premise of a syllogism is probably acceptable to most readers, you may not have to develop it in detail. The minor premise, however, will need extended development and explanation, and will require one or two paragraphs or even an entire section. Your conclusion, in turn, may become the premise of another syllogism after being combined with another compatible premise. This syllogism, in turn, may produce another conclusion that will clarify or expand an earlier point in the essay. Each premise and conclusion can be clarified in separate paragraphs. If all of this sounds too theoretical and even confusing, applying it to a writing assignment should make it clear.

Suppose that you want to write an essay urging your readers to protest an increase in the tuition at your college. Your thesis statement might read, "If the proposed increase in tuition is approved, many able students will have to drop out of college." This thesis is a reworded version of the conclusion of the syllogism:

*Major premise:* The poor students at our college cannot pay higher tuition.
*Minor premise:* Many of our able students are poor.
*Conclusion:* Many of our able students cannot pay higher tuition.

This syllogism has to be adapted to serve as the basis of a persuasive essay. The major premise implies but does not state flatly that *all* poor students cannot pay higher tuition. Such a sweeping generalization would probably be inaccurate (presumably some poor students would borrow from relatives or get loans in order to pay the higher tuition), and such a sweeping statement would be offensive to some readers (they would object to the categorical statement that *no* poor students could afford higher tuition). As already mentioned, the best you can usually hope for in such premises is strong probability or likelihood. In this case it is probable that most (if not all) poor students cannot pay higher tuition.

The minor premise is the key to the argument; if you cannot prove it, the syllogism collapses. What kind of proof would be sufficient to convince skeptical readers that many of the able students are poor? An interview with the financial aid officer at your college could provide statistics and data showing that many of the low-income students are receiving top grades. Students on the dean's list or honor roll could be interviewed and asked about their income. By examining a number of particular cases and arriving at the conclusion that many able students are poor, you would be using inductive reasoning. Persuasive writing incorporates both inductive reasoning and deductive reasoning (your conclusion becomes the minor premise in your syllogism).

The conclusion (the thesis of your essay) grows naturally out of the preceding premises: if poor students at your college can't pay higher tuition (major premise), and if many students with ability at your college are poor (minor premise), then many able students cannot pay higher tuition (conclusion). To make the conclusion more dramatic and effective as a thesis statement, you can rewrite it for greater impact: "If the Board of Trustees raises the tuition, many of our best students will have to drop out of college." This conclusion can, in turn, serve as the major premise for another premise and syllogism that will expand on the consequences of the proposed tuition increase ("Many able students can't pay higher tuition; many able students will have to drop out of college; our nation will lose the potential contributions of many of its brightest citizens."). This syllogism can be expanded and can become part of your essay.

An essay organized along the lines sketched here is easy to follow and, if supported with enough evidence and proof, can be very persuasive.

### Strengthening Your Argument by Avoiding Logical Fallacies

Your readers will not be persuaded if they detect mistakes in your logic or reasoning. Such flaws are called *logical fallacies;* conclusions reached using them are invalid. Avoid these common logical fallacies and keep your arguments persuasive.

*Hasty Generalization.* A hasty generalization is one based on an inadequate number of examples or on examples that are not typical or representative. "A local surgeon in my city reports that the number of heart surgeries performed at his hospital last year was down ten percent from the previous year. Americans are starting to live healthier lives." But the number of surgeries performed in only one hospital is hardly the basis of an inductive leap to a conclusion applying to an entire nation.

*Post Hoc, Ergo Propter Hoc.* This is a Latin expression meaning, "After this, therefore because of this." This fallacy occurs when we assume that what comes after an event is necessarily the *result* of that event. "Marcus was assigned the number 13 for his uniform, and now he can't hit an outside jumper." Just because one event follows or precedes another does not necessarily mean there is a causal relationship. In fact, there are usually several causes or effects in a relationship.

*False Analogy.* An analogy is a comparison used to explain or illustrate an idea. When you make comparisons that are not relevant to the issue or make misleading comparisons between logically unconnected ideas, you employ a false analogy: "I think he'll make a great President. After all, he started his own company and became a billionaire." The skills used in being a President are not necessarily the same skills used in running your own business.

*False Dilemmas (Either-Or Fallacies).* This means presenting an issue as having only two sides, and ignoring the possibility of a middle ground between two extremes. "People are either religious fanatics or atheists." "If we don't come to the aid of that country right now, the entire region will fall into chaos and civil war." Such statements fail to acknowledge that other choices exist.

*Non Sequitur.* This is a Latin expression for "It does not follow." This fallacy occurs when a conclusion does not follow from the premises that are supplied. "Why should police officers in America carry guns? Bobbies in England still walk their beats unarmed." The conditions in England that allow bobbies to be unarmed do not exist in America.

*Begging the Question.* Using one of your premises as the point that you are actually trying to prove is termed "begging the question." In other words, you assume the truth of something that you actually need to prove. "Everyone should be required to learn a second language; therefore, we should begin foreign language education early in primary schools." "When are these irrelevant history courses going to be dropped from the curriculum?" But should people be required to know a second language? And are history courses really irrelevant?

*Ignoring the Question.* This fallacy occurs in several forms; two of the most common are:

1. *Argumentum ad hominem* ("Argument to the man"), which is an attack not on the issue itself, but on the person who supports a certain view; and
2. *Glittering generalities,* using "fancy" words instead of evidence.

As an example of (1): "The voters should reject this proposition. One of its supporters is Glenn Monnier, who wears a bad toupee and is fat." An example of (2): "The voters should embrace this proposition because it stands for family values and maintaining the American way of life." In both instances the argument ignores the issue and tries to divert attention to irrelevant issues.

### Strengthening Your Argument by Confronting the Opposition

In addition to arguing logically, you can strengthen your position by anticipating the arguments of your opposition. Your object is to convey the impression that you have listened to your opponents, considered their views, examined their evidence, and then concluded that your arguments are more persuasive. By confronting the opposition, you will gain the respect of your readers who will be impressed by your honesty and fairness.

As pointed out in the "Concession and Rebuttal" section later in this chapter, the best place to dispose of your opponent's arguments is usually before you present your main argument. If the topic is relatively simple and the opposing arguments are few, you can summarize them in one paragraph before demolishing them. If the opposing arguments are more complex and detailed, you can introduce them point by point and answer each in its turn. In both cases, the use of expressions such as "nevertheless," "but," "however," and "after all" will help you structure your argument into a series of assertions and refutations that your reader can easily follow.

Assume that you are arguing against the abolition of the death penalty. If you present your thesis statement (assertion) and then launch immediately into your proof and evidence without considering the arguments of those who oppose capital punishment, your essay will be one-sided and unconvincing. But if you state, calmly and fairly, the arguments most often advanced by opponents of the death penalty, you will demonstrate your honesty and make the presentation of your own case more effective.

Most opponents of the death penalty advance four arguments, and you would do well to acknowledge and refute each before moving into the body of your essay. Notes for such a strategy might look like this:

*Thesis:* The death penalty should not be abolished.
*First opposing argument:* The death penalty is based on revenge.
*Refutation:* The death penalty is not rooted in revenge any more than a jail sentence for a drunk driver; it is based on the desire to protect others. Anger and vindication are not involved.

Second opposing
argument:   The death penalty does not deter.
Refutation:   This is not the point; capital punishment deters the killer from killing again.

Third opposing
argument:   Innocent men are sometimes executed.
Refutation:   This criticism is misdirected; the weakness lies with the judicial system, not with capital punishment. We need to improve our jury system, the rules of evidence, the machinery of appeal, etc.

Fourth opposing
argument:   The death penalty goes against the sanctity of life.
Refutation:   The sanctity of *whose* life? The murderer's or the victim's? If there is true merit to this argument, then armies and abortions should be outlawed. Furthermore, is a life sentence respectful of the sanctity of life?

After acknowledging the opposing arguments, you are ready to move into the body of your paper and present your evidence: the statistics, facts, examples, and other proof that support your thesis. You have shown your reader that you considered the views of your opponents, and that you found them unconvincing.

## E X E R C I S E 4

Identify the logical fallacy in each of the following arguments. Explain how each assertion goes astray, and whether it can be corrected or rewritten.

1. I think that heavy metal music must be evil. I heard that some kid committed suicide after listening to one album nonstop for several hours.
2. Jane Fonda should never receive an Oscar for her work in films because of what she did during the Vietnam war.
3. There's never anything good on TV. That show "The Lewis Files" last night was terrible.
4. Anybody over the age of ten who watches cartoons is just plain stupid.
5. How could William Shakespeare have written the plays as everyone claims? After all, he didn't go to Oxford or Cambridge.
6. I never listen to Rush Limbaugh because he's such a blowhard.
7. Why marry someone you're already sleeping with? After all, if you've got the cow, why pay for the milk?
8. After Buffalo lost the Super Bowl again, I figured they must be incompetent.

9. People from Ivy League schools are snobs.
10. If you fail this course, you'll wind up a failure in life.
11. The best teachers should be awarded merit pay.
12. Ever since the Supreme Court banned prayer in school, test scores have been on the decline nationwide, so we should bring prayer back into the classroom.
13. While this witness was near the scene of the crime, she is a member of several left-wing organizations and her testimony is therefore suspect.
14. Actors in Hollywood are among the most immoral people in the world. My friend Jody lives in LA, and she told me so.
15. I like the way she drives. I get the sense that she's a woman with a lot of self-confidence and pride.
16. Why should students be required to take worthless general education courses when all they want to take is courses in their majors?
17. I survived a winter in Syracuse, so dealing with the heat in Arizona should be no big deal.
18. There are Americans and then there are Democrats.
19. Mutts make the best dogs. All three dogs I have owned have been mutts.
20. Distinguished Americans such as Norman Schwarzkopf should be properly recognized.

---

## Organizing the Persuasive Essay

After you have sharpened your assertion, assembled your strongest arguments, and tested your logic, you are ready to organize your persuasive essay. Most experienced writers arrange their ideas in the following pattern:

Introduction
Assertion
Concession and rebuttal
Proof
Conclusion

The third section, "Concession and rebuttal," is sometimes introduced before the assertion or after the proof. Your own experience will be your best guide to deciding where to place this section.

### Introduction

Your persuasive essay should open with a clear explanation of the controversy. Your reader may not be familiar enough with the subject to have an opinion, or may not have recent information on which to base a decision. Your introduction brings the reader up to date and "sets the stage." This is also the section of your paper where you define the key or controversial terms that will be important to your argument.

If your paper argues, for instance, for a change in zoning regulations to allow homeowners to rent rooms to students, you should briefly summarize the debate: who opposes the proposed regulations and who supports them; the actions the city council or zoning commission has taken; and the timetable or agenda when a vote will be taken. If you will be using controversial terms, this is the place to define them.

By clearly and succinctly stating the problem or controversy, you have prepared the reader for your assertion.

## Assertion

After stating the controversy, you should clearly present your assertion, which will be expressed in your thesis statement. Your reader should know what you propose without any doubt. Be careful, however, to avoid a pugnacious or belligerent tone; that will only offend uncommitted readers. Remember, too, this early section is not the place to offer your proof. Before doing that, you must acknowledge opposing points of view in the concession and rebuttal section.

## Concession and Rebuttal

You have to acknowledge that there are other views that differ from yours. As noted previously (page 227), if you fail to include them your readers will assume that you are either ignorant of opposing arguments or that you are dishonest and are pretending that they do not exist.

It is important that you do not exaggerate or distort your opponents' arguments or resort to name-calling or scare tactics. If, for example, you are arguing for the legalization of laetrile as a possible cure for cancer, it would be unwise to begin your concession with a statement such as "My opponents claim that laetrile is too expensive to produce, but they don't know what they are talking about." A more effective statement might begin with something like "Opponents of laetrile claim that the drug is prohibitively expensive to manufacture. This argument, however, is not supported by the evidence that I have gathered." Words such as "admittedly," "although," "I realize," and "even though" suggest a moderate and reasonable stance and imply an open mind.

## Proof

This will be the longest section of your paper. It is similar to the body of the expository essay, which presents the thesis statement's support. In a persuasive essay it presents the evidence for your assertion. As you saw in the discussion of inductive and deductive reasoning, your proof and arguments can be arranged in either of two ways. You can support your opening generalization or assertion with a series of facts, examples, instances, and observations. If you use this method, the best arrangement is in order of increasing importance, saving your best or most dramatic arguments for last. Or you can arrange your proof in the form of a syllogism, with the body of your paper developing the major and minor premises. If you use this method, you will probably use more than one syllogism, with separate paragraphs or sections for each premise and conclusion.

If you use ethical and emotional appeals, be sure that they are supported by sound reasoning. If used judiciously, they can strengthen the impact of your logic.

### Conclusion

The conclusion of your persuasive essay should contain a brief but compelling restatement of your assertion. Try to avoid merely stating it in the same words. Present it in a fresh and pointed way so that your readers will remember it and reflect on it. As in the conclusion to the expository essay, do not introduce new arguments or facts in your ending. Its purpose is simply to draw together what you have said so that the reader has a clear idea of your intentions.

## The Traits of an Effective Persuasive Essay

An effective persuasive essay encourages the reader to accept the writer's thesis or assertion. It accomplishes this by clearly stating the issue and showing how it is related to the reader's interest. It offers a solution, avoids a "know-it-all" or offensive tone, yet conveys the impression of certainty. To be convincing, it presents the opponents' views fairly and demonstrates that the writer has examined their claims and found them weak. It provides the reader with convincing evidence: sound logic, examples, facts, testimony of authority, statistics, and reasons. An effective persuasive essay avoids logical fallacies and does not call names, exaggerate, or distort evidence. Finally, an effective persuasive essay concludes with a forceful restatement of the essay's assertion so that the reader knows exactly what the writer believes and why the assertion should be accepted.

## Student Essay

The following persuasive essay was written by a freshman supporting the assertion, "The current welfare system is ripe for fraud and abuse and needs to be reformed to protect the truly needy and require those who are able to rejoin the workforce."

The outline that precedes the essay points out the organization of its major sections, including the statement of the problem, the assertion, the concession, the proof, and the conclusion.

Welfare: Neither Well Nor Fair
Paragraph 1.
    Statement of the problem
    Evidence that the problem exists: use of statistics
    Statement of assertion
Paragraph 2.
    Concession: opposing arguments
Paragraph 3.
    Rebuttal of opposing arguments
    Inconsistencies in opposing arguments noted
    Benefits of reform: use of examples
Paragraph 4.
    Series of examples of benefits: appeal to authorities
Paragraph 5.
    Rebuttal of opposing argument: appeal to authority
Paragraph 6.
    Additional proof of assertion: examples
Paragraph 7.
    Additional proof
    Emotional appeal
Paragraph 8
    Conclusion: consequences of opposing argument

---

Welfare: Neither Well Nor Fair

1.    At the top of the conservatives' list of villains is the welfare mother. Portrayed as lazy yet fertile, the welfare mother allegedly revolves her life around government handout programs, living in public housing, having children to increase her benefits, and steadfastly refusing gainful employment if offered, all at great cost to the taxpayers. They note that the system, which hopes to help people, sees the mother as a victim of society, impoverished through no fault of her own, unable to help herself, who must be cared for and nurtured at public expense. The result has been the creation of a welfare system that encourages dependence. Opponents of welfare have developed the harsh response proposing to drastically cut benefits or eradicate welfare completely, believing that by making welfare less attractive, fewer will turn to it. But a different course can and must be charted. Although the current welfare system is indeed ripe for fraud and

abuse, the system can be reformed to protect the truly needy and still require those who are able to rejoin the workforce.

2.     Opponents of welfare have arguments that range from the fiscal to the spiritual. Welfare opponents see the programs as a drain on budgets. At a time of belt tightening at all levels of government, they argue that welfare is an ineffective program that wastes money. By cutting welfare payments, local and state governments would have additional revenue for other programs such as increased police or fire protection. Welfare also promotes a culture of laziness and victimization; welfare recipients grow accustomed to being dependent and lose all sense of self-esteem and ambition that would help them rise above their circumstances. Better, they argue, to not help at all than to help in this manner.

3.     Certainly, the conservative argument has a great deal of appeal. Who wouldn't like to save money? Perhaps a tax cut would result if welfare payments were stopped. If not, at least the tax money could be spent on expenses like police and fire protection. Certainly increased police would be necessary since without social services, the police would be the front line of contact with America's underclass. Desperation for money might drive some to crime; certainly prostitution and drug use would increase as single parents without marketable job skills try to raise cash to support themselves and their children. Some might even turn to robbery or burglary. Of course, not all welfare recipients are potential criminals, but the truth is that without government transfer payments, some current recipients are bound to turn to crime.

4.     Another problem with the conservative solution is that it fails to recognize the roots of poverty. While they correctly note that many poor people lack a strong work ethic, they do little to help change that. The conservatives assume that these people will magically turn around and find gainful employment. We need to recognize, however, that work ethics are learned, not innate. The rewards of work come not to all who work, but to all who work at jobs that produce rewards, including monetary. Many of the poor do work, in fact, yet they lack education and job skills, and find themselves in jobs with little potential for advancement beyond low-skill, minimum-wage jobs. Shaking our collective finger and saying, "Tsk, tsk, you should have done better at school" will change nothing in these people's lives now. These people need help, not scoldings.

5.     Opponents see the expansion of welfare to include job training and placement as throwing gasoline on a raging fire, but only by

taking such measures is there any hope of attacking the funda
mental problems of the working poor. Job training will give people the opportunity to move into jobs that can take them off the
welfare rolls. They can become tax payers, not tax recipients.
Job placement is necessary as well. By working with the private
sector, the government should help identify areas of job need,
train people for such jobs, and help place people in jobs that are
appropriate. A cost-saving measure could be to utilize private job
training and placement services if that is a practical alternative.
At any rate, the attitude of the government should be to assist
these people to enter the workplace in meaningful jobs.

6.   All the training programs and placements will not work though
without accessible, affordable day care. The need for day care is
also obvious: a large percentage of welfare recipients are single
mothers with few job skills, and the only way to move them into
the workforce is to have day care that is affordable and accessible.
Vouchers for day care services could be made available, re-
deemable only at licensed day-care centers. This would have a
twofold effect: (1) mothers could go to work with confidence,
knowing that their children are well taken care of and (2) an in-
centive to create more day-care services would be given to the private sector, which could also benefit working mothers who are not
on welfare. If anything, the need for day care is growing in this
country, and government support for this service is essential.

7.   Finally, we as a society need to look into our hearts, not just our
pocketbooks. No one wants to be played for a fool, giving money to
a person who will spend it on drugs or alcohol. Too often, it seems
that our efforts to help the poor have no effect except to help keep
them poor and to anger us. However, deep down, we want to help.
There is a sense that as Americans we should help take care of
each other, that the less fortunate desire our help. Most of us like
to think of ourselves as potential Good Samaritans, and taxes paid
into welfare programs can help accomplish this if used properly.

8.   If welfare can be made temporary, by supporting people while
they are retrained and placed in a job, by helping put their children into day-care facilities, then the government will have done
some good for the poor of this country. Lately, we are faced with
the attitude that the government can do no right; this attitude can
only be changed if we have the courage to change the way government works. However, the harsh, inhumane stripping of welfare payments will only create more bitterness and dependency;
the total elimination of welfare would invite a return to Charles
Dickens–style poverty. Only a thoughtful, thorough reform of welfare will improve the way we deal with our nation's poor. Then
the American people as a whole will feel better about welfare.

## E X E R C I S E 5

Select one of the topics in Exercise 2 for which you wrote an assertion or select one of the topics below, write an assertion, and develop it into a persuasive essay. Use the suggestions in this chapter, including the student example. After you write your first draft, read the checklist below.

1.  The information superhighway
2.  Affirmative action
3.  Genetic engineering
4.  Zoos
5.  Ethnic holidays
6.  The business of weddings
7.  Ross Perot
8.  AIDS hospices
9.  Nuclear war
10. Indian gaming
11. The disabled
12. Corporate farming
13. Bilingual education
14. Fashion models
15. Travel
16. White noise
17. Artificial intelligence
18. Contemporary art
19. Lobbyists
20. Social Security benefits

## R E V I S I O N  C H E C K L I S T

### The Persuasive Essay

After you have written the first draft of your persuasive essay, read this checklist carefully. Also consult Chapter 7, "Revising and Editing the Essay."

*1. What is the argumentative position or assertion taken in your essay? Does it discuss an issue that can be debated, or is it merely a fact that cannot be disputed?*
*2. Is your assertion clearly stated? Could it be improved? Is it too combative in tone?*
*3. Does your introduction summarize the controversy clearly so that an uninformed reader would immediately be familiar with the problem?*

4. *Is your acknowledgment of the opposing viewpoint stated calmly? Do you state opposing arguments fairly, or do you distort or misstate those views?*

5. *Is your evidence and proof clear and convincing? Is it presented in the most convincing order? Could it be arranged more effectively?*

6. *Can you think of any other examples, statistics, or evidence that would strengthen your argument?*

7. *Have you been careful to avoid the logical fallacies explained on pages 225–227?*

8. *Have you avoided name-calling, exaggeration, personal attacks, or other unfair techniques of argument?*

9. *Does your conclusion emphasize the assertion, leaving your reader with a clear idea of your assertion and why it should be accepted?*

## COMPUTER EXERCISE

Using the broadcast function, share your essay with the class. Have the class read the paper silently. Then, ask if they can identify your thesis sentence. If they cannot, you have trouble. You can continue to ask questions or your instructor may wish to ask questions, particularly those from the Revision Checklist on page 144. What is important at this stage is that you, the writer, ask questions and get the feedback you need from other students so that you can develop a sense of whether your essay is persuading your audience. Of lesser importance are matters of grammar, spelling, and punctuation, which you will clean up during the editing process.

# 11

# *Writing the Term Paper*

Writing the term paper is an extension of the skills and techniques you have learned in the preceding chapters. In fact, it is often the "grand finale" because it is the last major assignment in many composition classes.

If you do not understand its benefits and purposes, writing the term paper can be frustrating and discouraging. If you approach it in the right way, however, it will be an exciting and informative experience.

## What Is the Term Paper?

Whether it is called a research paper, reference paper, library paper, or term paper, it typically presents the results of the writer's investigation on a specific topic. It can range from 1,500 to 3,000 words, or approximately six to twelve typewritten pages. As presented in this chapter, the paper follows the guidelines set forth in the Modern Language Association *MLA Handbook for Writers of Research Papers* (1995), which reflects the practices required by most college instructors throughout the United States and Canada. Some instructors, particularly those in the social sciences and physical sciences, want their students to follow the guidelines in the *Publication Manual of the American Psychological Association* (1983).

The term paper written for most composition classes will usually be one of two kinds: a report or a thesis paper. A *report* is essentially a survey of facts and opinions; it does not offer an argument. Rather, it informs the reader, usually from a fresh point of view. The *thesis* paper does considerably more. It argues a point by presenting and evaluating facts to persuade the reader to accept a particular hypothesis or to take a certain course of action.

If you are writing a report, your instructor does not want a collection of quotations and paraphrases that you have pasted together that do not represent your own conclusions. If you are writing a thesis paper, your instructor does not expect you to present a brilliant new solution to a problem or the answer to an age-old question. In both cases what your instructor *does* expect is a studious inquiry into a subject in which you evaluate and interpret information and offer your audience evidence to support a thesis or point of view.

## The Benefits of the Term Paper

Because term papers require you to locate and investigate sources of information other than your opinion or personal knowledge, you will derive several benefits from the assignment. The most obvious is that you will learn a great deal about a topic that interests you. You will learn how to find information in the library (and sometimes how to find information that is *not* in the library). You will learn to evaluate, summarize, and synthesize a large body of material, reading it analytically and critically and presenting it in an organized and readable form, documenting your sources in acceptable style.

Writing term papers has some long-range benefits as well. After learning research techniques, you will be able to identify a problem, process information, and develop critical thinking skills. These are all benefits that extend beyond the college classroom. And, of course, there is the sense of accomplishment that comes from doing a challenging job to the best of your ability.

## Choosing and Limiting a Topic

The first step in writing the term paper is choosing and limiting your topic. Of course, if your instructor has assigned your topic, that step has been taken care of for you. But if you are given the responsibility for determining your topic, you are immediately faced with opportunities as well as dangers. We will consider both.

The best topic for a term paper is usually one that you are interested in and want to learn more about. It could be a subject that was mentioned in a class lecture, or something that has been on your mind and has aroused your curiosity. It might be a subject that has been written about in magazines and newspapers. Or it might be related to a hobby or interest that you have. But what if you can't think of a topic? You might try the following techniques.

One of the best sources of topics for a term paper is the *Library of Congress Subject Headings,* a large, red, two-volume set usually found near the card catalog or catalog computer in most libraries. It is the standard guide used by most libraries to catalog books according to the Library of Congress system. It lists subjects as they appear in the card catalog or catalog computer, as well as related headings and subtopics. By glancing through it you will see hundreds of possible topics that you might want to investigate in your term paper. When you find a topic that interests you, check the card catalog to see whether your library has books on it.

Page 240 shows a very small excerpt from the hundreds of topics listed under "Environment" in the *Library of Congress Subject Headings.*

Another source of topics is the encyclopedia. The *Columbia Encyclopedia* and *The Random House Encyclopedia* are both single volumes and are therefore convenient for a random search for an interest-

Environment
    *See* Acclimatization
        Adapation (Biology)
        Anthropo-geography
        Ecology
        Euthenics
        Human ecology
        Man—Influence of environment
        Man—Influence on nature
        Nature and nurture
        *subdivision* Environmental aspects
           *under special subjects, e.g.*
           Agricultural chemicals—
           Environmental aspects; Atomic
           power-plants—Environmental
           aspects; *and headings beginning with*
           *the word* Environmental
Environment, College
    *See* College environment
Environment, High school
    *See* High school environment
Environment, Human
    *See* Human ecology
Environment, School
    *See* School environment
Environment, Space
    *See* Space environment
**Environment (Art)** *(Direct)*
    *xx* Art, Modern—20th century
        Assemblage (Art)
Environment and mass media
    *See* Mass media and the environment
Environment and state
    *See* Environmental policy
Environment simulations (Teaching method)
    *See* Simulated environment (Teaching
        method)
Environment testing
    *See* Environmental testing
Environmental control
    *See* Environmental engineering
        Environmental law
        Environmental policy
Environmental education
    *See* Conservation of natural resources—
        Study and teaching
        Ecology—Study and teaching
        Human ecology—Study and teaching
Environmental effects
    *See* Environmental engineering
**Environmental engineering**
    *sa* Electric power-plants—Environmental
        aspects
        Environmental health
        Environmental policy

Environmental protection
Environmental testing
Extraterrestrial bases
Human engineering
Life support systems (Space
    environment)
Motor-trucks—Environmental aspects
Noise control
Petroleum chemicals industry—
    Environmental aspects
Pollution
Sanitary engineering
Space simulators
*subdivision* Influence of environment
    *under subjects, e.g.* United States.
    Army—Ordnance and ordnance
    stores—Influence of environment
  *x* Environmental control
    Environmental effects
    Environmental management
    Environmental stresses
 *xx* Design, Industrial
    Engineering
    Engineering meteorology
    Environmental health
    Environmental protection
    Pollution
    Testing
—Computer programs
—Information services *(Direct)*
—Research *(Direct)*
—Research grants *(Direct)*
—Vocational guidance
    *See* Environmental engineering as a
        profession
**Environmental engineering (Buildings)**
    *sa* Air conditioning
        Architectural acoustics
        Buildings—Vibration
        Clean rooms
        Heating
        Interior decorations
        Lighting
        Sanitation, Household
        Ventilation
   *x* Buildings—Environmental engineering
  *xx* Architecture
    Building
    Sanitation, Household
—Problems, exercises, etc.
—Tables, calculations, etc.
**Environmental engineering as a profession**
   *x* Environmental engineering —
        Vocational guidance

ing topic. By looking through either encyclopedia, you will come across many suggestions for further investigation.

Your textbooks can often yield topics for term papers. Suggestions for research are often placed at the end of chapters or units, and the table of contents may also give you some ideas.

There are certain kinds of topics to avoid as you make your choice. The first is a topic on which your library has no books or articles. This is not likely to be a problem if you have access to a major university library; smaller libraries with limited holdings, however, may lack enough material for some topics. Another topic to avoid is the "single-source" topic—one that could be exhausted by consulting only one book. An example is the biography of a famous person. The life of former President Lyndon B. Johnson, for instance, could easily be derived from a single book, but a comparison of his first hundred days in office with the first hundred days of Franklin Delano Roosevelt's first term would be based on several sources.

Be careful, too, of topics that have become clichés. Examples include the effect of television on violence, the debate over capital punishment, and the history of jazz. These are painfully familiar to most experienced instructors and will possibly evoke little more than a yawn. On the other hand, don't select a topic that is so new that no books have been written on it yet. It is doubtful, for example, that you could find many books on the implications of the most recent congressional elections in the United States.

You must be careful that your topic is specific enough to be covered in a paper of the length assigned. The suggestions for narrowing a topic given in Chapter 4 apply to term paper topics as well. Some of the steps you took to select your topic will also be helpful in narrowing it. For example, the *Library of Congress Subject Headings*, because it divides and subdivides topics, can help you narrow your topic to manageable proportions. The index of an encyclopedia will often list subjects of a larger subject that are suitable for a paper.

Other ways to narrow the topic include studying the subheadings of the topic in the card catalog, the *Reader's Guide to Periodical Literature*, and *The New York Times Index*. All of these break topics up into additional subtopics that are often narrow enough for a term paper.

## Determining Your Purpose and Audience

If your term paper is a report, your purpose will be to inform your audience by presenting information on a topic. Knowing something about your audience will help determine the kind of information you include and the way you present it. What can you expect your readers to know already about your topic? Do not bore readers with material that is already well-known. Readers should learn about new information instead. What terms or concepts will you have to define or explain? By keeping your audience in mind as you write, you will make your paper clearer and more informative.

In addition to the questions the report writer must ask, if your paper argues a point—if your purpose is to persuade the reader—you will have to investigate and present the claims and arguments of your opposition. By confronting the opposition, you will impress skeptical readers and convince your audience that you are fair and informed. (See pages 227–228 in Chapter 10, "Writing the Persuasive Essay.")

## Stating Your Purpose

When you have narrowed your topic, you will be ready to determine the main point you hope to make in your paper. Notice that it is *preliminary;* you will probably change it as you read further, enlarging or restricting its scope as you develop new information and ideas.

The value of knowing your purpose now—even if it is only preliminary—is that it will steer you away from books and articles that will not be useful and toward those that will be helpful in writing your paper. You will be able to select only those items that contribute to your central idea, and ignore those that are off the subject. (Most of the ideas in Chapter 4 for developing the thesis statement apply to the term paper, with one exception: because of its length and complexity, the thesis of the term paper may be more than one sentence long. Its purpose, however, is the same: to give your paper a focus.)

If you are writing a *report,* you may wish to relate facts and clear up superficial or erroneous notions about a subject that is unfamiliar or unknown to most of your readers. The following statement would be appropriate for this kind of paper: "The purpose of this paper is to list and describe the nineteenth-century suffragettes, the precursors of today's feminist movement." This paper intends only to inform, not to persuade.

If you are writing a *thesis* paper, you will probably attempt to argue a point or defend a particular hypothesis in order to persuade your reader. The following thesis reflects this kind of paper: "The Social Security system must be revised drastically to prevent it from going bankrupt." Such a statement is designed to encourage the reader to accept the writer's argument.

You don't have to worry about the precise wording of your thesis statement at this stage. The main thing is to have a reasonably clear idea of where you are heading. By knowing what the purpose of your paper is, you will be better able to determine the worth of the books and articles you find in the next step: the search strategy.

## The Search Strategy: Gathering Material

Too many students lose time "spinning their wheels" in confusion at the library as they try to find books and articles dealing with the topic of their term paper. They do not realize that by following a "search strategy"—a step-by-step process of collecting and evaluating information—they can save time and find the most useful and relevant information on their topic. In that sense the search strategy preceding the writing of the term paper is comparable to the prewriting stage of an essay. In both cases, the time spent searching for material and ideas is one of the most essential steps in the writing process. The search strategy explained here is an organized and systematic plan in which you move from general to more specific information. If you follow this sequence you will find the material you need with a minimum of difficulty and make the best use of your time.

You will notice that the search strategy takes you first to the reference section or room of your library. This—and *not* the card catalog or catalog computer, as many students think—is the best place to look for information for your term paper. By beginning with encyclopedias and the other general reference works listed below, you will have an overview of your subject and see its relationship to other topics. Then you can consult the card catalog or catalog computer, periodical and newspaper indexes, and more specialized sources.

Here are the basic steps in the search strategy, followed by an explanation of each step.

1. Consult a general or special encyclopedia for an overview of your topic. Look for bibliographies at the end of the encyclopedia article or for recommended readings.
2. If appropriate, consult biographical reference works, atlases, gazetteers, yearbooks, and subject dictionaries associated with your topic.
3. Use the bibliographies from the above sources to begin your search for books by author or title in the card catalog. Use the *Library of Congress Subject Headings* to find the subject headings for your topic in the card catalog.

4. Use relevant terms found in the encyclopedias, dictionaries, and other reference works in periodical and newspaper indexes for journal article citations.

## Encyclopedias

The best place to start your background reading is the encyclopedia. Although your instructor may not want you to quote from it in your term paper, the encyclopedia will give you an overview of your topic and provide plenty of leads for further reading.

When looking for information in the encyclopedia, always consult the index first. The index will list two kinds of entries: those subjects that have a separate article, and those subjects covered in the encyclopedia but as part of another entry.

At the end of most encyclopedia articles you will find a list of books and articles on the topic. These are very helpful because they guide you to other reliable sources of information. Make a note of those titles that sound interesting and promising. On a separate card for each, write *the author's name, the title of the article or book,* and *the facts of publication.* These cards (called *bibliography cards*) will form the basis of the list of books and articles that you must turn in with your term paper. (See page 251 for examples of bibliography cards for magazines and books.)

### General Encyclopedias

These give a summary of what is known on a subject, as well as bibliographies. They are the best place to start. Always use the most recent edition.

> *The Encyclopedia Americana.* 30 vols. New York: Grolier, 1994. It is particularly useful for its articles on science and mathematics, as well as for its biographies. Volume 30 is the index. Revised Annually.
>
> *Encyclopaedia Britannica.* 32 vols. Chicago: Encyclopaedia Britannica, 1991. The most scholarly of the general encyclopedias, it is divided into four sections: (1) the *Propaedia,* a one-volume outline of knowledge, (2) the *Micropaedia,* a ten-volume set of short articles; (3) the *Macropaedia,* a seventeen-volume set of longer, detailed articles; and (4) a two volume index.
>
> *Collier's Encyclopedia.* 24 vols. New York: Crowell-Collier, 1991. The articles are less detailed and usually briefer than those in the above encyclopedias, but easier to read. Volume 24 is the index.

*New Columbia Encyclopedia.* 2nd ed. 1 vol. New York: Columbia UP, 1989. This is a reliable one-volume reference work that will give you condensed information on a topic.

*Random House Encyclopedia.* 1 vol. New York: Random, 1990. Like the encyclopedia above, this is a reliable desk encyclopedia designed for quick reference.

### Specialized Encyclopedias and Dictionaries

Although general encyclopedias may not always be appropriate for use in a college term paper, specialized encyclopedias and dictionaries may be excellent references for college papers. Specialized encyclopedias and dictionaries are reference works that cover just one area of knowledge. The following list is merely a sampler; special encyclopedias are available for almost every important subject. To find the encyclopedia you need, check the latest edition of Eugene P. Sheehy's *Guide to Reference Books,* available in most libraries. Like the general encyclopedias listed above, special encyclopedias and dictionaries have bibliographies and lists of recommended readings. As you look at them, make a bibliography card for each title that looks helpful.

### The Arts

*Encyclopedia of World Art.* 17 vols. New York: McGraw, 1959-87.

Lucas, Edna Louise. *Art Books: A Basic Bibliography of Monographs on Artists.* Greenwich: New York Graphic Soc., 1968.

Maillard, Robert, ed. *New Dictionary of Modern Sculpture.* Trans. Bettina Wadia. New York: Amiel, 1971.

Myers, Bernard S. *Encyclopedia of Painting.* New York: Crown, 1955.

*New Grover Dictionary of Music and Musicians.* 4 vols. Washington, D.C.: Grove's Dictionaries of Music, 1986.

### Business

Buell, Victor P., ed. *Handbook of Modern Marketing.* 2nd. ed. New York: McGraw, 1986.

Graham, Irwin. *Encyclopedia of Advertising.* 2nd ed. New York: Fairchild, 1969.

Lazarus, Harold. *American Business Directory.* New York: Philosophical Library, 1957.

Munn, Glenn G. *Encyclopedia of Banking and Finance.* 9th ed. Ed. G. G. Munn. Boston: Bankers, 1991.

Sloan, Harold S., and Arnold Zurcher. *A Dictionary of Economics.* 5th ed. New York: Barnes, 1970.

## History

*American Historical Association: Guide to Historical Literature.* New York: Macmillan, 1961.

Commager, Henry Steele, and Milton Cator. *Documents of American History.* 10th ed. 2 vols. New York: Appleton, 1988.

Friedl, Frank, ed. *Harvard Guide to American History.* Rev. ed. Cambridge: Belknap Press of Harvard UP, 1974.

Hodge, Frederick W. *Handbook of American Indians North of Mexico.* 2 vols. 1910. Washington, D.C.: Rowman, 1975.

Ketz, Louise B., ed. *Dictionary of American History.* 2nd ed. 6 vols. New York: Scribner's, 1976.

Martin, Michael R., et al. *An Encyclopedia of Latin-American History.* Indianapolis: Bobbs, 1968.

Miller, Elizabeth. *The Negro in America: A Bibliography.* Cambridge: Harvard UP, 1970.

## Literature

Baugh, Albert C., et. al., eds. *Literature History of England.* 2nd ed. 4 vols. New York: Appleton, 1967.

Blanck, Jacob N. *Bibliography of American Literature.* 8 vols. New Haven: Yale UP, 1990.

Drabble, Margaret. *The Oxford Companion to English Literature.* 5th ed. New York: Oxford UP, 1985.

Hart, James D. *The Oxford Companion to American Literature.* 5th ed. New York: Oxford UP, 1983.

Spiller, Robert, et al. *Literary History of the United States.* 4th ed. 2 vols. New York: Macmillan, 1974.

Watson, George, ed. *The New Cambridge Bibliography of English Literature.* 5 vols. Cambridge UP, 1969–1977.

## Music and Dance

Blom, Eric. *Everyman's Dictionary of Music.* New York: New American Library, 1973.

Chujoy, Anatole, and P. W. Manchester. *The Dance Encyclopedia.* New York: Simon, 1967.

Randel, Don Michael. *The Harvard Dictionary of Music.* Cambridge: Harvard UP, 1986.

Stambler, Irwin. *Encyclopedia of Pop, Rock, and Soul.* New York: St. Martin's, 1989.

Thompson, Oscar. *Interntional Cyclopedia of Music and Musicians.* 11th ed. New York: Dodd, 1985.

## Religion and Philosophy

Buttrick, George A. and Keith Crim, eds. *The Interpreter's Dictionary of the Bible,* 5 vols. New York: Abingdon, 1976.

Edwards, Paul, ed. *The Encyclopedia of Philosophy.* 4 vols. New York: Macmillan, 1973.

Eliade, Mircea, ed. *The Encyclopedia of Religion.* 16 vol. New York: MacMillan, 1987.

*New Catholic Encyclopedia.* 15 vols. New York: Thomas Nelson, 1981.

Roth, Cecil, ed. *The New Standard Jewish Encyclopedia.* 5th ed. New rev. ed. edited by Geoffrey Wigoder. Garden City: Doubleday, 1977.

## Social Sciences

Beigel, Hugo G. *A Dictionary of Psychology and Related Fields.* New York: Frederick Ungar, 1974.

Kreslins, Janis A., ed. *Foreign Affairs Bibliography.* New York: Bowker, 1976.

*McGraw-Hill Dictionary of Modern Economics.* New York: McGraw, 1983.

Mitchell, G. Duncan, ed. *A Dictionary of Sociology.* Chicago: Aldine, 1967.

Sills, David L., ed. *International Encyclopedia of the Social Sciences.* 8 vols. New York: Free Press, 1977.

Webb, William H., ed. *Sources of Information in the Social Sciences: A Guide to the Literature.* 3rd ed. Chicago: ALA, 1986.

## Sciences

Considine, Douglas, M., and Glenn D. Considine, eds. *The Encyclopedia of Chemistry.* 4th ed. New York: Van Nostrand Reinhold, 1984.

Fairbridge, Rhodes W., ed. *The Encyclopedia of Oceanography.* New York: Van Nostrand Reinhold, 1966.

Gray, Peter. *The Encyclopedia of Biological Sciences.* 2nd ed. New York: Van Nostrand Reinhold, 1970.

*The International Dictionary of Physics and Electronics.* 2nd ed. Princeton: Nostrand Reinhold, 1961.

Parker, Sybil P. *The McGraw-Hill Encyclopedia of Science and Technology.* 6th ed. New York: McGraw, 1987.

Thewlis, J., ed. *Encyclopaedic Dictionary of Physics.* 9 vols. Elmsford: Pergamon, 1971.

## English Language

*The Oxford English Dictionary.* 2nd ed. 20 vols. plus supplements. New York: Oxford UP, 1989.

*Webster's Third New International Dictionary of the English Language.* Springfield: Merriam, 1986.

# Biographical Works, Atlases, Gazetteers, and Other Reference Works

## Biographical Reference Works

Although your instructor may not allow you to write a term paper based on the life of a person, you may find it necessary to consult biographical reference works.

## For Living People

*American Men and Women of Science.* 17th ed. 8 vols. New York: Bowker, 1989.

*Contemporary Authors.* 44 vols. Detroit: Gale, 1965–73. Supplements published annually.

*Current Biography.* New York: Wilson, published annually since 1940.

*Who's Who in America.* 2 vols. Chicago: Marquis Who's Who, published biennially since 1899.

*Who's Who of American Women.* Chicago: Marquis Who's Who, published biennially since 1958.

## For People No Longer Living

*Dictionary of American Biography.* 18 vols. plus supplements. New York: Scribner's, 1957–88.

*Dictionary of National Biography* (British). 22 vols. plus supplements. London: Smith, published annually since 1908.

## Atlases and Gazetteers

An atlas is a bound collection of maps; a gazetteer is a geographical dictionary.

*Atlas of American History.* Ed. Kenneth T. Jackson. 2nd Rev. ed. New York: Scribner's, 1984.

*Encyclopaedia Britannica World Atlas International.* Chicago: Encyclopaedia Britannica, 1974.

*National Geographic Atlas of the World.* 4th ed. Washington, D.C.: National Geographic Society, 1981.

*The New York Times Atlas of the World.* New York: Times Books, 1981.

*Rand-McNally Cosmopolitan World Atlas.* Rev. ed. Chicago: Rand, 1981.

*Rand-McNally Goode's World Atlas.* 16th ed. Chicago: Rand, 1990.

*The Times Atlas of the World.* 8th Comprehensive ed. New York: Times Books, 1990.

### *Almanacs and Yearbooks*

These are published annually and record information about the previous calendar year: charts, lists, facts, statistics, and dates on a variety of subjects.

*Britannica Book of the Year.* Chicago: Encyclopaedia Britannica, published annually since 1938.

*Facts on File Yearbook.* New York: Facts on File, published annually since 1940.

*World Almanac and Book of Facts.* New York: Newspaper Enterprise Association, published annually sincd 1868.

## *The Card Catalog*

By this time you have accumulated several leads for finding material for your topic. You have read articles in the general and specialized encyclopedias and other reference works. You have looked over the bibliographies and lists of recommended readings in those reference works, noting on separate cards any titles that sounded helpful, following the style of the sample bibliographical cards on page 251. Now you are ready to go to the card catalog or catalog computer to find those books you have noted and to find other books on your subject.

Your library will have an alphabetical listing for its books either on computers or in card catalogs. For purposes of our discussion, we will look in-depth only at how card catalogs are organized. If your library does use computers, familiarize yourself with your library's computer system. Many libraries offer orientation tours for this purpose, or a librarian may be available to show you how to use the system. Libraries that still use card catalogs have differences in their systems as well. For example, some list books and journals; others list books, journals, and phonograph records; and some list only books.

Each book is listed on at least three separate cards: by its *author,* by its *title,* and by its *subject.* Each card contains the same information, except that the title card has the book title at the top and the subject card lists the subject at the top of the card. (See page 251 for examples of the three types of cards.)

Libraries that have "divided" catalogs place the author and title cards together alphabetically in one section and the subject cards in another. Libraries that have "dictionary" catalogs combine all three—author, title, and subject—into a single alphabet.

*Author cards.* Author cards are arranged alphabetically under the author's last name (Wright, Richard). If the author has written more than one book, the author cards are arranged alphabetically by title under the author's name.

*Title cards.* Title cards are arranged alphabetically under the first world of the title, except for articles (*A, An,* and *The*). Thus, *A History of Irish Literature* would be filed under *H* and *The Life of Marco Polo* would be filed under *L.*

*Subject Cards.* The heading or top line of a subject card lists the subject of the book. Subject cards are arranged alphabetically by the first word of the heading on the card.

Two kinds of information on the card are particularly important. The *call number* is the book's library address; it tells you where the book can be found. Refer to the lists below for Dewey Decimal System and Library of Congress System call numbers. At the bottom of the card you will often see additional subjects mentioned; you should look under these headings in the subject cards for additional books on your topics. These listings, called "tracings," are extremely helpful when you are trying to find additional information on your subject.

## Dewey Decimal System

000 General Works
100 Philosophy
200 Religion
300 Social Sciences
400 Language
500 Natural Sciences
600 Technology and Applied Sciences
700 Fine Arts
800 Literature
900 History, Geography, Biography.

```
PN4121
.E36      Ehninger, Douglas.
1984           Principles of speech communication / Douglas Ehninger,
          Bruce E. Gronbeck, Alan H. Monroe. – 9th brief ed. – Glen-
          view, Ill. : Scott, Foresman, c1984.

               383 p. : ill. ; 21 cm.

               Includes bibliographies and index.
               ISBN 0-673-15877-2 : $11.95 (est.)

               1. Public Speaking.    I. Gronbeck, Bruce E.    II. Monroe, Alan Houston,
          1903-       .  III. Title
          PN4121.E36   1984                    808.5'1–dc                  83-11578
                                                                      AACR 2  MARC
          Library of Congress
```

```
                          Principles of speech communication
PN4121
.E36      Ehninger, Douglas,
1984           Principles of speech communication / Douglas Ehninger,
          Bruce E. Gronbeck, Alan H. Monroe. – 9th brief ed. – Glen-
          view, Ill. : Scott, Foresman, c1984.

               383 p. : ill. ; 21 cm.

               Includes bibliographies and index.
               ISBN 0-673-15877-2 : $11.95 (est.)

               1. Public Speaking.    I. Gronbeck, Bruce E.    II. Monroe, Alan Houston,
          1903-       .  III. Title
          PN4121.E36   1984                    808.5'1–dc                  83-11578
                                                                      AACR 2  MARC
          Library of Congress
```

```
          PUBLIC SPEAKING
PN4121
.E36      Ehninger, Douglas.
1984           Principles of speech communication / Douglas Ehninger,
          Bruce E. Gronbeck, Alan H. Monroe. – 9th brief ed. – Glen-
          view, Ill. : Scott, Foresman, c1984.

               383 p. : ill. ; 21 cm.

               Includes bibliographies and index.
               ISBN 0-673-15877-2 : $11.95 (est.)

               1. Public Speaking.    I. Gronbeck, Bruce E.    II. Monroe, Alan Houston,
          1903-       .  III. Title
          PN4121.E36   1984                    808.5'1–dc                  83-11578
                                                                      AACR 2  MARC
          Library of Congress
```

### Library of Congress System

| | | | |
|---|---|---|---|
| A | General Works | M | Music |
| B | Philosophy, Psychology, Religion | N | Fine Arts |
| | | P | Language, Literature |
| C | General History | Q | Science |
| D | Foreign History | R | Medicine |
| E–F | American History | S | Agriculture |
| G | Geography, Anthropology | T | Technology |
| | | U | Military Science |
| H | Social Science | V | Naval Science |
| J | Political Science | Z | Bibliography, Library Science |
| K | Law | | |
| L | Education | | |

When you know the title or author of a book, it is a simple matter to go to the title of author card, copy down the call number, and locate the book in the library. But if you do not have a particular author or title in mind, you have to consult the subject cards. This is a time when the Library of Congress Subject Headings (LCSH) can be very helpful. It gives the subject headings and subheadings in the card catalog, as well as cross-references. By listing every imaginable subject and then showing what other subject the entry might be classified under, this reference work can send you to additional books that you would probably have missed. For example, if you look up "Death Penalty" in your college library subject catalog but do not find any books, you can look up "Death Penalty" in the LCSH, which will send you to "Capital Punishment."

As you examine the cards in the catalog, you should make a bibliography card or entry in a notebook devoted exclusively to the term paper assignment for every book that looks helpful for your paper. Your job now is not to read them, but merely to select the most promising; you will examining them in detail later to determine their relevance to your subject.

In general, you should select the most recently published books on your topic. The reason is obvious: you will have up-to-date information. Imagine writing an article about corruption in American politics without consulting any books published after Watergate. Or imagine working on a paper about the Social Security system using only books written before 1980. Papers on many topics, such as environmental issues or political situations, demand the most current possible sources. Older sources on such topics may only be useful as historical references.

Another yardstick for determining whether to select book is its relevance to your subject. Because titles are sometimes deceiving (one reader thought that *Animal Farm* was about raising pigs!), you should read the table of contents and preface carefully in order to decide whether a book will be helpful.

## *Periodical Indexes*

The books that you have found will contain a great deal of material, but you will need to find articles for current information. Even if your topic has to do with the Ancient Roman Empire, you will want the most recent theories or findings on the subject. To find articles, you will need to consult the periodical indexes.

Some indexes include abstracts. An abstract is a short summary of an article. The abstract should not be used as a source itself, but it can be helpful in determining whether a particular article will be of value to you.

The steps for finding an article on your subject in a magazine or journal are simple:

1. Determine which periodical index you need. Almost every discipline or academic subject has its own index, and you should locate the one that lists articles on your topic.
2. Look under the subject headings for articles on your topic. The subject headings in indexes are similar to those in the subject card catalog.
3. Make a bibliography card for each promising article. If you don't understand the abbreviations used in the entry, look at the inside front cover of the index for an explanation.
4. Find out whether your library has a copy of the periodical you want by looking in the Periodicals Catalog. It contains a list of every periodical in the library and tells you where it may be found.

### *The Readers' Guide*

If your topic has been treated in a popular magazine, you should start with the *Readers' Guide to Periodical Literature,* which indexes articles from more than 150 magazines of general interest: *Readers' Digest, Time, Cosmopolitan, Ebony, Esquire,* and so on. It is the most popular and widely used periodical index.

The *Readers' Guide* is published every two weeks and then gathered in large, cumulative volumes covering a year or more. To find an article on a particular subject, you should consult several of the most recent issues. Articles are listed twice: by author and under a subject heading. Like the subject card catalog, it will often refer you to another subject entry by printing *see* or *see also* before an entry.

Here is a sample entry from the *Readers' Guide.*

**John F. Kennedy Space Center**
Status report—Kennedy Space Center. R. S. Wagner. *Space World* T-2-230:34 F '83
Status report—KSC. R. S. Wagner. *Space World* T-1-229:31 Ja '83
Wildlife abounds around the Cape [Merritt Island National Wildlife Refuge] R. S. Wagner. il *Space World* T-3-231:26 Mr '83
**John Jay French House (Beaumont, Tex.)** *See* Historic houses, sites, etc.—Texas
**John Paul II, Pope, 1920-**
*about*
The agenda for 1983. *America* 148:3 Ja 1-8 '83
Bishops' summit. F. O'Sullivan. *Commonweal* 110:37 Ja 28 '83
Cardinal Wyszynski's spirituality of work. R. Barta and W. Droel. *America* 148:11-12 Ja 1-8 '83
**Assassination attempt, May 13, 1981**
The Bulgarian connection. *America* 148:23 Ja 15 '83
The Bulgarian connection. S. Gilbert. il *Macleans* 96:21 Ja 17 '83
A cardinal sin to be atoned [KGB involvement] B. Amiel. il *Macleans* 96:9 Ja 17 '83
The defector's tale [implicating KGB] F. Willey. il *Newsweek* 101:42 Ap 4 '83
Kremlin papers. Natl Rev 35:15 Ja 21 '83
New pieces for the puzzle. J. B. Kelly. il *Time* 121:36 F 7 '83
New twists in the plot to kill the Pope. K. Rogal. *Newsweek* 101:31-2 F 7 '83
The plot sickens [possibility of Soviet involvement] *New Repub* 188:7-8 Ja 24 '83
Pope's shooting: a global hot potato [Soviet involvement] il por *U S News World Rep* 94:8 Ja 10 '83
The undiplomatic Bulgarian [alleged Soviet involvement in attempted assassination of John Paul II; views of I. Mantarov] J. Kelly. il *Time* 121:38-9 Ap 4 '83
*Reporters and reporting*
Counterattack [Soviet reaction to accusations of KGB involvement] il *Time* 121:30 Ja 17 '83
Equal time [French communists protest anti-Soviet bias in press coverage of KGB involvement in shooting of John Paul II] *Time* 121:31 Ja 10 '83
**Travel**
Globe-trotting Pope: what drives him? J. Mann. il por *U S New World Rep* 94:22 Mr 21 '83
**Visit to Central America, 1983**
Central American pietà. S. Christian. *New Repub* 188:12-14 Ap 4 '83

## Specialized Indexes

For articles on specialized subjects, the *Readers' Guide* will not be adequate. You should consult the appropriate subject index. Each index lists articles restricted to the topic implied in its title. The date in parentheses indicates when the index began publication.

*American Indian Index* (1953–)
*Applied Science and Technology Index* (1958–)
*Art Index* (1929–)
*Biography Index* (1947–)
*Biological and Agricultural Index* (1947–)
*Black Information Index* (1970–)

*Book Review Digest* (1905–)
*Business Periodicals Index* (1958–)
*Chicano Periodical Index* (1967–)
*Dramatic Index* (1909–1949)
*Education Index* (1929–)
*Film Literature Index* (1973–)
*General Science Index* (1978–)
*Humanities Index* (1974–)
*Index to Religious Periodical Literature* (1954–)
*International Index to Film Periodicals* (1972–)
*Monthly Catalog of United States Government Publications* (1895–)
*Music Index* (1949–)
*Poole's Index for Periodical Literature* (1802–1907)
*Psychological Abstracts* (1975–)
*Public Affairs Information Service Bulletin* (1915–)
*Social Sciences and Humanities Index* (1965–1974)
*Social Sciences Index* (1974–)
*Sociological Abstracts* (1975–)
*United Nations Documents Index* (1950–)
*Women's Studies Abstracts* (1972–)

## Current Events

For current subject or events, the following reference guides are helpful:

*Facts on File.* This is a weekly digest of world news, with an annual index, that began in 1940.

*The New York Times Index.* This index enables you to locate stories published in *The Times* since 1913.

*Newsbank.* This unique reference work reproduces on microfiche selected articles on urban and public affairs from newspapers in 103 cities and indexes them under major subject areas.

## Electronic Databases

A growing trend in libraries is to have databases available through a computer, either on CD-ROM or as part of a larger network. These databases can be an excellent resource for research. Electronic databases may include access to periodical indexes, abstracts, tables of contents, catalog holdings at other universities, or even full texts of articles on a subject. Be sure to consult your own college library to find out what is available to you on your campus. Some well-known databases include:

*ABI/Inform.* This is an index with abstracts to more than 800 business-related periodicals and specialty publications since 1986.

*Academic Abstracts.* This service uses CD-ROM to provide an index with abstracts of articles from a wide range of magazines and scholarly journals.

*Applied Science and Technology Index.* This is an index to articles published in major technology and applied science periodicals since October, 1983.

*ArticleFirst.* This is an author, title, subject index to articles in more than 11,500 scholarly journals with emphasis on the natural sciences, technology, and medicine.

*Business Abstracts.* This is an index, with abstracts, to material published in major business periodicals since July, 1982.

*ContentsFirst.* This provides access to the table of contents of more than 11,500 scholarly journals emphasizing the natural sciences, technology, and medicine.

*Dialog.* This service provides access to over 500 databases on almost every subject possible, including business, the humanities, social sciences, psychology, science, and engineering. This research-oriented service also includes bibliographies and abstracts, full texts of 60 newspapers, and information from over one million periodicals.

*Dissertation Abstracts International.* This is an index to doctoral dissertations and masters' theses in a full range of academic disciplines offered at over 550 universities.

*ERIC.* This is an index to educational journal articles and documents. It provides summaries of the articles and documents and contains citations back to 1966.

*Expanded Academic Index.* This is an index to articles in over 900 scholarly and general interest periodicals focusing on topics in the social sciences, humanities, and non-technical general science areas.

*GIN.* The Government Information Network work stations can provide access to the most popular U.S. government databases, including: 1990 Census; National Economic, Social and Environmental Data Bank; National Trade Data Bank; Foreign Traders Index; United States Exports; United States Imports; and others.

*Health and Psychological Instruments (HAPI).* This is a database of information about research and survey instruments, such as questionnaires, rating scales, checklist, surveys, interview forms, and so on.

*Infotrac.* This service provides indexes on CD-ROM that are updated every two to three months. Infotrac offers general interest indexes such as Magazine Plus, and the General Periodical Index, as well as other, more academically oriented indexes.

*Lexis/Nexis.* This database includes the full text of a wide variety of government information, including proposed and enacted federal and state legislation, the *Congressional Record*, Congressional member information, federal regulations, Executive agency publications, and news services.

*Marcive GPO CAT/PAC.* This indexes many U.S. government publications issued from July, 1976 to the present.

*Medline.* This is an index, with abstracts, to journal articles published in health, medicine, nursing, and dentistry since 1988.

*MLA International Bibliography.* This is an international index to literature, language, linguistics, and folklore. It indexes articles, books, book chapters, dissertations, and conference proceedings.

*National Newspaper Index.* This is an index to articles published over the past three years in five national newspapers: *The New York Times, The Wall Street Journal, The Washington Post, The Christian Science Monitor,* and *The Los Angeles Times.*

*Newspapers Abstracts.* This is an index to articles in seven major regional, national, and ethnic newspapers since 1989.

*Periodical Abstracts.* This is an index to articles in nearly 1,000 general interest, academic, and business periodicals, and transcripts of more than 30 television broadcasts since 1986.

*PsycLit.* This is an index, with abstracts, to the world's serial and book literature in psychology and related disciplines published since 1974.

*Uncover.* This database provides table of contents information for over 16,000 journals in all disciplines. Coverage for most journals begins with 1989.

*United Nations Index.* This is an index primarily to General Assembly and Security Council documents issued since 1990.

*Wilson.* This service provides indexes such as Reader's Guide to Periodical Literature or the Social Science Index on computer. By placing these indexes on computer, Wilson makes multiple subject searches easy.

## Reading and Taking Notes

If you followed the strategy outlined in the preceding section, you are now faced with an imposing stack of books and articles. You will discover that not all of this material is usable, and you will come across more leads as you continue to work on your paper. Right now, however, it's time to start reading and taking notes.

As you begin reading, you will need a stock of index cards to keep a record of the books and articles that you use and to record accurately and concisely the ideas and facts from your sources. You will compile two kinds of cards: *bibliography* cards and *subject* cards.

For every article or book that you consult, fill out a separate *bibliography* card. This means that if you use two works by the same author, you will need two separate cards. For each book or article, write the call number in the top left corner of the card; this will save time later. When arranged alphabetically, your bibliography cards will form the basis of the list of works at the end of your paper. See pages 259–260 for examples of bibliography cards.

As you read each book or article, the notes that you take will be written on your *subject* cards. You will take three kinds of notes: *quotations, paraphrases,* and *summaries.*

*Quotations* are the actual words (including the spelling and punctuation) of the author. You should place quotation marks around them to remind yourself that they are from the original work, and write the page number(s) of the source where the quotation can be found. Quote the words of the original exactly, being certain not to change the meaning of the passage. If you omit words from the quotation, use ellipses (. . .); if you insert your own words in the quotation, use brackets ([]). See the handbook for a discussion of the use of ellipses and brackets.

Most of your subject cards will contain *paraphrases* and *summaries.* Use direct quotations only when the original words will create an impact or lend authority to the passage or when you intend to analyze it in detail. Paraphrasing material is restating the author's ideas in your own words. Paraphrasing is useful because it keeps you from being too dependent on the words of the original, and it forces you to digest the ideas in the original in order to express them in your own words. Be certain that you don't distort or exaggerate the ideas in the original passage when rewriting them.

Summaries present the key ideas in a brief condensation of the original in your own words. In that sense, they are shorter versions of paraphrased passages. The difference is not too important; in both cases you are using your own words.

Here are a few suggestions for note cards:

1. Keep a separate bibliography card for each source. This will simplify alphabetizing the list of "Works Cited" at the end of your paper.
2. Write the call number of every book or bound magazine on its bibliography card so that you can find it later without too much trouble.
3. Limit each subject card to one idea; this will make it easier to arrange and rearrange your ideas when planning your paper. To adjust your plan, simply adjust your cards.
4. On the top of each subject card put the first item from the bibliography card—the name or title. This will be enough to identify the source and will prepare you for the citations in the text.

R 726
M 28

Maguire, Daniel C.
Death by Choice
New York: Doubleday
1974

5. Supply page references for all quotations, summaries, and paraphrases.
6. Write in ink (pencil often smudges) and do *not* write on the back of a card (you may forget to turn it over).

Example bibliography and subject cards appear on pages 259 and 260.

## Plagiarism

Plagiarism is presenting someone's ideas or words as your own without giving proper credit. It is stealing, and many colleges and universities discuss it in their catalogs or student codes.

To avoid plagiarism, document the following material from your reading:

1. *All directly quoted material.* Enclose all quoted passages within quotation marks and document them according to the guidelines on pages 268–269. An exception would be well-known proverbs, expressions, or famous lines from literature ("To be or not to be; that is the question").
2. *All paraphrased and summarized material.* Because the words are your own, you do not place quotation marks around them, but you have an obligation to cite your sources whenever you paraphrase or summarize another person's words or ideas.

Tipler, Frank. "We Are Alone."
Discover Mar. 1983: 56-60

Tipler 56

"At least one intelligent species exists, namely the human race. I claim that we are probrably the only intelligent species ever to exist in our galaxy, and quite possibly the only such species that has ever existed in the known universe."

3. *Information that is not generally known.* Facts not generally available or widely known should be documented. If you state, "Over 33,000 Turks and their allies were drowned in the Battle of Lepanto in the straits of the Gulf of Corinth," your reader has a right to ask, "Says who? How do you know that? What's your

source?" On the other hand, facts that are common knowledge ("The sun rises in the east") do not have to be documented.

For the correct way to document your sources, see pages 269–273.

Most students know that when they copy another person's ideas word for word, they must acknowledge their source. Failure to do so is plagiarism. Some students, however, do not realize that when they paraphrase—when they restate or summarize information from a source in their own words—they still have an obligation to acknowledge their source.

These examples illustrate the difference between an unacceptable paraphrase (plagiarism) and an acceptable paraphrase.

### Original Source

Frederick the Great, King of Prussia, came to power in 1740. Although he is remembered in history books mostly for his military astuteness, he was also devoted to the life of the mind and the spirit. His court in Potsdam was one of the great centers of intellectual activity in Europe in the eighteenth century. The celebrated mathematician Leonhard Euler spent twenty-five years there. Many other mathematicians and scientists came, as well as philosophers—including Voltaire and La Mettrie, who wrote some of their most influential works while there. (from Douglas R. Hofstadter, *Gödel, Escher, Bach: An Eternal Golden Braid*, p. 3)

### Unacceptable Paraphrase (Plagiarism)

Although Frederick the Great, the King of Prussia, is remembered in history books for his military ability, he was devoted to activities of the mind and spirit. One of the great centers of intellectual activities in Europe during the eighteenth century was his royal court at Potsdam. Among the famous mathematicians, scientists, and philosophers who were at his court were the celebrated mathematician Leonhard Euler, who spent twenty-five years there, and the philosophers Voltaire and La Mettrie, who wrote some of their most important works while there.

*Comment:* Except for of a few word changes ("military ability" for "military astuteness," "activities of the mind" for "life of the mind," "most important works" for "most influential works") and a few slightly altered sentences, this passage has been copied from Hofstadter. By failing to credit the source or use quotation marks, the writer implies that the ideas and words are original.

### Acceptable Paraphrase

As Douglas Hofstadter points out, Frederick the Great attracted some of the greatest thinkers of eighteenth-century Europe to his court at Potsdam. Despite his encouragement and patronage of many prominent mathematicians, scientists, and philosophers, however, "he is remembered in history books mostly for his military astuteness" (3).

*Comment:* The writer acknowledges indebtedness to the source by mentioning Hofstadter's name, placing quotation marks around the passage that has been used from the source, and identifying the page number from which the quoted passage was taken in parentheses. With the exception of the quoted passage, the paragraph is the student's.

Another set of examples illustrates how a student may attempt to note where the original material came from, but still fail to properly distinguish between the original author's ideas and his or her own.

### Original Source

Many among the present Hispanic leadership, however, are now refusing assimilation and demanding that Hispanic immigrant children have their Spanish language and culture maintained in perpetuity in public schools at taxpayers' expense. This has never happened before. (from Richard Grenier, "Language Barriers to Leaving the Barrio" *Insight* June 15, 1992, p. 22)

### Unacceptable Student Text

Nevertheless, many leaders of Hispanics today do not agree with the idea of assimilating into the dominant culture and want children of Hispanic immigrants to learn Spanish and their own culture in public schools. This would mean, of course, that the taxpayers pay. According to Richard Grenier, however, such a thing has never happened before (22).

*Comment:* This paragraph is still plagiarism. Even though the last sentence is correctly documented, the first two sentences are a virtual copy of the original material. Again, as in the earlier example of an unacceptable paraphrase, words have been only slightly modified. Again, the failure to credit the first two sentences suggests that the ideas and words are the writer's; clearly, however, they are not.

### Acceptable Student Text

One of the problems this country faces with immigration comes from a refusal by many Hispanics to learn English and adopt the culture of the majority. According to Richard Grenier, the current Hispanic leaders do not wish to assimilate into the dominant culture. He states that they are "demanding that Hispanic immigrant children have their Spanish language and culture maintained in perpetuity in public schools at taxpayers' expense." Grenier opposes this move by declaring that the assimilation pattern of Hispanics is not too different from that of other immigrants (22). The United States cannot afford, nor would it be wise, to treat Hispanic immigrants any differently than any other group of immigrants that have come to America over the years. Ultimately, the Hispanic immigrants will benefit from being a part of a larger America, just as Italians, Jews, Irish, and others have done before.

*Comment:* Since all of the paraphrased and quoted material comes from the same page, there is no need to make frequent page references.

However, note that each sentence refers to Grenier so that the logical train of credit is maintained. This particular passage has a topic sentence by the writer and some commentary after the material from Grenier. Avoid paragraphs in which only material from other sources is presented. Writers should strive to engage the material, to critique and analyze it for the reader.

## *Organizing and Outlining Your Paper*

The best time to outline your paper is after you have completed most of your reading. When you have accumulated a sizeable stack of subject cards, you can use them as the basis for organizing your paper. By sorting them into stacks by topics, you will develop the major headings of your paper. You will notice topics that are too thin and will require some development. You will also see that some ideas have bulged out and need pruning. Still others are off the subject, not supporting the thesis statement or contributing anything to the controlling idea of your paper. As painful as it may be, you should remove them from your collection.

You can prepare a rough outline at this point by arranging your subject cards in the order in which you want to present your ideas. (See Chapter 4 for examples of rough outlines.) As you develop more ideas and information, your outline will become increasingly detailed. Your instructor may want you to turn in a more detailed *formal outline*, written just before you write the final copy of your term paper. (See page 276 for an example of a formal outline for a term paper.)

If you have to write a formal outline, begin with your thesis statement. If it is sharply focused, it will contain key words that suggest ways to divide the outline into manageable parts or sections. Using those key words as guides, make a list of all the major ideas that develop the thesis. They are represented by Roman numerals (I, II, III, and so on). The minor ideas that support the major ideas are represented by uppercase letters (A, B, C, and so on). This system lets you see at a glance whether ideas are in the right place, whether less important ideas are given too much prominence, and whether your paper has gotten sidetracked by unimportant or trivial facts and ideas.

When you outline, you divide larger ideas or topics into smaller ones. This means that every idea or topic will be divided into at least two parts. If you have a Roman numeral I, you must have at least II; if you have an A, you must have a B, and so on. Your instructor may ask you to write either a *topic* or a *sentence* outline; the two types differ chiefly in the way they express each idea or thought.

In the *topic outline,* a phrase or even a single word serves to indicate an idea in the essay. In the *sentence outline* each thought or idea is stated in a complete sentence. Obviously, the topic outline is briefer and more general; it is convenient if you are concerned with facts more than with ideas. When writing a topic outline, be sure that you don't include sentences. Further, don't mix grammatical forms—that is, if Roman numeral I is a prepositional phrase, make sure that all of the other Roman numerals contain prepositional phrases; if A and B under I are nouns, the capital letters under the other major headings should also be nouns.

The *sentence outline* is more detailed and makes writing the essay easier. Unlike the topic outline, each major and minor idea is expressed in a sentence. The sentence outline is often used when the subject is complicated and when the relationships among the ideas are subtle. Regardless of which type you use, a good outline will give your term paper a sense of direction. It will also test the relevance of your notes, revealing the relationship of your ideas to your controlling idea or thesis statement.

---

## Writing the First Draft

---

After you have arranged your subject cards in the order in which you wish to present your material and have written an outline to guide you as you write, you should take another glance at your thesis statement. It should reflect precisely the point you want to make in your paper, the goal that all of your facts, ideas, impressions, and conclusions are aiming toward. By focusing your thesis statement sharply now, you have another way to test the relevance and relationship of your ideas.

As you write the first draft of your paper, you will continue to add, delete, and adjust. Therefore, leave abundant space at the top, bottom, and sides of each page. Don't try to include in your paper every note from every card merely because you hate to see it wasted. If it is irrelevant, it will stick out in your paper. On the other hand, if you see that more facts or ideas are needed in a particular section, make a note to remind yourself that you should go back to your books and articles for additional information.

After any borrowed information you have in the rough draft put the identifying item from the subject card—the name or title—and the page number from which the information came. Detailed instructions for documenting your sources are on pages 267–269; for the time being, your goal is to make sure that you don't omit or lose this information while writing your first draft.

## Revising and Editing Your Term Paper

After writing the first draft, set your term paper aside for a day or two before beginning your revision. This will allow you to return to it with a fresh perspective and to see your paper again from an objective distance. As pointed out in Chapter 7 ("Revising the Essay"), every piece of writing can profit by careful revision.

Before beginning your revision, look over the checklists on pages 142 and 144. Then read your paper aloud, listening for the flow of ideas, smooth sentences, and the right word choice. As you reconsider your paper, keep a pair of scissors and a roll of Scotch tape or a stapler handy so that you can cut, rearrange, delete, or add material. As Chapter 7 illustrates, there are different levels of revising. As you go through your paper the first time, make certain that you have enough material and that it is in the right order. Be sure that your paper makes a point—that it informs the reader clearly and without confusion, or that it offers a persuasive argument that is logical and fair.

Working on computers can save you a great deal of time during this phase. Using spell-check programs is faster than looking up individual words in a dictionary. Also, unlike using a typewriter, which forces students to retype each draft, once a change is made, it can be saved permanently and new drafts can be printed with a few keystrokes. Nevertheless, as you learned in Chapter 7, computers will not recognize all possible errors in spelling or usage, so be sure to check over all your work for any errors that may have slipped through. For many students, checking a printed copy is easier than checking the text on the computer screen, especially for detecting problems with format.

An important part of the revising process is checking your paper for mistakes in spelling, grammar, or punctuation. Errors in these areas can detract from the overall impact of an otherwise excellent term paper. If you are uncertain about the spelling of a word, look it up in a dictionary. For problems or uncertainties in punctuation, consult the handbook.

After you have carefully reread your paper for completeness, organization, smoothness, and mechanical correctness, you are ready to prepare your final copy.

### Format

Unless your instructor specifies otherwise, you term paper should including the following parts:

1. *A title page.* The title page includes the title of your paper about a third of the way down the page, your name about two inches

below the title, and starting about two inches below your name, the name of the course, the instructor, and the date.

2. *An outline.* If your instructor requests an outline, place it between the title page and the first page of the text. If it is two or more pages long, number the pages with small Roman numerals (for example "ii," "iii") beginning with the first page of the outline, placing your last name and the numerals at the top righthand corner of the page.

3. *The text of the paper.* If the paper does not require a title page and table of contents or outline, you can put your name, the instructor's name, course identification, and date in the upper left corner of the page. Two lines below that the title of the paper will be centered on the page. Four lines below that the text begins. Put your last name and the page number in the upper right corner of the first page of the text. If the paper has a title page and other front matter, follow the style of the sample papers at the end of this chapter. The text should be double-spaced. Leave a margin of one inch at the top, bottom, and both sides of the text. Indent the first word of a paragraph five spaces from the left margin. Begin numbering with the first page of the text and continue throughout the paper, including any appendices, endnotes and the "Works Cited" page.

4. *Content notes page.* Occasionally you may find it necessary to add a note of explanation or commentary that you cannot logically fit into the body of your paper. Examples of the kind of information typically included in a content note are suggestions for further reading, an explanation of a particular procedure or term, a comment about an apparent conflict between sources, or other matters not directly related to the text. Content notes can be placed at the bottom of the page as footnotes, or they can be placed on a separate page following the last page of your text as endnotes. Label this page with the word "Notes" centered one inch from the top of the page. The first note should begin two spaces below this heading. Using raised superscript numerals, number your notes in sequence so that they match those in your text. Double-space all entires and double-space between the entires. See pages 269–270 for examples of content notes.

5. *"Works Cited" page.* At the end of your term paper you should include a list of all the source materials actually cited in your paper, as well as those sources mentioned in your content endnotes. The items should be arranged alphabetically, placing the first line of each entry flush with the left margin and indenting succeeding lines five spaces. Double-space each entry and double-space between entries. Place the title "Works

Cited" one inch from the top of the page and leave two spaces between it and the first entry. See pages 270–273 for the correct format for books and other sources listed in the "Works Cited," and see page 284 for a sample "Works Cited" page.

### How to Handle Quotations Within the Text of Your Paper

As you write your term paper, you will frequently incorporate quoted material directly into your text. A quotation should be introduced smoothly into the text so that it does not clash or conflict with the surrounding passage, yet it should contribute forcefully and convincingly to the paper.

If a quotation takes up *no more than four lines* in your paper, place it in the body of the text and enclose it within quotation marks. If a quotation is *longer than four lines,* it should be indented ten spaces from the left margin and double-spaced, *without* quotation marks.

Shorter quotations should be introduced by the name of the author, when possible, and a verb such as *states, claims, declares,* or *adds.* If the quotation forms a grammatical part of the sentence in which it occurs, the first word of the quotation does not have to be capitalized, even though it might be capitalized in the original. Note the following example:

> Typical of the optimism expressed in recent weeks concerning the economic future is the statement of Richard Curtin who claims that "we are talking about a surge in consumer confidence that has never been seen before" (19).

If the quotation follows a formal introduction set off by a comma or colon, you should capitalize the first word as in the original:

> Typical of the optimism expressed in recent weeks concerning the economic future is the statement of Richard Curtin: "We are talking about a surge in consumer confidence that has never been seen before" (19).

Longer quotations should be introduced by the author's name, when possible, and by a colon or comma. The entire quoted passage should be double-spaced. If the quoted material is a single paragraph, do not indent the first line. If two or more paragraphs are quoted consecutively, indent the first line of each an additional three spaces.

Below is an example of a quotation that exceeds four lines.

---

. . . undertook to determine whether the universe really was expanding. As Jastrow has pointed out, Hubble took a series of logical steps:

Hubble's first step was to find out what the mysterious spiral "nebulas" were. Photographing these objects with the 100-inch telescope, he found that they contained vast numbers of individual stars. Hubble's photographs convinced astronomers that spiral nebulas were true galaxies, or island universes.

Hubble's next step was to find out how far away the galaxies were. He proceeded to measure their distances, using, as a yardstick, a certain kind of star called a Cepheid, whose true brightness was known from studies of similar stars in our own galaxy. (491)

From the degree of faintness of Cepheid stars in other galaxies, Hubble was able to estimate the distance to these galaxies. His . . .

---

## *Parenthetical Documentation*

With the exception of content notes (described on page 269), endnotes and footnotes are no longer necessary for identifying a source in a term paper. The system set forth in the *MLA Handbook* (1995) specifies that the source for each quotation and paraphrase must be included within the text in parentheses by author or short title and page. Any (or all) of these elements should be omitted if they are mentioned in the body of your paper. Because the "Works Cited" will list only general information about the books and articles you used, you must include within the text the specific page in the source.

For quotations of four lines or less, the parenthesis is placed after the closing quotation mark but before the end punctuation.

According to Alvin Toffler, "We develop a self-image by assuming the roles of others" (*Learning* 21).

The writer mentions Toffler's first name because this is the first reference to the author; subsequent references will dispense with the first name. Because there is more than one work by Toffler cited in the paper, the writer includes a shortened version of the title in question. Notice the page reference follows the title and is not separated by a comma. Here is another example.

As Wills points out, "Revolution was a respectable term in eighteenth-century English" (52).

Because the writer has previously identified Gary Wills, he does not repeat his first name. Because only one work by Wills is cited in the paper, the writer does not include the title of the work he is quoting from. The same is true of the next example.

Suzuki claims that Zen differs from all other philosophic and religious meditation practices (21).

The writer is presenting an indirect quotation from a book by Suzuki. The reader can turn to the list of "Works Cited" at the end of the term paper for further information, including the title, publisher, and date of publication.

To document longer quotations, omit quotation marks and indicate the page in parentheses after the final period. Below is an example of this style; notice that the writer has identified the author and title of the selection in the body of the term paper.

---

. . . and the relationship between style and art is pointed out by Susan Sontag in <u>Against Interpretation</u>:

> All works of art are found on a certain distance from the lived reality which is represented. This "distance" is, by definition, inhuman or impersonal to a certain degree; for in order to appear to us as art, the work must restrict sentimental intervention and emotional participation, which are functions of "closeness." It is the degree and manipulating of this distance, the conventions of distance, which constitute the style of the work. In the final analysis, "style" <u>is</u> art. And art is nothing more or less than various modes of stylized, dehumanized representation. (39)

According to Sontag, style is the principle of decision in a work of art, the signature of the artist's will. And as the human will . . .

---

Notice that the page reference follows the final period. To document an electronic source that uses paragraph numbers instead of page numbers, use the abbreviation "par." or "pars." before the relevant paragraph number.

The sample term paper on pages 275–284 contains additional examples of the MLA documentation style.

## Sample Content Notes

Content notes contain comments, explanations, and other information that you cannot fit into the text of your paper. They should be placed at the end of the text (as an endnote) or at the bottom of the page (as a footnote) on a separate page following the last page of your text. As in the case of your citations within the text of your paper, content notes must be fully documented in your Works Cited."

Here are some typical endnotes:

1. On this point see Highet (76) and Murray (191).
2. For an opposing point of view, see Ogilvie (211).
3. For the behaviorist response to Chomsky's theories, see Skinner (78–83).

## Preparing Your "Works Cited" Page

The final section of your term paper, "Works Cited," is an alphabetical list of the source materials you used when writing your paper. If you have kept your bibliography cards up-to-date, it is an easy matter to arrange them alphabetically. Be sure to include those works mentioned in your content endnotes.

Most entires are arranged alphabetically by the author's last name. If the work is anonymous or unsigned, its place is determined by the first word of the title (other than *A, An,* and *The*). The first line of each entry should be flush with the left margin, and succeeding lines should be indented five spaces. Double-space each entry and double-space between entires.

The MLA system requires that you omit unnecessary clutter from citations and the list of works cited. Items such as "p." (for "page") are not needed. However, commonly understood abbreviations, such as the postal forms for states (CA, WI) and the short forms for days and months (but not May, June, and July), should be used in documentation, but not in the text of the paper.

## Bibliography Form: Books

**Book With One Author**

> Winzerling, Oscar W. *Acadian Odyssey.* Baton Rouge: Louisiana State UP, 1955.

[If you use more than one work from the same author or source, it is not necessary to repeat the name with each entry. Instead, type three hyphens flush with the left margin, followed by a period, as in the following example.]

> ---. *The Settling of Belize.* New York: Holt, 1981.

**Book with Two or Three Authors**

> Mead, Margaret, and Rhoda Metraux. *A Way of Seeing.* New York: Morrow, 1968.

**Book with More Than Three Authors**
Turk, Amos, et al. *Environmental Science.* Philadelphia: Saunders, 1978.

**Book with a Corporate Author**
The Association for Educational Communications and Technology. *Research, Principles, and Practices in Visual Communication.* Washington: The Association for Educational Communications and Technology, 1960.

**Edition After the First**
Coleman, James C., James N. Butcher, and Robert C. Carson. *Abnormal Psychology and Modern Life.* 6th ed. Glenview: Scott, 1980.

**Edited Collection**
Valdez, Luis, and Stan Steiner, eds. *Aztlan: An Anthology of Mexican American Literature.* New York: Knopf, 1972.

**Story or Article from an Anthology**
Spark, Muriel. "The Twins." *Fiction 100: An Anthology of Short Stories.* Ed. James H. Pickering. New York: Macmillan, 1982. 132–45.

**Translation**
deCervantes Saavedra, Miguel. *Don Quixote of La Mancha.* Trans. Walter Starkie. New York: Macmillan, 1982.

**Work in More Than One Volume**
Washburn, Wilcomb E. *The American Indian and the United States.* 2 vols. New York: Random, 1973.

**Reprint**
Bury, J. B. *The Idea of Progress.* 1932. New York: Dover, 1955.

**Book with an Editor and an Author**
Newman, John Henry. *Apologia Pro Vita Sua.* Ed. David J. DeLaura. New York: Norton, 1968.

## *Bibliography Form: Reference Books*

Articles in reference works are similar to articles in anthologies. The author's name should be listed first, followed by the title of the article in quotation marks. (Sometimes only the author's initials are given with the article; the full name can be located elsewhere in the book.) The editor of the reference work should be omitted. If the work is arranged alphabetically, page numbers are omitted.

**Signed Article in an Encyclopedia**
> Ogilvie, R. M. "Livy." *Encyclopaedia Britannica: Macropedia.* 1974 ed.

**Unsigned Article in an Encyclopedia**
> "Cyclone." *Encyclopedia Americana.* 1981 ed.

**Unsigned Article in an Almanac**
> "Notable Sports Personalities." *World Almanac and Book of Facts.* 1981 ed. 815–17.

## *Bibliography Form: Periodicals*

The entry for a periodical shares some similarities with the entry for a book, but it also contains some differences. The arrangement of the lines is the same. The title of the article, in quotation marks, comes between the name of the author and the name of the journal or magazine. The original punctuation at the end of the article title should be used (a question mark, for example), or a period should be inserted inside the closing quotation mark. The name of the periodical from which the article is taken should be underlined, with any introductory articles omitted (*New York Times,* not *The New York Times*), followed by the volume and number, date of publication, a colon, and the page numbers for the entire article. If the article is not printed on consecutive pages, write only the first page number and the plus sign (A1+). Daily, weekly, and monthly periodicals omit the volume and parentheses.

**Signed Article in a Weekly Magazine**
> Barber, Benjamin. "Beyond the Feminist Mystique."*New Republic* 11 July 1983: 26–32.

**Signed Article in a Monthly Magazine**
> Christian, Shirley. "El Salvador's Divided Military." *Atlantic* June 1983: 50–60.

**Signed Article in a Daily Newspaper**
> Ostrow, Ronald J. "Cuban Refugees Get Due-Process Rights." *Los Angeles Times* 8 July 1983: A14.

**Editorial**
> "Power Defined Is Not Power Lost." Editorial. *New York Times* 3 July 1983: D12.

**Signed Article in a Journal with Continuous Pagination**
> O'Reilley, Mary Rose. "The Peaceable Classroom." *College English* 46 (1984): 103–12.

**Signed Article in a Journal with Separate Pagination**
> Kane, Declan F. "Irish Place Names." *Gaelic Studies* 14.1 (1956): 29–33.

**Unsigned Article**

> "London Express." *Time* 6 June 1983: 45–46.
> "British Doctors Report New Infant Disease." *San Diego Union* 9 July 1983: A10.

## *Bibliography Form: Other Sources*

An entry for material obtained from an electronic database should be presented like one for materials gathered from printed sources, but should also include information necessary to trace the entry through the database. This information will generally include the name of the database, the publication date, the name of the vendor (if relevant), and the electronic publication date.

**Electronic Database**

> Gogek, Jim. "We've Gotton Tough, But Not Smart, on Crime." *San Diego Union-Tribune.* 17 Jan. 1994: A–2. *San Diego Union-Tribune on CD-ROM.* CD-ROM. June 1994.

**Government Document**

> United States. Department of Health, Education, and Welfare. *Ethical Issues in Health Services.* Washington: GPO, 1970.

**Pamphlet**

> *Proposed Changes in Rules and Regulations for Secondary School Teams.* California Soccer Referees' Assn., 1983.

**Unpublished Dissertation**

> Willis, Veronica. "An Investigation of the Use of the Documented Research Paper in College Sources." Diss. United States International U, 1970.

**Television or Radio Program**

> "A Town Like Alice." *Masterpiece Theater.* PBS. WMVS, Milwaukee. 3 July 1983.
> Keillor, Garrison, host. *A Prairie Home Companion.* NPR. KPBS-FM, San Diego. 10 Feb. 1984.

**Film**

> *Return of the Jedi.* Dir. Richard Marquand. Twentieth-Century Fox, 1983.

**Recording**

> Fleetwood Mac. *Rumors.* Warner, 1977.

**Interview Conducted by the Researcher**

> Hogins, James B. Personal interview. 1 Apr. 1983.

# COMPUTER EXERCISE

Consulting pages 270–273 or the *MLA Handbook for Writers of Research Papers,* 4th ed., arrange the following items into the proper sequence for a Works Cited page. Your instructor will check your work.

**Unsigned Article in Magazine**

pages 400–403 *Consumer Reports* "Air-Conditioners for Big Spaces" June, 1994

**Reprint of Book with One Author (also, book with an Editor)**

Theodore Dreiser Houghton Mifflin Company *Sister Carrie* Boston 1959 Reprinted from 1900 edition Edited by Claude Simpson

**Book with two or three authors (also, Edition After the First)**

Robert E. Yarber Third Edition HarperCollins U.S.A. Andrew J. Hoffman *Writing for College* 1996

**Signed Article from a Daily Newspaper**

*New York Times* Gustav Niebuhr "Seeking Solace and Spirituality, Many Turn to Meditation Books" pages A-1 and A-10 August 10, 1991

**Interview Conducted by the Researcher**

Talked to Scott Ellis in person on August 16, 1994

**Signed Article in a Journal with Continuous Pagination**

pages 289–295 Volume 38 Year 1991 *Journal of Counseling Psychology* "Personality Differences of First-Time and Repeat Offenders Arrested for Driving While Intoxicated" Jams R. Reynolds, Joseph T. Kunce, Corrine S. Cope.

**Story or Article from an Anthology**

"Man Must Kill" by Adolf Hitler HarperCollins Edited by Jeanne Gunner and Ed Frankel pg. 168–9 *A Course of Ideas* Second Edition U.S.A. 1991

## Sample Term Papers

Two sample term papers follow. The first is a persuasive paper that argues a thesis. This paper follows the most commonly used documentation system described by the MLA.

The second paper is a report. It uses a short-cut system for documentation that resembles those used in the sciences. In both cases the form for the bibliography is the same. The only difference is the way the sources are cited in the text.

Tobacco Termination Techniques


by
Anna Kalina


English 101
Mr. Hoffman
10 December 1993

Outline

Thesis:  The "cold turkey" method of quitting smoking and the "Smoke No More" program are more effective and successful than the use of nicotine gum or of a nicotine patch.

I.  Nicotine Gum
   A.  Description and intent of nicotine gum
   B.  Problems with acidic beverages and gum
   C.  Problems with chewing and absorption
   D.  Effectiveness of nicotine gum

II.  Nicotine Patch
   A.  Description and intent of nicotine patch
   B.  Troubling side effects
   C.  Lack of psychological satisfaction
   D.  Effectiveness of nicotine patch

III.  "Smoke No More" Program
   A.  Description and intent of the program
   B.  Teaches looking at entire health of smoker
   C.  Effectiveness of the program

IV.  "Cold Turkey" approach
   A.  Description and intent of "cold turkey" approach
   B.  Effectiveness of this approach is superior to others

Kalina 1

Tobacco Termination Techniques

Cigarette smoking has had a striking effect on life in our country. According to the Scripps Clinic and Research Foundation, one out of every four adults in the United States smokes cigarettes. Considering that the ill effects of cigarette smoking are well known to the public, this percentage may come as somewhat of a surprise. As for why more people do not quit smoking, Cheryl Wuchina, Smoking Cessation Coordinator at Sharp Center for Health Promotion, notes that the nicotine found in cigarettes is "as addictive as heroin or cocaine" (8). Quitting smoking would seem to be a horrendous and painful task. As Wuchina points out, "of the 17 million American adults who attempt to quit each year, only 1.3 million are successful" (8). This is a relatively poor success rate, yet smokers' hopes of stopping have not ceased. In fact, a new industry has developed to help smokers quit. Some of the most commonly employed strategies of quitting smoking include use of nicotine gum, the nicotine patch, a smoking cessation program such as "Smoke No More," or the old-fashioned method of going "cold turkey." The "cold turkey" method of quitting smoking is more successful than the use of nicotine gum, a nicotine patch, or a smoking cessation program.

Nicotine gum is a popular method of quitting smoking because it allows the smoker to receive nicotine without smoking. Sheldon Saul Hender, M.D., Ph.D., tells the story of patient who beat addictions to alcohol, cocaine, and heroin on his own, but couldn't kick nicotine. Part of Hendler's prescription to break the habit involved the use of nicotine gum (137–38). This approach acknowledges that "nicotine is one of the most addictive substances known to man" (Hendler 139). However, those who choose this method should expect to pay a lot. In a telephone interview, Greg Hardesty, sales associate at Omega Drug, stated that nicotine gum can be found in drug stores and obtained by the prescription of a doctor for about $44 a package. This is not inexpensive.

The intent of nicotine gum is to wean smokers gradually from cigarettes by fueling their bodies with decreasing amounts of nicotine until the act of smoking has ceased. Wuchina notes that "nicotine gum released nicotine into the body through the membrane between the cheek and gums" (8). This elementary process, however, is frequently the cause of significant problems that can arise with the use of nicotine gum.

Drinking acidic beverages while using the gum is one common problem. According to the article "Nicotine-Gum Users: Watch What You Drink," when the mouth is rinsed with such common beverages as coffee and cola, the nicotine found in the gum is "virtually eliminated" (220). Since coffee and cola are such commonly consumed beverages, one may assume that misuse of nicotine gum in this way occurs regularly.

Other typical, though presumably inadvertent, misapplications of the nicotine gum reside in the specific chewing technique necessary for the intended function of the gum. According to Fiore, "Patients familiar with chewing regular gum may chew nicotine gum too rapidly . . . resulting in most of the available nicotine being swallowed" (2690). The flavor of the nicotine gum has also led to some ill-usage of it. Fiore points out that "many report the taste to be aversive, and thus fail to use the gum enough during the day to ensure adequate nicotine replacement" (2690). Carol Johnson, who has been a cigarette smoker for approximately thirty years, tried the nicotine gum several years ago and reports the gum as being "insignificant." She claims that nicotine gum did not have much of an effect on her except for inducing fatigue and headaches. The easy misuse of nicotine gum makes the gum seem laden with potential problems; as Richard E. Johnson notes, "Providers should educate their patients in the techniques that maximize the use and effectiveness of nicotine gum in smoking cessation" (1598). Invariably, if something can be misused, it will be, and nicotine gum is no exception.

Nicotine gum use in smoking cessation can help, but the drawback lies in how the gum works. On the positive side of using nicotine gum, as noted in the article "Nicotine-Gum Users: Watch What You Drink," nicotine gum "can reduce tobacco withdrawal, a desire to smoke, and such side effects as weight gain--but only when sufficient nicotine is absorbed" (220). Nicotine gum can be effective; however, the proper use is essential. Even though people using nicotine gum are still acquiring nicotine, the form and administration techniques differ greatly from actually smoking. Jack E. Henningfield, Ph.D., writes that nicotine gum "does not, however, produce the sharp plasma level spike achieved when smoking cigarettes" (1560). As a consequence, many people trying to quit smoking feel the loss of the rush cigarettes seem to offer.

The ultimate question is, of course, how effective nicotine gum is for stopping smoking. John R. Hughes, M.D., reports in a recent study that "nicotine gum did no better than a placebo in helping smokers stop smoking" (1531). Henningfield speculates on a possible and perhaps probable explanation for why nicotine gum has been such a poor remedy: "the problem may have been the failure to obtain the medication in sufficient doses and not the medication per se" (1560). In other words, the nicotine gum is used improperly.

Another distinct disadvantage of nicotine gum is that it tends solely to the physical addiction of smoking, ignoring psychological addiction. Fiore reports that "success rates are much higher when nicotine gum is incorporated into a comprehensive smoking cessation program" (2691). Perhaps the very function of nicotine gum is misinterpreted. People may chew the gum and expect it to instantly cure their addiction when more than just the physical addiction to cigarettes must be addressed.

The nicotine patch is another method. The patch was developed in 1992 (Fiore 2687). According to Sheryl Nance-Nash, nicotine patches can be obtained by getting a prescription from a doctor (38). Isadore Rosenfeld, M.D., urges people who are considering using the patch to keep in mind that "nicotine patches are not cheap. The number required for the ten weeks of treatment costs around three hundred dollars" (414). He reports that concerning the use and dosage of nicotine in the patch, there are "three different strengths--21 mg, 14 mg, and 7 mg"; an individual is to begin treatment with the highest nicotine dose, 21 mg, and then gradually decrease the intake of nicotine (414). Rusty Unger points out that the lowest dose, 7 mg, is "equal to about seven cigarettes" (22). In the United States, there are four different brands of approved nicotine patches, including Habitrol, Nicoderm, Nicotrol, and PROSTEP, all of which are basically equivalent to each other (Fiore 2689).

The intent of the nicotine patch is to decrease slowly the intake of nicotine into a person's body. Nicotine patches are essentially "adhesive patches, which release a controlled amount of nicotine through the skin into the bloodstream" (Unger 22). Simply adhering a nicotine-ridden patch to the body and then waiting for the effects seems almost too effortless of a task in quitting smoking. There are indeed several potential problems and disadvantages with using a nicotine patch.

A number of fairly troubling side effects are frequently reported with the use of the nicotine patch. Fiore notes some of the most common unpleasant consequences of the patch are "a local skin reaction" and "sweating, nervousness, vivid and/or disturbing dreams" and "mild to moderate insomnia" (2690). Another important factor to be aware of with the nicotine patch is the grave danger of smoking cigarettes while simultaneously wearing the patch. Rosenfeld writes, "This is not a good idea, because smoking may boost the nicotine level already present in the bloodstream to dangerous concentrations. . . . There have been heart attacks in such cases" (414). Rosenfeld also points out that nicotine patches are not for every smoker trying to quit; there are several situations in which the patch may do more harm than good. She notes that those who should avoid the patch include:

> pregnant women because nicotine in any form can harm the fetus. . . . People with an overactive thyroid gland or who have insulin-dependent diabetes should also be careful with the patch. Nicotine causes the adrenal glands to release hormones that can worsen both conditions. (414).

The nicotine patch must be used with care and caution for the maximum probability of success.

Although the nicotine patch physically does the equivalent of a cigarette, the patch is not the same as a cigarette psychologically. The nicotine patch introduces nicotine into the bloodstream as a cigarette would, "but it does deprive the addict of the high he or she enjoys when a slug of nicotine hits the brain seven seconds after a deep inhalation of smoke. This pleasurable feeling is what addicts miss most" (Rosenfeld 414). Another discrepancy is that people seem frequently to expect too much of the patch. According to "The Truth About the Nicotine Patch," one of the biggest misconceptions about the patch is that it is an instant cure for nicotine addiction (6). Richard Ritson, who tried to quit smoking with the aid of a nicotine patch, said in a personal interview that he wanted to smoke cigarettes even while using the patch. He felt that he probably expected too much from the nicotine patches. The use of the nicotine patch is apparently a more complex activity than it would initially appear to be.

When the nicotine patch is put to use, the effectiveness of the patch is questionable. Rosenfeld reports on the success rates of the nicotine patch: "Seventy-five percent of the people who try to quit smoking [with the nicotine patch] do so for an average of only three months, but the odds improve with psychological counseling" (414). An unsigned article titled "Patching a Habit" in Better Homes and Gardens says that "over a six-month period, the so-called nicotine patch (plus counseling) helped twice as many stay off tobacco as counseling by itself" (62). The nicotine patch seems to be not a cure for cigarette addiction, but a helpful component of the generally arduous process of quitting smoking.

Several programs designed to help people quit smoking have been developed throughout the United States. One such is the reputable "Smoke No More" program which was developed by the Health Resource Center of Scripps Clinic in San Diego, California. The fee is $175 (Scripps Clinic and Research Foundation). A distinct advantage of this program, according to Carol Johnson who joined the program after failing to quit by using nicotine gum, is that after one has paid the initial cost of the program, even if one is not successful, the first time around, the program allows and welcomes return members.

The organization of the "Smoke No More" program is simple as well as fairly extensive. "Smoke No More" is separated into a series of classes that come in two phases. According to literature from the Scripps Clinic and Research Foundation, "The first phase is an intensive, four-week course" in which members of a class of fifteen to twenty others meet biweekly for two and a half hours. Scripps Clinic reports that "these classes form the core of the program and provide the necessary tools for [one] to become a non-smoker." Scripps Clinic's literature states that the second phase places more focus on providing an "on-going follow-up to ensure that [members] remain smoke-free" as well as "to share each member's successes, discuss problems and add new skills."

The "Smoke No More" program places specified emphasis on several issues of pertinence to people quitting smoking. In a telephone interview with Cathy Cobble, who was a member of a "Smoke No More" class, she said that the program placed importance on maintaining a healthy diet, relaxation techniques, awareness of one's smoking habits, support from the group as well as family and friends, and determination to keep on trying. The "Smoke No More" program seems to make a genuine effort to encompass as many facets as are feasible within the program.

The "Smoke No More" classes are directed and instructed by specified, knowledgeable individuals as well. Scripps Clinic states that these qualified people include "the program specialist . . . a pulmonary physician, a stress management counselor, an exercise physiologist and a clinical dietitian." The "Smoke No More" program attempts to tend to the physical needs as well as the psychological needs of an individual who is trying to quit smoking.

Scripps Clinic and Research Foundation has apparently designed an effective program with "Smoke No More." According to the Scripps Clinic, in the national average of other smoking cessation programs, only about thirty percent of the members are successful after one year, and the annual success rate of the "Smoke No More" program is over fifty percent. While considering these statistics, "Smoke No More" does not seem like a poor choice of methods or programs at all. Nevertheless, that means one in two people continue to smoke. Carol Johnson continued to smoke after the "Smoke No More" program even though she testified that it is a better method than using nicotine gum or a nicotine patch. No program can promise complete success.

The "cold turkey" method of quitting smoking refers to the attempt by people to stop smoking on their own, presumably without any specialized techniques, programs, or classes. This is undoubtedly the most frugal technique for stopping smoking, though perhaps not always the most appropriate. As Wuchina points out, "While going cold turkey may be easy for one person, the next person may experience strong cravings for cigarettes" or other symptoms related to nicotine withdrawal (8). According to the American Medical Association or AMA, these symptoms include "restlessness and irritability, trouble concentrating, difficulty sleeping, hunger and weight gain, headaches and fatigue,

Kalina 7

sweating, dizziness, and a rapid heartbeat" and "cravings for a cigarette that may intensify at times (but won't go on forever)." The fact that these rather unpleasant symptoms do indeed cease is quite encouraging and makes the act and efforts of quitting smoking all the more worthwhile.

Although quitting smoking completely may seem to be a drastic and not a potentially wise move, the "cold turkey" method is reported as superior to all others that have been developed. According to the AMA, "most smokers are able to stop smoking 'cold turkey.'" The AMA also advises smokers that "Your best chance of success is to make a clean break with cigarettes" rather than gradually weaning oneself off of them. "The Truth About the Nicotine Patch" in <u>Hope Health Letter</u> states that "an estimated 90% of America's 40 million ex-smokers have quit on their own" (6). This statement makes the "cold turkey" method seem not only feasable but simply the most effective strategy for quitting smoking as well.

From schools to the United States Congress, people have talked about the dangers of smoking. According to Scripps Clinic, "There are 35,000 unnecessary deaths of smokers each year in the U.S." Millions who smoke are trying to quit, either with nicotine gum, the nicotine patch, a smoking cessation program, or just going "cold turkey." The numbers show that the "cold turkey" method of quitting smoking is more effective than the use of nicotine gum, the nicotine patch, or a smoking cessation program. Carol Johnson, among other millions of smokers trying to break the habit, will be better off quitting on her own.

Kalina 8

Works Cited

American Medical Association. <u>Stop for Good.</u> N.p.: AMA, 1993.
    N. pag.

Cobble, Cathy. Telephone interview. 7 Dec. 1993.

Fiore, Michael O., et al. "Tobacco Dependence and the Nicotine
    Patch." <u>Journal of the American Medical Association</u> 268
    (1992): 2687–94.

Hardesty, Greg. Telephone interview. 3 Dec. 1993.

Hendler, Sheldon Saul. <u>The Purification Prescription.</u> New·York:
    Morrow, 1991.

Henningfield, Jack E., et al. "Drinking Coffee and Carbonated
    Beverages Blocks Absorption of Nicotine from Nicotine
    Polacrilex Gum." <u>Journal of the American Medical
    Association</u> 264 (1990): 1560–64.

Hughes, John R. "Nicotine Gum in General Practice." <u>Journal of
    the American Medical Association</u> 264 (1990): 1531.

Johnson, Carol. Personal interview. 30 Nov. 1993.

Johnson, Richard E., et al. "Nicotine Chewing Gum Use in the
    Outpatient Care Setting." <u>Journal of the American Medical
    Association</u> 267 (1992): 1598.

Nance-Nash, Sheryl. "Making a Patch Work for You." <u>Money</u>
    Oct. 1992: 38.

"Nicotine-Gum Users: Watch What You Drink." <u>Science News</u> 138
    (1990): 220.

"Patching a Habit." <u>Better Homes and Gardens</u> Apr. 1992: 62.

Ritson, Richard. Personal interview. 2 Dec. 1993.

Rosenfeld, Isadore. "What to Expect from the Nicotine Patch."
    <u>Vogue</u> Sept. 1992: 414.

Scripps Clinic and Research Foundation. <u>Smoke No More.</u> San
    Diego: Scripps, 1992. No. pag.

"The Truth About the Nicotine Patch." <u>Hope Health Letter</u> n.d.:
    6.

Unger, Rusty. "Power Patch." <u>New York</u> 27 Apr 1992: 22.

Wuchina, Cheryl. "The Nicotine Patch: Is It for You?" <u>Sharp
    Health Care</u> San Diego: Sharp, 1993.

The Demaree Method of Swarm Control

by
Maria Chavez

English 208
Ms. Welles
April 15, 1988

### Summary

Swarming, though a natural method by which bees reproduce a colony, lessens the value of a colony for the beekeeper. Overcrowding is probably the chief cause. The beekeeper must be alert for the signs of swarming, such things as queen cells and lethargic performance by a healthy colony. The principle of the Demaree method of swarm control is to provide the queen more space for brood and the workers more space for honey. The method is more suitable for small than large apiaries.

Table of Contents

1

Introduction

Swarming is the natural method by which colonies of honey bees divide themselves and, by doing so, perpetuate the race. But, when a swarm occurs, the original colony is reduced in size and may not produce the amount of honey that the original colony could have in a season. For this reason, it is important that the beekeeper try to reduce the number of swarms and keep colonies strong. The purpose of this report is to describe the causes for and signs of swarming and one traditional way of preventing it called the Demaree method.

Background

It is well known that an otherwise ordinary colony will sometimes swarm when the hive is greatly disturbed, such as by livestock or a wild animal. Also, colonies that are troubled by stress or disease will completely empty a hive. This is not, in the usual sense, a swarm, but rather an extraordinary and accidental situation that causes a colony to move to a new location. The term "abscond" is used to describe this occurrence (see also "swarm" in the Glossary).

Swarming, on the other hand, is not an accident but something the colony plans, usually in the late spring:

> Swarming is a natural process whereby a colony divides so that part of its leaves for a new homesite, usually with the old queen, while the remaining members continue at the original site with a newly emerged . . . queen. In this manner, a single unit becomes two. (1, 73)

Swarming, then, is a form of reproduction, a way for the colony to have more chances to make its way in the world.

In a managed apiary the colonies of bees gather much more honey than they can use, and the beekeeper takes the surplus from them in the late summer and fall, leaving the bees just enough honey to tide them through the winter. The hives are then reduced to a size small enough to contain the bees and some food. Although a number of bees die over the winter, an average colony will begin to stir when the day lengthens and the plants begin to flower in the spring. This stimulates the queen to begin laying eggs. If the beekeeper does not provide additional space for the colony to grow, the result is overcrowding in the hive and preparation for swarming (2, 31).

2

<u>Causes of Swarming</u>

One reason for swarming, then, is a combination of the natural process and a shortage of space to live in. But there are
other situations that may increase a colony's inclination to
swarm. One has to do with the queen's age:

> Colonies with queens one or more years old, whose egg-laying
> powers are diminishing, swarm more readily than colonies
> with young laying queens. (4, 377)

Although it is desirable to have a strong colony in preparation
for the honey flow, it is possible to have the population build up
too quickly and plan to swarm before it is noticed. Crowding and
a lessening of the queen's vigor are the usual reasons offered
for swarming, but some writers have also mentioned overheating, poor ventilation, inclement weather, diseases, and poor
comb conditions as additional reasons why a colony might decide
to swarm (1, 73-4; 5, 95-96). Some of these eventualities the
beekeeper can't plan for, except for giving the bees good conditions and the best equipment to work in.

Less understood are some chemical substances called
"pheromones," glandular secretions which are said to bind the
colony together. If a queen does not produce a sufficient amount
to distribute to workers in the hive (perhaps because of age or
injury), there is a tendency to swarm (6, 356). There could be
some question as to whether this is a cause or an effect.

<u>The Signs of Swarming</u>

Some signs of swarm preparation can be detected without
opening a hive, but waiting until they are confirmed may make
it too late to do anything about it. "A badly crowded colony often
has bees clustered on the landing board and on the front of the
hive near the entrance," as one author describes it (3, 74). But
this could be confused with clustering caused by a hive being
overheated because it gets too much sun. (Overheating can also
cause swarming, but overheating usually occurs later in the
summer, when the usual time for swarms is past.)

Another external sign of swarming, one that is harder to
spot but seems accurate, is a slow down by the workers. They
may be seen "idling" around the front of the hive on a good for-
aging day, seemingly not much interested in work (8, 253). This
may be confirmed when the hive is opened and the beekeeper

3

notices less honey and wax production. In fact, one European researcher has noticed that the shape of the combs changes when a colony is planning to swarm. First, more drone cells begin to appear, and the combs are also more blunt on the bottom (8, 254-55).

Only if a hive is opened will a beekeeper be able to see for certain what the colony is planning. The most striking and obvious indication is queen cells on the bottom edges of frames of comb. As many as sixteen of these cells have been observed in a hive (7, 260). Noticing their location is important; queen cells located in the center of a comb, usually in the brood area, are usually an indication of the colony's plan to "supersede" the queen, rather than swarm.

If the queen cells are accompanied by a lack of freshly laid eggs in cells, and a lack of young brood generally, this is also an indication that the queen is not planning to stay (1, 74).

Another internal sign is a number of workers gorged with honey and lined up "like soldiers" on the top edge of the frames in the hive (8, 254).

Preparation for Swarm Prevention

The efficient beekeeper will have extra equipment available should a colony appear to be planning to swarm. The most obvious would be to have several extra "supers" with some drawn comb available, which will prove handy for preventing swarming or hiving a swarm after it leaves. Frequent checks of hives during late spring and early summer, when most of the swarming occurs, will help too. Since a queen can be raised in sixteen days (9, 103), hives should be opened at regular intervals. When it is clear that a hive is preparing to swarm, the beekeeper should have a strategy such as the Demaree method in mind.

The Demaree Method

This method is hardly new. According to The ABC and XYZ of Bee Culture, Mr. Demaree began talking about it in 1884. Articles on it appeared in the American Bee Journal in 1884, 1892, and 1894, and it was modified again in 1985 (9, 190-91). The method is succinctly described by Roger A. Morse in The Complete Guide to Beekeeping:

4

Basically the method involves confining the queen in the lowest super with a queen excluder and placing the brood in the third or fourth super above the bottom board. (10, 63-64)

This is elaborated on by Cale et al., who state that queen cells should also be destroyed when the brood are moved up. The single super to which the queen is confined should be supplied with one frame containing unsealed brood and eggs and the rest empty combs (4, 381).

Unfortunately, this is not a one-shot cure for swarming. The hive should be checked again in ten days and any queen cells that are located should be destroyed.

One reason this method works is that it frees space in the lower area for the queen to lay additional eggs. The brood combs that were moved upward in the hive were likely to be "honey bound." That is, in addition to the brood that were in the combs, the workers had already begun collecting and storing honey. Moving the brood up produces another effect. The newly hatched brood in the upper combs turn around and begin to fill them with honey. Suddenly, all of the bees have room to work--the queen to lay eggs and the workers to fill cells with honey (9, 191). The hive then seems less crowded and the colony is less likely to swarm.

Criticism of the Method

The method is not free from criticism. Hugh Maxwell, a Florida beekeeper, claims that the Demaree method is a queen raising system rather than a swarm control system:

The Demaree system was essentially separating the queen and the open brood. It was a troubled measure to cope with swarming in comb honey production around 75 to 100 years ago. When the queen is removed from the larvae, even though still in the same hive, the nurse bees immediately start queen cells around young larvae of the proper age. Under other labels, the Demaree system is described as a way to raise queens in a queen-right colony. (11, 420)

Although generally describing it as a successful method of swarm control, Sammataro and Avitabile suggest that having to find the queen is a disadvantage. Also, it is time-consuming and requires many manipulations of the hive and visits one, three, and four weeks afterward (1, 77).

5

<u>Conclusion</u>

As described by a number of authors, the Demaree method appears to be a workable method for controlling swarms. The objection brought up by Maxwell is partly answered by a modification Demaree announced in 1895, which involved putting only <u>sealed</u> brood above the queen excluder (<u>9</u>, 191).

The objection that the procedure is time-consuming is harder to ignore. Morse tends to agree with the idea that it is not a method suitable "on a commercial basis; however, for the hobbyist it may be a practical and sound method of colony management" (<u>10</u>, 63).

But the method offered by Demaree in the 1880s and 90s for controlling swarms seems to have stood the test of time and remains usable, if not by large commercial operations, at least by smaller beekeepers.

6

Glossary

abscond:  "under certain conditions, the entire original colony may depart their home forever without leaving a new queen behind" (<u>1</u>, 74)

pheromone:  "'chemical messengers' that are secreted externally and elicit intra-specific behavioral or physiological responses" (<u>12</u>, 255)

prime swarm:  "When the old queen is involved in this swarming process, it is called a 'prime' swarm" (<u>14</u>, 79)

super:  hive body part; "its dimensions are precise: 9 1/2 inches deep, 18 1/2 inches long, and 14 5/8 inches wide" (<u>15</u>, 34)

supersede:  "a young queen is reared to replace the old one but the colony does not divide" (<u>7</u>, 263)
"supersedure cells . . . are few in number, are usually located away from the comb edges, and contain larvae of approximately the same age" (<u>1</u>, 82)

swarm:  "swarming consists of the departure of the old queen with most of the workers from the hive, leaving behind the brood, including queen cells, some adult bees and the store, except such honey as the workers are able to carry in their honeystomachs" (<u>13</u>, 71-2)

swarm cells:  "usually hang from the lower edges of a comb, are numerous, and contain larvae of different ages" (<u>1</u>, 82)

7

Works Cited

1. Sammataro, Diana, and Alphonse Avitable. <u>The Beekeeper's Handbook.</u> New York: Charles Scribner's Sons, 1978.

2. Kauffeld, Norbert M. "Seasonal Cycle of Activities in Honey Bee Colonies." United States. Department of Agriculture. Science and Education Administration. <u>Beekeeping in the United States.</u> Washington, DC: GPO, 1980. 30-2.

3. Jaycox, Elbert R. <u>Beekeeping in the Midwest.</u> Urbana, IL: Univ. of Illinois, 1981.

4. Cale, Gladstone H., Robert Banker, and Jim Powers. "Management for Honey Production." <u>The Hive and the Honey Bee.</u> Rev. ed. Hamilton, IL: Dadant & Sons, 1975. 355–412.

5. Vivian, John. <u>Keeping Bees.</u> Charlotte, VT: Williamson Publishing, 1986.

6. Mobus, Bernard. "The Swarm Dance and Other Swarm Phenomena: Conclusion." <u>American Bee Journal</u> May 1987: 356-62.

7. Ribbands, C. R. <u>The Behavior and Social Life of Honey Bees.</u> New York: Dover, 1964.

8. Mobus, Bernard. "The Swarm Dance and Other Swarm Phenomena: Part I." <u>American Bee Journal</u> Apr. 1987: 249-55.

9. <u>The ABC and XYZ of Bee Culture.</u> Medina, OH: A. I. Root Co., 1945.

10. Morse, Roger A. <u>The Complete Guide to Beekeeping.</u> Rev. ed. New York: Dutton, 1974.

11. Maxwell, Hugh. "The Classroom." <u>American Bee Journal</u> June 1987: 419-21.

12. Gary, Norman E. "Activities and Behavior of Honey Bees." <u>The Hive and the Honey Bee.</u> Rev. ed. Hamilton, IL: Dadant & Sons, 1975. 185-264.

13. Phillips, Everett Franklin. <u>Beekeeping.</u> New York: Macmillan, 1939.

14. Killion, Eugene E. <u>Honey in the Comb.</u> Hamilton, IL: Dadant & Sons, 1981.

15. Longgood, William. <u>The Queen Must Die: And Other Affairs of Bees and Men.</u> New York: W. W. Norton, 1985.

# 12

# Writing Essay Examinations, Business Letters, and Résumés

Some of the most important writing you will do in college will be essay examinations; some of the most important writing you will do *after* college will be writing business letters, including letters of application and résumés. These special kinds of writing require the same skills you have been developing writing expository and persuasive essays. They must be clear, well organized, and correct.

## Writing Essay Examinations

Many of the examinations that you will take in college will require you to write an answer of several paragraphs. Your success or failure on the examination will often depend as much on your writing skills as on your mastery of the subject.

Writing an essay examination answer can best be done by dividing the task into manageable steps. You have seen that writing an essay is a process; so, too, is writing an essay exam. Here are the four steps in that process:

### Step 1: Understanding What an Essay Examination Requires

### Step 2: Preparing for an Essay Examination

### Step 3: Prewriting the Essay Examination

### Step 4: Writing the Essay Examination

Steps 1 and 2 have to be done *before* you attend class the day of the examination; steps 3 and 4 are completed *in class* on the day of the examination.

### Step 1: Understanding What an Essay Examination Requires

An essay written in response to an examination question is usually a discussion or an analysis of a topic. It is usually three or four paragraphs long and is written within a time limit. An instructor gives an essay exam to test your ability to recall certain facts. He or she may also want to test your ability to understand relationships, to organize the material in a new and different way, to separate the important from the unimportant, to solve problems, and to recognize new trends. In addition to all of these purposes, your instructor may ask you to make a judgment or draw a logical conclusion on the basis of the facts you present.

To accomplish all of these tasks, you have to provide more than a recitation of facts. Essay examinations measure your ability to assimilate, organize, and synthesize the material your instructor has presented. If you cram your head full of facts and just spill them all out on the test paper, you will probably fail to answer the questions adequately.

## Step 2: Preparing for an Essay Examination

When studying for an essay examination, follow these steps:

1. Review your lecture notes and the text material carefully. Take notes as you read. Notice chapter headings and their subtopics. Try to discover relationships between ideas and headings. Recite the subtopics to yourself as a review.

2. There is no substitute for being able to quote names, dates, places, numbers, and events. This lends authenticity to your statements. Therefore, review your notes regularly and memorize the facts. If possible, review the material with another person. An active recitation can help both memorization and understanding.

3. Discover the patterns in your study material. Decide which facts are related to other facts, and thereby contribute to an overall design. Make sample questions and answer them. Posing your own questions will help you organize the material in new and different ways.

4. To clarify your understanding of the material, write outlines and summaries. This will help you organize and capsulate information. As a result, you will acquire an overview and control of the material.

5. Review the following "command" words. Remember, different commands require different procedures and responses. These command words are those most often used in essay examination questions.

*To compare* means to give both the similarities and the differences; *to contrast* means to give the differences.

> Compare a femur and a humerus. (from an anatomy course)

> Contrast Leonardo's treatment of "The Last Supper" with the one done fifty years earlier by Andrea del Castagno. (from an art history course)

*To define* means to state accurately the meaning of a word or a concept and to include an example when possible.

> Define the term "insanity" as it is used by psychologists. (from a psychology course)

> What is a rhymed couplet? (from a poetry course)

*To describe* means to tell the qualities of a thing in such a way that your reader can visualize it.

> Describe the behavior of an atom in orbit around a nucleus. (fro ma physics course)

> Describe the effects on our economy if the money supply were increased by ten percent in one year. (from an economics course)

*To discuss* means to examine the subject in detail, giving as much information as you can in the time allotted. It may also include your reaction to the subject where appropriate.

> Discuss the effect of Darwin's theories on contemporary culture. (from a sociology course)

> Discuss this statement: "Computer languages should be considered the equivalent of human languages." (from a linguistics course)

*To explain* means to make clear by giving details, by giving reasons, or by showing cause and effect.

> Explain the importance of biodiversity on the maintenance of a healthy environment. (from a biology course)

> Explain the chemical reaction that occurs when an acid and a base are mixed. (from a chemistry course)

*To identify* (or *to define*) means to name, to classify, to give the *who, what, when, where,* and *why* of your subject. A brief description is also necessary.

> Identify the five steps of Maslow's hierarchy of needs. (from a psychology course)

> Define the term *anti-hero,* giving an example. (from a literature course)

*To illustrate* means to give examples.

> By referring to several novels, illustrate how the presence of nu-clear weapons has influenced post–World War II literature. (from a literature course)

> Illustrate divergent, convergent, and parallel evolution. (from a biology course)

*To trace* means to show the development of a subject or a process in time or space.

> Trace the history of the papacy from the break with the Eastern Church in 1054 to the Council of Trent in 1545–63. (from a history class)

> Trace the steps necessary for a bill to become law in the federal government. (from a political science course)

---

## Step 3: Prewriting the Essay Examination

---

Here are four things to do when the examination begins:

1. As soon as you receive the examination, glance over the entire set of questions. Notice how many questions are to be an-swered. Some instructors ask for only a certain number out of the total number of questions. For example, an instructor might ask you to respond to only three out of five questions. If no more credit is earned for answering five than for answering three, you should direct all of your time and effort toward those three only. If you answer more, you will have wasted valuable time.

   Budget your time. Notice the number of points assigned to each question and the time limit (if any) for each. If a time limit is specified, it is a clue to what the instructor expects for a com-plete answer. A ten-minute limit is usually given for identifi-cation or short-answer questions. They can be answered with a single paragraph or five or six sentences. A twenty-minute time limit would indicate two or three paragraphs, and a thirty-minute time limit would require three or four para-graphs. Therefore, budget your time according to the ques-tions you must answer. Remember, there is usually no addi-tional time allowed for revising.

Notice which questions are easier and which are more difficult for you. Answer the easier ones first. This will boost your
self-confidence and also prod your recall of other related facts
and information.

2. Read the question. Then read it a second time. Look for the
"command" words. Notice the limiting phrases and clauses.
For example:

> "Compare how Lyndon Johnson's Great Society programs
> dealt with the problems of poverty with the way Franklin Roo-
> sevelt's New Deal programs did and determine which were
> more effective in attacking the root causes of poverty." (from a
> history course)

> The command word in this question is, of course, "compare."
> This means that you must give similarities and differences be-
> tween Johnson's Great Society programs and Roosevelt's New
> Deal programs as they dealt with poverty. Your answer will be
> made more specific by the words "determine" (meaning "to de-
> cide"), "effective" (in what respect), and "root causes" (what
> kind of underlying conditions create poverty). Be sure that you
> understand what the question calls for, and then plot your
> strategy for answering.

3. Jot notes for your essay answer on scratch paper. Jot key ideas
(this is where your memorization of chapter headings and
subheadings will help), specific terms, names of people and
places, dates, events, and statistics. Don't panic if you see a
question about which you think you know absolutely nothing.
If you attended all the classes, listened to the lectures, and read
the assigned material, you are sure to be able to recall something about the topic. Leave it for the moment, and come back
to it later. Answering the easier questions first will jog your
memory for the difficult one.

4. Organize your main points (key ideas) into a brief outline for
your essay answer. Then decide what specific details and examples you will include under each main point. Check the
question again to see if you have included all the specific tasks
required. If you simply write everything you know about the
topic, you may still receive a low grade because you did not
show that you saw relationships or recognized larger patterns
in the course material. You might set up a relationship by
showing cause and effect, contrast, example, analogy, or order
of importance. These are not all-inclusive, but they suggest
some ways for developing an essay answer. Using transitional
expressions such as "therefore," "on the other hand," "as a re-

sult of," and "in addition to," will emphasize connections and make your essay easier to read.

---

## Step 4: Writing the Essay Examination

Begin your essay with a thesis statement (see Chapter 4). You will always have a beginning if you incorporate part of the question in your answer. To do this, begin your essay with key words of the question but turn them into a statement. For example:

| | |
|---|---|
| *Question:* | How do nuclear power plants differ from coal-fueled power plants? |
| *Thesis statement:* | Nuclear power plants differ from coal-fueled power plants in three important ways. |

This technique assures your reader that you have a strategy for answering the question. Your thesis statement gives direction to your answer. Changes of direction confuse your reader. Therefore, know how you are going to answer the question before you begin to write. Having jotted down what came to mind and rearranged it in rough outline in your prewriting stage, you can now develop your answer in the same way that you would write a longer essay.

As you write, be sure to include supporting statements and specific details. Explain, expand, and clarify. Omitting an important point can lower your grade. On the other hand, don't pad. Your instructor will not be impressed with mere words. Write only what is relevant to your topic. If you want to add material after you have moved on to another section, use an asterisk and then write an addendum at the bottom of the page, or attach a second page with a note to indicate the proper place for the addition.

Finally, edit your paper *as you write* because there is not time for rewriting a final draft. Check for the mistakes you usually make in spelling, capitalization, and punctuation. For example, if you frequently confuse *it's* and *its, their* and *there, affect* and *effect,* or use *must of* for *must have,* check for these errors. Look for omissions such as the second set of quotation marks in a title or quotation. Cross out vague words and expressions such as "kind of," "sort of," and "thing." A simple line through a word or phrase indicates to your reader that you want the item to be deleted.

Regardless of what students think, instructors do not grade examination papers capriciously. There is a reason for the grade you receive. When your instructor reads your paper, he or she is looking for particular facts and ideas, relationships and applications, judgments and conclusions—*not* wordiness, padding, and hot air.

### Sample Questions and Answers

Here are several typical examination questions and sample answers. Read each and decide which is the better essay. Then read the accompanying discussion of each answer.

*Sample*      "Identify the three originators of Modern Art, and
*Questions "A":*      evaluate a major work of each."

*Answer 1.* The three originators of Modern Art were Goya, David, and Constable. Goya painted the *Maja Nude* which hangs in the Prado in Spain. It is the mate to another painting, the *Maja Clothed*, which I think I like better.

David painted the *Death of Marat* which I find startling but dreary because the entire upper half of the picture is empty. The dedication at the bottom of the picture, "To Marat," with "David" underneath it, strikes me as unnecessary.

Constable painted the *View at Stoke*. This is an oil sketch which seems to need more delineation as I can't make out a lot of what is in the picture except for a house to the left and an animal of some kind standing in front of it. The whole painting needs more elaboration.

*Answer 2.* The three originators of Modern Art were Francisco Goya of Spain (1746–1828), Jacques Louis David of France (1748–1825), and John Constable of England (1776–1837).

Goya represents the beginning of modern painting because he depicts man and society from the scientific viewpoint. For example, in the *Family of Charles IV*, painted in 1800, he conveys realistically the insanity of the king and the ambition of his queen. This rendition does not glorify the royal family, or even offer a humanizing treatment. However, it is Goya's strength that he painted his subjects as he knew them to be, not as they appeared to be. Therefore, his painting conveys a combination of psychological analysis and scientific dissection.

David's most famous painting is the *Oath of the Horatii*, which depicts a stern Roman father asking his sons to make a self-sacrificing pledge, probably for a military battle. The diagonal lines in the painting convey movement of legs, arms, and swords. This movement contrasts with the background of vertical columns and horizontal masonry. The women grieving at the right of the picture help to complete the artist's protest against war. There are large areas in the painting that seem to exist only to emphasize the main action, which is a departure from the usual formal aspects of balance and style. The painting, therefore, contributes a revolutionary theme of lines and shapes to nineteenth-century art.

John Constable, the third originator of modern art, is known for his paintings of the English landscape. His *The Leaping Horse* shows a deep reverence for nature. The child and his horse are communing with nature in an almost religious simplicity. Man and nature seem to be united, but this is only part of the picture. A large part of the scene is given to the rendition of light and clouds. In fact, if it were not for the sky, the horse and rider would not even be evident in the pastoral scene. It is the light from the heavens that focuses the viewer's attention on horse and rider. The light and clouds are an important part of this painting, not just a background. Therefore, *The Leaping Horse* introduces an important idea to modern landscape painting—concentration on the use of light.

*Criticism of Answers.* Answer 2 is better for several reasons. First, it incorporates the key words of the question in the answer. Second, it acknowledges the meaning of the command words "identify" and "evaluate." Answer 2 immediately gives the *who, what, when,* and *where*. Through the use of classification it suggests an organizational pattern for the essay. Goya, David, and Constable will be discussed in order. The essay then proceeds to give both the strengths and the weaknesses of a specific work by each painter. Answer 2 was obviously the result of careful planning, because the main points and subpoints can be readily seen.

Answer 1 has made a stab at organization, but it is superficial in its discussion of the paintings. The answer does not fulfill the task of identification. It answers the command word "identify" only superficially. The essay does not support the thesis statement with specific facts or information; it offers, instead, a series of subjective reactions and irrelevant information. For example, where the *Maja Nude* hangs is extraneous to the question, as is the fact that it has a mate. Vague generalities and asides follow each other in a haphazard order, creating the impression that the writer really hadn't looked at the paintings carefully. In short, the answer fails to give a specific evaluation of any major work as specified by the question.

*Sample* "Explain some of the differences between *attitudes* and
*Question "B":* opinions."

*Answer 1.* Although people frequently use *attitudes* and *opinions* interchangeably, there are important differences between the two terms. Opinions are cognitive, that is, they are the result of a mental operation, not an emotional one. For example, it is my *opinion* that Chicago is less humid in August than St. Louis. If someone shows me meteorological records to the category, I will change my opinion. Opinions can be changed if irrefutable evidence is presented.

Attitudes are based on emotional reactions, combined with cognitive and action components. For example, if a person has a positive attitude toward animals, then he has favorable opinions (the cognitive component) about them. He is happy to be around them (the emotional component), and he spends some time with them (the action component). Because attitudes are more complicated than opinions, they last longer and are usually more difficult to change.

*Answer 2.* The difference between *attitudes* and *opinions* is not always easy to discover. For example, if a person holds the opinion that Chinese are shorter than Americans, this is not the same as a person calling all Mexicans shiftless and lazy.

*Criticism of Answers.* Answer 1 is better because it is specific. It tells what an opinion is and is not. It furnishes a simple, clear example. The term "attitude" receives a more specific treatment in accordance with its more complex nature. It is also accompanied by an example. Answer 2 is completely unsatisfactory. It has an inadequate thesis statement and gives no examples, definition, or explanation. It careens off into an illustration that is incorrect.

*Sample*
*Question "C":*     "Identify the following terms: *acids, base*, and *salt*."

*Answer 1.* An acid is a chemical compound that has a sharp, sour taste, will corrode metals, and will turn blue litmus red. Some examples are sulfuric, nitric, and hydrochloric acids.

A base is a chemical compound sometimes called an alkali. It feels soapy to the touch and turns red litmus to blue. It can neutralize an acid when mixed with it, thereby forming a salt. Some examples are soda, lime, and ammonia.

A salt is a crystalline substance produced by mixing an acid and a base. A salt is soluble in water and has a salty taste. It has none of the characteristics of the acid or base from which it is formed. Some examples are alum, borax, and common table salt.

*Answer 2.* Acids, bases, and salts are all related. They react differently on litmus paper and all have a different taste. Mixing two of these together will result in the third. It's never a good idea to mix chemicals together without first reading the label.

*Criticism of Answers.* Answer 1 is better because it uses classification, description, and examples as it formulates its clear, organized response. An acid or a base is a "chemical compound"; a salt is a "chemical substance." Answer 1 follows this information with a description of how acids, bases, and salts work. Then the essay gives examples of each. Answer 2 attempts to explain too much at once. Before any relationship is made, the terms need to be identified. This answer, however, fails to show how acids, bases, and salts are all related, despite its thesis statement. The discussion of each item is vague, and the last sentence is irrelevant and unnecessary. Consequently, it is a very unsatisfactory answer.

*Some Final Words About Writing Essay Examinations*

Writing an essay examination and writing an expository or persuasive essay for your English class share several steps. In both cases it is necessary to do some prewriting: gathering ideas, developing a thesis statement, and organizing the material. The wording of the essay examination question will usually dictate the method of development for the test essay, but the importance of coherence, unity, clarity, and correctness is identical in both assignments. Learning the "command" words and the unique requirements of each will be helpful to you, as will the other suggestions in this section.

## Writing Business Letters

A business letter initiates or transacts business. It asks someone to do something for you: fill an order, handle a complaint, give you a job, furnish information, answer a claim, or correct a mistake. Regardless of its purpose, a business letter requires the same kind of exactness and clarity that all good writing does. It must be clear, well organized, interesting, and grammatically correct. And because a business letter is often sent to someone you don't know—someone who may judge you in part by the appearance of your letter—it must follow certain expected patterns or conventions.

### Appearance and Format of the Business Letter

Business letters are typed on $8^1/_2$" × 11" unlined white paper of good quality. Your letters should be single-spaced and limited, if possible, to a single page. If you write more than one page, number the pages. Double-space between paragraphs. Center the letter, leaving margins at least $1^1/_2$" at the top and bottom and 1" on the sides. If your letter is brief, the top and bottom margins will be larger.

Most business letters follow either the *block style* or the *semi-block style*. In the block style, which is the most formal, all parts of the letter, including the first lines of paragraphs, are flush with the left margin. The letter on page 309 is written in block style.

The semi-block style, which is the format most widely used today in American business correspondence, is essentially the same as the block style except for the location of the heading, complimentary close, and signature, which are toward the right half of the page. All other parts of the letter are flush with the left margin. The letter on page 312 follows the semi-block style.

Regardless of its style, the business letter has six basic parts:

1. Heading
2. Inside Address
3. Salutation or Greeting
4. Body
5. Complimentary Close
6. Signature

*Heading.* If you are typing a letter on a letterhead that is preprinted with the name and address of the company or organization, type the date directly beneath the letterhead. If you are using plain white stationery, start 1 $1/_2$" from the top. The heading consists of your address (street, city, state ZIP code) and the date. With the exception of the two-letter abbreviations approved by the postal service, do not use any abbreviations in the heading.

If you follow the block style and are using plain white stationery, all lines in the heading should be flush with the left margin (see page 309). If you are following the semi-block style, the longest line in the heading should be flush with the right margin (see page 312). In both cases you should not use end punctuation. Here is an example of a heading:

> 2342 Maplehurst Drive
> Memphis, TN 38127
> July 17, 1994

*Inside Address.* The inside address gives the name and address of the company or person to whom you are writing. It contains the full name of the person or firm and the complete mailing address. Type the person's title, if appropriate (Mrs., Ms., Mr., Dr., and so on). It is always more effective to address a letter to a specific person than to a company. As in the case of the heading, do not use any abbreviations except for the two-letter abbreviation for the state.

The location of the inside address is the same for the block style and the semi-block style. It should be flush with the left margin and from two to four lines below the heading, as in the following example:

> Ms. Susan Thompson
> President
> Ivy Hill Book Binding
> 3535 Lark Street
> Clarion, PA 16214

*Salutation.* The salutation or greeting begins two spaces below the inside address and is followed by a colon. In both the block style and the semi-block style it is flush with the left margin.

If you have used the addressee's name in the inside address, use it in the salutation: "Dear Mr. Jones," "Dear Mrs. Edwards," and so on. If you are uncertain about the marital status of a woman, you may use "Ms.," which is widely accepted today. You may also use professional titles in your salutation: "Dear Dr. Ellis," "Dear Professor Dreyfus," and so on. If you do not know the name or sex or your addressee, you may use the unnamed person's job title instead.

The following forms are correct:

> Dear Ms. Clark:
> Dear Professor Newman:

Dear Mrs. Fieger:
Dear Dr. Cooper:

*Body.* Begin the body of your letter two spaces below the salutation. In both the block style and semi-block style, all paragraphs begin flush with the left margin. Paragraphs should be single-spaced, with double-spacing between paragraphs. The content of the body is discussed below.

*Complimentary Close.* If you are following the block style, begin the complimentary close two or three lines below the last line of the body, typed flush with the left-hand margin (see page 309). In the semi-block style, it is typed to the right of the letter in alignment with the heading (see page 315).

The most common forms of the complimentary close are "Sincerely yours," "Yours truly," "Sincerely," and "Cordially." Capitalize only the first word and place a comma after the complimentary close.

*Signature.* Type your name four to six spaces directly below the complimentary close. In the space above the typed signature, sign your name legibly in ink in longhand. When typing your name, do not put a professional title in front of it (Dr., Rev., etc.) or degrees after it (M.A., Ph.D., etc.). Some medical doctors make an exception to this rule, placing "M.D." after their typed name. Beneath your typed signature you may indicate your official capacity (Chairman of the Board, Athletic Director, or Sales Manager). A married woman uses her own first name, not that of her husband. A woman may indicate the title she prefers to be addressed by in her typed signature: (Miss) Joan Reiter; (Mrs.) Irene Farber; (Ms.) Rita Touhill.

## General Guidelines for Effective Business Writing

In addition to arranging the parts of your letters according to the standard form, the grammar and style must also fulfill the recipient's expectations. Your reader expects your letter to be accurate, concise, and clear. He or she must be able to grasp its contents immediately, without confusion or ambiguity. Misspellings, careless punctuation, or faulty grammar will keep your reader from taking you seriously. The tone of the letter should be appropriate to the subject and the situation. If the reader does not like the way you say it, your message will not be received favorably.

Your letters will be more effective if you follow these guidelines:

**1.** Write to express, not to impress. Present your ideas simply and directly. The writer who makes the best impression is the one who can express complex ideas in a simple way.

2. State the purpose of your letter in the first paragraph. Your reader is busy; don't keep him or her guessing. If you are applying for a job, name the position. By getting to the point, you will let the personnel manager know which position you are interested in.
3. Write in a natural, informal tone. Avoid business jargon. In particular, avoid such hackneyed phrases as "Enclosed please find," "I beg to acknowledge," "Contents noted," and so on.
4. Keep your sentences short. For easy reading, sentences should vary in length and structure, but reading is hard when sentences average more than twenty words.
5. Prefer the simple to the complex. Avoid words, phrases, and constructions that are too complicated. If there's a simpler way to say something, use it.
6. Avoid unnecessary words. Make every word in a business letter carry its own weight; get rid of any you don't need.
7. The tone of your letter should be courteous.
8. Put action in your verbs. The heaviness of much business writing comes from overworking passive verb forms. Active verbs put life into your writing.
9. Make it clear what you expect from your reader. Ask for an appointment or mention when you will be calling.
10. Read and reread your letter, checking for errors in spelling, punctuation, and grammar.

### Types of Business Letters

There are as many types of business letters as there are business situations. This section discusses three of the most common types: an order, a claim or letter of complaint, and a job application.

*The Order Letter.* An order letter is from a person who wants to buy something. The most important requirement in such a letter is that it state clearly and accurately (1) what is wanted, (2) how it will be paid for, and (3) how and where it is to be delivered.

Make sure that you describe the item that you want precisely and accurately. Give the name of the product, the model or stock number, and the quantity desired. Specify the color, size, finish, and weight as necessary.

Mention the price and the method of payment. If you have enclosed a check or money order, mention that fact. If the purchase is to be charged to your account or credit card, give the account number or name.

Tell where you want the item shipped and how you want it shipped (parcel post, air express, etc.). If you need it by a certain date, let the seller know.

An example of an order letter follows. Notice that it is written in the block style and is centered on the page.

---

3792 Brenner Drive
Santa Barbara, CA 93105
December 16, 1994

Mrs. Ellen Fowles, Manager
Morton's Kids' Furniture
876 West 92nd Street
Los Angeles, CA 90022

Dear Mrs. Fowles:

I would like to order the children's desk and dresser set advertised on page 12 in your 1994 Christmas catalogue. The set is called "Young Boy's Get-Started Set," item number 4756-2, and includes not only the desk and dresser, but also a chair. I prefer the blue model; if it is unavailable, the burgundy is acceptable.

The sales price indicated for 4756-2 is $249. I am enclosing a personal check for $309.23, which includes the $40 rush delivery charge and a seven percent state sales tax. I plan to give this set as a Christmas gift to my son, so I would appreciate it if you could process this order quickly. Send the set to the above address.

Sincerely yours,

*Victor D. Puppo*

Victor D. Puppo

---

# E X E R C I S E 1

Write a letter to a company in another city ordering a customized frame for a poster or painting you own, a pair of hiking boots for youself, or an appliance for your kitchen. Be sure to include all the information listed on page 308.

---

*The Claim or Letter of Complaint.* The purpose of a claim or complaint letter is to correct a situation. It usually arises from what the buyer regards as an error on the part of the merchant: an overcharge, the wrong size, style, or color, a delayed or missent shipment, or similar complaints. Regardless of the problem, the writer's immediate reaction usually is to send an angry letter "telling off" the merchant. Although such a letter might make the writer feel better, it's not likely to correct the situation. In fact, it will probably make the merchant unsympathetic to the buyer's complaint.

Claim letters and complaints that follow these guidelines will usually accomplish the writer's goal:

1. Describe the transaction completely; give identifying information such as the date, model and serial numbers, style, color, brand name, price, your check number, and so on.
2. Explain the problem in detail. Write in a calm, courteous, and factual style.
3. Tell the recipient of the letter how you think the situation should be corrected. If you want a replacement or a refund, state your reasons.
4. Above all, avoid sarcasm, threats, and name-calling. Most companies want to be fair.

The following letter was the first version of a complaint written by Carrie T. More, a student who had ordered a computer printer by mail from a catalog. As you read it, imagine that you are the recipient of the letter. What would your reaction be to Carrie's complaint? If you were to give her advice on rewriting her letter, what suggestions would you make?

You probably noticed several weaknesses in Carrie's letter that were guaranteed to irritate the recipient of her complaint. The most obvious is the sarcasm and anger that almost smother the letter. Such a tone would put the reader on the defensive and make him unsympathetic to Carrie's problem. Another problem with the letter is the series of spelling and grammatical errors ("If I had know," "I never would had ordered," "it smeers" and so on). Finally, her letter loses its impact because it is not directed to anyone specifically: "To Whom It May Concern" is such a vague greeting that no one would feel personally responsible for the sender's complaint.

Luckily, Carrie showed the draft of her letter to a couple of friends who suggested some changes. One suggestion was to learn the name of the manager or owner so that Carrie could address her letter to a specific person. Another idea was to adopt a calmer, more reason-

35351 San Marcos Way
Irvine, CA 92714
June 2, 1994

Berry Brothers Inc.
31 Mercury Lane
Amarillo, TX 72450

To Whom It May Concern:

I want you to send my money back on a computer printer I ordered from your catalog. If I had know it was damaged, I never would had ordered the thing. Your ad says that it has "beautiful, near-laser quality printing." Only an insane person could think the smudges and streaks this printer puts out are beautiful. In fact, the printer doesn't print; it smeers. I sent you a check which you quickly cashed over four weeks ago, according to my bank, and if I don't get my money back quickly, I'm going to sue. I've got a friend whose sister just passed the bar and I know she'd represent me for a percentage of what we recover from you. So send my money back quickly, or else.

                                        Yours truly,

                                        *Carrie T. More*
                                        Carrie T. More

able tone and to propose the specific adjustment that she wanted. Also, the threat to sue was dropped. Another suggestion was to follow a more conventional form for her letter (you may have noticed that her letter was a mixture of the block and semi-block styles). After Carrie thought about these ideas, she rewrote her letter.

As you read her revised letter, compare your reaction to it with your reaction to her earlier version. Which letter is likely to get the desired results?

35351 San Marcos Way
Irvine, CA 92714
June 2, 1994

Mr. Dennis Berry, Vice-President
Beryy Brothers Inc.
31 Mercury Lane
Amarillo, TX 72450

Dear Mr. Berry:

Today I received by UPS the computer printer that I had ordered from your 1994 Berry brothers catalogue. The printer is
the HQ 917 Printer described on page 20 of the catalogue.

Upon unpacking the printer I found that several of the parts
were broken and that both rollers inside the printer had deep,
uneven gouges. The printer is impossible to use. I would like a
replacement for this printer at your earliest convenience. If a
printer of identical quality is not available, I wish a complete refund. A photocopy of my check for $497.31 is enclosed.

I would appreciate your prompt response to this letter.

Yours truly,

*Carrie T. More*

Carrie T. More

# E X E R C I S E 2

Write a letter to a local cable TV company in which you complain
about a mistake in your bill. Before writing, review the guidelines
on page 310.

*The Letter of Application.* One of the most important business letters that
you will ever write is the letter of application. It will accompany your
résumé, a list of your experiences and qualifications for a job. Although the résumé is very important, it is the covering letter of application that your prospective employer will see first. The application

follows the format already described for the business letter. ___ cause it has a unique purpose, it follows additional guidelines.

*Guidelines for the Letter of Application*

1. Be specific about the position for which you are applying. Begin your letter by mentioning the person or advertisement that informed you of the job opening.
2. Emphasize your experience that is relevant to the job. You can be brief, because your résumé will provide details. Nevertheless, point out any practical experience that you have.
3. Mention your interest in the company; show that you are familiar with its products or its reputation. Explain how your experience and education can help the company.
4. Keep in mind that your letter will be your introduction to its reader. Be certain that it is neat, readable, concise, and correct.
5. Ask for an interview. Tell your prospective employer when you can be reached and when you are available for an interview.

On the next pages are two letters of application for the same position. Which person would you interview, based only on the letters?

## The Résumé

The résumé is a one- or two-page list of your achievements and qualifications. Its purpose is to give your prospective employer enough information about your background to help him or her determine your potential as an employee. The most qualified people don't always get the job. It goes to the person who present him- or herself most persuasively in person and on paper. That is why it is very important that your résumé and letter of application be carefully written.

Résumés vary in their content and format, but most of them present the following information: personal data, job objective, education, work experience, extracurricular activities, and references. The résumés on pages 316–317 follow the most popular formats.

### Information in the Résumé

*Personal information.* Federal guidelines prevent hiring on the basis of your race, religion, national origin, or sex. Many applicants, however, include this information on their résumés; in any event, you should include your name, address, and telephone number. Other items com-

23 Davison
Chicago, IL 38088
May 30, 1994

W. Crane
  Director of Personnel
  Madison County General Hospital
   77 Lilac Street
    Madison, WI 37559

Dear Mr. Crane:

I read in one of the trades a few weeks ago that you have a position or two available for the position of a physical therapist on your staff, with a salary starting at $24,500. I want to apply for that job. I am currently attending Northwestern University, and I expect to graduate this spring, even though if you look at my manuscripts I am about 19 semester units short (I'm taking all 19 semester this spring, so you know that I am a hard worker). I am interested in physical therapy because it seems like a good field in the health industry to make some decent money and help other people out in the process (without having to go to med school).

While attending Northwestern, I was very active in my fraternity Omega Omega Zeta. My junior year I was in charge of the fraternity's recreation program. That same year I changed my major from a pre-med biology major to physical therapy. My senior year I relinquished my job as recreation chief to better my G.P.A., and I think you can see from my transcripts that since doing so, my grades have shown remarkable improvement. The strengths that I bring with me are a real knowledge of people and a willingness to work really hard. I hope that you can call me up for an interview because I believe I look a lot better in person even if some others look better on paper. Please respond soon as I have several other applications going as well and I need to make an important decision about my future.

                              Yours truly,

                              *Sam Drabble*

                              Sam Drabble

889 Crusoe Lane
Omaha, NE 68133
May 8, 1994

Wilma Crane
Director of Personnel
Madison County Veteran's Administration Hospital
77 Lilac Street
Madison, WI 37559

Dear Ms. Crane:

Your advertisement in last week's <u>Hospital Employment Weekly</u> indicates that there is an entry level opening on your staff for a physical therapist. I would like to apply for that position.

As the accompanying résumé demonstrates, I have extensive academic and professional experience in the field of physical therapy that would qualify me for this position. I will be receiving my Bachelor of Science degree in Physical Therapy in a few weeks from Creighton University. In addition, for the past two years, I have been working as a physical therapist assistant at St. Victor's Hospital in Omaha, Nebraska.

I have heard that Madison County's VA Hospital has long been one of the leaders in developing new treatments for patients in need of physical therapy. During my years of service in the military, I knew at least three people who were treated at your facilities, and all had only the best things to say about your hospital and the people who work there. That is the reason for my interest in Madison County VA.

If I can provide information not specified on the Résumé, I shall be glad to do so. I am available for an interview at your convenience. I can be reached by phone at (402) 555-7873.

Sincerely yours,

*Nicholas W. Fisher*

Nicholas W. Fisher

Nicholas W. Fisher

889 Crusoe Lane                                         (402) 555-7873
Omaha, NE 68133

### Education

1990-94:    Creighton University, Omaha, Nebraska.
            Received B.B. in Physical Therapy

1982-86:    Drake High School, Flint, Michigan. Took college
            preparatory courses.

### Military Experience

1986-90:    United States Army. Received honorable discharge
            June 1990 with rank of Lance Corporal. Served in
            infantry unit as communications specialist.

### Work Experience

1993-       St. Victor's Hospital, Omaha, Nebraska. Currently
present      working as a physical therapy assistant. My duties
            included aiding the physical therapist in instructing
            the patients on how to perform their exercises,
            working with patients directly on their exercises,
            and explaining the use and care of wheelchairs,
            braces, canes and crutches, and artificial limbs.
            Also, I managed hospital paperwork including in-
            surance forms, transfer of patient requests, refer-
            rals, and inquiries. I will take the Physical Therapy
            license examination this coming September.

1990-93     Student Union bookstore, Omaha, Nebraska. Worked
            in the bookstore at Creighton University stacking
            books, taking book orders from faculty, and pro-
            cessing bills from distributors.

References are available upon request.

RÉSUMÉ
Carrie T. More
35351 San Marcos Way
Irvine, CA 92714
(714) 555-7621

| | |
|---|---|
| Job Objective | Dental hygienist for private dental practice |
| Education | |
| 1992-1994 | Allan Hancock College, Santa Maria, California<br>Degree: Associate of Sciences<br>Major: Dental Services |
| 1988-1992 | Bishop Diego High School, Santa Barbara, California<br>Graduated with honors in June, 1991. |
| License | Received California State Dental Services License July, 1994. |
| Work Experience | |
| Sept. 1992<br>to present | Sales clerk (part-time), Sears<br>Santa Maria, California |
| Summer 1992 | Waitress, Chase Bar and Grill<br>Santa Barbara, CA |
| Sept. 1990-<br>June 1992 | Waitress (part-time), Swenson's Ice Cream<br>Santa Barbara, CA |
| Extracurricular | Women's Volleyball team, Allan Hancock College (1992-1994) |
| Activities | Girl's Volleyball team, Bishop Diego High School (1988-1992) |
| | Honor Society, Bishop Diego High School (1988-1992) |
| References | Mr. Stan Tysell, Manager<br>Swenson's Ice Cream<br>3386 State Street<br>Santa Barbara, CA 93105<br>(805) 555-1209 |
| | Ms. Beryl Amendola, Coach<br>Bishop Diego High School<br>Santa Barbara, CA 93105<br>(805) 555-4388 |
| | Dr. Janet Waxman, Chairperson<br>Dental Services Department<br>Allan Hancock College<br>Santa Maria, CA<br>(805) 922-6966 |

monly listed in this section are height, weight, marital status, and condition of health.

*Job objective.* List either the actual position you are seeking or your long-range objective. If you name the latter, your covering letter of application should specify the position you are applying for.

*Education.* Begin by giving the date of attendance at the college you are currently enrolled in and work backwards to the high school from which you graduated. Mention the degree or certificate you received, your major, and the name and location of each institution. Mention your grade-point average (GPA) if it was high.

*Work experience.* List in reverse chronological order—most recent first—your full-time and part-time jobs. Tell when you held the job and list your former employers' names and addresses. If one of the jobs was similar to the job you are applying for, describe your duties.

*Extracurricular activities.* This section gives you a chance to list any related hobbies, memberships in organizations, and skills that might be useful in the job you are applying for. If you have been active in community activities or civic organizations that have given you experience in leadership, mention them. If you are a recent graduate and do not have much work experience, mention any campus clubs and organizations you belonged to, offices you held, and awards you received. Do not list political or religious affiliations; they are irrelevant in the hiring process.

*References.* In this section you have a choice: you can simply state, "References on request," or you can list from three to five people who know you. These can be of several kinds. You can list former or present employers, coworkers, prominent people in your community who know you, or instructors. In each case, list the name, title, address, and telephone number. Make certain that you obtain permission to use a person's name before listing it in your résumé.

### Some Reminders When Writing the Résumé

1. The appearance of your résumé is very important. It should be attractive, organized, and readable. It should have no spelling or grammatical mistakes or erasures.
2. Your résumé should be easy to read. Type on white paper, using wide margins and lots of white space between sections. Never send a carbon copy; photocopies are acceptable, however.
3. Underline or capitalize headings to make them stand out on the page. Don't use complete sentences; phrases and clauses are satisfactory and require less room.

4. As mentioned above, list your education and work experience in reverse order.
5. Don't pad your résumé with inflated language; keep your writing style simple.

Study the résumés on pages 316–317; then follow the suggestions in this chapter.

## E X E R C I S E    3

Write a résumé for yourself that includes the information listed on pages 313–318. Then write a letter of application to accompany your resume.

## C O M P U T E R    E X E R C I S E

Do any of the exercises on the computer and share the letters with your partner, your group, or the entire class using the broadcast function or an overhead projector. What is good about your letter? What needs to be improved?

# A Handbook

# of Grammar

# and Graphics:

# Usage

# and Puncuation

## A Guide to Editing: Usage and Punctuation

To be an effective writer, you will have to follow certain principles of *standard written English,* the kind of writing used in practically all public communication. In conversation, of course, many of these principles can be ignored. "I be going" and "He stay," for example, are perfectly acceptable to speakers of Black American English. *Written* English, however, is more standardized and conservative; it follows certain predictable guidelines that often conflict with your own speaking dialect.

If your sentences—including your punctuation—do not follow or conform to these guidelines or standards, there is a good chance they will not be read. If read, there is a likelihood that they will confuse or mislead your reader. In either case, you will have failed in your effort to communicate.

Many of the guidelines that regulate written English deal with sentence structure and punctuation. This handbook deals with major problems that you are going to encounter in those areas as you revise and edit your papers. The emphasis is on recognizing the problems and then learning how to correct them.

## Common Problems with Sentences

Surveys of employers, research by scholars, and the day-to-day experiences of your instructors support the notion that most writers have the following problems in their writing: incomplete sentences (or fragments), comma splices, run-on sentences, lack of subject-verb agreement, misplaced modifiers, faulty pronoun usage, and shifts in tense, voice, and person. This is not a complete list of all the possible errors, but it includes the most serious. We will examine each of these errors in turn.

### Sentence Fragments

A sentence is a group of words containing at least one independent clause and conveying a certain sense of completeness. In other words, it has a subject and a verb and is capable of standing alone. A sentence fragment is a group of words that lacks an independent clause—it looks like a sentence because it begins with a capital letter and ends with a period or other end punctuation, but it leaves the reader "hanging," waiting for more to follow.

Notice the sense of "incompleteness" in the following italicized fragments:

> Larry told a joke. *Which embarrassed everyone.*
> Many of Shakespeare's plays have been made into films. *Such as Romeo and Juliet.*

*Although he should have known better.* Con tried to jump over the glass coffee table.

Fragments are common in speech, particularly in informal conversations when they serve as responses to what someone else has said or as additions to something we have just said. The use of fragments in writing can sometimes be justified by an experienced writer when the meaning is clear and when the writer is striving for a particular effect or purpose. In general, however, fragments should be voided in writing. They imply that the writer is careless or uninformed (or both). They distract readers and create confusion.

There are two types of fragments: *dependent clauses* and *phrases.* Dependent clauses have subjects and verbs, but they cannot stand alone—they depend on independent clauses to complete their meaning. Dependent clauses can be spotted by the kinds of words that introduce them, making them dependent. The technical terms for these introductory words are *subordinating conjunctions* and *relative pronouns.* In the following fragments, notice that each begins with such a word:

> *When* the ceasefire was announced.
> *Before* the first guest arrived at the party.
> *Which* was enough to do the job.

If you read each fragment aloud, you will detect its sense of incompleteness.

The following list contains the most common dependent clause introducing words. Whenever a clause begins with one of these words (unless it is a question), it is a *dependent clause* and cannot stand alone.

| | | |
|---|---|---|
| after | in order that | where, wherever |
| although | since | whether |
| as, as if | that | which, whichever |
| because | unless | while |
| before | until | who, whose |
| how | what, whatever | whom |
| if | when, whenever | |

Notice what happens to the following independent clause when words from the list above are placed in front of it.

*Indepenent*
  *clause:*  **We studied for our finals.**

> *After* we studied for our finals. (*fragment*)
> *Although* we studied for our finals. (*fragment*)
> *As we* studied for our finals. (*fragment*)
> *Because* we studied for our finals. (*fragment*)
> *Before* we studied for our finals. (*fragment*)

*If* we studied for our finals. (*fragment*)
*Unless* we studied for our finals. (*fragment*)

As you can see, the independent clause has been changed into a series of dependent clauses. Each dependence clause is fragment, even though it is punctuated like a sentence. To correct this kind of fragment, simply add an independent clause:

After we studied for our finals, *we ate pizza.*
Although we studied for our finals, *we were still nervous.*
As we studied for our finals, *we listened to the radio.*
Because we studied for our finals, *we felt prepared.*

Here are some examples of dependent clause fragments along with their corrections.

*Dependent*
   *clause:*  Although the price had been lowered. (*fragment*)
  *Revised:*  Although the price had been lowered, the house remained unsold.

*Dependent*
   *clause:*  While they were watching the movie. (*fragment*)
  *Revised:*  Their car was stolen while they were watching the movie.

*Dependent*
   *clause:*  After she served in public office. (*fragment*)
  *Revised:*  After she served in public office, she retired to her farm.

The other kind of sentence fragment is the *phrase*. The phrase fragment is a group of words that is missing a subject or a verb or both, and therefore does not make sense by itself. Here are some examples of phrase fragments:

Quebec, the oldest city in Canada and the capital city of the province of Quebec. (*fragment*)
Attracted by the tales of adventures and the rumors of gold. (*fragment*)
Soaring above the crowd. (*fragment*)
The fans in the stands. (*fragment*)

Phrase fragments can be corrected in two ways:

**1.** By supplying the missing part:

Quebec, the oldest city in Canada, *is* the capital city of the province of Quebec. (*adding a verb*)
*The miners were* attracted by the tales of adventures and the rumors of gold. (*adding a subject and verb*)

**2.** By tying the fragment to a complete sentence:

> Soaring above the crowd, the dirigible relayed the radio signal.
> He waves to his teammates, to the cameras, and to the fans in
> the stands.

Sentence fragments can usually be detected when they are read aloud because they convey a sense of incompleteness—you are left waiting for more to follow. Don't rely on your ear, however. When revising your writing, make certain that every sentence contains at least one independent clause.

### Comma Splices and Run-on Sentences

A *comma splice* results when two independent clauses are mistakenly connected ("spliced") with a comma instead of being separated into two sentences or joined with a conjunction or a semicolon. (See page 343 for a discussion of this use of the semicolon.) If the independent clauses are run together without a conjunction or punctuation, the result is a *run-on* sentence.

Here are examples of both errors:

*Comma splice:* Synthetic furs are widely used for winter coats, they are gradually replacing genuine animal pelts.

*Run-on sentence:* Synthetic furs are widely used for winter coats they are gradually replacing genuine animal pelts.

You should avoid common splices and run-on sentences in your writing for the same reasons that you should avoid sentence fragments: they are hard to read, they confuse your reader, they suggest that you are careless, and they indicate that you do not know what a sentence is. English instructors rarely regard them as indications of creativity.

Comma splices and run-on sentences can be corrected in four ways.

**1.** By using a period between the independent clauses, making them two sentences.

> Synthetic furs are widely used for winter coats. They are gradually replacing genuine animal pelts.

**2.** By inserting a semicolon between the independent clauses.

> Synthetic furs are widely used for winter coats; they are gradually replacing genuine animal pelts.

**3.** By placing a comma and a coordinating conjunction (*and, but, for, or, yet, so*) between the independent clauses.

> Synthetic furs are widely used for winter coats, **and** they are gradually replacing genuine animal pelts.

4. By using one of the dependent words (or subordinating conjunctions) from the list on page 322, making one of the clauses dependent.

> **Because** synthetic furs are widely used for winter coats, they are gradually replacing genuine animal pelts.

## E X E R C I S E 1

The word groups below contain sentence fragments, comma splices, and run-on sentences. Following the suggestions given above, correct the errors. If a sentence is correct, mark it "C."

1. Some fans believe that Michael Jordan is the greatest basketball player of all time, others would name Magic Johnson.
2. Ernest Hemingway was an expatriate living in Paris after World War I, F. Scott Fitzgerald lived there also.
3. Although Israel and the PLO signed agreements covering Palestinian self-rule in Jericho and Gaza.
4. The flower arrangements had obviously taken a great deal of time, the judges, however, still seemed unimpressed with the overall preparation.
5. Murder, rape, kidnapping, some of the most heinous crimes known to humanity.
6. She told us that the divorce would be final next month.
7. As the cherry blossoms bloomed and the gentle breeze caressed our faces and whispered sweet suggestions, until we could no longer stand apart.
8. The price of fish has increased in recent years this is due to its increasing popularity among health-conscious consumers.
9. She had read his autobiography and seen the film about his life, still, Malcolm X seemed to be an elusive figure.
10. Drinking until dawn, sleeping until afternoon, eating hot dogs and chips daily throughout his brief college career.
11. Although the Dead Sea, despite its name, is actually a lake.
12. Because most of the vitamins in rice are concentrated in the husk, and ninety-five percent of the world crop is grown in the Orient.
13. As the language grows and adds new words, it drops other words no longer used.
14. Mel thought he had returned the library book, however, he found it in the trunk of his car.
15. Groucho Marx had been an entertainer for almost seventy years, he died when he was eighty-six.
16. Many schools now have computer terminals in their libraries, some of them have been donated by computer manufacturers.

17. Mrs. Sheehan gave a lecture on the history of the calendar, I was surprised to learn of its changes throughout the ages.
18. Claire works for a printer that specializes in restaurant menus.
19. His blood pressure went down it was because of his salt-free diet.
20. The rain, dripping slowly from the leak in the porch roof and onto the porch swing.

---

## Subject-Verb Agreement

Mistakes in subject-verb agreement are among the most common writing errors, and they are particularly irritating to readers. They are often the result of carelessness. Sometimes, however, they are caused by the writer's confusion concerning the subject and the verb.

Subjects and verbs must agree in two important ways: in *number* and in *person*. To help you understand the distinction, here are two rules:

Rule 1:  The subject and the verb must agree in number. A singular subject takes a singular verb.

> The muffler *rattles* when the car *goes* over forty miles per hour.

A plural subject takes a plural verb.

> The sparkplugs *are* expensive but they *make* the engine more efficient.

Rule 2:  The subject and the verb must agree in person. First person:

> I stay [not *stays*] with my uncle when I visit [not *visits*] Baltimore.
> We stay [not *stays*] away from strange-looking weeds because we are [not *is*] afraid of poison ivy.

Second person:

> You are [not *be* or *is*] one of the most helpful friends I have.
> You throw [not *throws*] the ball just like your sister.

Third person:

> Judith and Dick decided to get married next month. They are [not *is*] very excited.
> Maggie is enrolled in a Chinese class. She enjoys [not *enjoy*] practicing the vocabulary drills.

To help you apply these rules, study the following suggestions:

1. A verb must agree with the subject—not with any words or phrases that follow the subject but are not part of it. These include terms such as *along with, together with, including, as well as*, and *in addition to*.

    Anita, as well as the other members of her family, is [not *are*] looking forward to the trip.
    I, together with Earl and Dave, am [not *are*] going to give a party for the custodian.

2. The verb must agree with the subject—not with words that rename it in the sentence.

    My favorite memory of the reunion was [not *were*] the hours spent talking to my newly-found relatives.
    Customers who want to exchange their purchases without a receipt are [not *is*] the biggest problem.

3. Don't be confused by sentences that do not follow the usual subject-verb pattern.

    Under the desk were [not *was*] the missing folders.
    Beyond the hills was [not *were*] the cottage.

4. Two or more subjects connected by "and" require a plural verb.

    His loud voice and bizarre behavior make [not *makes*] him unpopular.

    *Note:* When the compound subject consists of two words of closely related meaning or of two nouns that name the same person, a singular verb is often used:

    Her wit and humor *is* known to everyone.

    The best athlete and scholar in the class *is* Mario.

5. Singular pronouns require singular verbs. The following pronouns are singular: *another, anybody, anyone, anything, each, either, everybody, everyone, everything, neither, nobody, no one, nothing, one, somebody, someone, something.*

    No one *was* able to solve the puzzle.
    Everybody *wants* to be the first in line.
    Something *tells* me I should study harder.

6. Some pronouns may be singular or plural in meaning. This means that verbs used with them depend on the noun or pronoun they refer to. Such pronouns include the following: *all, any, more, most, none, some, that, which,* and *who.*

    All of the tools *were* missing.
    All of the ice *was* melted.

Most of the speakers *were* interesting.
Most of the ice cream *was* eaten.

None of the students *were* in their seats.
None of this candy *is* any good.

7. When subjects are connected by "either-or" or "neither-nor," the verb agrees with the subject that is closer to it.

> Neither the driver nor the passengers *were* able to tell what happened.
> Either the passengers or the driver *is* to blame.

8. Some nouns plural in form but singular in meaning require a singular verb. These include *economics, news, mathematics, physics, politics, headquarters, electronics.*

> The news from the lab *was* encouraging.
> Physics *is* a required course for premed students.

9. Subjects that indicate distance, measure, money, or time require a singular verb.

> Six miles *was* the longest race he had ever run.
> Four quarts of oil *is* the capacity of the motor.
> To a child, fifty cents *seems* like a fortune.
> Forty minutes *is* a long time to wait for a taxi.

10. A collective noun (a word singular in form but referring to a group of people or things) takes a singular verb when the group is regarded as a unit, and a plural verb when the individuals of the group are regarded separately. Some common collective nouns are *army, assembly, committee, company, couple, crowd, faculty, family, flock, group, herd, jury, pair, squad,* and *team.*

> The *couple* was seated at the head table.
> The couple *were* unable to agree on which wine to order with their meal.
> The faculty *was* given a raise.
> The faculty *were* assigned their parking spaces.

11. Subjects plural in form that indicate a quantity or number take a singular verb if the subject is considered a unit but a plural verb if the individuals of the subject are regarded separately.

> Three-fourths of the earth's surface *is* covered with water.
> Three-fourths of the words in the spelling list *were* of Latin or Greek origin.

12. When *a number* is used as the subject, it requires a plural verb. *The number* is always singular.

A number of tourists *are* always surprised by the size of the Grand Canyon.

The number of tourists visiting the Grand Canyon *is* quite large.

# E X E R C I S E 2

*subject is right in the beginning*

Find the subject in each of the following sentences and determine whether it is singular or plural. Then select the correct verb.

1. The scoutmaster, as well as the young scouts, (was, were) disappointed by the rain.
2. The Olympic decathlon, more than all other events, (determine, determines) the world's greatest athlete.
3. Marc, like thousands of other surfers, (wants, want) to travel to the exotic locations shown in surfer films.
4. Among the many disappointments (was, were) a rejection slip from *The New Yorker.*
5. Larry Bird, no longer playing pro basketball, (appear, appears) in television commercials.
6. My father, along with thousands of other fathers, (participates, participate) in an annual "Bring Your Daughter to Work" day.
7. A sheet of directions accompanying the snow chains (explain, explains) how to install them.
8. One of the best places for taking pictures (are, is) Niagara Falls.
9. Under the eaves (was, were) a nest of hornets.
10. In this bed (has, have) slept several famous presidents.
11. An attorney from one of the most distinguished law firms in the city (represent, represents) the suspect.
12. Drowning out the boss (was, were) the applause of her admirers.
13. In contrast to the urging of her friends (was, were) the cautions of her family.
14. Two members of the exploration party (has, have) been commended for bravery.
15. Each participant, as well as the members of his family, (receive, receives) bonus points that can be applied to the next drawing.

# E X E R C I S E 3

Select the correct verb in the following sentences.

1. A toy truck, as well as other gifts, (was, were) given to Sean on his first birthday.

2. Although his mother is a professor, Jaime claims that academics (is, are) less important than athletics.
3. Most of the military in Russia (fears, fear) that their careers are in jeopardy because of budget cuts.
4. None of the students (wants, want) to be called on by the teacher.
5. All of the anger expressed by the senior citizens (was, were) directed at their congressman.
6. Neither a fine nor incarceration (bothers, bother) hardened criminals.
7. Either the artist or his students (is, are) expected to write a response to the critical review of his latest show.
8. A couple from Iowa (has, have) won the jackpot.
9. None of the winners of the Ugly Man on Campus contest (wants, want) their names announced.
10. A group of dissastisfied customers (is, are) suing the utility company.
11. The psychologist said that most of the anxiety experienced by the children (is, are) caused by their parents' absence.
12. Professor Carman stated that anyone in the class who (turn, turns) in a late paper will fail.
13. Neither the tornadoes nor the flood (has, have) succeeded in destroying the spirits of the townspeople.
14. Chili powder and cayenne pepper (provide, provides) the tang in my chili.
15. All of the visitors (agree, agrees) that they were unprepared for the extreme heat.

---

## Misplaced and Dangling Modifiers

Modifiers are words that describe other words in a sentence. They may be single words or groups of words, and they may come before the word they modify or they may follow it. In either case, the modifiers should appear *near* the word it modifies to avoid confusion.

A *misplaced modifier* is one that is separated from the word it modifies and as a result modifies the wrong word. Sentences with misplaced modifiers are usually confusing and often humorous because of the unintended meaning. Carefully read the following examples of sentences containing misplaced modifiers:

> Craig bought a motorcycle for his wife with an electric starter.

> The pizza was served by an unsmiling waiter covered with anchovies, tomato sauce, and mushrooms.

By placing the modifier next to the word it modifies or by rewording the sentence, we can make the meaning of such sentences clear to the reader:

| | |
|---|---|
| *Revised:* | Craig bought a motorcycle with an electric starter for his wife. |
| *Revised:* | The pizza, covered with anchovies, tomato sauce, and mushrooms, was served by an unsmiling waiter. |

A *dangling modifier* is a word or group of words that does not modify the proper word in the sentence. The result is uncertainty, as in the following:

Planning for months and reading about the countries to be visited, Bob's vacation was unforgettable.

Frightened and alone, our walk through the cemetery was terrifying.

Sentences with dangling modifiers can be corrected by inserting the missing word to be modified, or by rewriting the sentence, making sure that each modifier is close to the word it should modify.

| | |
|---|---|
| *Revised:* | Because we had planned for months and read about the countries to be visited, our vacation was unforgettable. |
| *Revised:* | Frightened and alone, we were terrified as we walked through the cemetery. |

### Faulty Pronoun Reference

Pronouns are words that stand for (or refer to) other words, called their *antecedents*. A pronoun must agree with its antecedent in number. This means that a singular antecedent should have a singular pronoun, and a plural antecedent should have a plural pronoun.

| | |
|---|---|
| *Singular antecedent and pronoun:* | Roger Maris set *his* record in 1961. |
| *Plural antecedent and pronoun:* | The players put on *their* uniforms before *they* left for the stadium. |

If you follow these rules, your pronouns will agree with their antecedents:

1. The antecedent should be specific rather than implied. The pronouns *that, this, it,* and *which* are often used to refer to an idea never mentioned in the sentence but only vaguely implied. In such cases give the pronoun a specific antecedent to refer to.

   | | |
   |---|---|
   | *Vague:* | My childhood hero was a chemist, which inspired me to major in it. |

    *Revised:*  My childhood hero was a chemist who inspired me to major in chemistry.

    *Vague:*  She arrived early at the surprise party, which was not her fault.

    *Revised:*  Her early arrival at the surprise party was not her fault.

2. Rewrite sentences in which there are two possible antecedents for a pronoun.

    *Confusing:*  Sylvia told Arlene that she had been mistaken.
    *Revised:*  Sylvia admitted to Arlene that she had been mistaken.
        Sylvia told Arlene, "I have been mistaken."
        Sylvia told Arlene, "You have been mistaken."

3. Use the correct pronoun when referring to animals, people, and things.
   Use *which* only for animals and things.

    The German shepherd, *which* is a good watchdog, can be trained easily.
    A fire, *which* had started in the cellar, destroyed the home.

    Use *who* and *whom* only for people.

    A person *who* does not smoke often receives a discount when applying for life insurance.
    Charles Lindbergh was a hero *whom* everyone admired.

    Use *that* for animals, people, and things.

    Dogs, children over five, and large containers *that* occupy a separate seat must have tickets.

Masculine pronouns (*he, him, his*) are often used when the gender of the antecedent is not specified, as in the following sentence:

    A student should turn in *his* work on time if *he* wants credit for it.

However, many writers object to the exclusive use of masculine pronouns. Students should attempt to use gender-inclusive pronouns whenever possible. One way to achieve this is to use the following form:

    A student should turn in *his or her* work on time if *he or she* wants credit for it.

Some writers and readers, while trying to avoid using only masculine pronouns, believe that the preceding sentence is awkward. Their suggestion is to rewrite the sentence by making the antecedent plural.

> *Students* should turn in *their* work on time if *they* want credit for it.

For a more detailed discussion of sexism in language, see page 198.

### Problems with Personal Pronouns

Problems often arise in the use of pronouns because many of them have different forms, depending on their use in the sentence. When you are not certain how a pronoun is used, you will be uncertain of which form to use.

The *subject* pronouns are used as the subject of a sentence or a clause and as a subject complement. (A *subject complement* is a noun, adjective, or pronoun used after a linking verb. After a linking verb, use only the subject form of a pronoun.)

| | |
|---|---|
| *As a subject:* | Marty and I [not *me*] stayed until the game was over. |
| | Who [not *Whom*] is going to pay for this? |
| *As a subject complement:* | It was they [not *them*] who ordered the new posters. |
| | That was he [not *him*] yelling at the dog. |

*Note:* Some exceptions to this rule are allowed in informal speech and writing. "It is me," "That's him," and "It was her," for example, are widely accepted in such situations. Careful speakers and writers, however, continue to use the subject form in more formal situations.

The *object* pronouns are used as direct objects, indirect objects, and objects of prepositions.

| | |
|---|---|
| *As a direct object:* | Rita suspected George and me [not *I*] of dropping the balloons filled with water. |
| | Whom [not *Who*] do you want? |
| *As an indirect object:* | When we were children, our parents gave my brothers and me [not *I*] an electric train. |
| *As the object of a preposition:* | The damage to the car was a surprise to Reggie and her [not *she*]. |
| | To whom [not *who*] do you wish to speak? |

The *possessive* form of a pronoun is usually used immediately before a noun ending in *-ing* (such nouns are called *gerunds,* and they are formed by adding *-ing* to verbs).

> My friends laughed at my [not *me*] singing.
> He resents your [not *you*] being taller than he is.

The possessive forms of *it, who,* and *you* cause problems for many writers. Remembers that the apostrophe in *it's, who's,* and *you're* indicates that these are contractions, not possessive forms.

I am fascinated by the history of Mexico and its [not *it's*] culture.

Any applicant whose [not *who's*] record includes a serious traffic violation will be disqualified.

You will always remember your [not *you're*] twenty-first birthday.

### Shifts in Tense, Voice, and Person

Your reader follows your ideas in your sentences much like someone follows you along an unfamiliar path. If you suddenly shift or head in a new direction, you will confuse or lose your reader. Three kinds of unnecessary shifts in a sentence are particularly distracting: shifts in *tense*, in *voice*, and in *person*.

*Shifts in Tense.* You tell your reader when an action takes place—in the past, at present, or in the future—by the tenses of your verbs. The first verb in a sentence usually affects all of the other verbs in the sentence or paragraph because it lays down a track or sequence for the events being described. A sentence that begins, "After I *bought* my ticket, I . . ." signals the reader that the incident will be told in the past tense because *bought* is a past tense verb. If, however, the sentence were to switch to the present tense, the result would be chaos: "After I bought my ticket, I *enter* the stadium and *try* to find my seat." Is the writer telling about a particular instance when he bought a ticket and tried to find his seat? Or is he describing his usual procedure: he buys a ticket, enters the stadium, and then tries to find the right seat? We don't know, because the writer has switched tenses. When relating an incident, keep in mind the tense forms you are using.

The most common kind of unnecessary shift—going from past to present and back again—usually happens when telling something that becomes so real that it seems to be happening to the narrator *now*. Notice what happens in the following paragraph when the writer forgets when the events took place.

> Because it *was* a beautiful day yesterday, I *decided* to wash my car. I no sooner *get* it washed off than it *begins* to rain. But this *isn't* the first time this *happened* to me. Last Monday evening, when I *was* watering the lawn, it *begins* to drizzle.

To avoid unnecessary shifts and to express your ideas more precisely, review the following summary of the six common tenses in English.

| | |
|---|---|
| *Present:* | I live (am living) |
| *Past:* | I lived (was living) |
| *Future:* | I will* live (will be living) |
| *Present Perfect:* | I have lived (have been living) |

*Past Perfect:*   I had lived (had been living)
*Future Perfect:*   I will* have lived (will have been living)

Each tense has a specific use and should not be confused with any other tense.

The *present tense* is used in the following situations:

> To express an action or condition that is going on or exists now.

> That music *is* too loud.
> The cream *tastes* sour.

> To express action that is habitual.

> Ed *plays* poker every Saturday night.
> He *strikes* out more often than any other player on the team.

> To express universal truths or ideas that are always true.

> The sun *sets* in the West.
> Silence *is* golden.

The *past tense* is used to express an action or condition completed in the past.

> Sam *divorced* her in 1989.
> President Truman's election in 1948 *was* a surprise.

The *future tense* is used to express an action that will take place in the future.

> We *will* arrive in Denver tomorrow night.
> The band *will by playing* four engagements next week.

The future may also be expressed by using the present tense and an adverb or adverb phrase.

> I *am going* to start my paper *tomorrow.*
> *Next Monday* we *leave* for Detroit.

The *present perfect tense* expresses an action or condition that started in the past and has been completed at some indefinite time or is still going on.

> Gwen *has seen* the Acropolis in Athens.
> George *has kept* the secret to himself for many years.

The *past perfect tense* expresses an action that was completed before another action in the past occurred.

---

* *Shall* is often substituted for *will* in the future and future perfect tenses.

Before she accepted the job, she *had investigated* the responsibilities and duties of the position.

Mary *had saved* her money for several years before she bought her new car.

*Note:* The simple past tense is sometimes used for the past perfect: Before she accepted the job, she *investigated* the responsibilities and duties of the position. Mary *saved* her money for several years before she bought her new car.

The *future perfect tense* indicates an action that will be complete before a particular time in the future.

We *will have lived* here six years next June.

Here are a few additional suggestions for using the correct tense.

Don't use the past tense of a verb when it should be present.

Last summer he visited New Orleans. He said that the old French section *was* interesting and picturesque. [*Incorrect.* The second sentence implies that the old French section has been destroyed. The correct verb is "is."]

Use the present infinitive (*to leave, to bring, to remember,* and so on) unless the action referred to was completed before the time expressed in the governing verb.

I wanted *to talk* [not *to have talked*] to her about it.
We are happy *to have had* [not *to have*] you stay with us.

When a narrative in the past tense is interrupted by a reference to a preceding event, use the past perfect tense.

Rachel repaired the bicycle that she *had broken.*
His letter stated that his father *had died.*

*Shift in Voice.* A sentence written in *active voice* contains a subject that performs an action expressed by an *active verb:*

The composer *wrote* the song as a tribute to his wife.

A sentence is in the *passive voice* when the subject is acted on by a *passive verb,* consisting of a form of *be* plus the past participle:

The song *was written* by the composer as a tribute to his wife.

As you saw in Chapter 8, passive voice constructions often lead to weak and wordy sentences. Another trap to avoid is shifting from one voice to another in the same sentence:

*Shift:*  The jury returned to the courtroom after their verdict had been reached. [*Confusing; it sounds as though the verdict were reached by someone else.*]

    *Revised:*    The jury returned to the courtroom after they had reached their verdict.

A shift in the voice usually creates a confusing or irritating shift in the subject:

    *Shift:*    When you look up into the night sky, a falling star is sometimes seen.
    *Revised:*    When you look up into the night sky, you can sometimes see a falling star.

*Shifts in Person.* Shifts in person occur when the writer shifts from one point of view to another. They happen because the writer forgets the subject of the sentence. The most common faulty shifts are from second person (*you*) to third (*he, she, they*) and from third person to second.

Here are some examples of confusing shifts in person:

    *Shift:*    A *person* should look both ways when *you* cross the street.
    *Revised:*    A *person* should look both ways when *he* crosses the street.
    *Shift:*    As *you* leave the freeway and enter the main business district, a *person* can see the damage caused by the twister.
    *Revised:*    As *you* leave the freeway and enter the main business district, *you* can see the damage caused by the twister.

These shifts in person occur within the same sentence. It is equally important that you avoid unnecessary shifts in person from one sentence to another, and from paragraph to paragraph. The best way to avoid such shifts is to decide in advance whom you are talking about—and stick with that point of view.

## E X E R C I S E 4

Correct any mistakes in the following sentences. If a sentence is correct, mark it "C."

1. An increase in student fees has been ordered, but they will not explain the reason for it.
2. Although rock music has been around for four decades, rock music is still viewed by some as the music of rebellious youth.
3. Angela's major was sociology because they study the way people live.
4. Ignoring the airplanes overhead, the open-air theater offered a terrific version of *As You Like It.*

5. The restaurant was doing poorly because of their poor service and high prices.
6. Colleen wore the sandals after they had repaired the buckle.
7. When you learn to drive a manual car first, one usually is a better driver overall.
8. Grunge fashions were popular for a while, but it is not as popular now.
9. Mozart is a prodigy because he learned to play the piano and compose music at such extremely early ages.
10. The L.A. riots shocked much of the middle class since they thought significant progress had been made in race relations.
11. My two sisters and me were punished for being out past curfew.
12. All candidates report the amount of campaign contributions they receive.
13. Trucks have been rumbling through the streets all day with dirt and rock.
14. Wailing and demanding its bottle, the sermon was interrupted.
15. Vince bites his fingernails, and he is trying to stop it.
16. Beverly admires her father, who is an architect, and that is the profession she plans to follow.
17. Last Monday was the deadline to register to vote in the primary election.
18. Julie and her mother are very close, and although she lives in Europe.
19. Acid rain has been studied by scientists which are unable to link it to any single cause.
20. Any animal who is caught without a license will be held in the animal pound.
21. As we entered the room, you could smell the fresh paint.
22. A student in a word-processing course has a good chance of employment when they graduate.
23. The drivers' licenses in some states are color coded for drivers of automobiles that wear eyeglasses.
24. Astrologers and clairvoyants are consulted by some people before they make an important decision.
25. My history prof said that if a person wants to understand the present, you should read about the past.

---

## A Guide to Punctuation and Capitalization

The purpose of punctuation and capitalization is to make your meaning clear to readers. Every mark of punctuation carries some meaning and gives hints about how to read written English. The capitalization of words, too, helps the reader and serves as a guide to meaning.

The wrong punctuation mark or incorrect capitalization can often change the meaning of a sentence; at the very least, it diverts the reader's attention from what you are saying and suggests that you are careless.

Learning to punctuate and capitalize correctly is not difficult. It does, however, require a little effort. In this section we will look at the most common situations in written English that require punctuation and capitalization.

## Punctuation

### The Period

1. Use the period at the end of a declarative sentence, a mild command, and an indirect question.

   *Declarative sentence*
   The Japanese consume more fish per capita than Americans do.

   *Mild command*
   Please write in ink.

   *Indirect question*
   I wonder where I put my wallet.

2. Use the period after most abbreviations.

   Mr.   St.   Nov.   P.M.   Weds.

   Periods do not usually follow abbreviations of organizations and government agencies.

   NFL   USA   CBS   UN   FBI

### The Question Mark

1. Use a question mark after a direct question.

   Are these your socks?

2. Use a question mark to indicate uncertainty about the accuracy of a date, word, or phrase.

   Hubert van Eyck (1366?–1426) was a founder of the Flemish School of painting.

### The Exclamation Point

Use an exclamation mark after a strong interjection or an expression of very strong feeling.

   Help!
   Darn it!

Don't overdo the use of exclamation points. Excessive use dulls their impact.

## The Comma

The comma is the punctuation mark most frequently used inside the sentence. It also offers the widest range of individual choice. Do not use a comma unless you have a definite reason for doing so. The following rules will help you avoid cluttering your sentences with unnecessary commas and will show you how to use commas to make your meaning clear.

1. Use a comma to separate independent clauses joined by *and, but, for, nor, or so,* and *yet.*

   She worked and saved for her children, but they did not appreciate it.
   The village centennial was approaching, and everyone was contributing ideas for the celebration.

   If the independent clauses are short, the comma may be omitted.

   I stayed but he left.

2. Use a comma to separate an introductory dependent clause from the main part of the sentence.

   Because Pete was only three when he left Vienna, he does not remember the city.

3. Use a comma to separate a long introductory prepositional phrase.

   Despite an exhausting and often confusing overnight journey, Randy volunteered to work at the picnic.

4. Use a comma to set off an introductory phrase containing a past or present participle or infinitive.

   Wanting to be remembered for his contribution to the arts, Mr. Crow named the symphony as the major recipient of his estate.
   To impress his girlfriend and to shock his parents, Andrew got a job.

5. Use a comma to set off items in a series.

   To be a successful salesman, you must have enthusiasm, confidence in your product, and a knowledge of psychology.

6. Use a comma to set off interrupting elements (also called parenthetical elements) such as the following: *as a matter of fact, at any rate, it appears, for instance, nevertheless, of course, however,* and *therefore.*

It would appear, nevertheless, that your efforts have failed.

Despite Senator Williams' campaign pledge, however, he voted for the tax increase.

7. Use commas to set off *nonessential* elements in a sentence. Nonessential elements are modifiers and appositives that are unnecessary to identify the term they refer to. They should be set off on both sides by commas unless they come at the beginning or end of a sentence. Do *not* set off essential modifiers and appositives with commas.

Abraham Lincoln, *the sixteenth President,* was a complex and often contradictory person. [The nonessential appositive merely gives additional information; the subject is identified by his name. Because the appositive is nonessential, it is set off.]

The poet *Wordsworth* is famous for his descriptions of nature. [The appositive is essential; if it were omitted, we would not know the poet referred to. Therefore, it is not set off with commas.]

New Orleans, *which is known for its jazz,* is a city I have always wanted to visit. [The clause is nonessential because the subject is fully identified; therefore, it is set off with commas.]

A city *that I have always wanted to visit* is New Orleans. [The clause is essential and therefore is not set off with commas.]

8. Use a comma to set off coordinate adjectives. Adjectives are coordinate if *and* can be placed between them.

It was a long, boring novel. [You can say "long *and* boring."] *But note:*

It was a long detective novel. [No comma: you would not say, "a long *and* detective novel."]

9. Use a comma to set off contrasted elements.

I ordered a steak, not oysters.

10. Use a comma to set off quoted material.

In a clear voice she announced, "I am resigning."

11. Use a comma in direct address.

Eddie, when are you leaving for Des Moines?

12. Use a comma in dates if the month is given first.

September 28, 1929

If the date is followed by the rest of the sentence, the year should also be followed by a comma.

December 7, 1941, is a day that will live in infamy.

13. Use a comma to separate the elements in an address.

United Nations Plaza, Riverside Drive, New York, New York

Within a sentence, place a comma after the final element in an address.

> His office at the United Nations Plaza on Riverside Drive, New York, is his headquarters.

**14.** Titles and degrees are set off by commas on both sides.

> James L. Tierney, Ph.D., was the graduation speaker.

**15.** Use a comma to prevent misreading.

> Although angry, Tim shook hands with his opponent.

*Misusing Commas.* The comma is misused more than any other punctuation mark. Too many commas can slow down thought or confuse meaning. The following list presents some of the frequent situations that might tempt you to use the comma.

**1.** Do not use a comma to separate the subject from its verb.

> *Incorrect:* A valid driver's license or credit card, is required.
> *Revised:* A valid driver's license or credit card is required.

**2.** Do not use a comma after the last item in a series of adjectives preceding the noun.

> *Incorrect:* She was a creative, imaginative, dedicated, dancer.
> *Revised:* She was a creative, imaginative, dedicated dancer.

**3.** Do not use a comma before indirect quotations.

> *Incorrect:* He said, that his favorite singer was Placido Domingo.
> *Revised:* He said that his favorite singer was Placido Domingo.

**4.** Do not use a comma between two words or phrases joined by a coordinator.

> *Incorrect:* Every applicant was asked to bring a résumé, and a photograph.
> *Revised:* Every applicant was asked to bring a résumé and a photograph.

**5.** Do not use a comma to separate a verb from a *that* clause.

> *Incorrect:* He often claimed, that he was a member of the royal family.
> *Revised:* He often claimed that he was a member of the royal family.

**6.** Do not use a comma to separate independent clauses.

> *Incorrect:* The average price of a personal computer is declining, more people are buying them for home use.
> *Revised:* The average price of a personal computer is declining; more people are buying them for home use. [There are

several ways to correct this comma splice; the use of a semicolon is only one. See pages 324–325 for others.]

## The Semicolon

**1.** Use a semicolon to separate two closely related independent clauses when there is no coordinating conjunction to join them.

You do not have to be a brute to hit a tennis ball a long distance; a flick of the wrist will do it.

**2.** Use a semicolon to separate items in a series if the items contain commas.

The winners of the raffle were Te Nguyen, an insurance agent from Garden Grove, California; Joyce Martin, a salesperson from Toledo, Ohio; Marino Garcia, a wrestling coach from St. Louis, Missouri; and Bill Hubbard, a butcher from Spokane, Washington.

## The Colon

**1.** Use a colon before a list of items introduced by an independent clause.

She had articles published in three popular magazines: *TV Guide, Reader's Digest,* and *Woman's Day.*

Do not place a colon between a verb and its objects or complements or between a preposition and its objects.

*Incorrect:*   The three magazines she has published in are: *TV Guide, Reader's Digest,* and *Woman's Day.*

*Incorrect:*   While in Washington we saw: the Vietnam War Memorial, the White House, and the Washington Monument.

*Incorrect:*   As a source of energy, coal has been partially replaced by: nuclear energy, solar energy, and oil.

**2.** Use a colon between two complete thoughts when the second explains the first.

He told me what I wanted to hear: my application had been accepted.

## Parentheses

Use parentheses to enclose unimportant information or comments that are not an essential part of the passage.

Some majors in college (English, for instance) require two years of a foreign language.

*Two warnings:* Never place a comma before a parenthesis. Always use parentheses in pairs.

### Dashes

1. Use a dash to mark an abrupt change in the thought or structure of a sentence.

   Last night I went to—but do you really want to hear about it?

2. Use dashes to make explanatory matter more prominent.

   T.S. Eliot—a native of the United States—was one of England's greatest modern poets.

   Dashes are used to make explanatory matter *stand out;* parentheses are used to bury it in the sentence.

3. Use a dash to set off an introductory series.

   Chinese, English, Hindu, Spanish, and Russian—these are the major world languages.

### Brackets

1. Use brackets to set off your own words that you have inserted into a quotation.

   "My favorite actors," the aging producer said, "are Ronnie [Reagan] and Helmut [Dantine]."

2. Use brackets to set off words and phrases that you have added for the purpose of explanation or identification.

   "Next year the G.N.P. [Gross National Product] will exceed our expectations," reported the Secretary of the Treasury.

### Quotation Marks

1. Use quotation marks around the exact words of a speaker.

   "I will be happy to give you a tour of the museum," she said.

   Do not use quotation marks for indirect quotations.

   She said that she would be happy to give us a tour of the museum.

2. Use quotation marks to call attention to words that are being used in an unusual sense and in definitions.

   Many people mispronounce "mischievous."

   *Note:* Some people prefer to italicize (underline) words when used in this way.

3. Use quotation marks to enclose titles of short poems, paintings, magazine articles, television episodes, short stories, songs, and any selection from a longer work.

> Dorothy's favorite poem is "Trees," by Joyce Kilmer.
> My favorite *Star Trek* episode is "The Trouble with Tribbles."
> "Stardust" is probably the most frequently recorded song in history.

## *Italics*

When words that would be italicized if printed are handwritten or typed, they should be underlined.

1. Italicize titles of books, plays, magazines, movies, television series, and newspapers.

> *Death Comes for the Archbishop*
> *Hamlet*
> *Time*
> *Detroit Free Press*
> *Casablanca*

2. Italicize foreign words and phrases that have not yet been adopted as English expression. If you are uncertain about the status of a particular word or phrase, check a good dictionary.

> *por favor*
> *C'est la guerre*

3. Use italics when referring to letters, numbers, and words.

> The professor gave only two *A*'s all year.
> All of the *9*'s were removed from the deck of cards.
> He always mispronounces *discipline*. [As noted under "Quotation marks," some writers prefer to enclose words used like this in quotes.]

4. Use italics for special emphasis.

> I know what I *should* do, but I don't *want* to do it.

## *Ellipsis*

Use an ellipsis (three periods) to indicate an omission of unnecessary or irrelevant material from a quotation. If the ellipsis occurs at the end of a sentence or the ellipsis eliminates words that include the end of a sentence, use four periods.

> The treaty stated, "The terms of this document . . . will be observed by both parties effective midnight. . . ."

## The Hyphen

The hyphen is used to set off certain prefixes, to separate certain compound words, and to show that a word is to be carried over to the next line.

**1.** After *ex-, self,-* and *all-* when they are prefixes.

> ex-wife
> self-hatred
> all-knowing

**2.** After prefixes that precede a proper noun or adjective.

> pro-Democratic
> un-American
> anti-Semitic

**3.** Between compound descriptions serving as a single adjective before a noun.

> dark-green water
> a hard-bitten sheriff
> a slow-starting pace

**4.** Between fractions and compound numbers from twenty-one through ninety-nine.

> five-eighths
> three-fourths
> fifty-two
> eighty-four

**5.** Between syllables for words at the end of a line. Never divide a one-syllable word. When you are uncertain about the use of the hyphen in the syllabication of a word or in compound words, consult a collegiate-level dictionary.

## The Apostrophe

The apostrophe is used for the possessive case (except for personal pronouns), to indicate an omitted letter or number, and to form the plural of numbers, specific words, and letters.

**1.** Use the apostrophe to form the possessive case.

> To form the possessive case of a singular person, thing, or indefinite pronoun, add *'s:*
>
> > Lou's parking space
> > the girl's job
> > the owl's hooting
> > anyone's duty

If a proper name already ends in *s* in its singular form and the adding of *'s* would make the pronunciation difficult, it is best to use the apostrophe only:

> Jesus' teachings [*Jesus's* would be difficult to pronounce but is acceptable]
> Charles' telephone number [*Charles's* is acceptable]

To form the possessive case of a plural noun ending in *s,* add an apostrophe only:

> the Smiths' new home
> the birds' songs

To form the possessive of a plural noun *not* ending in *s,* add *'s:*

> the children's program
> men's obligations

To form the possessives of compound words, use the apostrophe according to the meaning of the construction:

> Sears and Roebuck's new stores [the new stores of Sears and Roebuck]
> J. C. Penney's and Montgomery Ward's stores [the stores of J. C. Penney and of Montgomery Ward]
> Her brother and sister's home [the home of her brother and sister]

2. Use an apostrophe to indicate an omitted letter or number.

> isn't
> the '90s

3. Use an apostrophe to form the plurals of letters, specific words, and numbers.

> Her *1*'s and *e*'s look the same to me. [Notice that they are italicized or underlined as well.]
> I counted forty *aye*'s and sixteen *nay*'s.
> Anyone who received a score in the *90*'s did not have to take the unit test.

*Note:* An apostrophe is not necessary for the plural of a year.

> The 1980s were a time of economic hardship for many.

4. The apostrophe should *not* be used with the possessive forms of personal and relative pronouns.

*Incorrect:*     it's, her's, your's, our's, who's [to show possession]

*Revised:*      its, hers, yours, ours, whose (possessive form)

Notice, however, that indefinite pronouns form the possessive case by adding *'s: one's, anyone's, someone's, everyone's,* and so on.

## Numbers

1. If a number requires no more than two words, it should be spelled out.

   seven hours    eleven million dollars    two hundred workers

2. Always write out a number beginning a sentence.

   *Incorrect:*     47 passengers were injured in a train crash this after-noon.
   *Revised:*      Forty-seven passengers were injured in a train crash this afternoon.

   If the number is a long one and spelling it would be awkward, reword the sentence so that the number comes later, in which case it can be stated as a figure.

   *Incorrect:*     Three hundred sixty-four thousand nine hundred forty-one voters had gone to the polls by ten o'clock this morn-ing.
   *Revised:*      By ten o'clock this morning 364,941 voters had gone to the polls.

3. Use figures when they are followed by A.M. or P.M.; write out whole hours.

   7 A.M., 12 A.M., 4:30 P.M.
   twelve midnight, nine o'clock

4. Figures can be made plural in either of two ways: by adding *-s*, or by adding *-'s*. Most writers prefer the latter *(-'s)*.

   several *3's*, four *10's*

   Notice that figures used in this sense are also italicized (underlined).
   Do not use an apostrophe when writing out a number in the plural.

   *Incorrect:*     several three's and ten's
   *Revised:*      several threes and tens

## *Capitalization*

The rules for capitalization are based, in general, on the following principle: the names of *specific* persons, places, and things (*proper* nouns) are capitalized; the names of *general* persons, places, and things (*common* nouns) are not capitalized.

1. Capitalize the first word in any sentence, including direct quotations that are complete sentences.

   > The waiter approached our table and asked, "Is Doctor Marshall with this group?"

2. Capitalize the first and last words in a title and all other words except *a, an, the,* and unimportant words with fewer than five letters.

   > One of the required texts in the course is titled *A Guide to the Principles of Ornithology.*

3. Capitalize the titles of relatives and professions only when they come before the person's name, or when they take the place of the person's name.

   > I'll see you next week, Aunt Bea.
   > Her aunt lived in Buenos Aires.
   > The recruits reported to Corporal Trujillo.
   > The corporal welcomed the recruits to the base.
   > Is your mother home?
   > Here's the magazine I was telling you about, Mother.

4. Capitalize the names of people, political, religious, and ethnic groups, languages, and nationalities, as well as adjectives derived from them.

   | | | |
   |---|---|---|
   | Republicans | French | Mexican food |
   | Mormons | Quakers | German wines |
   | Chicanos | Chinese | Polish names |

5. Capitalize the names of particular streets, buildings, bridges, rivers, cities, states, nations, specific geographical features, schools, and other institutions.

   | | |
   |---|---|
   | Wilshire Boulevard | Ireland |
   | Merchandise Mart | Monks' Mounds |
   | Eads Bridge | Julliard School of Music |
   | Fox River | the United States Senate |
   | Philadelphia | the Alps |

6. Capitalize directions only when they refer to specific regions.

   > People who live in the West have language differences from those who live in the East.

*But:* The plane turned north.

7. Capitalize the days of the week, months of the year, and names of holidays.

   The Fourth of July was observed on the first Monday of the month this year.

8. Capitalize the names of particular historical events and eras.

   the First World War
   the Roaring Twenties
   the Age of Reason

9. Capitalize the names of school subjects only if they are proper nouns or if they are followed by a course number.

   a biology course          Economics 102
   Biology 215               French
   the economics professor   English

## E X E R C I S E    5

The paragraph below lacks correct punctuation and capitalization. Copy it, making the necessary corrections.

   The american indian has had to endure bad housing lack of jobs dismal health conditions and poor education the present plight of the red man is in contrast to his condition four hundred and fifty years ago at first the newly discovered indians were respected and admired christopher columbus sir walter raleigh and the french philosopher michel de montaigne spoke highly of them the puritans in new england however regarded indians as stubborn animals that refused to acknowledge the obvious blessings of white civilization in 1637 a group of puritans surrounded the pequot indian village and set fire to it about 500 indians were burned to death or shot when the puritan preacher cotton mather heard about the raid he wrote in his diary on this day we have sent six hundred heathen souls to hell after the war of 1812 the conditions of the indians declined rapidly pressures increased to get the indians off the lands the whites had appropriated from them almost all of the indians were cleared from the east the experience of the indians west of the mississippi was only a sad duplication of what had happened east of it warfare broken treaties expropriation of land rebellion and ultimately defeat as president cleveland remarked the hunger and thirst of the white man for the indians land is almost equal to his hunger and thirst after righteousness the indian problem still nags at the american conscience in the

1990s indians exist as the most manipulated people on earth and yet our indian policy has produced only failure after failure.

## E X E R C I S E   6

Add any missing commas and delete those that are unnecessary in the following sentences. If a sentence is punctuated correctly, mark it "C."

1. Needing desperately to get some sleep and having his new-born twins crying at all hours the frustrated father checked into a motel room for the night.
2. Each week while she prepared the status report on the project she noted how far behind schedule and over budget the program was.
3. A hauberk a tunic of chain mail worn by soldiers in the Middle Ages can be seen at the local museum.
4. If you try to go without a good breakfast you will get tired and very hungry, when you should be wide awake and satisfied.
5. Because of her allergy to peanuts, her children never experienced the joys of peanut butter sandwiches until they moved away for college.
6. Many programs offer to increase your self-esteem but some are prohibitively expensive and sometimes have disreputable finances.
7. Not merely lucky the rich entrepreneur worked many, long, hard, hours.
8. Miami, which has a large Cuban population is on the east coast of Florida.
9. Lacking the confidence to sing in public and believing that everyone was ridiculing him the tenor abandoned his career, and returned to Casper Wyoming.
10. According to Abraham Maslow one of the giants of modern psychology, productive individuals share certain common traits.
11. The technology needed to make atom bombs is available to almost any country or terrorist and some critics fear eventual nuclear blackmail.
12. According to Isaac Asimov science fiction is the only literature, that is based firmly on scientific thought.
13. Some parishioners wanted a modernistic design for the new church however, others preferred a traditional plan.
14. The Cuyahoga River in Ohio is so terribly polluted, that it actually caught fire.
15. Children on an Israeli kibbutz do not live with their parents, they are raised in groups.

## E X E R C I S E 7

Some of the apostrophes in the following sentences are unnecessary, and some are missing. Make the necessary corrections.

1. Some people think in todays' Hollywood, the movie stars are too ordinary, ugly, or graceless compared to the ones' in the 1930s and 1940s.
2. Societies determination of being hip or un-hip seems to rest on its' current standards of material success.
3. The Demlingers' party on New Years' Eve was a brawling, drunken riot.
4. The carpenter's tools were more expensive than the electricians.
5. The three actors robes' were made from Victorias' old curtains.
6. I recognized your cat by it's diamond-studded collar.
7. The professors' students remarked that she was a brilliant lecturer but somewhat reluctant to answer anyone's questions after class.
8. Americans who remember the '30s often refer to the Depression and to those who's fortunes were wiped out.
9. Gloria Steinem is an eloquent speaker for womens rights.
10. Biblical archaeologists do not know the location of Moses' grave.

## E X E R C I S E 8

The sentences below require capital letters, quotation marks, or additional punctuation.

1. Traci has seen all of the original Star Trek episodes and once met William Shatner.
2. My favorite movie is casablanca and my favorite song is stop! in the name of love by diana ross and the supremes.
3. Christine had taken professor Gilleran's English 101 course so many times that she could mouth the lectures before professor Gilleran said them.
4. After adjusting his microphone Mr. Maynard began his lecture by saying I firmly believe that a solid understanding of the world begins with the study of ancient Sanskrit texts.
5. The gap between the have's and the have-nots in this country is increasing, according to a local columnist who had just read a study of wealth distribution in the us.
6. George Eliot born Mary Anne Evans is the author of the novel Adam Bede.

7. The emotional responses evoked by Bach's music are different from those triggered by Chuck Berry's song Maybellene.
8. Shakespeare, the author of the play Hamlet wrote a sonnet that begins Shall I compare thee to a summers day.
9. One of the great philosophers of the middle ages was saint Thomas Aquinas.
10. After living in the west since the beginning of world war II, aunt Marilyn longed for the sights and sounds of the east particularly the lovely New Jersey cities of fort Lee and Secaucus.

# A

## A Glossary
## of Usage

Here is a list of words that are often confused by college writers. If you want to know more about these (or other) words, consult one of the collegiate dictionaries recommended in Chapter 1, or Webster's Third *New International Dictionary*.

*accept, except*  *Accept* is a verb meaning "to receive," and *except* is a preposition meaning "but," or a verb meaning "to exclude."

> "We wanted to *accept* his offer, but we were unable to."
> "All of the countries *except* Peru were represented."
> "The committee decided to *except* the officers from the meeting."

*adapt, adopt*  To *adapt* something is to change it for a purpose; to *adopt* something is to control or possess it.

> "She *adapted* the words of the song to her own meaning."
> "She *adopted* the words of the song as her philosophy."

*advice, advise*  *Advice* is an opinion you offer; *advise* means to recommend.

> "The coach's *advice* was ignored."
> "My teacher can *advise* you of the best novel to read."

*affect, effect*  To *affect* is to change or modify; to *effect* is to bring about or cause something; an *effect* is a result.

> "The fog will *affect* traffic conditions."
> "The doctor will try to *effect* a change in his patient's condition."
> "The *effect* of the treatment was not noticeable."

*aggravate, annoy*  To *aggravate* is to make a condition worse; to *annoy* is to irritate.

> "The treatment only *aggravated* his condition."
> "The ticking clock *annoyed* Dean as he read."

*ain't*  *Ain't* is a nonstandard word never used by educated or careful speakers or writers except to achieve a deliberate humorous effect. Avoid the word.

*all ready, already*  *All ready* shows preparedness; *already* is an adverb meaning "before or by the time mentioned."

> "The troops were *all ready* for inspection."
> "It was *already* six o'clock when darkness came."

*all right, alright*  *All right* is the correct form; do not use *alright*, which is nonstandard.

*all together, altogether*  *All together* means "all at once or at the same time." *Altogether* means "completely" or "entirely."

> "The family are *all together* in the living room."
> "You are *altogether* correct."

*allusion, illusion*  An *allusion* is an indirect reference to something. An *illusion* is a false image or impression.

"He made an *allusion* to his parents' wealth."
"It is an *illusion* to think that I will be a millionaire."

**among,
between**  Use *among* when referring to more than two items and *between* when referring to two.

"Sandy was *among* the four finalists."
"Sid can't decide *between* a green or a blue shirt."

**amount,
number**  *Amount* refers to a quantity or to things in the aggregate; *number* refers to objects that you can count.

"A large *amount* of work remains to be done."
"A *number* of jobs are still unfilled."

**anyone,
any one**  *Anyone* means "any person at all," and *any one* means any single person.

"I will talk to *anyone* who answers the phone."
"*Any one* of these players can teach you the game in minutes."

**anyways,
anywheres**  These are nonstandard forms for *anyway* and *anywhere*, and they should be avoided.

**bad, badly**  *Bad* is an adjective, and *badly* is an adverb.

"Her pride was hurt *badly* [not *bad*]."
"She feels *bad* [not *badly*]."

**being as,
being that**  These are nonstandard terms and should be avoided. Use *since* or *because*.

**beside, besides**  *Beside* is a preposition meaning "by the side of." *Besides* may be a preposition or an adverb meaning "in addition to" or "also."

"The doctor sat *beside* the bed talking to the patient."
"*Besides* my homework, I have some letters to write."

**can, may**  *Can* refers to ability, and *may* refers to permission.

"Henry *may* go with us if he wants to."
"Henry *can* go with us now that he feels better."

**can't hardly,
barely**  These are double negatives and are to be avoided. Use *can hardly* and *can barely* or *can't*.

**complement,
compliment**  To *complement* is to balance or complete; to *compliment* is to flatter.

"Her new shoes *complement* her outfit."
"He *complimented* her for her ability to yodel."

**conscience,
conscious**  A *conscience* is a sense of right or wrong. To be *conscious* is to be aware.

"His *conscience* wouldn't allow him to cheat on the test."
"I was not *conscious* of the noise in the background."

**continual,**  *Continual* means "repeated frequently," and *continu-*

| | |
|---|---|
| *continuous* | *ous* "without interruptions." |
| | "We heard a series of *continual* beeps in the background." |
| | "I was lulled to sleep by the *continuous* hum of the motor below deck." |
| *could of* | This is a nonstandard form. Use *could have*. |
| *council,*<br>*counsel* | A *council* is a body of people; *counsel* refers to an advisor or to advice. |
| | "The city *council* voted itself a pay hike." |
| | "The trial was interrupted by her *counsel's* sudden illness." |
| | "Her lawyer gave her excellent *counsel*." |
| *different from,*<br>*different than* | Use *different from* to note a difference. *Different than* is a colloquial substitute. |
| | "Moscow is different from Kiev." |
| | "Moscow is different than Kiev." |
| *disinterested,*<br>*uninterested* | To be *disinterested* is to be impartial. *Uninterested* means "not interested." |
| | "The losing team thought that the referee was not *disinterested*." |
| | "It was easy to tell by his falling asleep that he was *uninterested*." |
| *enormity,*<br>*enormousness* | *Enormity* means "atrociousness"; *enormousness* means "of great size." |
| | "The *enormity* of the crime staggered the sheriff." |
| | "Because of the *enormousness* of his feet, it was impossible to fit him with shoes." |
| *farther,*<br>*further* | Use *farther* for physical distance and *further* for degree or quantity. |
| | "They live *farther* from the center of town than we do." |
| | "Their proposal was a *further* attempt to reach an agreement." |
| *fewer, less* | Although these words are often used interchangeably, careful speakers and writers still use *fewer* to refer to things that are readily distinguishable or in the plural (*fewer jobs, calories, hairpins*) and *less* to things that are singular or are not ordinarily capable of being separated (*less energy, money, freedom*). |
| | "*Fewer* [not *less*] accidents were reported because of the new stop sign." |
| | "*Less* [not *fewer*] traffic congestion has been one of the effects of the new stop sign." |
| *flaunt, flout* | To *flaunt* is to show off; to *flout* is to defy. |
| | "He *flaunted* his knowledge of several languages." |
| | "The tourists *flouted* the local laws." |

| | |
|---|---|
| *formally,*<br>*formerly* | *Formally* refers to conventional behavior. *Formerly* refers to action in the past.<br><br>"We dressed *formally* for Lou's wedding."<br>"Shelley *formerly* lived in Ohio." |
| *good, well* | *Good* is an adjective, never an adverb. *Well* is an adverb and an adjective; as an adjective it means "in a state of good health."<br><br>"She performs *well* [not *good*] in that role."<br>"I am *well* now, although last week I didn't feel very *good*." |
| *hanged, hung* | Criminals are *hanged* for their crimes; pictures are *hung*. |
| *imply, infer* | To *imply* means "to hint strongly"; to *infer* means "to derive the meaning by induction." You *infer* the meaning of a passage when you read or hear it; the writer or speaker *implies* it.<br><br>"He *implied* that he was only thirty-nine."<br>"We *inferred* from his remarks that he would not change his mind." |
| *insure, ensure* | To *insure* means "to give, take, or procure insurance on or for something" or "to make certain or safe, especially with extra steps or precautions." To *ensure* means "to make certain or safe" but without the extra steps or precautions *insure* implies.<br><br>The state requires that you *insure* your car.<br>He *ensured* his promotion when he broke the company's sales record for the month of July. |
| *irregardless* | Nonstandard. Use *regardless*. |
| *its, it's* | *Its* is the possessive form; *it's* is a contraction for *it is* or *it has*. There is no word spelled *its'*.<br><br>"What was *its* price before it went on sale?"<br>"*It's* going to be a long day at the rate we're going."<br>"*It's* been a long day." |
| *lie, lay* | You *lay* or set something down; yesterday you *laid* it down. You *lie* down or rest, yesterday you *lay* down; you have *lain* down for an hour. |
| *loose, lose* | To *loose* means "to unite or unfasten"; to *lose* it "to misplace." *Loose* as an adjective means "unfastened" or "unattached."<br><br>"His necktie was *loose*."<br>"Did he *lose* his necktie?" |
| *maybe, may*<br>*be* | *Maybe* means "perhaps"; *may be* is a verb phrase.<br>"*Maybe* he'll come tomorrow."<br><br>"We *may be* surprised at the results." |

*myself*   Correct when used as a reflexive: "I hurt *myself*," "I helped *myself*," etc. May also be used as an intensive pronoun for emphasis: "I *myself* baked the cake." Colloquial when used as a substitute for *I* or *me* as in the following:

> "My sister and *myself* were raised in Wisconsin."
> "He spoke to my sister and *myself*."

*precede,*   To *precede* means "to go before or in front of"; to
*proceed*   *proceed* is "to continue moving ahead."

> "Poverty and hunger often *precede* revolutions."
> "They *proceeded* down the aisle as if nothing had happened."

*principal,*   *Principal* has two meanings: "The administrator of a
*principle*   school," and "most important." *Principle* means "rule or theory."

> "Mr. Lewis is the *principal* of our high school."
> "The *principal* reason I can't swim is that I'm afraid of the water."
> "The *principles* of geometry are too subtle for me."

*set, sit*   To *sit* means "to occupy a seat"; the past tense is *sat* and the past participle is also *sat.* The present participle is *sitting.* To *set* means "to place something somewhere," and its principal parts are *set, set,* and *setting.*

> "Please *sit* down and have a cup of coffee."
> "He *sat* here for an hour waiting for you."
> "Please *set* the box on the desk."
> "She *set* her packages on the kitchen table when she came home."

*their, there*   Note carefully the following sentences:
*they're*   "They were shocked to find *their* house on fire."

> "Please stay *there* while I make a phone call."
> "It looks as though *they're* going to be late."

*these kind,*   Both expressions are nonstandard. Use "that kind,"
*those kind*   "this kind," "those kinds," and "these kinds."

*who's, whose*   *Who's* is a contraction meaning "who is" or "who has"; *whose* is the possessive form of *who.*

> "*Who's* going with me?"
> "*Who's* been eating my porridge?"
> "*Whose* book is this?"

*your, you're*   Similar to the preceding pair. *Your* is the possessive form of *you; you're* is a contraction for *you are.*

> "Are these *your* gloves?"
> "*You're* going to get a sunburn if you stay out much longer."

# B

## 300
## *Writing Topics*

When asked to select their own writing topics, some students panic. If you are one of them, this list may help. It contains 300 topics—some general, others more specific—that you may want to write about or that may trigger, through association, another idea that you can develop into an essay.

vitamins
NAFTA
euphemisms
Norther Ireland
mental illness
antibiotics
cures for baldness
celebrity trials
liberals
Madonna
virtual reality
billionaires
nostalgia craze
Quebec separatism
numismatics
VA benefits
political correctness
Prozac
Sudden Infant Death
  Syndrome
Health risks in the
  Information Age
incompetence in the
  workplace
artificial intelligence
New York Stock
  Exchange
corporate espionage
Persian Gulf War
crimes by children
Disney movies
androgyny
baseball strikes
existentialism
compute animation
child-care centers
first day of college
foreign holidays cele-
  brated in the U.S.

maquiladores
breast implants
indoor pollution
LSD
tabloids
lack of courtesy
honeymoons
controversial NEA
  grants
recycling
hypochondriacs
New World Order
sex scandals
regrets
Easter or Holy Week
  celebrations
liberal arts versus vo-
  cational education
wine tasting
blind dates
recycling
exotic places
my church
a death in the family
parapsychology
a secret prejudice
pets
famous monuments
childhood dreams
diets
games
self-help books
acting
television
dissent
pollution
being a stranger
being organized
autistic children

lies
*Playboy*
classical music
scientific
  experiments
rejection
high-school cliques
Elvis Presley
the CIA
car mechanics
fancy cooking
graffiti
the Civil War
magazines
cosmetics
weightlifting
the beach
pay raises
a surprise party
teachers' grading
  standards
making a cake
hunting without a
  gun
saving a life
skiing
writing music
astrology
birth control
Judaism
my first kiss
archaeology
my boss
affirmative action
prostitution
student rights
prisons
motorcycles
insurance

family history
veterinarians
forests
bartending
child support
Chinese food
nonsmokers
competition
airplanes
gangsters
astronomy
Zionism
MTV
addictions
life on other planets
living alone
Calvin and Hobbes
perfume ads
science fiction
song lyrics
town characters
humor
clothing styles
cheating
old cars
hobbies for profit
painting
yoga
whales
model airplanes
funerals
breaking the law
making movies
memories
patriotism
on being
   handicapped
campus slang
computers
the exercise epidemic
black athletes
the "thin" craze
sexism in language
heroes
John Lennon

life after death
nuclear freeze
creationism
stepfathers
amusement parks
welfare cheaters
waiting tables
local elections
news anchorpersons
the nation
foreign customs
surveys
weddings
leaving home
swimming suits
dictators
objectionable
   commercials
a change in religion
labor unions
sex education
backpacking
our court system
being a worry-wart
the Equal Rights
   Amendment
vegetarianism
Bill Clinton
stress
Woody Allen
automation
cats versus dogs
collecting antiques
large families
country living
job interviews
draft registration
phonies
first love
dirty movies
waitresses
ethnic customs
smoking
gay liberation
violence in America

a bore I know
Miss America
condominiums
doublespeak
libraries
Shakespeare
rhythm and blues
conservatives
athletes and grades
blue jeans
prayer
the American Indian
Generation X
drive-in movies
Star Trek
the space shuttle
inflation
cable TV
electronic music
teenage drinking
witchcraft
shopping malls
foreign travels
bigotry
terminal illness
phobias
in-laws
capital punishment
dreams
genetic engineering
Vietnam
an objectionable
   roommate
flying saucers
embarrassing
   moments
privacy versus
   security
gun control
censorship on
   campus
drugs in sports
the population
   explosion
radioactive waste

airports
foreign trade
euthanasia
sociobiology
subliminal
    advertising
movie starlets
scandal magazines
punk rock
Groucho Marx
gambling
hobbies
second marriages
IQ tests
adoption
terrorism
migrant workers
the Third World
newspapers
parking regulations
photography
race problems
Social Security
insurance men

Chris Berman
living together
brain-washing
clones
local politicians
cults
night people
jogging
cafeteria food
small cars
Christmas
grunge
parents
fear of math
swimming lessons
fathers and sons
the English language
nursery rhymes
the metric system
modern novelists
phrenology
opera singers
boycotts
a high-school teacher

a favorite author
people-watching
the life of the party
best friend
worthless cures
being shy
suicide
reincarnation
the Super Bowl
anti-vivisectionism
the Bible
car dealers
birthdays
shock therapy
famous hoaxes
holy shrines
a threatening
    situation
my secret ambition
the pleasures of my
    youth
the joy of cooking

# Index